100

PERSIAN VERBS

Fully Conjugated in the Most Common Tenses

Nazanin Mirsadeghi

Bahar Books

www.baharbooks.com

Mirsadeghi, Nazanin
    100 Persian Verbs-Fully Conjugated in the Most Common Tenses(Farsi-English Bi-lingual Edition)/Nazanin Mirsadeghi

ISBN-10: 1939099099
ISBN-13: 978-1-939099-09-9

Published by Bahar Books, White Plains, New York

INTRODUCTION

This book of *100 Persian Verbs* provides students with immediate access to correct verb forms of the Persian language.

Finding the Persian verb conjunctions is not usually an easy task. Using the verbs in their correct forms might be a challenge for students, regardless of the learning system.

This book has been designed to be used as a quick and easy way to find the full conjunction of the most common Persian verbs you need to use in a conversation or in your writing. In order to use this book effectively, you must be able to read and write in Persian, and be familiar with the grammar and the basic structure of the Persian language. However, in the beginning of the book, some essential materials regarding the Persian alphabet, pronunciation of the Persian letters, the definition of different Persian verb tenses and their uses have been provided.

It is hoped that those who are learning the Persian language could use this book as a reference and find it helpful as they advance their language skills.

Nazanin Mirsadeghi

Pronunciation Guide for the Persian Letters

ă like the "a" in arm	آ – ا *
b like the "b" in boy	بـ – ب
p like the "p" in play	پـ – پ
t like the "t" in tree	تـ – ت
s like the "s" in sun	ثـ – ث
j like the "j" in jam	جـ – ج
č like the "ch" in child	چـ – چ
h like the "h" in hotel	حـ – ح
ǩ like "ch" in the German word *bach*, or Hebrew word *smach*.	خـ – خ
d like the "d" in door	د
z like the "z" in zebra	ذ
r like the "r" in rabbit	ر
z like the "z" in zebra	ز
ž like the "z" in zwago	ژ
s like the "s" in sun	سـ – س
š like the "sh" in shell	شـ – ش
s like the "s" in sun	صـ – ص
z like the "z" in zebra	ضـ – ض

t like the "t" in tree	ط
z like the "z" in zebra	ظ
ʻ is a glottal stop, like between the syllables of "uh-oh".	ع – ﻌ – ﻊ
ğ like the "r" in French word *merci*	غ – ﻐ – ﻎ
f like the "f" in fall	ف – ﻓ
ğ like the "r" in French word *merci*	ق – ﻗ
k like the "k" in kite	ک – ﻛ
g like the "g" in game	گ – ﮔ
l like the "l" in lost	ل – ﻟ
m like the "m" in master	م – ﻣ
n like the "n" in night	ن – ﻧ
v like the "v" in van	و
o like the "o" in ocean	و
On some occasions, it has no sound and becomes silent.	و
u like the "u" in sure	* او – و
h like the "h" in hotel	ه – ﻬ – ﻫ – ﻪ
e like the "e" in element	ﻪ – ﻬ
y like the "y" in yellow	ﻳ – ی
i like the "ee" in need	* ﺍﻳ – ﻳ – ی – ﺍی

* long vowels

Represents doubled consonants.	ّ

a like the "a" in animal	ـَ اَ **
o like the "o" in ocean	ـُ اُ **
e like the "e" in element	ـِ اِ ** ـِ

** short vowels

Persian Letters with the Same Pronunciation

t like the "t" in tree	ت – ط ط
ğ like the "r" in French word *merci*	ق – ق غ – غـ – ـغ
h like the "h" in hotel	حـ – ح هـ – ـهـ – ـه – ه
s like the "s" in sun	ث – ث سـ – س صـ – ص
z like the "z" in zebra	ذ ز ض ظ

vi

Names Given to the Persian Letters

alef	‏ا - آ‏
be	‏بـ - ب‏
pe	‏پـ - پ‏
te	‏تـ - ت‏
se	‏ثـ - ث‏
jim	‏جـ - ج‏
če	‏چـ - چ‏
he	‏حـ - ح‏
ke	‏خـ - خ‏
dăl	‏د‏
zăl	‏ذ‏
re	‏ر‏
ze	‏ز‏
že	‏ژ‏
sin	‏سـ - س‏
šin	‏شـ - ش‏
săd	‏صـ - ص‏
zăd	‏ضـ - ض‏
tă	‏ط‏

ză	ظ
eyn	ع – ـع – ـ
ğeyn	غ – ـغ – ـ
fe	ف – ـف
ğăf	ق – ـق
kăf	ک – ـک
găf	گ – ـگ
lăm	ل – ـل
mim	م – ـم
noon	ن – ـن
văv	و
he	ه – ـه – ـ – ـ
ye	ی – ـی

Persian Pronouns

Plural		Singular	
We = ما		**I** = من	
/mă/		/man/	
You = شما		**You** = تو	
/šo.mă/		/to/	
They = آنها		**She – He/ It** = او/آن	
/ăn.hă/		/u/ ăn/	

Persian Verb Tenses

__Simple Present__

مضارع اخباری(حال ساده)

It is used to indicate one of the following:

a) An action at the present time.

> Example:

من دعوت تو را قبول می کنم.

/man- daˁ.va.te- to- ră- ğa.bul- mi.ko.nam/

I *accept* your invitation.

b) A habitual action.

> Example:

من هر روز به مادرم تلفن می کنم.

/man- har- ruz- be- mă.da.ram- te.le.fon- mi.ko.nam/

I *call* my mother every day.

c) An action in the future.

> Example:

پدرم یک ماه دیگر از ایران برمی گردد.

/pe.da.ram- yek- mă.he- di.gar- az- i.răn- bar.mi.gar.dad/

My father *will return* from Iran in a month.

Present Subjunctive
مضارع التزامی

It is used after a verb that expresses one of the following:

a) A suggestion.

    Example:

بهتر است اوّل به مدرسه *تلفن بکنی*.

/beh.tar- ast- av.val- be- mad.re.se- te.le.fon- be.ko.ni/

It's better that (you) *call* the school first.

b) A wish.

    Example:

من امیدوارم که تو دخترت را به مهمانی *بیاوری*.

/man- o.mid.vă.ram- ke- to- doǩ.ta.rat- ră- be- meh.mă.ni- bi.yă.va.ri/

I hope that you *bring* your daughter to the party.

c) A preference.

    Example:

سارا ترجیح می دهد که سام با ما *بیاید*.

/să.ră- tar.jih- mi.da.had- ke- săm- bă- mă- bi.yă.yad/

Sara prefers that Sam *come* with us.

d) A doubt.

    Example:

من شک دارم دوستانت به دیدن ما *بیایند*.

/man- šak- dă.ram- dus.tă.nat- be- di.da.ne- mă- bi.yă.yand/

I doubt that your friends *come* to visit us.

e) A necessity.

    Example:

من باید به مدرسه *بروم*.

/man- bă.yad- be- mad.re.se- be.ra.vam/

I *have to go* to school.

X

Present Progressive

مضارع مستمر(در جریان)

It is used to describe an action that is an on-going action and that is happening right now. The simple present tense of the verb "داشتن" is always used to conjugate all verbs in the present progressive tense.

Example:

سارا دارد با برادرت می رقصد.

/să.ră- dă.rad- bă- ba.ră.da.rat- mi.rağ.sad/

Sara *is dancing* with your brother.

Simple Past

ماضی مطلق(گذشته ساده)

It is used to express an action that has happened in the past.

Example:

خواهرم کتابش را به من داد.

/kă.ha.ram- ke.tă.baš- ră- be- man- dăd/

My sister *gave* me her book.

Imperfect Indicative

ماضی استمراری

(The English equivalent: simple past OR past progressive OR "used to" + infinitive)

It is used to express an action that is one of the following:

a) Was continuous in the past.

Example:

ما قبلاً در آپارتمان زندگی می کردیم.

/mă- ğab.lan- dar- ă.păr.te.măn- zen.de.gi- mi.kar.dim/

We *used to live* in an apartment.

b) Done by someone habitually in the past.

Example:

وقتی در تهران بودم، هر روز در پارک راه می رفتم.

/vağ.ti- dar- teh.răn- bu.dam- har- ruz- dar- părk- răh- mi.raf.tam/

When (I) was in Tehran, (I) *walked* in the park every day.

Present Perfect

ماضی نقلی

It is used to express an action that has happened in the past but its effect or result continues to the present time.

Example:

من تمام سوالات را جواب داده ام.

/man- ta.mă.me- so.ă.lăt- ră- ja.văb- dă.de.am/

I *have answered* all the questions.

Past Perfect

ماضی بعید

It is used to express an action which took place in the past before another past action.

Example:

قبل از اینکه به هاوایی بروم، هیچوقت ساحلی به این زیبایی ندیده بودم.

/ğabl- az- in.ke- be- hă.vă.i- be.ra.vam- hič.vağt- să.he.li- be- in- zi.bă.yi- na.di.de- bu.dam/

(I) *had* never *seen* such a beautiful beach, before (I) went to Hawaii.

Past Subjunctive

ماضی التزامی

It is used to express an action that might have happened in the past.

Example:

ممکن است مادرم با مادرت حرف زده باشد.

/mom.ken- ast- mă.da.ram- bă- mă.da.rat- harf- za.de- bă.šad/

My mother *might have talked* to your mother.

Past Progressive

ماضی مستمر(در جریان)

It is used to describe an action that was in progress at some point in the past. The simple past tense of the verb "داشتن" is always used to conjugate all verbs in the past progressive tense.

Example:

وقتی آمدی، داشتم کتاب می خواندم.

/vağ.ti- ă.ma.di- dăš.tam- ke.tăb- mi.kăn.dam/

When (you) came, (I) *was reading* a book.

Simple Future

آینده ساده

It is used to express an action that will take place at some pont in time in the future. The simple present tense of the verb "خواستن" without "می" is always used to conjugate all verbs in the future tense.

Example:

سارا باز هم قلبت را خواهد شکست.

/să.ră- băz- ham- ğal.bat- ră- k̆ă.had- še.kast/

Sara *will break* your heart again.

Command

امر

It is used:

a) To express a command.

Example:

در را بازکن!

/dar- ră- băz- kon/

Open the door!

b) To demand the acceptance of a condition.

Example:

آماده باش!

/ă.mă.de- băš/

Be prepared!

What this book provides:

- To facilitate the search, the verbs in *100 Persian Verbs* have been arranged based on their English translation in alphabetical order.

- The phonetic transcriptions for all Persian verbs and their conjunctions have been provided in different tenses.

- If a verb in a particular tense could be conjugated in more than one form, the additional form has been cited as a foot note.

- If the conjunction of a verb in a particular tense is not commonly used, the tables containing those conjugated forms have been shaded out.

Important note: There are two types of "infinitives" in the Persian language:

1) Verbs ending in: /dan/
2) Verbs ending in: /tan/

100

PERSIAN VERBS

Fully Conjugated in the Most Common Tenses

to accept

قَبول کَردَن

/ğa.bul- kar.dan/

Plural	Singular
Simple Present	
مضارع اخباری(حال ساده)	
(ما) قبول می کنیم	(من) قبول می کنم
/(mǎ) ğa.bul- mi.ko.nim/	/(man) ğa.bul- mi.ko.nam/
(شما) قبول می کنید	(تو) قبول می کنی
/(šo.mǎ) ğa.bul- mi.ko.nid/	/(to) ğa.bul- mi.ko.ni/
(آنها) قبول می کنند	(او/آن) قبول می کند
/(ǎn.hǎ) ğa.bul- mi.ko.nand/	/(u/ ǎn) ğa.bul- mi.ko.nad/
Present Subjunctive	
مضارع التزامی	
(ما) قبول بکنیم	(من) قبول بکنم
/(mǎ) ğa.bul- be.ko.nim/	/(man) ğa.bul- be.ko.nam/
(شما) قبول بکنید	(تو) قبول بکنی
/(šo.mǎ) ğa.bul- be.ko.nid/	/(to) ğa.bul- be.ko.ni/
(آنها) قبول بکنند	(او/آن) قبول بکند
/(ǎn.hǎ) ğa.bul- be.ko.nand/	/(u/ ǎn) ğa.bul- be.ko.nad/
Present Progressive	
مضارع مستمر(در جریان)	
(ما) داریم قبول می کنیم	(من) دارم قبول می کنم
/(mǎ) dǎ.rim- ğa.bul- mi.ko.nim/	/(man) dǎ.ram- ğa.bul- mi.ko.nam/
(شما) دارید قبول می کنید	(تو) داری قبول می کنی
/(šo.mǎ) dǎ.rid- ğa.bul- mi.ko.nid/	/(to) dǎ.ri- ğa.bul- mi.ko.ni/
(آنها) دارند قبول می کنند	(او/آن) دارد قبول می کند
/(ǎn.hǎ) dǎ.rand- ğa.bul- mi.ko.nand/	/(u/ ǎn) dǎ.rad- ğa.bul- mi.ko.nad/

<table>
<tr><td colspan="2" align="center">

Simple Past

ماضی مطلق (گذشته ساده)

</td></tr>
<tr>
<td align="center">

(ما) قبول کردیم

/(mă) ğa.bul- kar.dim/

</td>
<td align="center">

(من) قبول کردم

/(man) ğa.bul- kar.dam/

</td>
</tr>
<tr>
<td align="center">

(شما) قبول کردید

/(šo.mă) ğa.bul- kar.did/

</td>
<td align="center">

(تو) قبول کردی

/(to) ğa.bul- kar.di/

</td>
</tr>
<tr>
<td align="center">

(آنها) قبول کردند

/(ăn.hă) ğa.bul- kar.dand/

</td>
<td align="center">

(او/آن) قبول کرد

/(u/ ăn) ğa.bul- kard/

</td>
</tr>
</table>

<table>
<tr><td colspan="2" align="center">

Imperfect Indicative   *used to ...*

ماضی استمراری

</td></tr>
<tr>
<td align="center">

(ما) قبول می کردیم

/(mă) ğa.bul- mi.kar.dim/

</td>
<td align="center">

(من) قبول می کردم

/(man) ğa.bul- mi.kar.dam/

</td>
</tr>
<tr>
<td align="center">

(شما) قبول می کردید

/(šo.mă) ğa.bul- mi.kar.did/

</td>
<td align="center">

(تو) قبول می کردی

/(to) ğa.bul- mi.kar.di/

</td>
</tr>
<tr>
<td align="center">

(آنها) قبول می کردند

/(ăn.hă) ğa.bul- mi.kar.dand/

</td>
<td align="center">

(او/آن) قبول می کرد

/(u/ ăn) ğa.bul- mi.kard/

</td>
</tr>
</table>

<table>
<tr><td colspan="2" align="center">

Present Perfect

ماضی نقلی

</td></tr>
<tr>
<td align="center">

(ما) قبول کرده ایم

/(mă) ğa.bul- kar.de.im/

</td>
<td align="center">

(من) قبول کرده ام

/(man) ğa.bul- kar.de.am/

</td>
</tr>
<tr>
<td align="center">

(شما) قبول کرده اید

/(šo.mă) ğa.bul- kar.de.id/

</td>
<td align="center">

(تو) قبول کرده ای

/(to) ğa.bul- kar.de.i/

</td>
</tr>
<tr>
<td align="center">

(آنها) قبول کرده اند

/(ăn.hă) ğa.bul- kar.de.and/

</td>
<td align="center">

(او/آن) قبول کرده است

/(u/ ăn) ğa.bul- kar.de- ast/

</td>
</tr>
</table>

<table>
<tr><td colspan="2" align="center">

Past Perfect

ماضی بعید

</td></tr>
<tr>
<td align="center">

(ما) قبول کرده بودیم

/(mă) ğa.bul- kar.de- bu.dim/

</td>
<td align="center">

(من) قبول کرده بودم

/(man) ğa.bul- kar.de- bu.dam/

</td>
</tr>
<tr>
<td align="center">

(شما) قبول کرده بودید

/(šo.mă) ğa.bul- kar.de- bu.did/

</td>
<td align="center">

(تو) قبول کرده بودی

/(to) ğa.bul- kar.de- bu.di/

</td>
</tr>
<tr>
<td align="center">

(آنها) قبول کرده بودند

/(ăn.hă) ğa.bul- kar.de- bu.dand/

</td>
<td align="center">

(او/آن) قبول کرده بود

/(u/ ăn) ğa.bul- kar.de- bud/

</td>
</tr>
</table>

3

<table>
<tr><td colspan="2" align="center">**Past Subjunctive**
ماضی التزامی</td></tr>
<tr>
<td align="center">(ما) قبول کرده باشیم
/(mǎ) ǧa.bul- kar.de- bǎ.šim/</td>
<td align="center">(من) قبول کرده باشم
/(man) ǧa.bul- kar.de- bǎ.šam/</td>
</tr>
<tr>
<td align="center">(شما) قبول کرده باشید
/(šo.mǎ) ǧa.bul- kar.de- bǎ.šid/</td>
<td align="center">(تو) قبول کرده باشی
/(to) ǧa.bul- kar.de- bǎ.ši/</td>
</tr>
<tr>
<td align="center">(آنها) قبول کرده باشند
/(ǎn.hǎ) ǧa.bul- kar.de- bǎ.šand/</td>
<td align="center">(او/آن) قبول کرده باشد
/(u/ ǎn) ǧa.bul- kar.de- bǎ.šad/</td>
</tr>
</table>

<table>
<tr><td colspan="2" align="center">**Past Progressive**
ماضی مستمر(در جریان)</td></tr>
<tr>
<td align="center">(ما) داشتیم قبول می کردیم
/(mǎ) dǎš.tim- ǧa.bul- mi.kar.dim/</td>
<td align="center">(من) داشتم قبول می کردم
/(man) dǎš.tam- ǧa.bul- mi.kar.dam/</td>
</tr>
<tr>
<td align="center">(شما) داشتید قبول می کردید
/(šo.mǎ) dǎš.tid- ǧa.bul- mi.kar.did/</td>
<td align="center">(تو) داشتی قبول می کردی
/(to) dǎš.ti- ǧa.bul- mi.kar.di/</td>
</tr>
<tr>
<td align="center">(آنها) داشتند قبول می کردند
/(ǎn.hǎ) dǎš.tand- ǧa.bul- mi.kar.dand/</td>
<td align="center">(او/آن) داشت قبول می کرد
/(u/ ǎn) dǎšt- ǧa.bul- mi.kard/</td>
</tr>
</table>

<table>
<tr><td colspan="2" align="center">**Simple Future**
مستقبل (آینده ساده)</td></tr>
<tr>
<td align="center">(ما) قبول خواهیم کرد
/(mǎ) ǧa.bul- ǩǎ.him- kard/</td>
<td align="center">(من) قبول خواهم کرد
/(man) ǧa.bul- ǩǎ.ham- kard/</td>
</tr>
<tr>
<td align="center">(شما) قبول خواهید کرد
/(šo.mǎ) ǧa.bul- ǩǎ.hid- kard/</td>
<td align="center">(تو) قبول خواهی کرد
/(to) ǧa.bul- ǩǎ.hi- kard/</td>
</tr>
<tr>
<td align="center">(آنها) قبول خواهند کرد
/(ǎn.hǎ) ǧa.bul-ǩǎ.hand- kard/</td>
<td align="center">(او/آن) قبول خواهد کرد
/(u/ ǎn) ǧa.bul-ǩǎ.had- kard/</td>
</tr>
</table>

<table>
<tr><td colspan="2" align="center">**Command**
امر</td></tr>
<tr>
<td align="center">* قبول بکنید!
/ǧa.bul- be.ko.nid/</td>
<td align="center">* قبول بکن!
/ǧa.bul- be.kon/</td>
</tr>
</table>

* also: قبول کن!   قبول کنید!

4

to answer

جَواب دادَن

/ja.văb- dă.dan/

Plural	*Singular*
Simple Present م... مضارع اخباری(حال ساده)	
(ما) جواب می دهیم /(mă) ja.văb- mi.da.him/	(من) جواب می دهم /(man) ja.văb- mi.da.ham/
(شما) جواب می دهید /(šo.mă) ja.văb- mi.da.hid/	(تو) جواب می دهی /(to) ja.văb- mi.da.hi/
(آنها) جواب می دهند /(ăn.hă) ja.văb- mi.da.hand/	(او/آن) جواب می دهد /(u/ ăn) ja.văb- mi.da.had/
Present Subjunctive مضارع التزامی	
(ما) جواب بدهیم /(mă) ja.văb- be.da.him/	(من) جواب بدهم /(man) ja.văb- be.da.ham/
(شما) جواب بدهید /(šo.mă) ja.văb- be.da.hid/	(تو) جواب بدهی /(to) ja.văb- be.da.hi/
(آنها) جواب بدهند /(ăn.hă) ja.văb- be.da.hand/	(او/آن) جواب بدهد /(u/ ăn) ja.văb- be.da.had/
Present Progressive مضارع مستمر(در جریان)	
(ما) داریم جواب می دهیم /(mă) dă.rim- ja.văb- mi.da.him/	(من) دارم جواب می دهم /(man) dă.ram- ja.văb- mi.da.ham/
(شما) دارید جواب می دهید /(šo.mă) dă.rid- ja.văb- mi.da.hid/	(تو) داری جواب می دهی /(to) dă.ri- ja.văb- mi.da.hi/
(آنها) دارند جواب می دهند /(ăn.hă) dă.rand- ja.văb- mi.da.hand/	(او/آن) دارد جواب می دهد /(u/ ăn) dă.rad- ja.văb- mi.da.had/

5

Simple Past
ماضی مطلق (گذشته ساده)

(ما) جواب دادیم	(من) جواب دادم
/(mǎ) ja.vǎb- dǎ.dim/	/(man) ja.vǎb- dǎ.dam/
(شما) جواب دادید	(تو) جواب دادی
/(šo.mǎ) ja.vǎb- dǎ.did/	/(to) ja.vǎb- dǎ.di/
(آنها) جواب دادند	(او/آن) جواب داد
/(ǎn.hǎ) ja.vǎb- dǎ.dand/	/(u/ ǎn) ja.vǎb- dǎd/

Imperfect Indicative
ماضی استمراری

used to

(ما) جواب می دادیم	(من) جواب می دادم
/(mǎ) ja.vǎb- mi.dǎ.dim/	/(man) ja.vǎb- mi.dǎ.dam/
(شما) جواب می دادید	(تو) جواب می دادی
/(šo.mǎ) ja.vǎb- mi.dǎ.did/	/(to) ja.vǎb- mi.dǎ.di/
(آنها) جواب می دادند	(او/آن) جواب می داد
/(ǎn.hǎ) ja.vǎb- mi.dǎ.dand/	/(u/ ǎn) ja.vǎb- mi.dǎd/

Present Perfect
ماضی نقلی

(ما) جواب داده ایم	(من) جواب داده ام
/(mǎ) ja.vǎb- dǎ.de.im/	/(man) ja.vǎb- dǎ.de.am/
(شما) جواب داده اید	(تو) جواب داده ای
/(šo.mǎ) ja.vǎb- dǎ.de.id/	/(to) ja.vǎb- dǎ.de.i/
(آنها) جواب داده اند	(او/آن) جواب داده است
/(ǎn.hǎ) ja.vǎb- dǎ.de.and/	/(u/ ǎn) ja.vǎb- dǎ.de- ast/

Past Perfect
ماضی بعید

(ما) جواب داده بودیم	(من) جواب داده بودم
/(mǎ) ja.vǎb- dǎ.de- bu.dim/	/(man) ja.vǎb- dǎ.de- bu.dam/
(شما) جواب داده بودید	(تو) جواب داده بودی
/(šo.mǎ) ja.vǎb-dǎ.de- bu.did/	/(to) ja.vǎb- dǎ.de- bu.di/
(آنها) جواب داده بودند	(او/آن) جواب داده بود
/(ǎn.hǎ) ja.vǎb- dǎ.de- bu.dand/	/(u/ ǎn) ja.vǎb- dǎ.de- bud/

Past Subjunctive	
ماضی التزامی	
(ما) جواب داده باشیم	(من) جواب داده باشم
/(mă) ja.văb- dă.de- bă.šim/	/(man) ja.văb- dă.de- bă.šam/
(شما) جواب داده باشید	(تو) جواب داده باشی
/(šo.mă) ja.văb- dă.de- bă.šid/	/(to) ja.văb- dă.de- bă.ši/
(آنها) جواب داده باشند	(او/آن) جواب داده باشد
/(ăn.hă) ja.văb- dă.de- bă.šand/	/(u/ ăn) ja.văb- dă.de- bă.šad/

Past Progressive	
ماضی مستمر(در جریان)	
(ما) داشتیم جواب می دادیم	(من) داشتم جواب می دادم
/(mă) dăš.tim- ja.văb- mi.dă.dim/	/(man) dăš.tam- ja.văb- mi.dă.dam/
(شما) داشتید جواب می دادید	(تو) داشتی جواب می دادی
/(šo.mă) dăš.tid- ja.văb- mi.dă.did/	/(to) dăš.ti- ja.văb- mi.dă.di/
(آنها) داشتند جواب می دادند	(او) داشت جواب می داد
/(ăn.hă) dăš.tand- ja.văb- mi.dă.dand/	/(u/ ăn) dăšt- ja.văb- mi.dăd/

Simple Future	
مستقبل (آینده ساده)	
(ما) جواب خواهیم داد	(من) جواب خواهم داد
/(mă) ja.văb- kă.him- dăd/	/(man) ja.văb- kă.ham- dăd/
(شما) جواب خواهید داد	(تو) جواب خواهی داد
/(šo.mă) ja.văb- kă.hid- dăd/	/(to) ja.văb- kă.hi- dăd/
(آنها) جواب خواهند داد	(او/آن) جواب خواهد داد
/(ăn.hă) ja.văb- kă.hand- dăd/	/(u/ ăn) ja.văb- kă.had- dăd/

Command	
امر	
جواب بدهید!	جواب بده!
/ja.văb- be.da.hid/	/ja.văb- be.de/

to ask

پُرسیدَن

/ por.si.dan/

Plural	*Singular*
Simple Present	
مضارع اخباری(حال ساده)	
(ما) می پرسیم	(من) می پرسم
/(mă) mi.por.sim/	/(man) mi.por.sam/
(شما) می پرسید	(تو) می پرسی
/(šo.mă) mi.por.sid/	/(to) mi.por.si/
(آنها) می پرسند	(او/آن) می پرسد
/(ăn.hă) mi.por.sand/	/(u/ ăn) mi.por.sad/

Plural	*Singular*
Present Subjunctive	
مضارع التزامی	
(ما) بپرسیم	(من) بپرسم
/(mă) be.por.sim/	/(man) be.por.sam/
(شما) بپرسید	(تو) بپرسی
/(šo.mă) be.por.sid/	/(to) be.por.si/
(آنها) بپرسند	(او/آن) بپرسد
/(ăn.hă) be.por.sand/	/(u/ ăn) be.por.sad/

Plural	*Singular*
Present Progressive	
مضارع مستمر(در جریان)	
(ما) داریم می پرسیم	(من) دارم می پرسم
/(mă) dă.rim- mi.por.sim/	/(man) dă.ram- mi.por.sam/
(شما) دارید می پرسید	(تو) داری می پرسی
/(šo.mă) dă.rid- mi.por.sid/	/(to) dă.ri- mi.por.si/
(آنها) دارند می پرسند	(او/آن) دارد می پرسد
/(ăn.hă) dă.rand- mi.por.sand/	/(u/ ăn) dă.rad- mi.por.sad/

<table>
<tr><td colspan="2" align="center">**Simple Past**
ماضی مطلق (گذشته ساده)</td></tr>
<tr>
<td align="center">(ما) پرسیدیم
/(mǎ) por.si.dim/</td>
<td align="center">(من) پرسیدم
/(man) por.si.dam/</td>
</tr>
<tr>
<td align="center">(شما) پرسیدید
/(šo.mǎ) por.si.did/</td>
<td align="center">(تو) پرسیدی
/(to) por.si.di/</td>
</tr>
<tr>
<td align="center">(آنها) پرسیدند
/(ǎn.hǎ) por.si.dand/</td>
<td align="center">(او/آن) پرسید
/(u/ ǎn) por.sid/</td>
</tr>
</table>

<table>
<tr><td colspan="2" align="center">**Imperfect Indicative**
ماضی استمراری</td></tr>
<tr>
<td align="center">(ما) می پرسیدیم
/(mǎ) mi.por.si.dim/</td>
<td align="center">(من) می پرسیدم
/(man) mi.por.si.dam/</td>
</tr>
<tr>
<td align="center">(شما) می پرسیدید
/(šo.mǎ) mi.por.si.did/</td>
<td align="center">(تو) می پرسیدی
/(to) mi.por.si.di/</td>
</tr>
<tr>
<td align="center">(آنها) می پرسیدند
/(ǎn.hǎ) mi.por.si.dand/</td>
<td align="center">(او/آن) می پرسید
/(u/ ǎn) mi.por.sid/</td>
</tr>
</table>

<table>
<tr><td colspan="2" align="center">**Present Perfect**
ماضی نقلی</td></tr>
<tr>
<td align="center">(ما) پرسیده ایم
/(mǎ) por.si.de.im/</td>
<td align="center">(من) پرسیده ام
/(man) por.si.de.am/</td>
</tr>
<tr>
<td align="center">(شما) پرسیده اید
/(šo.mǎ) por.si.de.id/</td>
<td align="center">(تو) پرسیده ای
/(to) por.si.de.i/</td>
</tr>
<tr>
<td align="center">(آنها) پرسیده اند
/(ǎn.hǎ) por.si.de.and/</td>
<td align="center">(او/آن) پرسیده است
/(u/ ǎn) por.si.de- ast/</td>
</tr>
</table>

<table>
<tr><td colspan="2" align="center">**Past Perfect**
ماضی بعید</td></tr>
<tr>
<td align="center">(ما) پرسیده بودیم
/(mǎ) por.si.de- bu.dim/</td>
<td align="center">(من) پرسیده بودم
/(man) por.si.de-bu.dam/</td>
</tr>
<tr>
<td align="center">(شما) پرسیده بودید
/(šo.mǎ) por.si.de- bu.did/</td>
<td align="center">(تو) پرسیده بودی
/(to) por.si.de- bu.di/</td>
</tr>
<tr>
<td align="center">(آنها) پرسیده بودند
/(ǎn.hǎ) por.si.de- bu.dand/</td>
<td align="center">(او/آن) پرسیده بود
/(u/ ǎn) por.si.de- bud/</td>
</tr>
</table>

Past Subjunctive
ماضی التزامی

(ما) پرسیده باشیم	(من) پرسیده باشم
/(mă) por.si.de- bă.šim/	/(man) por.si.de- bă.šam/
(شما) پرسیده باشید	(تو) پرسیده باشم
/(šo.mă) por.si.de- bă.šid/	/(to) por.si.de- bă.ši/
(آنها) پرسیده باشند	(او/آن) پرسیده باشد
/(ăn.hă) por.si.de- bă.šand/	/(u/ ăn) por.si.de- bă.šad/

Past Progressive
ماضی مستمر(در جریان)

(ما) داشتیم می پرسیدیم	(من) داشتم می پرسیدم
/(mă) dăš.tim- mi.por.si.dim/	/(man) dăš.tam- mi.por.si.dam/
(شما) داشتید می پرسیدید	(تو) داشتی می پرسیدی
/(šo.mă) dăš.tid- mi.por.si.did/	/(to) dăš.ti- mi.por.si.di/
(آنها) داشتند می پرسیدند	(او/آن) داشت می پرسید
/(ăn.hă) dăš.tand - mi.por.si.dand/	/(u/ ăn) dăšt- mi.por.sid/

Simple Future
مستقبل (آینده ساده)

(ما) خواهیم پرسید	(من) خواهم پرسید
/(mă) kă.him- por.sid/	/(man) kă.ham- por.sid/
(شما) خواهید پرسید	(تو) خواهی پرسید
/(šo.mă) kă.hid- por.sid/	/(to) kă.hi- por.sid/
(آنها) خواهند پرسید	(او/آن) خواهد پرسید
/(ăn.hă) kă.hand- por.sid/	/(u/ ăn) kă.had- por.sid/

Command
امر

بپرسید!	بپرس!
/be.por.sid/	/be.pors/

to be

بودَن

/bu.dan/

	Plural		Singular
Simple Present			
مضارع اخباری(حال ساده)			
* (ما) هستیم		* (من) هستم	
/(mǎ) has.tim/		/(man) has.tam/	
* (شما) هستید		* (تو) هستی	
/(šo.mǎ) hast.tid/		/(to) has.ti/	
* (آنها) هستند		* (او/آن) هست	
/(ǎn.hǎ) has.tand/		/(u/ ǎn) hast/	

	Plural		Singular
Present Subjunctive			
مضارع التزامی			
(ما) باشیم		(من) باشم	
/(mǎ) bǎ.šim/		/(man) bǎ.šam/	
(شما) باشید		(تو) باشی	
/(šo.mǎ) bǎ.šid/		/(to) bǎ.ši/	
(آنها) باشند		(او/آن) باشد	
/(ǎn.hǎ) bǎ.šand/		/(u/ ǎn) bǎ.šad/	

	Plural		Singular
Present Progressive			
مضارع مستمر(در جریان)			
(ما) داریم می باشیم		(من) دارم می باشم	
/(mǎ) dǎ.rim- mi.bǎ.šim/		/(man) dǎ.ram- mi.bǎ.šam/	
(شما) دارید می باشید		(تو) داری می باشی	
/(šo.mǎ) dǎ.rid- mi.bǎ.šid/		/(to) dǎ.ri- mi.bǎ.ši/	
(آنها) دارند می باشند		(او/آن) دارد می باشد	
/(ǎn.hǎ) dǎ.rand- mi.bǎ.šand/		/(u/ ǎn) dǎ.rad- mi.bǎ.šad/	

11

	Simple Past ماضی مطلق (گذشته ساده)	
(ما) بودیم /(mǎ) bu.dim/		(من) بودم /(man) bu.dam/
(شما) بودید /(šo.mǎ) bu.did/		(تو) بودی /(to) bu.di/
(آنها) بودند /(ǎn.hǎ) bu.dand/		(او/آن) بود /(u/ ǎn) bud/

	Imperfect Indicative ماضی استمراری	
(ما) می بودیم /(mǎ) mi.bu.dim/		(من) می بودم /(man) mi.bu.dam/
(شما) می بودید /(šo.mǎ) mi.bu.did/		(تو) می بودی /(to) mi.bu.di/
(آنها) می بودند /(ǎn.hǎ) mi.bu.dand/		(او/آن) می بود /(u/ ǎn) mi.bud/

	Present Perfect ماضی نقلی	
(ما) بوده ایم /(mǎ) bu.de.im/		(من) بوده ام /(man) bu.de.am/
(شما) بوده اید /(šo.mǎ) bu.de.id/		(تو) بوده ای /(to) bu.de.i/
(آنها) بوده اند /(ǎn.hǎ) bu.de.and/		(او/آن) بوده است /(u/ ǎn) bu.de- ast/

	Past Perfect ماضی بعید	
(ما) بوده بودیم /(mǎ) bu.de- bu.dim/		(من) بوده بودم /(man) bu.de- bu.dam/
(شما) بوده بودید /(šo.mǎ) bu.de- bu.did/		(تو) بوده بودی /(to) bu.de- bu.di/
(آنها) بوده بودند /(ǎn.hǎ) bu.de- bu.dand/		(او/آن) بوده بود /(u/ ǎn) bu.de- bud/

<table>
<tr><td colspan="2" align="center">**Past Subjunctive**
ماضی التزامی</td></tr>
<tr>
<td align="center">(ما) بوده باشیم
/(mǎ) bu.de- ba.šim/</td>
<td align="center">(من) بوده باشم
/(man) bu.de- ba.šam/</td>
</tr>
<tr>
<td align="center">(شما) بوده باشید
/(šo.mǎ) bu.de- ba.šid/</td>
<td align="center">(تو) بوده باشی
/(to) bu.de- ba.ši/</td>
</tr>
<tr>
<td align="center">(آنها) بوده باشند
/(ǎn.hǎ) bu.de- ba.šand/</td>
<td align="center">(او/آن) بوده باشد
/(u/ ǎn) bu.de- ba.šad/</td>
</tr>
</table>

<table>
<tr><td colspan="2" align="center">**Past Progressive**
ماضی مستمر(در جریان)</td></tr>
<tr>
<td align="center">(ما) داشتیم می بودیم
/(mǎ) daš.tim- mi.bu.dim/</td>
<td align="center">(من) داشتم می بودم
/(man) daš.tam- mi.bu.dam/</td>
</tr>
<tr>
<td align="center">(شما) داشتید می بودید
/(šo.mǎ) daš.tid- mi.bu.did/</td>
<td align="center">(تو) داشتی می بودی
/(to) daš.ti- mi.bu.di/</td>
</tr>
<tr>
<td align="center">(آنها) داشتند می بودند
/(ǎn.hǎ) daš.tand- mi.bu.dand/</td>
<td align="center">(او/آن) داشت می بود
/(u/ ǎn) dašt- mi.bud/</td>
</tr>
</table>

<table>
<tr><td colspan="2" align="center">**Simple Future**
مستقبل (آینده ساده)</td></tr>
<tr>
<td align="center">(ما) خواهیم بود
/(mǎ) ǩǎ.him- bud/</td>
<td align="center">(من) خواهم بود
/(man) ǩǎ.ham- bud/</td>
</tr>
<tr>
<td align="center">(شما) خواهید بود
/(šo.mǎ) ǩǎ.hid- bud/</td>
<td align="center">(تو) خواهی بود
/(to) ǩǎ.hi- bud/</td>
</tr>
<tr>
<td align="center">(آنها) خواهند بود
/(ǎn.hǎ) ǩǎ.hand- bud/</td>
<td align="center">(او/آن) خواهد بود
/(u/ ǎn) ǩǎ.had- bud/</td>
</tr>
</table>

<table>
<tr><td colspan="2" align="center">**Command**
امر</td></tr>
<tr>
<td align="center">باشید!
/bǎ.šid/</td>
<td align="center">باش!
/bǎš/</td>
</tr>
</table>

* also: (آنها) اَند   (شما) اید   (ما) ایم   (او/آن) اَست   (تو) ای   (من) اَم

to be able to

تَوانِستَن

/ta.vǎ.nes.tan/

Plural	*Singular*
Simple Present <div dir="rtl">مضارع اخباری(حال ساده)</div>	
<div dir="rtl">(ما) می توانیم</div> /(mǎ) mi.ta.vǎ.nim/	<div dir="rtl">(من) می توانم</div> /(man) mi.ta.vǎ.nam/
<div dir="rtl">(شما) می توانید</div> /(šo.mǎ) mi.ta.vǎ.nid/	<div dir="rtl">(تو) می توانی</div> /(to) mi.ta.vǎ.ni/
<div dir="rtl">(آنها) می توانند</div> /(ǎn.hǎ) mi.ta.vǎ.nand/	<div dir="rtl">(او/آن) می تواند</div> /(u/ ǎn) mi.ta.vǎ.nad/
Present Subjunctive <div dir="rtl">مضارع التزامی</div>	
<div dir="rtl">(ما) بتوانیم</div> /(mǎ) be.ta.vǎ.nim/	<div dir="rtl">(من) بتوانم</div> (man) be.ta.vǎ.nam/
<div dir="rtl">(شما) بتوانید</div> /(šo.mǎ) be.ta.vǎ.nid/	<div dir="rtl">(تو) بتوانی</div> /(to) be.ta.vǎ.ni/
<div dir="rtl">(آنها) بتوانند</div> /(ǎn.hǎ) be.ta.vǎ.nand/	<div dir="rtl">(او/آن) بتواند</div> /(u/ ǎn) be.ta.vǎ.nad/
Present Progressive <div dir="rtl">مضارع مستمر(در جریان)</div>	
<div dir="rtl">(ما) داریم می توانیم</div> /(mǎ) dǎ.rim- mi.ta.vǎ.nim/	<div dir="rtl">(من) دارم می توانم</div> /(man) dǎ.ram- mi.ta.vǎ.nam/
<div dir="rtl">(شما) دارید می توانید</div> /(šo.mǎ) dǎ.rid- mi.ta.vǎ.nid/	<div dir="rtl">(تو) داری می توانی</div> /(to) dǎ.ri- mi.ta.vǎ.ni/
<div dir="rtl">(آنها) دارند می توانند</div> /(ǎn.hǎ) dǎ.rand- mi.ta.vǎ.nand/	<div dir="rtl">(او/آن) دارد می تواند</div> /(u/ ǎn) dǎ.rad- mi.ta.vǎ.nad/

<table>
<tr><td colspan="2" align="center">**Simple Past**
ماضی مطلق (گذشته ساده)</td></tr>
<tr>
<td align="center">(ما) توانستیم
/(mă) ta.vă.nes.tim/</td>
<td align="center">(من) توانستم
/(man) ta.vă.nes.tam/</td>
</tr>
<tr>
<td align="center">(شما) توانستید
/(šo.mă) ta.vă.nes.tid/</td>
<td align="center">(تو) توانستی
/(to) ta.vă.nes.ti/</td>
</tr>
<tr>
<td align="center">(آنها) توانستند
/(ăn.hă) ta.vă.nes.tand/</td>
<td align="center">(او/ آن) توانست
/(u/ ăn) ta.vă.nest/</td>
</tr>
</table>

<table>
<tr><td colspan="2" align="center">**Imperfect Indicative**
ماضی استمراری</td></tr>
<tr>
<td align="center">(ما) می توانستیم
/(mă) mi.ta.vă.nes.tim/</td>
<td align="center">(من) می توانستم
/(man) mi.ta.vă.nes.tam/</td>
</tr>
<tr>
<td align="center">(شما) می توانستید
/(šo.mă) mi.ta.vă.nes.tid/</td>
<td align="center">(تو) می توانستی
/(to) mi.ta.vă.nes.ti/</td>
</tr>
<tr>
<td align="center">(آنها) می توانستند
/(ăn.hă) mi.ta.vă.nes.tand/</td>
<td align="center">(او/ آن) می توانست
/(u/ ăn) mi.ta.vă.nest/</td>
</tr>
</table>

<table>
<tr><td colspan="2" align="center">**Present Perfect**
ماضی نقلی</td></tr>
<tr>
<td align="center">(ما) توانسته ایم
/(mă) ta.vă.nes.te.im/</td>
<td align="center">(من) توانسته ام
(man) ta.vă.nes.te.am/</td>
</tr>
<tr>
<td align="center">(شما) توانسته اید
/(šo.mă) ta.vă.nes.te.id/</td>
<td align="center">(تو) توانسته ای
/(to) ta.vă.nes.te.i/</td>
</tr>
<tr>
<td align="center">(آنها) توانسته اند
/(ăn.hă) ta.vă.nes.te.and/</td>
<td align="center">(او/آن) توانسته است
/(u/ ăn) ta.vă.nes.te- ast/</td>
</tr>
</table>

<table>
<tr><td colspan="2" align="center">**Past Perfect**
ماضی بعید</td></tr>
<tr>
<td align="center">(ما) توانسته بودیم
/(mă) ta.vă.nes.te- bu.dim/</td>
<td align="center">(من) توانسته بودم
(man) ta.vă.nes.te- bu.dam/</td>
</tr>
<tr>
<td align="center">(شما) توانسته بودید
/(šo.mă) ta.vă.nes.te- bu.did/</td>
<td align="center">(تو) توانسته بودی
/(to) ta.vă.nes.te- bu.di/</td>
</tr>
<tr>
<td align="center">(آنها) توانسته بودند
/(ăn.hă) ta.vă.nes.te- bu.dand/</td>
<td align="center">(او/ آن) توانسته بود
/(u/ ăn) ta.vă.nes.te- bud/</td>
</tr>
</table>

Past Subjunctive	
ماضی التزامی	
(ما) توانسته باشیم	(من) توانسته باشم
/(mǎ) ta.vǎ.nes.te- bǎ.šim/	/(man) ta.vǎ.nes.te- bǎ.šam/
(شما) توانسته باشید	(تو) توانسته باشی
/(šo.mǎ) ta.vǎ.nes.te- bǎ.šid/	/(to) ta.vǎ.nes.te- bǎ.ši/
(آنها) توانسته باشند	(او/ آن) توانسته باشد
/(ǎn.hǎ) ta.vǎ.nes.te- bǎ.šand/	/(u/ ǎn) ta.vǎ.nes.te- bǎ.šad/

Past Progressive	
ماضی مستمر(در جریان)	
(ما) داشتیم می توانستیم	(من) داشتم می توانستم
/(mǎ) dǎš.tim- mi.ta.vǎ.nes.tim/	/(man) dǎš.tam- mi.ta.vǎ.nes.tam/
(شما) داشتید می توانستید	(تو) داشتی می توانستی
/(šo.mǎ) dǎš.tid- mi.ta.vǎ.nes.tid/	/(to) dǎš.ti- mi.ta.vǎ.nes.ti/
(آنها) داشتند می توانستند	(او/ آن) داشت می توانست
/(ǎn.hǎ) dǎš.tand- mi.ta.vǎ.nes.tand/	/(u/ ǎn) dǎšt- mi.ta.vǎ.nest/

Simple Future	
مستقبل (آینده ساده)	
(ما) خواهیم توانست	(من) خواهم توانست
/(mǎ) ǩǎ.him- ta.vǎ.nest/	/(man) ǩǎ.ham- ta.vǎ.nest/
(شما) خواهید توانست	(تو) خواهی توانست
/(šo.mǎ) ǩǎ.hid- ta.vǎ.nest/	/(to) ǩǎ.hi- ta.vǎ.nest/
(آنها) خواهند توانست	(او/ آن) خواهد توانست
/(ǎn.hǎ) ǩǎ.hand- ta.vǎ.nest/	/(u/ ǎn) ǩǎ.had- ta.vǎ.nest/

Command	
امر	
بتوانید!	بتوان!
/be.ta.vǎ.nid/	/be.ta.vǎn/

16

to become

شُدَن

/šo.dan/

Plural	Singular
Simple Present مضارع اخباری(حال ساده)	
(ما) می شویم /(mă) mi.ša.vim/	(من) می شوم /(man) mi.ša.vam/
(شما) می شوید /(šo.mă) mi.ša.vid/	(تو) می شوی /(to) mi.ša.vi/
(آنها) می شوند /(ăn.hă) mi.ša.vand/	(او/آن) می شود /(u/ ăn) mi.ša.vad/
Present Subjunctive مضارع التزامی	
(ما) بشویم /(mă) be.ša.vim/	(من) بشوم /(man) be.ša.vam/
(شما) بشوید /(šo.mă) be.ša.vid/	(تو) بشوی /(to) be.ša.vi/
(آنها) بشوند /(ăn.hă) be.ša.vand/	(او/آن) بشود /(u/ ăn) be.ša.vad/
Present Progressive مضارع مستمر(در جریان)	
(ما) داریم می شویم /(mă) dă.rim- mi.ša.vim/	(من) دارم می شوم /(man) dă.ram- mi.ša.vam/
(شما) دارید می شوید /(šo.mă) dă.rid- mi.ša.vid/	(تو) داری می شوی /(to) dă.ri- mi.ša.vi/
(آنها) دارند می شوند /(ăn.hă) dă.rand- mi.ša.vand/	(او/آن) دارد می شود /(u/ ăn) dă.rad- mi.ša.vad/

Simple Past	
ماضی مطلق (گذشته ساده)	
(ما) شدیم	(من) شدم
/(mǎ) šo.dim/	/(man) šo.dam/
(شما) شدید	(تو) شدی
/(šo.mǎ) šo.did/	/(to) šo.di/
(آنها) شدند	(او/آن) شد
/(ǎn.hǎ) šo.dand/	/(u/ ǎn) šod/

Imperfect Indicative	
ماضی استمراری	
(ما) می شدیم	(من) می شدم
/(mǎ) mi.šo.dim/	/(man) mi.šo.dam/
(شما) می شدید	(تو) می شدی
/(šo.mǎ) mi.šo.did/	/(to) mi.šo.di/
(آنها) می شدند	(او/آن) می شد
/(ǎn.hǎ) mi.šo.dand/	/(u/ ǎn) mi.šod/

Present Perfect	
ماضی نقلی	
(ما) شده ایم	(من) شده ام
/(mǎ) šo.de.im/	/(man) šo.de.am/
(شما) شده اید	(تو) شده ای
/(šo.mǎ) šo.de.id/	/(to) šo.de.i/
(آنها) شده اند	(او/آن) شده است
/(ǎn.hǎ) šo.de.and/	/(u/ ǎn) šo.de- ast/

Past Perfect	
ماضی بعید	
(ما) شده بودیم	(من) شده بودم
/(mǎ) šo.de- bu.dim/	/(man) šo.de- bu.dam/
(شما) شده بودید	(تو) شده بودی
/(šo.mǎ) šo.de- bu.did/	/(to) šo.de- bu.di/
(آنها) شده بودند	(او/آن) شده بود
/(ǎn.hǎ) šo.de- bu.dand/	/(u/ ǎn) šo.de- bud/

<table>
<tr><td colspan="2" align="center">**Past Subjunctive**
ماضی التزامی</td></tr>
<tr>
<td align="center">(ما) شده باشیم
/(mă) šo.de- bă.šim/</td>
<td align="center">(من) شده باشم
/(man) šo.de- bă.šam/</td>
</tr>
<tr>
<td align="center">(شما) شده باشید
/(šo.mă) šo.de- bă.šid/</td>
<td align="center">(تو) شده باشی
/(to) šo.de- bă.ši/</td>
</tr>
<tr>
<td align="center">(آنها) شده باشند
/(ăn.hă) šo.de- bă.šand/</td>
<td align="center">(او/آن) شده باشد
/(u/ ăn) šo.de- bă.šad/</td>
</tr>
</table>

<table>
<tr><td colspan="2" align="center">**Past Progressive**
ماضی مستمر(در جریان)</td></tr>
<tr>
<td align="center">(ما) داشتیم می شدیم
/(mă) dăš.tim- mi.šo.dim/</td>
<td align="center">(من) داشتم می شدم
/(man) dăš.tam- mi.šo.dam/</td>
</tr>
<tr>
<td align="center">(شما) داشتید می شدید
/(šo.mă) dăš.tid- mi.šo.did/</td>
<td align="center">(تو) داشتی می شدی
/(to) dăš.ti- mi.šo.di/</td>
</tr>
<tr>
<td align="center">(آنها) داشتند می شدند
/(ăn.hă) dăš.tand- mi.šo.dand/</td>
<td align="center">(او/آن) داشت می شد
/(u/ ăn) dăšt- mi.šod/</td>
</tr>
</table>

<table>
<tr><td colspan="2" align="center">**Simple Future**
مستقبل (آینده ساده)</td></tr>
<tr>
<td align="center">(ما) خواهیم شد
/(mă) ǩă.him- šod/</td>
<td align="center">(من) خواهم شد
/(man) ǩă.ham- šod/</td>
</tr>
<tr>
<td align="center">(شما) خواهید شد
/(šo.mă) ǩă.hid- šod/</td>
<td align="center">(تو) خواهی شد
/(to) ǩă.hi- šod/</td>
</tr>
<tr>
<td align="center">(آنها) خواهند شد
/(ăn.hă) ǩă.hand- šod/</td>
<td align="center">(او/آن) خواهد شد
/(u/ ăn) ǩă.had- šod/</td>
</tr>
</table>

<table>
<tr><td colspan="2" align="center">**Command**
امر</td></tr>
<tr>
<td align="center">بشوید!
/be.ša.vid/</td>
<td align="center">بشو!
/be.šo/</td>
</tr>
</table>

to break

شِکَستَن

/še.kas.tan/

Plural	Singular
Simple Present مضارع اخباری(حال ساده)	
(ما) می شکنیم /(mǎ) mi.še.ka.nim/	(من) می شکنم /(man) mi.še.ka.nam/
(شما) می شکنید /(šo.mǎ) mi.še.ka.nid/	(تو) می شکنی /(to) mi.še.ka.ni/
(آنها) می شکنند /(ǎn.hǎ) mi.še.ka.nand/	(او/آن) می شکند /(u/ ǎn) mi.še.ka.nad/
Present Subjunctive مضارع التزامی	
(ما) بشکنیم /(mǎ) be.še.ka.nim/	(من) بشکنم /(man) be.še.ka.nam/
(شما) بشکنید /(šo.mǎ) be.še.ka.nid/	(تو) بشکنی /(to) be.še.ka.ni/
(آنها) بشکنند /(ǎn.hǎ) be.še.ka.nand/	(او/آن) بشکند /(u/ ǎn) be.še.ka.nad/
Present Progressive مضارع مستمر(در جریان)	
(ما) داریم می شکنیم /(mǎ) dǎ.rim- mi.še.ka.nim/	(من) دارم می شکنم /(man) dǎ.ram- mi.še.ka.nam/
(شما) دارید می شکنید /(šo.mǎ) dǎ.rid- mi.še.ka.nid/	(تو) داری می شکنی /(to) dǎ.ri- mi.še.ka.ni/
(آنها) دارند می شکنند /(ǎn.hǎ) dǎ.rand- mi.še.ka.nand/	(او/آن) دارد می شکند /(u/ ǎn) dǎ.rad- mi.še.ka.nad/

<table>
<tr><td colspan="2" align="center">**Simple Past**
ماضی مطلق (گذشته ساده)</td></tr>
<tr><td align="center">(ما) شکستیم
/(mǎ) še.kas.tim/</td><td align="center">(من) شکستم
/(man) še.kas.tam/</td></tr>
<tr><td align="center">(شما) شکستید
/(šo.mǎ) še.kas.tid/</td><td align="center">(تو) شکستی
/(to) še.kas.ti/</td></tr>
<tr><td align="center">(آنها) شکستند
/(ǎn.hǎ) še.kas.tand</td><td align="center">(او/آن) شکست
/(u/ ǎn) še.kast/</td></tr>
</table>

<table>
<tr><td colspan="2" align="center">**Imperfect Indicative**
ماضی استمراری</td></tr>
<tr><td align="center">(ما) می شکستیم
/(mǎ) mi.še.kas.tim/</td><td align="center">(من) می شکستم
/(man) mi.še.kas.tam/</td></tr>
<tr><td align="center">(شما) می شکستید
/(šo.mǎ) mi.še.kas.tid/</td><td align="center">(تو) می شکستی
/(to) mi.še.kas.ti/</td></tr>
<tr><td align="center">(آنها) می شکستند
/(ǎn.hǎ) mi.še.kas.tand/</td><td align="center">(او/آن) می شکست
/(u/ ǎn) mi.še.kast/</td></tr>
</table>

<table>
<tr><td colspan="2" align="center">**Present Perfect**
ماضی نقلی</td></tr>
<tr><td align="center">(ما) شکسته ایم
/(mǎ) še.kas.te.im/</td><td align="center">(من) شکسته ام
/(man) še.kas.te.am/</td></tr>
<tr><td align="center">(شما) شکسته اید
/(šo.mǎ) še.kas.te.id/</td><td align="center">(تو) شکسته ای
/(to) še.kas.te.i/</td></tr>
<tr><td align="center">(آنها) شکسته اند
/(ǎn.hǎ) še.kas.te.and/</td><td align="center">(او/آن) شکسته است
/(u/ ǎn) še.kas.te- ast/</td></tr>
</table>

<table>
<tr><td colspan="2" align="center">**Past Perfect**
ماضی بعید</td></tr>
<tr><td align="center">(ما) شکسته بودیم
/(mǎ) še.kas.te- bu.dim/</td><td align="center">(من) شکسته بودم
/(man) še.kas.te- bu.dam/</td></tr>
<tr><td align="center">(شما) شکسته بودید
/(šo.mǎ) še.kas.te- bu.did/</td><td align="center">(تو) شکسته بودی
/(to) še.kas.te- bu.di/</td></tr>
<tr><td align="center">(آنها) شکسته بودند
/(ǎn.hǎ) še.kas.te- bu.dand/</td><td align="center">(او/آن) شکسته بود
/(u/ ǎn) še.kas.te- bud/</td></tr>
</table>

Past Subjunctive	
ماضی التزامی	
(ما) شکسته باشیم	(من) شکسته باشم
/(mǎ) še.kas.te- bǎ.šim/	/(man) še.kas.te- bǎ.šam/
(شما) شکسته باشید	(تو) شکسته باشی
/(šo.mǎ) še.kas.te- bǎ.šid/	/(to) še.kas.te- bǎ.ši/
(آنها) شکسته باشند	(او/آن) شکسته باشد
/(ǎn.hǎ) še.kas.te- bǎ.šand/	/(u/ ǎn) še.kas.te- bǎ.šad/

Past Progressive	
ماضی مستمر(در جریان)	
(ما) داشتیم می شکستیم	(من) داشتم می شکستم
/(mǎ) dǎš.tim- mi.še.kas.tim/	/(man) dǎš.tam- mi.še.kas.tam/
(شما) داشتید می شکستید	(تو) داشتی می شکستی
/(šo.mǎ) dǎš.tid- mi.še.kas.tid/	/(to) dǎš.ti- mi.še.kas.ti/
(آنها) داشتند می شکستند	(او/آن) داشت می شکست
/(ǎn.hǎ) dǎš.tand- mi.še.kas.tand/	/(u/ ǎn) dǎšt- mi.še.kast/

Simple Future	
مستقبل (آینده ساده)	
(ما) خواهیم شکست	(من) خواهم شکست
/(mǎ) kǎ.him- še.kast/	/(man) kǎ.ham- še.kast/
(شما) خواهید شکست	(تو) خواهی شکست
/(šo.mǎ) kǎ.hid- še.kast/	/(to) kǎ.hi- še.kast/
(آنها) خواهند شکست	(او/آن) خواهد شکست
/(ǎn.hǎ) kǎ.hand- še.kast/	/(u/ ǎn) kǎ.had- še.kast/

Command	
امر	
بشکنید!	بشکن!
/be.še.ka.nid/	/be.še.kan/

to bring

آوَردَن

/ă.var.dan/

Plural	Singular
Simple Present مضارع اخباری(حال ساده)	
(ما) می آوریم /(mă) mi.ă.va.rim/	(من) می آورم /(man) mi.ă.va.ram/
(شما) می آورید /(šo.mă) mi.ă.va.rid/	(تو) می آوری /(to) mi.ă.va.ri/
(آنها) می آورند /(ăn.hă) mi.ă.va.rand/	(او/آن) می آورد /(u/ ăn) mi.ă.va.rad/
Present Subjunctive مضارع التزامی	
(ما) بیاوریم /(mă) bi.yă.va.rim/	(من) بیاورم /(man) bi.yă.va.ram/
(شما) بیاورید /(šo.mă) bi.yă.va.rid/	(تو) بیاوری /(to) bi.yă.va.ri/
(آنها) بیاورند /(ăn.hă) bi.yă.va.rand/	(او/آن) بیاورد /(u/ ăn) bi.yă.va.rad/
Present Progressive مضارع مستمر(در جریان)	
(ما) داریم می آوریم /(mă) dă.rim- mi.ă.va.rim/	(من) دارم می آورم /(man) dă.ram- mi.ă.va.ram/
(شما) دارید می آورید /(šo.mă) dă.rid- mi.ă.va.rid/	(تو) داری می آوری /(to) dă.ri- mi.ă.va.ri/
(آنها) دارند می آورند /(ăn.hă) dă.rand- mi.ă.va.rand/	(او/آن) دارد می آورد /(u/ ăn) dă.rad- mi.ă.va.rad/

Simple Past
ماضی مطلق (گذشته ساده)

(ما) آوردیم	(من) آوردم
/(mǎ) ǎ.var.dim/	/(man) ǎ.var.dam/
(شما) آوردید	(تو) آوردی
/(šo.mǎ) ǎ.var.did/	/(to) ǎ.var.di/
(آنها) آوردند	(او/آن) آورد
/(ǎn.hǎ) ǎ.var.dand/	/(u/ ǎn) ǎ.vard/

Imperfect Indicative
ماضی استمراری

(ما) می آوردیم	(من) می آوردم
/(mǎ) mi.ǎ.var.dim/	/(man) mi.ǎ.var.dam/
(شما) می آوردید	(تو) می آوردی
/(šo.mǎ) mi.ǎ.var.did/	/(to) mi.ǎ.var.di/
(آنها) می آوردند	(او/آن) می آورد
/(ǎn.hǎ) mi.ǎ.var.dand/	/(u/ ǎn) mi.ǎ.vard/

Present Perfect
ماضی نقلی

(ما) آورده ایم	(من) آورده ام
/(mǎ) ǎ.var.de.im/	/(man) ǎ.var.de.am/
(شما) آورده اید	(تو) آورده ای
/(šo.mǎ) ǎ.var.de.id/	/(to) ǎ.var.de.i/
(آنها) آورده اند	(او/آن) آورده است
/(ǎn.hǎ) ǎ.var.de.and/	/(u/ ǎn) ǎ.var.de- ast/

Past Perfect
ماضی بعید

(ما) آورده بودیم	(من) آورده بودم
/(mǎ) ǎ.var.de- bu.dim/	/(man) ǎ.var.de- bu.dam/
(شما) آورده بودید	(تو) آورده بودی
/(šo.mǎ) ǎ.var.de- bu.did/	/(to) ǎ.var.de- bu.di/
(آنها) آورده بودند	(او/آن) آورده بود
/(ǎn.hǎ) ǎ.var.de- bu.dand/	/(u/ ǎn) ǎ.var.de- bud/

Past Subjunctive	
ماضی التزامی	
(ما) آورده باشیم	(من) آورده باشم
/(mă) ă.var.de- bă.šim/	/(man) ă.var.de- bă.šam/
(شما) آورده باشید	(تو) آورده باشی
/(šo.mă) ă.var.de- bă.šid/	/(to) ă.var.de- bă.ši/
(آنها) آورده باشند	(او/آن) آورده باشد
/(ăn.hă) ă.var.de- bă.šand/	/(u/ ăn) ă.var.de- bă.šad/

Past Progressive	
ماضی مستمر(در جریان)	
(ما) داشتیم می آوردیم	(من) داشتم می آوردم
/(mă) dăš.tim- mi.ă.var.dim/	/(man) dăš.tam- mi.ă.var.dam/
(شما) داشتید می آوردید	(تو) داشتی می آوردی
/(šo.mă) dăš.tid- mi.ă.var.did/	/(to) dăš.ti- mi.ă.var.di/
(آنها) داشتند می آوردند	(او/آن) داشت می آورد
/(ăn.hă) dăš.tand- mi.ă.var.dand/	/(u/ ăn) dăšt- mi.ă.vard/

Simple Future	
مستقبل (آینده ساده)	
(ما) خواهیم آورد	(من) خواهم آورد
/(mă) kă.him- ă.vard/	/(man) kă.ham- ă.vard/
(شما) خواهید آورد	(تو) خواهی آورد
/(šo.mă) kă.hid- ă.vard/	/(to) kă.hi- ă.vard/
(آنها) خواهند آورد	(او/آن) خواهد آورد
/(ăn.hă) kă.hand- ă.vard/	/(u/ ăn) kă.had- ă.vard/

Command	
امر	
بیاورید!	بیاور!
/bi.yă.va.rid/	/bi.yă.var/

to buy

خَریدَن

/ǩa.ri.dan/

Plural	Singular
Simple Present	
مضارع اخباری(حال ساده)	
(ما) می خریم	(من) می خرم
/(mǎ) mi.ǩa.rim/	/(man) mi.ǩa.ram/
(شما) می خرید	(تو) می خری
/(šo.mǎ) mi.ǩa.rid/	/(to) mi.ǩa.ri/
(آنها) می خرند	(او/آن) می خرد
/(ǎn.hǎ) mi.ǩa.rand/	/(u/ ǎn) mi.ǩa.rad/
Present Subjunctive	
مضارع التزامی	
(ما) بخریم	(من) بخرم
/(mǎ) be.ǩa.rim/	/(man) be.ǩa.ram/
(شما) بخرید	(تو) بخری
/(šo.mǎ) be.ǩa.rid/	/(to) be.ǩa.ri/
(آنها) بخرند	(او/آن) بخرد
/(ǎn.hǎ) be.ǩa.rand/	/(u/ ǎn) be.ǩa.rad/
Present Progressive	
مضارع مستمر(در جریان)	
(ما) داریم می خریم	(من) دارم می خرم
/(mǎ) dǎ.rim- mi.ǩa.rim/	/(man) dǎ.ram- mi.ǩa.ram/
(شما) دارید می خرید	(تو) داری می خری
/(šo.mǎ) dǎ.rid- mi.ǩa.rid/	/(to) dǎ.ri- mi.ǩa.ri/
(آنها) دارند می خرند	(او/آن) دارد می خرد
/(ǎn.hǎ) dǎ.rand- mi.ǩa.rand/	/(u/ ǎn) dǎ.rad- mi.ǩa.rad/

Simple Past
ماضی مطلق (گذشته ساده)

(ما) خریدیم	(من) خریدم
/(mă) ǩa.ri.dim/	/(man) ǩa.ri.dam/
(شما) خریدید	(تو) خریدی
/(šo.mă) ǩa.ri.did/	/(to) ǩa.ri.di/
(آنها) خریدند	(او/آن) خرید
/(ăn.hă) ǩa.ri.dand/	/(u/ ăn) ǩa.rid/

Imperfect Indicative
ماضی استمراری

(ما) می خریدیم	(من) می خریدم
/(mă) mi.ǩa.ri.dim/	/(man) mi.ǩa.ri.dam/
(شما) می خریدید	(تو) می خریدی
/(šo.mă) mi.ǩa.ri.did/	/(to) mi.ǩa.ri.di/
(آنها) می خریدند	(او/آن) می خرید
/(ăn.hă) mi.ǩa.ri.dand/	/(u/ ăn) mi.ǩa.rid/

Present Perfect
ماضی نقلی

(ما) خریده ایم	(من) خریده ام
/(mă) ǩa.ri.de.im/	/(man) ǩa.ri.de.am/
(شما) خریده اید	(تو) خریده ای
/(šo.mă) ǩa.ri.de.id/	/(to) ǩa.ri.de.i/
(آنها) خریده اند	(او/آن) خریده است
/(ăn.hă) ǩa.ri.de.and/	/(u/ ăn) ǩa.ri.de- ast/

Past Perfect
ماضی بعید

(ما) خریده بودیم	(من) خریده بودم
/(mă) ǩa.ri.de- bu.dim/	/(man) ǩa.ri.de- bu.dam/
(شما) خریده بودید	(تو) خریده بودی
/(šo.mă) ǩa.ri.de- bu.did/	/(to) ǩa.ri.de- bu.di/
(آنها) خریده بودند	(او/آن) خریده بود
/(ăn.hă) ǩa.ri.de- bu.dand/	/(u/ ăn) ǩa.ri.de- bud/

27

Past Subjunctive		
ماضی التزامی		
(ما) خریده باشیم		(من) خریده باشم
/(mǎ) ǩa.ri.de- bǎ.šim/		/(man) ǩa.ri.de- bǎ.šam/
(شما) خریده باشید		(تو) خریده باشی
/(šo.mǎ) ǩa.ri.de- bǎ.šid/		/(to) ǩa.ri.de- bǎ.ši/
(آنها) خریده باشند		(او/آن) خریده باشد
/(ǎn.hǎ) ǩa.ri.de- bǎ.šand/		/(u/ ǎn) ǩa.ri.de- bǎ.šad/

Past Progressive		
ماضی مستمر(در جریان)		
(ما) داشتیم می خریدیم		(من) داشتم می خریدم
/(mǎ) dǎš.tim- mi.ǩa.ri.dim/		/(man) dǎš.tam- mi.ǩa.ri.dam/
(شما) داشتید می خریدید		(تو) داشتی می خریدی
/(šo.mǎ) dǎš.tid- mi.ǩa.ri.did/		/(to) dǎš.ti- mi.ǩa.ri.di/
(آنها) داشتند می خریدند		(او/آن) داشت می خرید
/(ǎn.hǎ) dǎš.tand- mi.ǩa.ri.dand/		/(u/ ǎn) dǎšt- mi.ǩa.rid/

Simple Future		
مستقبل (آینده ساده)		
(ما) خواهیم خرید		(من) خواهم خرید
/(mǎ) ǩǎ.him- ǩa.rid/		/(man) ǩǎ.ham- ǩa.rid/
(شما) خواهید خرید		(تو) خواهی خرید
/(šo.mǎ) ǩǎ.hid- ǩa.rid/		/(to) ǩǎ.hi- ǩa.rid/
(آنها) خواهند خرید		(او/آن) خواهد خرید
/(ǎn.hǎ) ǩǎ.hand- ǩa.rid/		/(u/ ǎn) ǩǎ.had- ǩa.rid/

Command		
امر		
بخرید!		بخر!
/be.ǩa.rid/		/be.ǩar/

to call

تلِفُن کَردَن

/te.le.fon- kar.dan/

Plural	Singular
Simple Present	
مضارع اخباری(حال ساده)	
(ما) تلفن می کنیم	(من) تلفن می کنم
/(mă) te.le.fon- mi.ko.nim/	/(man) te.le.fon- mi.ko.nam/
(شما) تلفن می کنید	(تو) تلفن می کنی
/(šo.mă) te.le.fon- mi.ko.nid/	/(to) te.le.fon- mi.ko.ni/
(آنها) تلفن می کنند	(او/آن) تلفن می کند
/(ăn.hă) te.le.fon- mi.ko.nand/	/(u/ ăn) te.le.fon- mi.ko.nad/
Present Subjunctive	
مضارع التزامی	
(ما) تلفن بکنیم	(من) تلفن بکنم
/(mă) te.le.fon- be.ko.nim/	/(man) te.le.fon- be.ko.nam/
(شما) تلفن بکنید	(تو) تلفن بکنی
/(šo.mă) te.le.fon- be.ko.nid/	/(to) te.le.fon- be.ko.ni/
(آنها) تلفن بکنند	(او/آن) تلفن بکند
/(ăn.hă) te.le.fon- be.ko.nand/	/(u/ ăn) te.le.fon- be.ko.nad/
Present Progressive	
مضارع مستمر(در جریان)	
(ما) داریم تلفن می کنیم	(من) دارم تلفن می کنم
/(mă) dă.rim- te.le.fon- mi.ko.nim/	/(man) dă.ram- te.le.fon- mi.ko.nam/
(شما) دارید تلفن می کنید	(تو) داری تلفن می کنی
/(šo.mă) dă.rid- te.le.fon- mi.ko.nid/	/(to)) dă.ri- te.le.fon- mi.ko.ni/
(آنها) دارند تلفن می کنند	(او/آن) دارد تلفن می کند
/(ăn.hă) dă.rand- te.le.fon- mi.ko.nand/	/(u/ ăn) dă.rad- te.le.fon- mi.ko.nad/

29

Simple Past
ماضی مطلق (گذشته ساده)

(ما) تلفن کردیم	(من) تلفن کردم
/(mǎ) te.le.fon- kar.dim/	/(man) te.le.fon- kar.dam/
(شما) تلفن کردید	(تو) تلفن کردی
/(šo.mǎ) te.le.fon- kar.did/	/(to) te.le.fon- kar.di/
(آنها) تلفن کردند	(او/آن) تلفن کرد
/(ǎn.hǎ) te.le.fon- kar.dand/	/(u/ ǎn) te.le.fon- kard/

Imperfect Indicative
ماضی استمراری

(ما) تلفن می کردیم	(من) تلفن می کردم
/(mǎ) te.le.fon- mi.kar.dim/	/(man) te.le.fon- mi.kar.dam/
(شما) تلفن می کردید	(تو) تلفن می کردی
/(šo.mǎ) te.le.fon- mi.kar.did/	/(to) te.le.fon- mi.kar.di/
(آنها) تلفن می کردند	(او/آن) تلفن می کرد
/(ǎn.hǎ) te.le.fon- mi.kar.dand/	/(u/ ǎn) te.le.fon- mi.kard/

Present Perfect
ماضی نقلی

(ما) تلفن کرده ایم	(من) تلفن کرده ام
/(mǎ) te.le.fon- kar.de.im/	/(man) te.le.fon- kar.de.am/
(شما) تلفن کرده اید	(تو) تلفن کرده ای
/(šo.mǎ) te.le.fon- kar.de.id/	/(to) te.le.fon- kar.de.i/
(آنها) تلفن کرده اند	(او/آن) تلفن کرده است
/(ǎn.hǎ) te.le.fon- kar.de.and/	/(u/ ǎn) te.le.fon- kar.de- ast/

Past Perfect
ماضی بعید

(ما) تلفن کرده بودیم	(من) تلفن کرده بودم
/(mǎ) te.le.fon- kar.de- bu.dim/	/(man) te.le.fon- kar.de- bu.dam/
(شما) تلفن کرده بودید	(تو) تلفن کرده بودی
/(šo.mǎ) te.le.fon- kar.de- bu.did/	/(to) te.le.fon- kar.de- bu.di/
(آنها) تلفن کرده بودند	(او/آن) تلفن کرده بود
/(ǎn.hǎ) te.le.fon- kar.de- bu.dand/	/(u/ ǎn) te.le.fon- kar.de- bud/

Past Subjunctive
ماضی التزامی

(ما) تلفن کرده باشیم	(من) تلفن کرده باشم
/(mă) te.le.fon- kar.de- bă.šim/	/(man) te.le.fon- kar.de- bă.šam/
(شما) تلفن کرده باشید	(تو) تلفن کرده باشی
/(šo.mă) te.le.fon- kar.de- bă.šid/	/(to) te.le.fon- kar.de- bă.ši/
(آنها) تلفن کرده باشند	(او/آن) تلفن کرده باشد
/(ăn.hă) te.le.fon- kar.de- bă.šand/	/(u/ ăn) te.le.fon- kar.de- bă.šad/

Past Progressive
ماضی مستمر(در جریان)

(ما) داشتیم تلفن می کردیم	(من) داشتم تلفن می کردم
/(mă) dăš.tim- te.le.fon- mi.kar.dim/	/(man) dăš.tam- te.le.fon- mi.kar.dam/
(شما) داشتید تلفن می کردید	(تو) داشتی تلفن می کردی
/(šo.mă) dăš.tid- te.le.fon- mi.kar.did/	/(to) dăš.ti- te.le.fon- mi.kar.di/
(آنها) داشتند تلفن می کردند	(او/آن) داشت تلفن می کرد
/(ăn.hă) dăš.tand- te.le.fon- mi.kar.dand/	/(u/ ăn) dăšt- te.le.fon- mi.kard/

Simple Future
مستقبل (آینده ساده)

(ما) تلفن خواهیم کرد	(من) تلفن خواهم کرد
/(mă) te.le.fon- kă.him- kard/	/(man) te.le.fon- kă.ham- kard/
(شما) تلفن خواهید کرد	(تو) تلفن خواهی کرد
/(šo.mă) te.le.fon- kă.hid- kard/	/(to) te.le.fon- kă.hi- kard/
(آنها) تلفن خواهند کرد	(او/آن) تلفن خواهد کرد
/(ăn.hă) te.le.fon- kă.hand- kard/	/(u/ ăn) te.le.fon- kă.had- kard/

Command
امر

* تلفن بکنید!	* تلفن بکن!
/te.le.fon- be.ko.nid/	/te.le.fon- be.kon/

*   also: تلفن کنید!   تلفن کن!

to catch

گِرِفتَن

/ge.ref.tan/

Plural	Singular
Simple Present	
مضارع اخباری(حال ساده)	
(ما) می گیریم	(من) می گیرم
/(mă) mi.gi.rim/	/(man) mi.gi.ram/
(شما) می گیرید	(تو) می گیری
/(šo.mă) mi.gi.rid/	/(to) mi.gi.ri/
(آنها) می گیرند	(او/آن) می گیرد
/(ăn.hă) mi.gi.rand/	/(u/ ăn) mi.gi.rad/

Plural	Singular
Present Subjunctive	
مضارع التزامی	
(ما) بگیریم	(من) بگیرم
/(mă) be.gi.rim/	/(man) be.gi.ram/
(شما) بگیرید	(تو) بگیری
/(šo.mă) be.gi.rid/	/(to) be.gi.ri/
(آنها) بگیرند	(او/آن) بگیرد
/(ăn.hă) be.gi.rand/	/(u/ ăn) be.gi.rad/

Plural	Singular
Present Progressive	
مضارع مستمر(در جریان)	
(ما) داریم می گیریم	(من) دارم می گیرم
/(mă) dă.rim- mi.gi.rim/	/(man) dă.ram- mi.gi.ram/
(شما) دارید می گیرید	(تو) داری می گیری
/(šo.mă) dă.rid- mi.gi.rid/	/(to) dă.ri- mi.gi.ri/
(آنها) دارند می گیرند	(او/آن) دارد می گیرد
/(ăn.hă) dă.rand- mi.gi.rand/	/(u/ ăn) dă.rad- mi.gi.rad/

Simple Past
ماضی مطلق (گذشته ساده)

(ما) گرفتیم	(من) گرفتم
/(mǎ) ge.ref.tim/	/(man) ge.ref.tam/
(شما) گرفتید	(تو) گرفتی
/(šo.mǎ) ge.ref.tid/	/(to) ge.ref.ti/
(آنها) گرفتند	(او/آن) گرفت
/(ǎn.hǎ) ge.ref.tand/	/(u/ ǎn) ge.reft/

Imperfect Indicative
ماضی استمراری

(ما) می گرفتیم	(من) می گرفتم
/(mǎ) mi.ge.ref.tim/	/(man) mi.ge.ref.tam/
(شما) می گرفتید	(تو) می گرفتی
/(šo.mǎ) mi.ge.ref.tid/	/(to) mi.ge.ref.ti/
(آنها) می گرفتند	(او/آن) می گرفت
/(ǎn.hǎ) mi.ge.ref.tand/	/(u/ ǎn) mi.ge.reft/

Present Perfect
ماضی نقلی

(ما) گرفته ایم	(من) گرفته ام
/(mǎ) ge.ref.te.im/	/(man) ge.ref.te.am/
(شما) گرفته اید	(تو) گرفته ای
/(šo.mǎ) ge.ref.te.id/	/(to) ge.ref.te.i/
(آنها) گرفته اند	(او/آن) گرفته است
/(ǎn.hǎ) ge.ref.te.and/	/(u/ ǎn) ge.ref.te- ast/

Past Perfect
ماضی بعید

(ما) گرفته بودیم	(من) گرفته بودم
/(mǎ) ge.ref.te- bu.dim/	/(man) ge.ref.te- bu.dam/
(شما) گرفته بودید	(تو) گرفته بودی
/(šo.mǎ) ge.ref.te- bu.did/	/(to) ge.ref.te- bu.di/
(آنها) گرفته بودند	(او/آن) گرفته بود
/(ǎn.hǎ) ge.ref.te- bu.dand/	/(u/ ǎn) ge.ref.te- bud/

Past Subjunctive	
ماضی التزامی	
(ما) گرفته باشیم	(من) گرفته باشم
/(mǎ) ge.ref.te- bǎ.šim/	/(man) ge.ref.te- bǎ.šam/
(شما) گرفته باشید	(تو) گرفته باشی
/(šo.mǎ) ge.ref.te- bǎ.šid/	/(to) ge.ref.te- bǎ.ši/
(آنها) گرفته باشند	(او/ آن) گرفته باشد
/(ǎn.hǎ) ge.ref.te- bǎ.šand/	/(u/ ǎn) ge.ref.te- bǎ.šad/

Past Progressive	
ماضی مستمر(در جریان)	
(ما) داشتیم می گرفتیم	(من) داشتم می گرفتم
/(mǎ) dǎš.tim- mi.ge.ref.tim/	/(man) dǎš.tam- mi.ge.ref.tam/
(شما) داشتید می گرفتید	(تو) داشتی می گرفتی
/(šo.mǎ) dǎš.tid- mi.ge.ref.tid/	/(to) dǎš.ti- mi.ge.ref.ti/
(آنها) داشتند می گرفتند	(او/آن) داشت می گرفت
/(ǎn.hǎ) dǎš.tand- mi.ge.ref.tand/	/(u/ ǎn) dǎšt- mi.ge.reft/

Simple Future	
مستقبل (آینده ساده)	
(ما) خواهیم گرفت	(من) خواهم گرفت
/(mǎ) ǩǎ.him- ge.reft/	/(man) ǩǎ.ham- ge.reft/
(شما) خواهید گرفت	(تو) خواهی گرفت
/(šo.mǎ) ǩǎ.hid- ge.reft/	/(to) ǩǎ.hi- ge.reft/
(آنها) خواهند گرفت	(او/آن) خواهد گرفت
/(ǎn.hǎ) ǩǎ.hand- ge.reft/	/(u/ ǎn) ǩǎ.had- ge.reft/

Command	
امر	
بگیرید!	بگیر!
/be.gi.rid/	/be.gir/

to change

عَوَض کَردَن

/aʿ.vaz- kar.dan/

Plural	Singular
Simple Present مضارع اخباری(حال ساده)	*(handwritten)* (I change)
(ما) عوض می کنیم /(mă) aʿ.vaz- mi.ko.nim/	(من) عوض می کنم /(man) aʿ.vaz- mi.ko.nam/
(شما) عوض می کنید /(šo.mă) aʿ.vaz- mi.ko.nid/	(تو) عوض می کنی /(to) aʿ.vaz- mi.ko.ni/
(آنها) عوض می کنند /(ăn.hă) aʿ.vaz- mi.ko.nand/	(او/آن) عوض می کند /(u/ ăn) aʿ.vaz- mi.ko.nad/
Present Subjunctive مضارع التزامی	*(handwritten)* I want / indecisive
(ما) عوض بکنیم /(mă) aʿ.vaz- be.ko.nim/	(من) عوض بکنم /(man) aʿ.vaz- be.ko.nam/
(شما) عوض بکنید /(šo.mă) aʿ.vaz- be.ko.nid/	(تو) عوض بکنی /(to) aʿ.vaz- be.ko.ni/
(آنها) عوض بکنند /(ăn.hă) aʿ.vaz- be.ko.nand/	(او/آن) عوض بکند /(u/ ăn) aʿ.vaz- be.ko.nad/
Present Progressive مضارع مستمر(در جریان)	*(handwritten)* I am changing
(ما) داریم عوض می کنیم /(mă) dă.rim- aʿ.vaz- mi.ko.nim/	(من) دارم عوض می کنم /(man) dă.ram- aʿ.vaz- mi.ko.nam/
(شما) دارید عوض می کنید /(šo.mă) dă.rid- aʿ.vaz- mi.ko.nid/	(تو) داری عوض می کنی /(to) dă.ri- aʿ.vaz- mi.ko.ni/
(آنها) دارند عوض می کنند /(ăn.hă) dă.rand- aʿ.vaz- mi.ko.nand/	(او/آن) دارد عوض می کند /(u/ ăn) dă.rad- aʿ.vaz- mi.ko.nad/

<table>
<tr><td colspan="2" align="center">**Simple Past**
ماضی مطلق (گذشته ساده)   _I changed_</td></tr>
<tr><td align="right">(ما) عوض کردیم</td><td align="right">(من) عوض کردم</td></tr>
<tr><td>/(mă) aʿ.vaz- kar.dim/</td><td>/(man) aʿ.vaz- kar.dam/</td></tr>
<tr><td align="right">(شما) عوض کردید</td><td align="right">(تو) عوض کردی</td></tr>
<tr><td>/(šo.mă) aʿ.vaz- kar.did/</td><td>/(to) aʿ.vaz- kar.di/</td></tr>
<tr><td align="right">(آنها) عوض کردند</td><td align="right">(او/آن) عوض کرد</td></tr>
<tr><td>/(ăn.hă) aʿ.vaz- kar.dand/</td><td>/(u/ ăn) aʿ.vaz- kard/</td></tr>
</table>

<table>
<tr><td colspan="2" align="center">**Imperfect Indicative**
ماضی استمراری   _I was changing_</td></tr>
<tr><td align="right">(ما) عوض می کردیم</td><td align="right">(من) عوض می کردم</td></tr>
<tr><td>/(mă) aʿ.vaz- mi.kar.dim/</td><td>/(man) aʿ.vaz- mi.kar.dam/</td></tr>
<tr><td align="right">(شما) عوض می کردید</td><td align="right">(تو) عوض می کردی</td></tr>
<tr><td>/(šo.mă) aʿ.vaz- mi.kar.did/</td><td>/(to) aʿ.vaz- mi. kar.di/</td></tr>
<tr><td align="right">(آنها) عوض می کردند</td><td align="right">(او/آن) عوض می کرد</td></tr>
<tr><td>/(ăn.hă) aʿ.vaz- mi.kar.dand/</td><td>/(u/ ăn) aʿ.vaz- mi.kard/</td></tr>
</table>

<table>
<tr><td colspan="2" align="center">**Present Perfect** _I have changed_
ماضی نقلی</td></tr>
<tr><td align="right">(ما) عوض کرده ایم</td><td align="right">(من) عوض کرده ام</td></tr>
<tr><td>/(mă) aʿ.vaz- kar.de.im/</td><td>/(man) aʿ.vaz- kar.de.am/</td></tr>
<tr><td align="right">(شما) عوض کرده اید</td><td align="right">(تو) عوض کرده ای</td></tr>
<tr><td>/(šo.mă) aʿ.vaz- kar.de.id/</td><td>/(to) aʿ.vaz- kar.de.i/</td></tr>
<tr><td align="right">(آنها) عوض کرده اند</td><td align="right">(او/آن) عوض کرده است</td></tr>
<tr><td>/(ăn.hă) aʿ.vaz- kar.de.and/</td><td>/(u/ ăn) aʿ.vaz- kar.de- ast/</td></tr>
</table>

<table>
<tr><td colspan="2" align="center">**Past Perfect** _I had changed_
ماضی بعید</td></tr>
<tr><td align="right">(ما) عوض کرده بودیم</td><td align="right">(من) عوض کرده بودم</td></tr>
<tr><td>/(mă) aʿ.vaz- kar.de- bu.dim/</td><td>/(man) aʿ.vaz- kar.de- bu.dam/</td></tr>
<tr><td align="right">(شما) عوض کرده بودید</td><td align="right">(تو) عوض کرده بودی</td></tr>
<tr><td>/(šo.mă) aʿ.vaz-kar.de- bu.did/</td><td>/(to) aʿ.vaz- kar.de- bu.di/</td></tr>
<tr><td align="right">(آنها) عوض کرده بودند</td><td align="right">(او/آن) عوض کرده بود</td></tr>
<tr><td>/(ăn.hă) aʿ.vaz- kar.de- bu.dand/</td><td>/(u/ ăn)aʿ.vaz- kar.de- bud/</td></tr>
</table>

<table>
<tr><td colspan="2" align="center">**Past Subjunctive**
ماضی التزامی</td></tr>
<tr>
<td align="center">(ما) عوض کرده باشیم
/(mă) aˈ.vaz- kar.de- bă.šim/</td>
<td align="center">(من) عوض کرده باشم
/(man) aˈ.vaz- kar.de- bă.šam/</td>
</tr>
<tr>
<td align="center">(شما) عوض کرده باشید
/(šo.mă) aˈ.vaz- kar.de- bă.šid/</td>
<td align="center">(تو) عوض کرده باشی
/(to) aˈ.vaz- kar.de- bă.ši/</td>
</tr>
<tr>
<td align="center">(آنها) عوض کرده باشند
/(ăn.hă) aˈ.vaz- kar.de- bă.šand/</td>
<td align="center">(او/آن) عوض کرده باشد
/(u/ ăn) aˈ.vaz- kar.de- bă.šad/</td>
</tr>
</table>

Past Progressive
ماضی مستمر(در جریان)   _I use to was changing_

<table>
<tr>
<td align="center">(ما) داشتیم عوض می کردیم
/(mă) dăš.tim- aˈ.vaz- mi.kar.dim/</td>
<td align="center">(من) داشتم عوض می کردم
/(man) dăš.tam- aˈ.vaz- mi.kar.dam/</td>
</tr>
<tr>
<td align="center">(شما) داشتید عوض می کردید
/(šo.mă) dăš.tid- aˈ.vaz- mi.kar.did/</td>
<td align="center">(تو) داشتی عوض می کردی
/(to) dăš.ti- aˈ.vaz- mi.kar.di/</td>
</tr>
<tr>
<td align="center">(آنها) داشتند عوض می کردند
/(ăn.hă) dăš.tand- aˈ.vaz- mi.kar.dand/</td>
<td align="center">(او/آن) داشت عوض می کرد
/(u/ ăn) dăšt- aˈ.vaz- mi.kard/</td>
</tr>
</table>

Simple Future
مستقبل (آینده ساده)   _I will change_

<table>
<tr>
<td align="center">(ما) عوض خواهیم کرد
/(mă) aˈ.vaz- ǩă.him- kard/</td>
<td align="center">(من) عوض خواهم کرد
/(man) aˈ.vaz- ǩă.ham- kard/</td>
</tr>
<tr>
<td align="center">(شما) عوض خواهید کرد
/(šo.mă) aˈ.vaz- ǩă.hid- kard/</td>
<td align="center">(تو) عوض خواهی کرد
/(to) aˈ.vaz- ǩă.hi- kard/</td>
</tr>
<tr>
<td align="center">(آنها) عوض خواهند کرد
/(ăn.hă) aˈ.vaz- ǩă.hand- kard/</td>
<td align="center">(او/آن) عوض خواهد کرد
/(u/ ăn) aˈ.vaz- ǩă.had- kard/</td>
</tr>
</table>

<table>
<tr><td colspan="2" align="center">**Command**
امر</td></tr>
<tr>
<td align="center">* عوض بکنید !
/aˈ.vaz- be.ko.nid/</td>
<td align="center">* عوض بکن !
/aˈ.vaz- be.kon/</td>
</tr>
</table>

* also: عوض کن !   عوض کنید !

to choose

انتِخاب کَردَن

/en.te.ǩăb- kar.dan/

Plural	Singular
Simple Present	
مضارع اخباری(حال ساده)	
(ما) انتخاب می کنیم	(من) انتخاب می کنم
/(mă) en.te.ǩăb- mi.ko.nim/	/(man) en.te.ǩăb- mi.ko.nam/
(شما) انتخاب می کنید	(تو) انتخاب می کنی
/(šo.mă) en.te.ǩăb- mi.ko.nid/	/(to) en.te.ǩăb- mi.ko.ni/
(آنها) انتخاب می کنند	(او/آن) انتخاب می کند
/(ăn.hă) en.te.ǩăb- mi.ko.nand/	/(u/ăn) en.te.ǩăb- mi.ko.nad/
Present Subjunctive	
مضارع التزامی	
(ما) انتخاب بکنیم	(من) انتخاب بکنم
/(mă) en.te.ǩăb- be.ko.nim/	/(man) en.te.ǩăb- be.ko.nam/
(شما) انتخاب بکنید	(تو) انتخاب بکنی
/(šo.mă) en.te.ǩăb- be.ko.nid/	/(to) en.te.ǩăb- be.ko.ni/
(آنها) انتخاب بکنند	(او/آن) انتخاب بکند
/(ăn.hă) en.te.ǩăb- be.ko.nand/	/(u/ ăn/) en.te.ǩăb- be.ko.nad/
Present Progressive	
مضارع مستمر(در جریان)	
(ما) داریم انتخاب می کنیم	(من) دارم انتخاب می کنم
/(mă) dă.rim- en.te.ǩăb- mi.ko.nim/	/(man) dă.ram- en.te.ǩăb- mi.ko.nam/
(شما) دارید انتخاب می کنید	(تو) داری انتخاب می کنی
/(šo.mă) dă.rid- en.te.ǩăb- mi.ko.nid/	/(to) dă.ri- en.te.ǩăb- mi.ko.ni/
(آنها) دارند انتخاب می کنند	(او/آن) دارد انتخاب می کند
/(ăn.hă) dă.rand- en.te.ǩăb- mi.ko.nand/	/(u/ ăn) dă.rad- en.te.ǩăb- mi.ko.nad/

<table>
<tr><td colspan="2" align="center">**Simple Past**
ماضی مطلق (گذشته ساده)</td></tr>
<tr>
<td align="center">(ما) انتخاب کردیم
/(mă) en.te.ǩăb- kar.dim/</td>
<td align="center">(من) انتخاب کردم
/(man) en.te.ǩăb- kar.dam/</td>
</tr>
<tr>
<td align="center">(شما) انتخاب کردید
/(šo.mă) en.te.ǩăb- kar.did/</td>
<td align="center">(تو) انتخاب کردی
/(to) en.te.ǩăb- kar.di/</td>
</tr>
<tr>
<td align="center">(آنها) انتخاب کردند
/(ăn.hă) en.te.ǩăb- kar.dand/</td>
<td align="center">(او/ آن) انتخاب کرد
/(u/ ăn) en.te.ǩăb- kard/</td>
</tr>
</table>

<table>
<tr><td colspan="2" align="center">**Imperfect Indicative**
ماضی استمراری</td></tr>
<tr>
<td align="center">(ما) انتخاب می کردیم
/(mă) en.te.ǩăb- mi.kar.dim/</td>
<td align="center">(من) انتخاب می کردم
/(man) en.te.ǩăb- mi.kar.dam/</td>
</tr>
<tr>
<td align="center">(شما) انتخاب می کردید
/(šo.mă) en.te.ǩăb- mi.kar.did/</td>
<td align="center">(تو) انتخاب می کردی
/(to) en.te.ǩăb- mi.kar.di/</td>
</tr>
<tr>
<td align="center">(آنها) انتخاب می کردند
/(ăn.hă) en.te.ǩăb- mi.kar.dand/</td>
<td align="center">(او/آن) انتخاب می کرد
/(u/ ăn) en.te.ǩăb- mi.kard/</td>
</tr>
</table>

<table>
<tr><td colspan="2" align="center">**Present Perfect**
ماضی نقلی</td></tr>
<tr>
<td align="center">(ما) انتخاب کرده ایم
/(mă) en.te.ǩăb- kar.de.im/</td>
<td align="center">(من) انتخاب کرده ام
(man) en.te.ǩăb- kar.de.am/</td>
</tr>
<tr>
<td align="center">(شما) انتخاب کرده اید
/(šo.mă) en.te.ǩăb- kar.de.id/</td>
<td align="center">(تو) انتخاب کرده ای
/(to) en.te.ǩăb- kar.de.i/</td>
</tr>
<tr>
<td align="center">(آنها) انتخاب کرده اند
/(ăn.hă) en.te.ǩăb- kar.de.and/</td>
<td align="center">(او/آن) انتخاب کرده است
/(u/ăn) en.te.ǩăb- kar.de- ast/</td>
</tr>
</table>

<table>
<tr><td colspan="2" align="center">**Past Perfect**
ماضی بعید</td></tr>
<tr>
<td align="center">(ما) انتخاب کرده بودیم
/(mă) en.te.ǩăb- kar.de- bu.dim/</td>
<td align="center">(من) انتخاب کرده بودم
/(man) en.te.ǩăb- kar.de- bu.dam/</td>
</tr>
<tr>
<td align="center">(شما) انتخاب کرده بودید
/(šo.mă) en.te.ǩăb- kar.de- bu.did/</td>
<td align="center">(تو) انتخاب کرده بودی
/(to) en.te.ǩăb- kar.de- bu.di/</td>
</tr>
<tr>
<td align="center">(آنها) انتخاب کرده بودند
/(ăn.hă) en.te.ǩăb- kar.de- bu.dand/</td>
<td align="center">(او/ آن) انتخاب کرده بود
/(u/ ăn) en.te.ǩăb- kar.de- bud/</td>
</tr>
</table>

<table>
<tr><td colspan="2" align="center">Past Subjunctive
ماضی التزامی</td></tr>
<tr>
<td align="center">(ما) انتخاب کرده باشیم
/(mă) en.te.ǩăb- kar.de- bă.šim/</td>
<td align="center">(من) انتخاب کرده باشم
/(man) en.te.ǩăb- kar.de- bă.šam/</td>
</tr>
<tr>
<td align="center">(شما) انتخاب کرده باشید
/(šo.mă) en.te.ǩăb- kar.de- bă.šid/</td>
<td align="center">(تو) انتخاب کرده باشی
/(to) en.te.ǩăb- kar.de- bă.ši/</td>
</tr>
<tr>
<td align="center">(آنها) انتخاب کرده باشند
/(ăn.hă) en.te.ǩăb- kar.de- bă.šand/</td>
<td align="center">(او/آن) انتخاب کرده باشد
/(u/ ăn) en.te.ǩăb- kar.de- bă.šad/</td>
</tr>
</table>

<table>
<tr><td colspan="2" align="center">Past Progressive
ماضی مستمر(در جریان)</td></tr>
<tr>
<td align="center">(ما) داشتیم انتخاب می کردیم
/(mă) dăš.tim- en.te.ǩăb- mi.kar.dim/</td>
<td align="center">(من) داشتم انتخاب می کردم
/(man) dăš.tam- en.te.ǩăb- mi.kar.dam/</td>
</tr>
<tr>
<td align="center">(شما) داشتید انتخاب می کردید
/(šo.mă) dăš.tid- en.te.ǩăb- mi.kar.did/</td>
<td align="center">(تو) داشتی انتخاب می کردی
/(to) dăš.ti- en.te.ǩăb- mi.kar.di/</td>
</tr>
<tr>
<td align="center">(آنها) داشتند انتخاب می کردند
/(ăn.hă) dăš.tand- en.te.ǩăb- mi.kar.dand/</td>
<td align="center">(او/آن) داشت انتخاب می کرد
/(u/ ăn) dăšt- en.te.ǩăb- mi.kard/</td>
</tr>
</table>

<table>
<tr><td colspan="2" align="center">Simple Future
مستقبل (آینده ساده)</td></tr>
<tr>
<td align="center">(ما) انتخاب خواهیم کرد
/(mă) en.te.ǩăb- ǩă.him- kard/</td>
<td align="center">(من) انتخاب خواهم کرد
/(man) en.te.ǩăb- ǩă.ham- kard/</td>
</tr>
<tr>
<td align="center">(شما) انتخاب خواهید کرد
/(šo.mă) en.te.ǩăb- ǩă.hid- kard/</td>
<td align="center">(تو) انتخاب خواهی کرد
/(to) en.te.ǩăb- ǩă.hi- kard/</td>
</tr>
<tr>
<td align="center">(آنها) انتخاب خواهند کرد
/(ăn.hă) en.te.ǩăb- ǩă.hand- kard/</td>
<td align="center">(او/آن) انتخاب خواهد کرد
/(u/ ăn) en.te.ǩăb- ǩă.had- kard/</td>
</tr>
</table>

<table>
<tr><td colspan="2" align="center">Command
امر</td></tr>
<tr>
<td align="center">* انتخاب بکنید!
/en.te.ǩăb- be.ko.nid/</td>
<td align="center">* انتخاب بکن!
/en.te.ǩăb- be.kon/</td>
</tr>
</table>

* also: انتخاب کن ! انتخاب کنید !

to close

بَستَن

/bas.tan/

Plural	Singular
Simple Present	
مضارع اخباری(حال ساده)	
(ما) می بندیم	(من) می بندم
/(mǎ) mi.ban.dim/	/(man) mi.ban.dam/
(شما) می بندید	(تو) می بندی
/(šo.mǎ) mi.ban.did/	/(to) mi.ban.di/
(آنها) می بندند	(او/آن) می بندد
/(ǎn.hǎ) mi.ban.dand/	/(u/ ǎn) mi.ban.dad/
Present Subjunctive	
مضارع التزامی	
(ما) ببندیم	(من) ببندم
/(mǎ) be.ban.dim/	/(man) be.ban.dam/
(شما) ببندید	(تو) ببندی
/(šo.mǎ) be.ban.did/	/(to) be.ban.di/
(آنها) ببندند	(او/آن) ببندد
/(ǎn.hǎ) be.ban.dand/	/(u/ ǎn) be.ban.dad/
Present Progressive	
مضارع مستمر(در جریان)	
(ما) داریم می بندیم	(من) دارم می بندم
/(mǎ) dǎ.rim- mi.ban.dim/	/(man) dǎ.ram- mi.ban.dam/
(شما) دارید می بندید	(تو) داری می بندی
/(šo.mǎ) dǎ.rid- mi.ban.did/	/(to) dǎ.ri- mi.ban.di/
(آنها) دارند می بندند	(او/آن) دارد می بندد
/(ǎn.hǎ) dǎ.rand- mi.ban.dand/	/(u/ ǎn) dǎ.rad- mi.ban.dad/

41

Simple Past
ماضی مطلق (گذشته ساده)

(ما) بستیم	(من) بستم
/(mǎ) bas.tim/	/(man) bas.tam/
(شما) بستید	(تو) بستی
/(šo.mǎ) bas.tid/	/(to) bas.ti/
(آنها) بستند	(او/ آن) بست
/(ǎn.hǎ) bas.tand/	/(u/ ǎn) bast/

Imperfect Indicative
ماضی استمراری

(ما) می بستیم	(من) می بستم
/(mǎ) mi.bas.tim/	/(man) mi.bas.tam/
(شما) می بستید	(تو) می بستی
/(šo.mǎ) mi.bas.tid/	/(to) mi.bas.ti/
(آنها) می بستند	(او/آن) می بست
/(ǎn.hǎ) mi.bas.tand/	/(u/ ǎn) mi.bast/

Present Perfect
ماضی نقلی

(ما) بسته ایم	(من) بسته ام
/(mǎ) bas.te.im/	/(man) bas.te.am/
(شما) بسته اید	(تو) بسته ای
/(šo.mǎ) bas.te.id/	/(to) bas.te.i/
(آنها) بسته اند	(او/آن) بسته است
/(ǎn.hǎ) bas.te.and/	/(u/ ǎn) bas.te- ast/

Past Perfect
ماضی بعید

(ما) بسته بودیم	(من) بسته بودم
/(mǎ) bas.te- bu.dim/	/(man) bas.te- bu.dam/
(شما) بسته بودید	(تو) بسته بودی
/(šo.mǎ) bas.te- bu.did/	/(to) bas.te- bu.di/
(آنها) بسته بودند	(او/آن) بسته بود
/(ǎn.hǎ) bas.te- bu.dand/	/(u/ ǎn) bas.te- bud/

	Past Subjunctive
	ماضی التزامی
(ما) بسته باشیم	(من) بسته باشم
/(mă) bas.te- bă.šim/	/(man) bas.te- bă.šam/
(شما) بسته باشید	(تو) بسته باشی
/(šo.mă) bas.te- bă.šid/	/(to) bas.te- bă.ši/
(آنها) بسته باشند	(او/آن) بسته باشد
/(ăn.hă) bas.te- bă.šand/	/(u/ ăn) bas.te- bă.šad/

	Past Progressive
	ماضی مستمر(در جریان)
(ما) داشتیم می بستیم	(من) داشتم می بستم
/(mă) dăš.tim- mi.bas.tim/	/(man) dăš.tam- mi.bas.tam/
(شما) داشتید می بستید	(تو) داشتی می بستی
/(šo.mă) dăš.tid- mi.bas.tid/	/(to) dăš.ti- mi.bas.ti/
(آنها) داشتند می بستند	(او/آن) داشت می بست
/(ăn.hă) dăš.tand- mi.bas.tand/	/(u/ ăn) dăšt- mi.bast/

	Simple Future
	مستقبل (آینده ساده)
(ما) خواهیم بست	(من) خواهم بست
/(mă) kă.him- bast/	/(man) kă.ham- bast/
(شما) خواهید بست	(تو) خواهی بست
/(šo.mă) kă.hid- bast/	/(to) kă.hi- bast/
(آنها) خواهند بست	(او/آن) خواهد بست
/(ăn.hă) kă.hand- bast/	/(u/ ăn) kă.had- bast/

	Command
	امر
ببندید!	ببند!
/be.ban.did/	/be.band/

to come

آمَدَن

/ă.ma.dan/

Plural	Singular
Simple Present	
مضارع اخباری(حال ساده)	
(ما) می آییم	(من) می آیم
/(mă) mi.ă.yim/	/(man) mi.ă.yam/
(شما) می آیید	(تو) می آیی
/(šo.mă) mi.ă.yid/	/(to) mi.ă.yi/
(آنها) می آیند	(او/آن) می آید
/(ăn.hă) mi.ă.yand/	/(u/ ăn) mi.ă.yad/

Plural	Singular
Present Subjunctive	
مضارع التزامی	
(ما) بیاییم	(من) بیایم
/(mă) bi.yă.yim/	/(man) bi.yă.yam/
(شما) بیایید	(تو) بیایی
/(šo.mă) bi.yă.yid/	/(to) bi.yă.yi/
(آنها) بیایند	(او/آن) بیاید
/(ăn.hă) bi.yă.yand/	/(u/ ăn) bi.yă.yad/

Plural	Singular
Present Progressive	
مضارع مستمر(در جریان)	
(ما) داریم می آییم	(من) دارم می آیم
/(mă) dă.rim- mi.ă.yim/	/(man) dă.ram- mi.ă.yam/
(شما) دارید می آیید	(تو) داری می آیی
/(šo.mă) dă.rid- mi.ă.yid/	/(to) dă.ri- mi.ă.yi/
(آنها) دارند می آیند	(او/آن) دارد می آید
/(ăn.hă) dă.rand- mi.ă.yand/	/(u/ ăn) dă.rad- mi.ă.yad/

44

<table>
<tr><td colspan="2" align="center">Simple Past
ماضی مطلق (گذشته ساده)</td></tr>
<tr><td align="center">(ما) آمدیم
/(mă) ă.ma.dim/</td><td align="center">(من) آمدم
/(man) ă.ma.dam/</td></tr>
<tr><td align="center">(شما) آمدید
/(šo.mă) ă.ma.did/</td><td align="center">(تو) آمدی
/(to) ă.ma.di/</td></tr>
<tr><td align="center">(آنها) آمدند
/(ăn.hă) ă.ma.dand/</td><td align="center">(او/آن) آمد
/(u/ ăn) ă.mad/</td></tr>
</table>

<table>
<tr><td colspan="2" align="center">Imperfect Indicative
ماضی استمراری</td></tr>
<tr><td align="center">(ما) می آمدیم
/(mă) mi.ă.ma.dim/</td><td align="center">(من) می آمدم
/(man) mi.ă.ma.dam/</td></tr>
<tr><td align="center">(شما) می آمدید
/(šo.mă) mi.ă.ma.did/</td><td align="center">(تو) می آمدی
/(to) mi.ă.ma.di/</td></tr>
<tr><td align="center">(آنها) می آمدند
/(ăn.hă) mi.ă.ma.dand/</td><td align="center">(او/آن) می آمد
/(u/ ăn) mi.ă.mad/</td></tr>
</table>

<table>
<tr><td colspan="2" align="center">Present Perfect
ماضی نقلی</td></tr>
<tr><td align="center">(ما) آمده ایم
/(mă) ă.ma.de.im/</td><td align="center">(من) آمده ام
/(man) ă.ma.de.am/</td></tr>
<tr><td align="center">(شما) آمده اید
/(šo.mă) ă.ma.de.id/</td><td align="center">(تو) آمده ای
/(to) ă.ma.de.i/</td></tr>
<tr><td align="center">(آنها) آمده اند
/(ăn.hă) ă.ma.de.and/</td><td align="center">(او/آن) آمده است
/(u/ ăn) ă.ma.de- ast/</td></tr>
</table>

<table>
<tr><td colspan="2" align="center">Past Perfect
ماضی بعید</td></tr>
<tr><td align="center">(ما) آمده بودیم
/(mă) ă.ma.de- bu.dim/</td><td align="center">(من) آمده بودم
/(man) ă.ma.de- bu.dam/</td></tr>
<tr><td align="center">(شما) آمده بودید
/(šo.mă) ă.ma.de- bu.did/</td><td align="center">(تو) آمده بودی
/(to) ă.ma.de- bu.di/</td></tr>
<tr><td align="center">(آنها) آمده بودند
/(ăn.hă) ă.ma.de- bu.dand/</td><td align="center">(او/آن) آمده بود
/(u/ ăn) ă.ma.de- bud/</td></tr>
</table>

Past Subjunctive	
ماضی التزامی	
(ما) آمده باشیم	(من) آمده باشم
/(mǎ) ǎ.ma.de- bǎ.šim/	/(man) ǎ.ma.de- bǎ.šam/
(شما) آمده باشید	(تو) آمده باشی
/(šo.mǎ) ǎ.ma.de- bǎ.šid/	/(to) ǎ.ma.de- bǎ.ši/
(آنها) آمده باشند	(او/آن) آمده باشد
/(ǎn.hǎ) ǎ.ma.de- bǎ.šand/	/(u/ ǎn) ǎ.ma.de- bǎ.šad/

Past Progressive	
ماضی مستمر(در جریان)	
(ما) داشتیم می آمدیم	(من) داشتم می آمدم
/(mǎ) dǎš.tim- mi.ǎ.ma.dim/	/(man) dǎš.tam- mi.ǎ.ma.dam/
(شما) داشتید می آمدید	(تو) داشتی می آمدی
/(šo.mǎ) dǎš.tid- mi.ǎ.ma.did/	/(to) dǎš.ti- mi.ǎ.ma.di/
(آنها) داشتند می آمدند	(او/آن) داشت می آمد
/(ǎn.hǎ) dǎš.tand- mi.ǎ.ma.dand/	/(u/ ǎn) dǎšt- mi.ǎ.mad/

Simple Future	
مستقبل (آینده ساده)	
(ما) خواهیم آمد	(من) خواهم آمد
/(mǎ) ǩǎ.him- ǎ.mad/	/(man) ǩǎ.ham- ǎ.mad/
(شما) خواهید آمد	(تو) خواهی آمد
/(šo.mǎ) ǩǎ.hid- ǎ.mad/	/(to) ǩǎ.hi- ǎ.mad/
(آنها) خواهند آمد	(او/آن) خواهد آمد
/(ǎn.hǎ) ǩǎ.hand- ǎ.mad/	/(u/ ǎn) ǩǎ.had- ǎ.mad/

Command	
امر	
بیایید !	بیا !
/bi.yǎ.yid/	/bi.yǎ/

to continue

اِدامه دادَن

/e.dă.me- dă.dan/

Plural	Singular
Simple Present مضارع اخباری(حال ساده)	
(ما) ادامه می دهیم /(mă) e.dă.me- mi.da.him/	(من) ادامه می دهم /(man) e.dă.me- mi.da.ham/
(شما) ادامه می دهید /(šo.mă) e.dă.me- mi.da.hid/	(تو) ادامه می دهی /(to) e.dă.me- mi.da.hi/
(آنها) ادامه می دهند /(ăn.hă) e.dă.me- mi.da.hand/	(او/آن) ادامه می دهد /(u/ ăn) e.dă.me- mi.da.had/
Present Subjunctive مضارع التزامی	
(ما) ادامه بدهیم /(mă) e.dă.me- be.da.him/	(من) ادامه بدهم /(man) e.dă.me- be.da.ham/
(شما) ادامه بدهید /(šo.mă) e.dă.me- be.da.hid/	(تو) ادامه بدهی /(to) e.dă.me- be.da.hi/
(آنها) ادامه بدهند /(ăn.hă) e.dă.me- be.da.hand/	(او/آن) ادامه بدهد /(u/ ăn) e.dă.me- be.da.had/
Present Progressive مضارع مستمر(در جریان)	
(ما) داریم ادامه می دهیم /(mă) dă.rim- e.dă.me- mi.da.him/	(من) دارم ادامه می دهم /(man) dă.ram- e.dă.me- mi.da.ham/
(شما) دارید ادامه می دهید /(šo.mă) dă.rid- e.dă.me- mi.da.hid/	(تو) داری ادامه می دهی /(to) dă.ri- e.dă.me- mi.da.hi/
(آنها) دارند ادامه می دهند /(ăn.hă) dă.rand- e.dă.me- mi.da.hand/	(او/آن) دارد ادامه می دهد /(u/ ăn) dă.rad- e.dă.me- mi.da.had/

Simple Past
ماضی مطلق (گذشته ساده)

(ما) ادامه دادیم	(من) ادامه دادم
/(mǎ) e.dǎ.me- dǎ.dim/	/(man) e.dǎ.me- dǎ.dam/
(شما) ادامه دادید	(تو) ادامه دادی
/(šo.mǎ) e.dǎ.me- dǎ.did/	/(to) e.dǎ.me- dǎ.di/
(آنها) ادامه دادند	(او/آن) ادامه داد
/(ǎn.hǎ) e.dǎ.me- dǎ.dand/	/(u/ ǎn) e.dǎ.me- dǎd/

Imperfect Indicative
ماضی استمراری

(ما) ادامه می دادیم	(من) ادامه می دادم
/(mǎ) e.dǎ.me- mi.dǎ.dim/	/(man) e.dǎ.me- mi.dǎ.dam/
(شما) ادامه می دادید	(تو) ادامه می دادی
/(šo.mǎ) e.dǎ.me- mi.dǎ.did/	/(to) e.dǎ.me- mi.dǎ.di/
(آنها) ادامه می دادند	(او/آن) ادامه می داد
/(ǎn.hǎ) e.dǎ.me- mi.dǎ.dand/	/(u/ ǎn) e.dǎ.me- mi.dǎd/

Present Perfect
ماضی نقلی

(ما) ادامه داده ایم	(من) ادامه داده ام
/(mǎ) e.dǎ.me- dǎ.de.im/	/(man) e.dǎ.me- dǎ.de.am/
(شما) ادامه داده اید	(تو) ادامه داده ای
/(šo.mǎ) e.dǎ.me- dǎ.de.id/	/(to) e.dǎ.me- dǎ.de.i/
(آنها) ادامه داده اند	(او/آن) ادامه داده است
/(ǎn.hǎ) e.dǎ.me- dǎ.de.and/	/(u/ ǎn) e.dǎ.me- dǎ.de- ast/

Past Perfect
ماضی بعید

(ما) ادامه داده بودیم	(من) ادامه داده بودم
/(mǎ) e.dǎ.me- dǎ.de- bu.dim/	/(man) e.dǎ.me- dǎ.de- bu.dam/
(شما) ادامه داده بودید	(تو) ادامه داده بودی
/(šo.mǎ) e.dǎ.me- dǎ.de- bu.did/	/(to) e.dǎ.me- dǎ.de- bu.di/
(آنها) ادامه داده بودند	(او/آن) ادامه داده بود
/(ǎn.hǎ) e.dǎ.me- dǎ.de- bu.dand/	/(u/ ǎn) e.dǎ.me- dǎ.de- bud/

Past Subjunctive	
ماضی التزامی	
(ما) ادامه داده باشیم	(من) ادامه داده باشم
/(mă) e.dă.me- dă.de- bă.šim/	/(man) e.dă.me- dă.de- bă.šam/
(شما) ادامه داده باشید	(تو) ادامه داده باشی
/(šo.mă) e.dă.me- dă.de- bă.šid/	/(to) e.dă.me- dă.de- bă.ši/
(آنها) ادامه داده باشند	(او/آن) ادامه داده باشد
/(ăn.hă) e.dă.me- dă.de- bă.šand/	/(u/ ăn) e.dă.me- dă.de- bă.šad/

Past Progressive	
ماضی مستمر(در جریان)	
(ما) داشتیم ادامه می دادیم	(من) داشتم ادامه می دادم
/(mă) dăš.tim- e.dă.me- mi.dă.dim/	/(man) dăš.tam- e.dă.me- mi.dă.dam/
(شما) داشتید ادامه می دادید	(تو) داشتی ادامه می دادی
/(šo.mă) dăš.tid- e.dă.me- mi.dă.did/	/(to) dăš.ti- e.dă.me- mi.dă.di/
(آنها) داشتند ادامه می دادند	(او/آن) داشت ادامه می داد
/(ăn.hă) dăš.tand- e.dă.me- mi.dă.dand/	/(u/ ăn) dăšt- e.dă.me- mi.dad/

Simple Future	
مستقبل (آینده ساده)	
(ما) ادامه خواهیم داد	(من) ادامه خواهم داد
/(mă) e.dă.me- ǩă.ham- dad/	/(man) e.dă.me- ǩă.ham- dad/
(شما) ادامه خواهید داد	(تو) ادامه خواهی داد
/(šo.mă) e.dă.me- ǩă.hid- dad/	/(to) e.dă.me- ǩă.hi- dad/
(آنها) ادامه خواهند داد	(او/آن) ادامه خواهد داد
/(ăn.hă) e.dă.me- ǩă.hand- dad/	/(u/ ăn) e.dă.me- ǩă.had- dad/

Command	
امر	
ادامه بدهید!	ادامه بده!
/e.dă.me- be.da.hid/	/e.dă.me- be.de/

to cook

پُختَن

/poǩ.tan/

Plural	*Singular*
Simple Present مضارع اخباری(حال ساده)	
(ما) می پزیم /(mǎ) mi.pa.zim/	(من) می پزم /(man) mi.pa.zam/
(شما) می پزید /(šo.mǎ) mi.pa.zid/	(تو) می پزی /(to) mi.pa.zi/
(آنها) می پزند /(ǎn.hǎ) mi.pa.zand/	(او/آن) می پزد /(u/ ǎn) mi.pa.zad/
Present Subjunctive مضارع التزامی	
(ما) بپزیم /(mǎ) be.pa.zim/	(من) بپزم /(man) be.pa.zam/
(شما) بپزید /(šo.mǎ) be.pa.zid/	(تو) بپزی /(to) be.pa.zi/
(آنها) بپزند /(ǎn.hǎ) be.pa.zand/	(او/آن) بپزد /(u/ ǎn) be.pa.zad/
Present Progressive مضارع مستمر(در جریان)	
(ما) داریم می پزیم /(mǎ) dǎ.rim- mi.pa.zim/	(من) دارم می پزم /(man) dǎ.ram- mi.pa.zam/
(شما) دارید می پزید /(šo.mǎ) dǎ.rid- mi.pa.zid/	(تو) داری می پزی /(to) dǎ.ri- mi.pa.zi/
(آنها) دارند می پزند /(ǎn.hǎ) dǎ.rand- mi.pa.zand/	(او/آن) دارد می پزد /(u/ ǎn) dǎ.rad- mi.pa.zad/

<table>
<tr><td colspan="2" align="center">**Simple Past**
ماضی مطلق (گذشته ساده)</td></tr>
<tr><td align="center">(ما) پختیم
/(mă) poǩ.tim/</td><td align="center">(من) پختم
/(man) poǩ.tam/</td></tr>
<tr><td align="center">(شما) پختید
/(šo.mă) poǩ.tid/</td><td align="center">(تو) پختی
/(to) poǩ.ti/</td></tr>
<tr><td align="center">(آنها) پختند
/(ăn.hă) poǩ.tand/</td><td align="center">(او/آن) پخت
/(u/ ăn) poǩt/</td></tr>
</table>

<table>
<tr><td colspan="2" align="center">**Imperfect Indicative**
ماضی استمراری</td></tr>
<tr><td align="center">(ما) می پختیم
/(mă) mi.poǩ.tim/</td><td align="center">(من) می پختم
/(man) mi.poǩ.tam/</td></tr>
<tr><td align="center">(شما) می پختید
/(šo.mă) mi.poǩ.tid/</td><td align="center">(تو) می پختی
/(to) mi.poǩ.ti/</td></tr>
<tr><td align="center">(آنها) می پختند
/(ăn.hă) mi.poǩ.tand/</td><td align="center">(او/آن) می پخت
/(u/ ăn) mi.poǩt/</td></tr>
</table>

<table>
<tr><td colspan="2" align="center">**Present Perfect**
ماضی نقلی</td></tr>
<tr><td align="center">(ما) پخته ایم
/(mă) poǩ.te.im/</td><td align="center">(من) پخته ام
/(man) poǩ.te.am/</td></tr>
<tr><td align="center">(شما) پخته اید
/(šo.mă) poǩ.te.id/</td><td align="center">(تو) پخته ای
/(to) poǩ.te.i/</td></tr>
<tr><td align="center">(آنها) پخته اند
/(ăn.hă) poǩ.te.and/</td><td align="center">(او/آن) پخته است
/(u/ ăn) poǩ.te- ast/</td></tr>
</table>

<table>
<tr><td colspan="2" align="center">**Past Perfect**
ماضی بعید</td></tr>
<tr><td align="center">(ما) پخته بودیم
/(mă) poǩ.te- bu.dim/</td><td align="center">(من) پخته بودم
/(man) poǩ.te- bu.dam/</td></tr>
<tr><td align="center">(شما) پخته بودید
/(šo.mă) poǩ.te- bu.did/</td><td align="center">(تو) پخته بودی
/(to) poǩ.te- bu.di/</td></tr>
<tr><td align="center">(آنها) پخته بودند
/(ăn.hă) poǩ.te- bu.dand/</td><td align="center">(او/آن) پخته بود
/(u/ ăn) poǩ.te- bud/</td></tr>
</table>

Past Subjunctive	
ماضی التزامی	
(ما) پخته باشیم	(من) پخته باشم
/(mǎ) poǩ.te- bǎ.šim/	/(man) poǩ.te- bǎ.šam/
(شما) پخته باشید	(تو) پخته باشی
/(šo.mǎ) poǩ.te- bǎ.šid/	/(to) poǩ.te- bǎ.ši/
(آنها) پخته باشند	(او/آن) پخته باشد
/(ǎn.hǎ) poǩ.te- bǎ.šand/	/(u/ ǎn) poǩ.te- bǎ.šad/

Past Progressive	
ماضی مستمر(در جریان)	
(ما) داشتیم می پختیم	(من) داشتم می پختم
/(mǎ) dǎš.tim- mi.poǩ.tim/	/(man) dǎš.tam- mi.poǩ.tam/
(شما) داشتید می پختید	(تو) داشتی می پختی
/(šo.mǎ) dǎš.tid- mi.poǩ.tid/	/(to) dǎš.ti- mi.poǩ.ti/
(آنها) داشتند می پختند	(او/آن) داشت می پخت
/(ǎn.hǎ) dǎš.tand- mi.poǩ.tand/	/(u/ ǎn) dǎšt- mi.poǩt/

Simple Future	
مستقبل (آینده ساده)	
(ما) خواهیم پخت	(من) خواهم پخت
/(mǎ) ǩǎ.him- poǩt/	/(man) ǩǎ.ham- poǩt/
(شما) خواهید پخت	(تو) خواهی پخت
/(šo.mǎ) ǩǎ.hid- poǩt/	/(to) ǩǎ.hi- poǩt/
(آنها) خواهند پخت	(او/آن) خواهد پخت
/(ǎn.hǎ) ǩǎ.hand- poǩt/	/(u/ ǎn) ǩǎ.had- poǩt/

Command	
امر	
بپزید!	بپز!
/be.pa.zid/	/be.paz/

to cry

گِریه کَردَن

/ger.ye- kar.dan/

Plural	Singular
Simple Present مضارع اخباری(حال ساده)	
(ما) گریه می کنیم /(mǎ) ger.ye- mi.ko.nim/	(من) گریه می کنم /(man) ger.ye- mi.ko.nam/
(شما) گریه می کنید /(šo.mǎ) ger.ye- mi.ko.nid/	(تو) گریه می کنی /(to) ger.ye- mi.ko.ni/
(آنها) گریه می کنند /(ǎn.hǎ) ger.ye- mi.ko.nand/	(او/آن) گریه می کند /(u/ ǎn) ger.ye- mi.ko.nad/
Present Subjunctive مضارع التزامی	
(ما) گریه بکنیم /(mǎ) ger.ye- be.ko.nim/	(من) گریه بکنم /(man) ger.ye- be.ko.nam/
(شما) گریه بکنید /(šo.mǎ) ger.ye- be.ko.nid/	(تو) گریه بکنی /(to) ger.ye- be.ko.ni/
(آنها) گریه بکنند /(ǎn.hǎ) ger.ye- be.ko.nand/	(او/آن) گریه بکند /(u/ ǎn) ger.ye- be.ko.nad/
Present Progressive مضارع مستمر(در جریان)	
(ما) داریم گریه می کنیم /(mǎ) dǎ.rim- ger.ye- mi.ko.nim/	(من) دارم گریه می کنم /(man) dǎ.ram- ger.ye- mi.ko.nam/
(شما) دارید گریه می کنید /(šo.mǎ) dǎ.rid- ger.ye- mi.ko.nid/	(تو) داری گریه می کنی /(to) dǎ.ri- ger.ye- mi.ko.ni/
(آنها) دارند گریه می کنند /(ǎn.hǎ) dǎ.rand- ger.ye- mi.ko.nand/	(او/آن) دارد گریه می کند /(u/ ǎn) dǎ.rad- ger.ye- mi.ko.nad/

Simple Past	
ماضی مطلق (گذشته ساده)	
(ما) گریه کردیم	(من) گریه کردم
/(mǎ) ger.ye- kar.dim/	/(man) ger.ye- kar.dam/
(شما) گریه کردید	(تو) گریه کردی
/(šo.mǎ) ger.ye- kar.did/	/(to) ger.ye- kar.di/
(آنها) گریه کردند	(او/آن) گریه کرد
/(ǎn.hǎ) ger.ye- kar.dand/	/(u/ ǎn) ger.ye- kard/

Imperfect Indicative	
ماضی استمراری	
(ما) گریه می کردیم	(من) گریه می کردم
/(mǎ) ger.ye- mi.kar.dim/	/(man) ger.ye- mi.kar.dam/
(شما) گریه می کردید	(تو) گریه می کردی
/(šo.mǎ) ger.ye- mi.kar.did/	/(to) ger.ye- mi.kar.di/
(آنها) گریه می کردند	(او/آن) گریه می کرد
/(ǎn.hǎ) ger.ye- mi.kar.dand/	/(u/ ǎn) ger.ye- mi.kard/

Present Perfect	
ماضی نقلی	
(ما) گریه کرده ایم	(من) گریه کرده ام
/(mǎ) ger.ye- kar.de.im/	/(man) ger.ye- kar.de.am/
(شما) گریه کرده اید	(تو) گریه کرده ای
/(šo.mǎ) ger.ye- kar.de.id/	/(to) ger.ye- kar.de.i/
(آنها) گریه کرده اند	(او/آن) گریه کرده است
/(ǎn.hǎ) ger.ye- kar.de.and/	/(u/ ǎn) ger.ye- kar.de- ast/

Past Perfect	
ماضی بعید	
(ما) گریه کرده بودیم	(من) گریه کرده بودم
/(mǎ) ger.ye- kar.de- bu.dim/	(man) ger.ye- kar.de- bu.dam/
(شما) گریه کرده بودید	(تو) گریه کرده بودی
/(šo.mǎ) ger.ye- kar.de- bu.did/	/(to) ger.ye- kar.de- bu.di/
(آنها) گریه کرده بودند	(او/آن) گریه کرده بود
/(ǎn.hǎ) ger.ye- kar.de- bu.dand/	/(u/ ǎn) ger.ye- kar.de- bud/

<table>
<tr><td colspan="2" align="center">

Past Subjunctive

ماضی التزامی

</td></tr>
<tr>
<td align="center">

(ما) گریه کرده باشیم

/(mǎ) ger.ye- kar.de- bǎ.šim/

</td>
<td align="center">

(من) گریه کرده باشم

/(man) ger.ye- kar.de- bǎ.šam/

</td>
</tr>
<tr>
<td align="center">

(شما) گریه کرده باشید

/(šo.mǎ) ger.ye- kar.de- bǎ.šid/

</td>
<td align="center">

(تو) گریه کرده باشی

/(to) ger.ye- kar.de- bǎ.ši/

</td>
</tr>
<tr>
<td align="center">

(آنها) گریه کرده باشند

/(ǎn.hǎ) ger.ye- kar.de- bǎ.šand/

</td>
<td align="center">

(او/آن) گریه کرده باشد

/(u/ ǎn) ger.ye- kar.de- bǎ.šad/

</td>
</tr>
</table>

<table>
<tr><td colspan="2" align="center">

Past Progressive

ماضی مستمر(در جریان)

</td></tr>
<tr>
<td align="center">

(ما) داشتیم گریه می کردیم

/(mǎ) dǎš.tim- ger.ye- mi.kar.dim/

</td>
<td align="center">

(من) داشتم گریه می کردم

/(man) dǎš.tam- ger.ye- mi.kar.dam/

</td>
</tr>
<tr>
<td align="center">

(شما) داشتید گریه می کردید

/(šo.mǎ) dǎš.tid- ger.ye- mi.kar.did/

</td>
<td align="center">

(تو) داشتی گریه می کردی

/(to) dǎš.ti- ger.ye- mi.kar.di/

</td>
</tr>
<tr>
<td align="center">

(آنها) داشتند گریه می کردند

/(ǎn.hǎ) dǎš.tand- ger.ye- mi.kar.dand/

</td>
<td align="center">

(او/آن) داشت گریه می کرد

/(u/ ǎn) dǎšt- ger.ye- mi.kard/

</td>
</tr>
</table>

<table>
<tr><td colspan="2" align="center">

Simple Future

مستقبل (آینده ساده)

</td></tr>
<tr>
<td align="center">

(ما) گریه خواهیم کرد

/(mǎ) ger.ye- ǩǎ.him- kard/

</td>
<td align="center">

(من) گریه خواهم کرد

/(man) ger.ye- ǩǎ.ham- kard/

</td>
</tr>
<tr>
<td align="center">

(شما) گریه خواهید کرد

/(šo.mǎ) ger.ye- ǩǎ.hid- kard/

</td>
<td align="center">

(تو) گریه خواهی کرد

/(to) ger.ye- ǩǎ.hi- kard/

</td>
</tr>
<tr>
<td align="center">

(آنها) گریه خواهند کرد

/(ǎn.hǎ) ger.ye- ǩǎ.hand- kard/

</td>
<td align="center">

(او/آن) گریه خواهد کرد

/(u/ ǎn) ger.ye- ǩǎ.had- kard/

</td>
</tr>
</table>

<table>
<tr><td colspan="2" align="center">

Command

امر

</td></tr>
<tr>
<td align="center">

* گریه بکنید!

/ger.ye- be.ko.nid/

</td>
<td align="center">

* گریه بکن!

/ger.ye- be.kon/

</td>
</tr>
</table>

* also: گریه کن!   گریه کنید!

to dance

رَقصیدَن

/rağ.si.dan/

Plural	Singular
Simple Present	
مضارع اخباری(حال ساده)	
(ما) می رقصیم	(من) می رقصم
/(mă) mi.rağ.sim/	/(man) mi.rağ.sam/
(شما) می رقصید	(تو) می رقصی
/(šo.mă) mi.rağ.sid/	/(to) mi.rağ.si/
(آنها) می رقصند	(او /آن) می رقصد
/(ăn.hă) mi.rağ.sand/	/(u/ ăn) mi.rağ.sad/

Plural	Singular
Present Subjunctive	
مضارع التزامی	
(ما) برقصیم	(من) برقصم
/(mă) be.rağ.sim/	/(man) be.rağ.sam/
(شما) برقصید	(تو) برقصی
/(šo.mă) be.rağ.sid/	/(to) be.rağ.si/
(آنها) برقصند	(او /آن) برقصد
/(ăn.hă) be.rağ.sand/	/(u/ ăn) be.rağ.sad/

Plural	Singular
Present Progressive	
مضارع مستمر(در جریان)	
(ما) داریم می رقصیم	(من) دارم می رقصم
/(mă) dă.rim- mi.rağ.sim/	/(man) dă.ram- mi.rağ.sam/
(شما) دارید می رقصید	(تو) داری می رقصی
/(šo.mă) dă.rid- mi.rağ.sid/	/(to) dă.ri- mi.rağ.si/
(آنها) دارند می رقصند	(او /آن) دارد می رقصد
/(ăn.hă) dă.rand- mi.rağ.sand/	/(u/ ăn) dă.rad- mi.rağ.sad/

	Simple Past
	ماضی مطلق (گذشته ساده)
(ما) رقصیدیم	(من) رقصیدم
/(mă) rağ.si.dim/	/(man) rağ.si.dam/
(شما) رقصیدید	(تو) رقصیدی
/(šo.mă) rağ.si.did/	/(to) rağ.si.di/
(آنها) رقصیدند	(او/آن) رقصید
/(ăn.hă) rağ.si.dand/	/(u/ ăn) rağ.sid/

	Imperfect Indicative
	ماضی استمراری
(ما) می رقصیدیم	(من) می رقصیدم
/(mă) mi.rağ.si.dim/	/(man) mi.rağ.si.dam/
(شما) می رقصیدید	(تو) می رقصیدی
/(šo.mă) mi.rağ.si.did/	/(to) mi.rağ.si.di/
(آنها) می رقصیدند	(او/آن) می رقصید
/(ăn.hă) mi.rağ.si.dand/	/(u/ ăn) mi.rağ.sid/

	Present Perfect
	ماضی نقلی
(ما) رقصیده ایم	(من) رقصیده ام
/(mă) rağ.si.de.im/	/(man) rağ.si.de.am/
(شما) رقصیده اید	(تو) رقصیده ای
/(šo.mă) rağ.si.de.id/	/(to) rağ.si.de.i/
(آنها) رقصیده اند	(او/آن) رقصیده است
/(ăn.hă) rağ.si.de.and/	/(u/ ăn) rağ.si.de- ast/

	Past Perfect
	ماضی بعید
(ما) رقصیده بودیم	(من) رقصیده بودم
/(mă) rağ.si.de- bu.dim/	/(man) rağ.si.de- bu.dam/
(شما) رقصیده بودید	(تو) رقصیده بودی
/(šo.mă) rağ.si.de- bu.did/	/(to) rağ.si.de- bu.di/
(آنها) رقصیده بودند	(او/آن) رقصیده بود
/(ăn.hă) rağ.si.de- bu.dand/	/(u/ ăn) rağ.si.de- bud/

Past Subjunctive	
ماضی التزامی	
(ما) رقصیده باشیم	(من) رقصیده باشم
/(mă) rağ.si.de- bă.šim/	/(man) rağ.si.de- bă.šam/
(شما) رقصیده باشید	(تو) رقصیده باشی
/(šo.mă) rağ.si.de- bă.šid/	/(to) rağ.si.de- bă.ši/
(آنها) رقصیده باشند	(او/آن) رقصیده باشد
/(ăn.hă) rağ.si.de- bă.šand/	/(u/ ăn) rağ.si.de- bă.šad/

Past Progressive	
ماضی مستمر(در جریان)	
(ما) داشتیم می رقصیدیم	(من) داشتم می رقصیدم
/(mă) dăš.tim- mi.rağ.si.dim/	/(man) dăš.tam- mi.rağ.si.dam/
شما داشتید می رقصیدید	(تو) داشتی می رقصیدی
/(šo.mă) dăš.tid- mi.rağ.si.did/	/(to) dăš.ti- mi.rağ.si.di/
(آنها) داشتند می رقصیدند	(او/آن) داشت می رقصید
/(ăn.hă) dăš.tand- mi.rağ.si.dand/	/(u/ ăn) dăšt- mi.rağ.sid/

Simple Future	
مستقبل (آینده ساده)	
(ما) خواهیم رقصید	(من) خواهم رقصید
/(mă) kă.him- rağ.sid/	/(man) kă.ham- rağ.sid/
(شما) خواهید رقصید	(تو) خواهی رقصید
/(šo.mă) kă.hid- rağ.sid/	/(to) kă.hi- rağ.sid/
(آنها) خواهند رقصید	(او/آن) خواهد رقصید
/(ăn.hă) kă.hand- rağ.sid/	/(u/ ăn) kă.had- rağ.sid/

Command	
امر	
برقصید!	برقص!
/be.rağ.sid/	/be.rağs/

to decide

تَصمیم گِرِفتَن

/tas.mim- ge.ref.tan/

Plural	Singular
Simple Present مضارع اخباری(حال ساده)	
(ما) تصمیم می گیریم /(mǎ) tas.mim- mi.gi.rim/	(من) تصمیم می گیرم /(man) tas.mim- mi.gi.ram/
(شما) تصمیم می گیرید /(šo.mǎ) tas.mim- mi.gi.rid/	(تو) تصمیم می گیری /(to) tas.mim- mi.gi.ri/
(آنها) تصمیم می گیرند /(ǎn.hǎ) tas.mim- mi.gi.rand/	(او/آن) تصمیم می گیرد /(u/ ǎn) tas.mim- mi.gi.rad/
Present Subjunctive مضارع التزامی	
(ما) تصمیم بگیریم /(mǎ) tas.mim- be.gi.rim/	(من) تصمیم بگیرم /(man) tas.mim- be.gi.ram/
(شما) تصمیم بگیرید /(šo.mǎ) tas.mim- be.gi.rid/	(تو) تصمیم بگیری /(to) tas.mim- be.gi.ri/
(آنها) تصمیم بگیرند /(ǎn.hǎ) tas.mim- be.gi.rand/	(او/آن) تصمیم بگیرد /(u/ ǎn) tas.mim- be.gi.rad/
Present Progressive مضارع مستمر(در جریان)	
(ما) داریم تصمیم می گیریم /(mǎ) dǎ.rim- tas.mim- mi.gi.rim/	(من) دارم تصمیم می گیرم /(man) dǎ.ram- tas.mim- mi.gi.ram/
(شما) دارید تصمیم می گیرید /(šo.mǎ) dǎ.rid- tas.mim- mi.gi.rid/	(تو) داری تصمیم می گیری /(to) dǎ.ri- tas.mim- mi.gi.ri/
(آنها) دارند تصمیم می گیرند /(ǎn.hǎ) dǎ.rand- tas.mim- mi.gi.rand/	(او/آن) دارد تصمیم می گیرد /(u/ ǎn) dǎ.rad- tas.mim- mi.gi.rad/

59

Simple Past
ماضی مطلق (گذشته ساده)

(ما) تصمیم گرفتیم	(من) تصمیم گرفتم
/(mǎ) tas.mim- ge.ref.tim/	/(man) tas.mim- ge.ref.tam/
(شما) تصمیم گرفتید	(تو) تصمیم گرفتی
/(šo.mǎ) tas.mim- ge.ref.tid/	/(to) tas.mim- ge.ref.ti/
(آنها) تصمیم گرفتند	(او/آن) تصمیم گرفت
/(ǎn.hǎ) tas.mim- ge.ref.tand/	/(u/ ǎn) tas.mim- ge.reft/

Imperfect Indicative
ماضی استمراری

(ما) تصمیم می گرفتیم	(من) تصمیم می گرفتم
/(mǎ) tas.mim- mi.ge.ref.tim/	/(man) tas.mim- mi.ge.ref.tam/
(شما) تصمیم می گرفتید	(تو) تصمیم می گرفتی
/(šo.mǎ) tas.mim- mi.ge.ref.tid/	/(to) tas.mim- mi.ge.ref.ti/
(آنها) تصمیم می گرفتند	(او/آن) تصمیم می گرفت
/(ǎn.hǎ) tas.mim- mi.ge.ref.tand/	/(u/ ǎn) tas.mim- mi.ge.reft/

Present Perfect
ماضی نقلی

(ما) تصمیم گرفته ایم	(من) تصمیم گرفته ام
/(mǎ) tas.mim- ge.ref.te.im/	/(man) tas.mim- ge.ref.te.am/
(شما) تصمیم گرفته اید	(تو) تصمیم گرفته ای
/(šo.mǎ) tas.mim- ge.ref.te.id/	/(to) tas.mim- ge.ref.te.i/
(آنها) تصمیم گرفته اند	(او/آن) تصمیم گرفته است
/(ǎn.hǎ) tas.mim- ge.ref.te.and/	/(u/ǎn) tas.mim- ge.ref.te- ast/

Past Perfect
ماضی بعید

(ما) تصمیم گرفته بودیم	(من) تصمیم گرفته بودم
/(mǎ) tas.mim- ge.ref.te- bu.dim/	/(man) tas.mim- ge.ref.te- bu.dam/
(شما) تصمیم گرفته بودید	(تو) تصمیم گرفته بودی
/(šo.mǎ) tas.mim- ge.ref.te- bu.did/	/(to) tas.mim- ge.ref.te- bu.di/
(آنها) تصمیم گرفته بودند	(او/آن) تصمیم گرفته بود
/(ǎn.hǎ) tas.mim- ge.ref.te- bu.dand/	/(u/ ǎn) tas.mim- ge.ref.te- bud/

<table>
<tr><td colspan="2" align="center">**Past Subjunctive**
ماضی التزامی</td></tr>
<tr>
<td>(ما) تصمیم گرفته باشیم
/(mă) tas.mim- ge.ref.te- bă.šim/</td>
<td>(من) تصمیم گرفته باشم
/(man) tas.mim- ge.ref.te- bă.šam/</td>
</tr>
<tr>
<td>(شما) تصمیم گرفته باشید
/(šo.mă) tas.mim- ge.ref.te- bă.šid/</td>
<td>(تو) تصمیم گرفته باشی
/(to) tas.mim- ge.ref.te- bă.ši/</td>
</tr>
<tr>
<td>(آنها) تصمیم گرفته باشند
/(ăn.hă) tas.mim- ge.ref.te- bă.šand/</td>
<td>(او/آن) تصمیم گرفته باشد
/(u/ ăn) tas.mim- ge.ref.te- bă.šad/</td>
</tr>
</table>

<table>
<tr><td colspan="2" align="center">**Past Progressive**
ماضی مستمر(در جریان)</td></tr>
<tr>
<td>(ما) داشتیم تصمیم می گرفتیم
/(mă) dăš.tim- tas.mim- mi.ge.ref.tim/</td>
<td>(من) داشتم تصمیم می گرفتم
/(man) dăš.tam- tas.mim- mi.ge.ref.tam/</td>
</tr>
<tr>
<td>(شما) داشتید تصمیم می گرفتید
/(šo.mă) dăš.tid- tas.mim- mi.ge.ref.tid/</td>
<td>(تو) داشتی تصمیم می گرفتی
/(to) dăš.ti- tas.mim- mi.ge.ref.ti/</td>
</tr>
<tr>
<td>(آنها) داشتند تصمیم می گرفتند
/(ăn.hă) dăš.tand- tas.mim- mi.ge.ref.tand/</td>
<td>(او/آن) داشت تصمیم می گرفت
/(u/ ăn) dăšt- tas.mim- mi.ge.reft/</td>
</tr>
</table>

<table>
<tr><td colspan="2" align="center">**Simple Future**
مستقبل (آینده ساده)</td></tr>
<tr>
<td>(ما) تصمیم خواهیم گرفت
/(mă) tas.mim- kă.him- ge.reft/</td>
<td>(من) تصمیم خواهم گرفت
/(man) tas.mim- kă.ham- ge.reft/</td>
</tr>
<tr>
<td>(شما) تصمیم خواهید گرفت
/(šo.mă) tas.mim- kă.hid- ge.reft/</td>
<td>(تو) تصمیم خواهی گرفت
/(to) tas.mim- kă.hi- ge.reft/</td>
</tr>
<tr>
<td>(آنها) تصمیم خواهند گرفت
/(ăn.hă) tas.mim- kă.hand- ge.reft/</td>
<td>(او/آن) تصمیم خواهد گرفت
/(u/ ăn) tas.mim- kă.had- ge.reft/</td>
</tr>
</table>

<table>
<tr><td colspan="2" align="center">**Command**
امر</td></tr>
<tr>
<td>تصمیم بگیرید!
/tas.mim- be.gi.rid/</td>
<td>تصمیم بگیر!
/tas.mim- be.gir/</td>
</tr>
</table>

to decrease

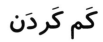

کَم کَردَن

/kam- kar.dan/

Plural	Singular
Simple Present	
مضارع اخباری(حال ساده)	
(ما) کم می کنیم	(من) کم می کنم
/(mǎ) kam- mi.ko.nim/	/(man) kam- mi.ko.nam/
(شما) کم می کنید	(تو) کم می کنی
/(šo.mǎ) kam- mi.ko.nid/	/(to) kam- mi.ko.ni/
(آنها) کم می کنند	(او/آن) کم می کند
/(ǎn.hǎ) kam- mi.ko.nand/	/(u/ ǎn) kam- mi.ko.nad/
Present Subjunctive	
مضارع التزامی	
(ما) کم بکنیم	(من) کم بکنم
/(mǎ) kam- be.ko.nim/	/(man) kam- be.ko.nam/
(شما) کم بکنید	(تو) کم بکنی
/(šo.mǎ) kam- be.ko.nid/	/(to) kam- be.ko.ni/
(آنها) کم بکنند	(او/آن) کم بکند
/(ǎn.hǎ) kam- be.ko.nand/	/(u/ ǎn) kam- be.ko.nad/
Present Progressive	
مضارع مستمر(در جریان)	
(ما) داریم کم می کنیم	(من) دارم کم می کنم
/(mǎ) dǎ.rim- kam- mi.ko.nim/	/(man) dǎ.ram- kam- mi.ko.nam/
(شما) دارید کم می کنید	(تو) داری کم می کنی
/(šo.mǎ) dǎ.rid- kam- mi.ko.nid/	/(to) dǎ.ri- kam- mi.ko.ni/
(آنها) دارند کم می کنند	(او/آن) دارد کم می کند
/(ǎn.hǎ) dǎ.rand- kam- mi.ko.nand/	/(u/ǎn) dǎ.rad- kam- mi.ko.nad/

Simple Past
ماضی مطلق (گذشته ساده)

(ما) کم کردیم	(من) کم کردم
/(mǎ) kam- kar.dim/	/(man) kam- kar.dam/
(شما) کم کردید	(تو) کم کردی
/(šo.mǎ) kam- kar.did/	/(to) kam- kar.di/
(آنها) کم کردند	(او/آن) کم کرد
/(ǎn.hǎ) kam- kar.dand/	/(u/ ǎn) kam- kard/

Imperfect Indicative
ماضی استمراری

(ما) کم می کردیم	(من) کم می کردم
/(mǎ) kam- mi.kar.dim/	/(man) kam- mi.kar.dam/
(شما) کم می کردید	(تو) کم می کردی
/(šo.mǎ) kam- mi.kar.did/	/(to) kam- mi.kar.di/
(آنها) کم می کردند	(او/آن) کم می کرد
/(ǎn.hǎ) kam- mi.kar.dand/	/(u/ ǎn) kam- mi.kard/

Present Perfect
ماضی نقلی

(ما) کم کرده ایم	(من) کم کرده ام
/(mǎ) kam- kar.de.im/	/(man) kam- kar.de.am/
(شما) کم کرده اید	(تو) کم کرده ای
/(šo.mǎ) kam- kar.de.id/	/(to) kam- kar.de.i/
(آنها) کم کرده اند	(او/آن) کم کرده است
/(ǎn.hǎ) kam- kar.de.and/	/(u/ ǎn) kam- kar.de- ast/

Past Perfect
ماضی بعید

(ما) کم کرده بودیم	(من) کم کرده بودم
/(mǎ) kam- kar.de- bu.dim/	/(man) kam- kar.de- bu.dam/
(شما) کم کرده بودید	(تو) کم کرده بودی
/(šo.mǎ) kam- kar.de- bu.did/	/(to) kam- kar.de- bu.di/
(آنها) کم کرده بودند	(او/آن) کم کرده بود
/(ǎn.hǎ) kam- kar.de- bu.dand/	/(u/ ǎn) kam- kar.de- bud/

Past Subjunctive	
ماضی التزامی	
(ما) کم کرده باشیم	(من) کم کرده باشم
/(mă) kam- kar.de- bă.šim/	/(man) kam- kar.de- bă.šam/
(شما) کم کرده باشید	(تو) کم کرده باشی
/(šo.mă) kam- kar.de- bă.šid/	/(to) kam- kar.de- bă.ši/
(آنها) کم کرده باشند	(او/آن) کم کرده باشد
/(ăn.hă) kam- kar.de- bă.šand/	/(u/ ăn) kam- kar.de- bă.šad/

Past Progressive	
ماضی مستمر(در جریان)	
(ما) داشتیم کم می کردیم	(من) داشتم کم می کردم
/(mă) dăš.tim- kam- mi.kar.dim/	/(man) dăš.tam- kam- mi.kar.dam/
(شما) داشتید کم می کردید	(تو) داشتی کم می کردی
/(šo.mă) dăš.tid- kam- mi.kar.did/	/(to) dăš.ti- kam- mi.kar.di/
(آنها) داشتند کم می کردند	(او/آن) داشت کم می کرد
/(ăn.hă) dăš.tand- kam- mi.kar.dand/	/(u/ ăn) dăšt- kam- mi.kard/

Simple Future	
مستقبل (آینده ساده)	
(ما) کم خواهیم کرد	(من) کم خواهم کرد
/(mă) kam- ǩă.him- kard/	/(man) kam- ǩă.ham- kard/
(شما) کم خواهید کرد	(تو) کم خواهی کرد
/(šo.mă) kam- ǩă.hid- kard/	/(to) kam- ǩă.hi- kard/
(آنها) کم خواهند کرد	(او/آن) کم خواهد کرد
/(ăn.hă) kam- ǩă.hand- kard/	/(u/ ăn) kam- ǩă.had- kard/

Command	
امر	
* کم بکنید!	* کم بکن!
/kam- be.ko.nid/	/kam- be.kon/

* also: کم کنید!   کم کن!

64

to deny

رَد گَردَن

/rad- kar.dan/

Plural	Singular
Simple Present مضارع اخباری(حال ساده)	
(ما) رد می کنیم /(mǎ) rd- mi.ko.nim/	(من) رد می کنم /(man) rad- mi.ko.nam/
(شما) رد می کنید /(šo.mǎ) rad- mi.ko.nid/	(تو) رد می کنی /(to) rad- mi.ko.ni/
(آنها) رد می کنند /(ǎn.hǎ) rad- mi.ko.nand/	(او/آن) رد می کند /(u/ ǎn) rad- mi.ko.nad/
Present Subjunctive مضارع التزامی	
(ما) رد بکنیم /(mǎ) rad- be.ko.nim/	(من) رد بکنم /(man) rad- be.ko.nam/
(شما) رد بکنید /(šo.mǎ) rad- be.ko.nid/	(تو) رد بکنی /(to) rad- be.ko.ni/
(آنها) رد بکنند /(ǎn.hǎ) rad- be.ko.nand/	(او/آن) رد بکند /(u/ ǎn) rad- be.ko.nad/
Present Progressive مضارع مستمر(در جریان)	
(ما) داریم رد می کنیم /(mǎ) dǎ.rim- rad- mi.ko.nim/	(من) دارم رد می کنم /(man) dǎ.ram- rad- mi.ko.nam/
(شما) دارید رد می کنید /(šo.mǎ) dǎ.rid- rad- mi.ko.nid/	(تو) داری رد می کنی /(to) dǎ.ri- rad- mi.ko.ni/
(آنها) دارند رد می کنند /(ǎn.hǎ) dǎ.rand- rad- mi.ko.nand/	(او/آن) دارد رد می کند /(u/ ǎn) dǎ.rad- rad- mi.ko.nad/

Simple Past	
ماضی مطلق (گذشته ساده)	
(ما) رد کردیم	(من) رد کردم
/(mă) rad- kar.dim/	/(man) rad- kar.dam/
(شما) رد کردید	(تو) رد کردی
/(šo.mă) rad- kar.did/	/(to) rad- kar.di/
(آنها) رد کردند	(او/آن) رد کرد
/(ăn.hă) rad- kar.dand/	/(u/ ăn) rad- kard/

Imperfect Indicative	
ماضی استمراری	
(ما) رد می کردیم	(من) رد می کردم
/(mă) rad- mi.kar.dim/	/(man) rad- mi.kar.dam/
(شما) رد می کردید	(تو) رد می کردی
/(šo.mă) rad- mi.kar.did/	/(to) rad- mi.kar.di/
(آنها) رد می کردند	(او/آن) رد می کرد
/(ăn.hă) rad- mi.kar.dand/	/(u/ ăn) rad- mi.kard/

Present Perfect	
ماضی نقلی	
(ما) رد کرده ایم	(من) رد کرده ام
/(mă) rad- kar.de.im/	/(man) rad- kar.de.am/
(شما) رد کرده اید	(تو) رد کرده ای
/(šo.mă) rad- kar.de.id/	/(to) rad- kar.de.i/
(آنها) رد کرده اند	(او/آن) رد کرده است
/(ăn.hă) rad- kar.de.and/	/(u/ ăn) rad- kar.de- ast/

Past Perfect	
ماضی بعید	
(ما) رد کرده بودیم	(من) رد کرده بودم
/(mă) rad- kar.de- bu.dim/	/(man) rad- kar.de- bu.dam/
(شما) رد کرده بودید	(تو) رد کرده بودی
/(šo.mă) rad- kar.de- bu.did/	/(to) rad- kar.de- bu.di/
(آنها) رد کرده بودند	(او/آن) رد کرده بود
/(ăn.hă) rad- kar.de- bu.dand/	/(u/ ăn) rad- kar.de- bud/

<table>
<tr><td colspan="2" align="center">**Past Subjunctive**
ماضی التزامی</td></tr>
<tr>
<td align="center">(ما) رد کرده باشیم
/(mă) rad- kar.de- bă.šim/</td>
<td align="center">(من) رد کرده باشم
/(man) rad- kar.de- bă.šam/</td>
</tr>
<tr>
<td align="center">(شما) رد کرده باشید
/(šo.mă) rad.de- bă.šid/</td>
<td align="center">(تو) رد کرده باشی
/(to) rad- kar.de- bă.ši/</td>
</tr>
<tr>
<td align="center">(آنها) رد کرده باشند
/(ăn.hă) rad- kar.de- bă.šand/</td>
<td align="center">(او/آن) رد کرده باشد
/(u/ ăn) rad- kar.de- bă.šad/</td>
</tr>
</table>

<table>
<tr><td colspan="2" align="center">**Past Progressive**
ماضی مستمر(در جریان)</td></tr>
<tr>
<td align="center">(ما) داشتیم رد می کردیم
/(mă) dăš.tim- rad- mi.kar.dim/</td>
<td align="center">(من) داشتم رد می کردم
/(man) dăš.tam- rad- mi.kar.dam/</td>
</tr>
<tr>
<td align="center">(شما) داشتید رد می کردید
/(šo.mă) dăš.tid- rad- mi.kar.did/</td>
<td align="center">(تو) داشتی رد می کردی
/(to) dăš.ti- rad- mi.kar.di/</td>
</tr>
<tr>
<td align="center">(آنها) داشتند رد می کردند
/(ăn.hă) dăš.tand- rad- mi.kar.dand/</td>
<td align="center">(او/آن) داشت رد می کرد
/(u/ ăn) dăšt- rad- mi.kard/</td>
</tr>
</table>

<table>
<tr><td colspan="2" align="center">**Simple Future**
مستقبل (آینده ساده)</td></tr>
<tr>
<td align="center">(ما) رد خواهیم کرد
/(mă) rad- kă.him- kard/</td>
<td align="center">(من) رد خواهم کرد
/(man) rad- kă.ham- kard/</td>
</tr>
<tr>
<td align="center">(شما) رد خواهید کرد
/(šo.mă) rad- kă.hid- kard/</td>
<td align="center">(تو) رد خواهی کرد
/(to) rad- kă.hi- kard/</td>
</tr>
<tr>
<td align="center">(آنها) رد خواهند کرد
/(ăn.hă) rad- kă.hand- kard/</td>
<td align="center">(او/آن) رد خواهد کرد
/(u/ ăn) rad- kă.had- kard/</td>
</tr>
</table>

<table>
<tr><td colspan="2" align="center">**Command**
امر</td></tr>
<tr>
<td align="center">* رد بکنید!
/rad- be.ko.nid/</td>
<td align="center">* رد بکن!
/rad- be.kon/</td>
</tr>
</table>

* also: رد کن!   رد کنید!

to do

گَردَن

/kar.dan/

Plural	Singular
Simple Present	
<div dir="rtl">مضارع اخباری(حال ساده)</div>	
<div dir="rtl">(ما) می کنیم</div> /(mă) mi.ko.nim/	<div dir="rtl">(من) می کنم</div> /(man) mi.ko.nam/
<div dir="rtl">(شما) می کنید</div> /(šo.mă) mi.ko.nid/	<div dir="rtl">(تو) می کنی</div> /(to) mi.ko.ni/
<div dir="rtl">(آنها) می کنند</div> /(ăn.hă) mi.ko.nand/	<div dir="rtl">(او/آن) می کند</div> /(u/ ăn) mi.ko.nad/
Present Subjunctive	
<div dir="rtl">مضارع التزامی</div>	
<div dir="rtl">(ما) بکنیم</div> /(mă) be.ko.nim/	<div dir="rtl">(من) بکنم</div> /(man) be.ko.nam/
<div dir="rtl">(شما) بکنید</div> /(šo.mă) be.ko.nid/	<div dir="rtl">(تو) بکنی</div> /(to) be.ko.ni/
<div dir="rtl">(آنها) بکنند</div> /(ăn.hă) be.ko.nand/	<div dir="rtl">(او/آن) بکند</div> /(u/ ăn) be.ko.nad/
Present Progressive	
<div dir="rtl">مضارع مستمر(در جریان)</div>	
<div dir="rtl">(ما) داریم می کنیم</div> /(mă) dă.rim- mi.ko.nim/	<div dir="rtl">(من) دارم می کنم</div> /(man) dă.ram- mi.ko.nam/
<div dir="rtl">(شما) دارید می کنید</div> /(šo.mă) dă.rid- mi.ko.nid/	<div dir="rtl">(تو) داری می کنی</div> /(to) dă.ri- mi.ko.ni/
<div dir="rtl">(آنها) دارند می کنند</div> /(ăn.hă) dă.rand- mi.ko.nand/	<div dir="rtl">(او/آن) دارد می کند</div> /(u/ ăn) dă.rad- mi.ko.nad/

Simple Past
ماضی مطلق (گذشته ساده)

(ما) کردیم	(من) کردم
/(mǎ) kar.dim/	/(man) kar.dam/
(شما) کردید	(تو) کردی
/(šo.mǎ) kar.did/	/(to) kar.di/
(آنها) کردند	(او/آن) کرد
/(ǎn.hǎ) kar.dand/	/(u/ ǎn) kard/

Imperfect Indicative
ماضی استمراری

(ما) می کردیم	(من) می کردم
/(mǎ) mi.kar.dim/	/(man) mi.kar.dam/
(شما) می کردید	(تو) می کردی
/(šo.mǎ) mi.kar.did/	/(to) mi.kar.di/
(آنها) می کردند	(او/آن) می کرد
/(ǎn.hǎ) mi.kar.dand/	/(u/ ǎn) mi.kard/

Present Perfect
ماضی نقلی

(ما) کرده ایم	(من) کرده ام
/(mǎ) kar.de.im/	/(man) kar.de.am/
(شما) کرده اید	(تو) کرده ای
/(šo.mǎ) kar.de.id/	/(to) kar.de.i/
(آنها) کرده اند	(او/آن) کرده است
/(ǎn.hǎ) kar.de.and/	/(u/ ǎn) kar.de- ast/

Past Perfect
ماضی بعید

(ما) کرده بودیم	(من) کرده بودم
/(mǎ) kar.de- bu.dim/	/(man) kar.de- bu.dam/
(شما) کرده بودید	(تو) کرده بودی
/(šo.mǎ) kar.de- bu.did/	/(to) kar.de- bu.di/
(آنها) کرده بودند	(او/آن) کرده بود
/(ǎn.hǎ) kar.de- bu.dand/	/(u/ ǎn) kar.de- bud/

Past Subjunctive	
ماضی التزامی	
(ما) کرده باشیم	(من) کرده باشم
/(mǎ) kar.de- bǎ.šim/	/(man) kar.de- bǎ.šam/
(شما) کرده باشید	(تو) کرده باشی
/(šo.mǎ) kar.de- bǎ.šid/	/(to) kar.de- bǎ.ši/
(آنها) کرده باشند	(او/آن) کرده باشد
/(ǎn.hǎ) kar.de- bǎ.šand/	/(u/ ǎn) kar.de- bǎ.šad/

Past Progressive	
ماضی مستمر(در جریان)	
(ما) داشتیم می کردیم	(من) داشتم می کردم
/(mǎ) dǎš.tim- mi.kar.dim/	/(man) dǎš.tam- mi.kar.dam/
(شما) داشتید می کردید	(تو) داشتی می کردی
/(šo.mǎ) dǎš.tid- mi.kar.did/	/(to) dǎš.ti- mi.kar.di/
(آنها) داشتند می کردند	(او/آن) داشت می کرد
/(ǎn.hǎ) dǎš.tand- mi.kar.dand/	/(u/ ǎn) dǎšt- mi.kard/

Simple Future	
مستقبل (آینده ساده)	
(ما) خواهیم کرد	(من) خواهم کرد
/(mǎ) ǩǎ.him- kard/	/(man) ǩǎ.ham- kard/
(شما) خواهید کرد	(تو) خواهی کرد
/(šo.mǎ) ǩǎ.hid- kard/	/(to) ǩǎ.hi- kard/
(آنها) خواهند کرد	(او/آن) خواهد کرد
/(ǎn.hǎ) ǩǎ.hand- kard/	/(u/ ǎn) ǩǎ.had- kard/

Command	
امر	
بکنید!	بکن!
/be.ko.nid/	/be.kon/

to drink

نوشیدَن

/nu.ši.dan/

	Plural	**Singular**
Simple Present مضارع اخباری(حال ساده)		
(ما) می نوشیم /(mǎ) mi.nu.šim/		(من) می نوشم /(man) mi.nu.šam/
(شما) می نوشید /(šo.mǎ) mi.nu.šid/		(تو) می نوشی /(to) mi.nu.ši/
(آنها) می نوشند /(ǎn.hǎ) mi.nu.šand/		(او/آن) می نوشد /(u/ ǎn) mi.nu.šad/

Present Subjunctive مضارع التزامی		
(ما) بنوشیم /(mǎ) be.bu.šim/		(من) بنوشم /(man) be.nu.šam/
(شما) بنوشید /(šo.mǎ) be.nu.šid/		(تو) بنوشی /(to) be.nu.ši/
(آنها) بنوشند /(ǎn.hǎ) be.nu.šand/		(او/آن) بنوشد /(u/ ǎn) be.nu.šad/

Present Progressive مضارع مستمر(در جریان)		
(ما) داریم می نوشیم /(mǎ) dǎ.rim- mi.nu.šim /		(من) دارم می نوشم /(man) dǎ.ram- mi.nu.šam/
(شما) دارید می نوشید /(šo.mǎ) dǎ.rid- mi.nu.šid/		(تو) داری می نوشی /(to) dǎ.ri- mi.nu.ši/
(آنها) دارند می نوشند /(ǎn.hǎ) dǎ.rand- mi.nu.šand/		(او/آن) دارد می نوشد /(u/ ǎn) dǎ.rad- mi.nu.šad/

	Simple Past ماضی مطلق (گذشته ساده)	
(ما) نوشیدیم /(mǎ) nu.ši.dim/	(من) نوشیدم /(man) nu.ši.dam/
(شما) نوشیدید /(šo.mǎ) nu.ši.did/	(تو) نوشیدی /(to) nu.ši.di/
(آنها) نوشیدند /(ǎn.hǎ) nu.ši.dand/	(او/آن) نوشید /(u/ ǎn) nu.šid/

	Imperfect Indicative ماضی استمراری	
(ما) می نوشیدیم /(mǎ) mi.nu.ši.dim/	(من) می نوشیدم /(man) mi.nu.ši.dam/
(شما) می نوشیدید /(šo.mǎ) mi.nu.ši.did/	(تو) می نوشیدی /(to) mi.nu.ši.di/
(آنها) می نوشیدند /(ǎn.hǎ) mi.nu.ši.dand/	(او/آن) می نوشید /(u/ ǎn) mi.nu.šid/

	Present Perfect ماضی نقلی	
(ما) نوشیده ایم /(mǎ) nu.ši.de.im/	(من) نوشیده ام /(man) nu.ši.de.am/
(شما) نوشیده اید /(šo.mǎ) nu.ši.de.id/	(تو) نوشیده ای /(to) nu.ši.de.i/
(آنها) نوشیده اند /(ǎn.hǎ) nu.ši.de.and/	(او/آن) نوشیده است /(u/ ǎn) nu.ši.de- ast/

	Past Perfect ماضی بعید	
(ما) نوشیده بودیم /(mǎ) nu.ši.de- bu.dim/	(من) نوشیده بودم /(man) nu.ši.de- bu.dam/
(شما) نوشیده بودید /(šo.mǎ) nu.ši.de- bu.did/	(تو) نوشیده بودی /(to) nu.ši.de- bu.di/
(آنها) نوشیده بودند /(ǎn.hǎ) nu.ši.de- bu.dand/	(او/آن) نوشیده بود /(u/ ǎn) nu.ši.de- bud/

<table>
<tr><td colspan="2" align="center">Past Subjunctive
ماضی التزامی</td></tr>
<tr>
<td align="center">(ما) نوشیده باشیم
/(mă) nu.ši.de- bă.šim/</td>
<td align="center">(من) نوشیده باشم
/(man) nu.ši.de- bă.šam/</td>
</tr>
<tr>
<td align="center">(شما) نوشیده باشید
/(šo.mă) nu.ši.de- bă.šid/</td>
<td align="center">(تو) نوشیده باشی
/(to) nu.ši.de- bă.ši/</td>
</tr>
<tr>
<td align="center">(آنها) نوشیده باشند
(ăn.hă) nu.ši.de- bă.šand/</td>
<td align="center">(او/آن) نوشیده باشد
/(u/ ăn) nu.ši.de- bă.šad/</td>
</tr>
</table>

<table>
<tr><td colspan="2" align="center">Past Progressive
ماضی مستمر(در جریان)</td></tr>
<tr>
<td align="center">(ما) داشتیم می نوشیدیم
/(mă) dăš.tim- mi.nu.ši.dim/</td>
<td align="center">(من) داشتم می نوشیدم
/(man) dăš.tam- mi.nu.ši.dam/</td>
</tr>
<tr>
<td align="center">(شما) داشتید می نوشیدید
/(šo.mă) dăš.tid- mi.nu.ši.did/</td>
<td align="center">(تو) داشتی می نوشیدی
/(to) dăš.ti- mi.nu.ši.di/</td>
</tr>
<tr>
<td align="center">(آنها) داشتند می نوشیدند
/(ăn.hă) dăš.tand- mi.nu.ši.dand/</td>
<td align="center">(او/آن) داشت می نوشید
/(u/ ăn) dăšt- mi.nu.šid/</td>
</tr>
</table>

<table>
<tr><td colspan="2" align="center">Simple Future
مستقبل (آینده ساده)</td></tr>
<tr>
<td align="center">(ما) خواهیم نوشید
/(mă) kă.him- nu.šid/</td>
<td align="center">(من) خواهم نوشید
/(man) kă.ham- nu.šid/</td>
</tr>
<tr>
<td align="center">(شما) خواهید نوشید
/(šo.mă) kă.hid- nu.šid/</td>
<td align="center">(تو) خواهی نوشید
/(to) kă.hi- nu.šid/</td>
</tr>
<tr>
<td align="center">(آنها) خواهند نوشید
/(ăn.hă) kă.hand- nu.šid/</td>
<td align="center">(او/آن) خواهد نوشید
/(u/ ăn) kă.had- nu.šid/</td>
</tr>
</table>

<table>
<tr><td colspan="2" align="center">Command
امر</td></tr>
<tr>
<td>بنوشید!
/be. nu.šid/</td>
<td>بنوش!
/be.nuš/</td>
</tr>
</table>

to drive

رانَندِگی کَردَن

/rǎ.nan.de.gi- kar.dan/

Plural	Singular
Simple Present	
مضارع اخباری(حال ساده)	
(ما) رانندگی می کنیم	(من) رانندگی می کنم
/(mǎ) rǎ.nan.de.gi- mi.ko.nim/	/(man) rǎ.nan.de.gi- mi.ko.nam/
(شما) رانندگی می کنید	(تو) رانندگی می کنی
/(šo.mǎ) rǎ.nan.de.gi- mi.ko.nid/	/(to) rǎ.nan.de.gi- mi.ko.ni/
(آنها) رانندگی می کنند	(او/آن) رانندگی می کند
/(ǎn.hǎ) rǎ.nan.de.gi- mi.ko.nand/	/(u/ ǎn) rǎ.nan.de.gi- mi.ko.nad/
Present Subjunctive	
مضارع التزامی	
(ما) رانندگی بکنیم	(من) رانندگی بکنم
/(mǎ) rǎ.nan.de.gi- be.ko.nim/	/(man) rǎ.nan.de.gi- be.ko.nam/
(شما) رانندگی بکنید	(تو) رانندگی بکنی
/(šo.mǎ) rǎ.nan.de.gi- be.ko.nid/	/(to) rǎ.nan.de.gi- be.ko.ni/
(آنها) رانندگی بکنند	(او/آن) رانندگی بکند
/(ǎn.hǎ) rǎ.nan.de.gi- be.ko.nand/	/(u/ ǎn) rǎ.nan.de.gi- be.ko.nad/
Present Progressive	
مضارع مستمر(در جریان)	
(ما) داریم رانندگی می کنیم	(من) دارم رانندگی می کنم
/(mǎ) dǎ.rim- rǎ.nan.de.gi- mi.ko.nim/	/(man) dǎ.ram- rǎ.nan.de.gi- mi.ko.nam/
(شما) دارید رانندگی می کنید	(تو) داری رانندگی می کنی
/(šo.mǎ) dǎ.rid- rǎ.nan.de.gi- mi.ko.nid/	/(to) dǎ.ri- rǎ.nan.de.gi- mi.ko.ni/
(آنها) دارند رانندگی می کنند	(او/آن) دارد رانندگی می کند
/(ǎn.hǎ) dǎ.rand- rǎ.nan.de.gi- mi.ko.nand/	/(u/ ǎn) dǎ.rad- rǎ.nan.de.gi- mi.ko.nad/

Simple Past
ماضی مطلق (گذشته ساده)

(ما) رانندگی کردیم	(من) رانندگی کردم
/(mă) ră.nan.de.gi- kar.dim/	/(man) ră.nan.de.gi- kar.dam/
(شما) رانندگی کردید	(تو) رانندگی کردی
/(šo.mă) ră.nan.de.gi- kar.did/	/(to) ră.nan.de.gi- kar.di/
(آنها) رانندگی کردند	(او/آن) رانندگی کرد
/(ăn.hă) ră.nan.de.gi- kar.dand/	/(u/ ăn) ră.nan.de.gi- kard/

Imperfect Indicative
ماضی استمراری

(ما) رانندگی می کردیم	(من) رانندگی می کردم
/(mă) ră.nan.de.gi- mi.kar.dim/	/(man) ră.nan.de.gi- mi.kar.dam/
(شما) رانندگی می کردید	(تو) رانندگی می کردی
/(šo.mă) ră.nan.de.gi- mi.kar.did/	/(to) ră.nan.de.gi- mi.kar.di/
(آنها) رانندگی می کردند	(او/آن) رانندگی می کرد
/(ăn.hă) ră.nan.de.gi- mi.kar.dand/	/(u/ ăn) ră.nan.de.gi- mi.kard/

Present Perfect
ماضی نقلی

(ما) رانندگی کرده ایم	(من) رانندگی کرده ام
/(mă) ră.nan.de.gi- kar.de.im/	/(man) ră.nan.de.gi- kar.de.am/
(شما) رانندگی کرده اید	(تو) رانندگی کرده ای
/(šo.mă) ră.nan.de.gi- kar.de.id/	/(to) ră.nan.de.gi- kar.de.i/
(آنها) رانندگی کرده اند	(او/آن) رانندگی کرده است
/(ăn.hă) ră.nan.de.gi- kar.de.and/	/(u/ ăn) ră.nan.de.gi- kar.de- ast/

Past Perfect
ماضی بعید

(ما) رانندگی کرده بودیم	(من) رانندگی کرده بودم
/(mă) ră.nan.de.gi- kar.de- bu.dim/	/(man) ră.nan.de.gi- kar.de- bu.dam/
(شما) رانندگی کرده بودید	(تو) رانندگی کرده بودی
/(šo.mă) ră.nan.de.gi- kar.de- bu.did/	/(to) ră.nan.de.gi- kar.de- bu.di/
(آنها) رانندگی کرده بودند	(او/آن) رانندگی کرده بود
/(ăn.hă) ră.nan.de.gi- kar.de- bu.dand/	/(u/ ăn) ră.nan.de.gi- kar.de- bud/

Past Subjunctive
ماضی التزامی

(ما) رانندگی کرده باشیم	(من) رانندگی کرده باشم
/(mǎ) rǎ.nan.de.gi- kar.de- bǎ.šim/	/(man) rǎ.nan.de.gi- kar.de- bǎ.šam/
(شما) رانندگی کرده باشید	(تو) رانندگی کرده باشی
/(šo.mǎ) rǎ.nan.de.gi- kar.de- bǎ.šid/	/(to) rǎ.nan.de.gi- kar.de- bǎ.ši/
(آنها) رانندگی کرده باشند	(او/آن) رانندگی کرده باشد
/(ǎn.hǎ) rǎ.nan.de.gi- kar.de- bǎ.šand/	/(u/ ǎn) rǎ.nan.de.gi- kar.de- bǎ.šad/

Past Progressive
ماضی مستمر(در جریان)

(ما) داشتیم رانندگی می کردیم	(من) داشتم رانندگی می کردم
/(mǎ) dǎš.tim- rǎ.nan.de.gi- mi.kar.dim/	/(man) dǎš.tam- rǎ.nan.de.gi- mi.kar.dam/
(شما) داشتید رانندگی می کردید	(تو) داشتی رانندگی می کردی
/(šo.mǎ) dǎš.tid- rǎ.nan.de.gi- mi.kar.did/	/(to) dǎš.ti- rǎ.nan.de.gi- mi.kar.di/
(آنها) داشتند رانندگی می کردند	(او/آن) داشت رانندگی می کرد
/(ǎn.hǎ) dǎš.tand- rǎ.nan.de.gi- mi.kar.dand/	/(u/ ǎn) dǎšt- rǎ.nan.de.gi- mi.kard/

Simple Future
مستقبل (آینده ساده)

(ما) رانندگی خواهیم کرد	(من) رانندگی خواهم کرد
/(mǎ) rǎ.nan.de.gi- ǩǎ.him- kard/	/(man) rǎ.nan.de.gi- ǩǎ.ham- kard/
(شما) رانندگی خواهید کرد	(تو) رانندگی خواهی کرد
/(šo.mǎ) rǎ.nan.de.gi- ǩǎ.hid- kard/	/(to) rǎ.nan.de.gi- ǩǎ.hi- kard/
(آنها) رانندگی خواهند کرد	(او/آن) رانندگی خواهد کرد
/(ǎn.hǎ) rǎ.nan.de.gi- ǩǎ.hand- kard/	/(u/ ǎn) rǎ.nan.de.gi- ǩǎ.had- kard/

Command
امر

* رانندگی بکنید!	* رانندگی بکن!
/rǎ.nan.de.gi- be.ko.nid/	/rǎ.nan.de.gi- be.kon/

* also: رانندگی کن !   رانندگی کنید !

76

to eat

خوردَن

/ǩor.dan/

Plural	*Singular*
Simple Present مضارع اخباری(حال ساده)	
(ما) می خوریم /(mă) mi.ǩo.rim/	(من) می خورم /(man) mi.ǩo.ram/
(شما) می خورید /(šo.mă) mi.ǩo.rid/	(تو) می خوری /(to) mi.ǩo.ri/
(آنها) می خورند /(ăn.hă) mi.ǩo.rand/	(او/آن) می خورد /(u/ ăn) mi.ǩo.rad/
Present Subjunctive مضارع التزامی	
(ما) بخوریم /(mă) be.ǩo.rim/	(من) بخورم /(man) be.ǩo.ram/
(شما) بخورید /(šo.mă) be.ǩo.rid/	(تو) بخوری /(to) be.ǩo.ri/
(آنها) بخورند /(ăn.hă) be.ǩo.rand/	(او/آن) بخورد /(u/ ăn) be.ǩo.rad/
Present Progressive مضارع مستمر(در جریان)	
(ما) داریم می خوریم /(mă) dă.rim- mi.ǩo.rim/	(من) دارم می خورم /(man) dă.ram- mi.ǩo.ram/
(شما) دارید می خورید /(šo.mă) dă.rid- mi.ǩo.rid/	(تو) داری می خوری /(to) dă.ri- mi.ǩo.ri/
(آنها) دارند می خورند /(ăn.hă) dă.rand- mi.ǩo.rand/	(او/آن) دارد می خورد /(u/ ăn) dă.rad- mi.ǩo.rad/

Simple Past	
ماضی مطلق (گذشته ساده)	
(ما) خوردیم	(من) خوردم
/(mă) ǩor.dim/	/(man) ǩor.dam/
(شما) خوردید	(تو) خوردی
/(šo.mă) ǩor.did/	/(to) ǩor.di/
(آنها) خوردند	(او/آن) خورد
/(ăn.hă) ǩor.dand/	/(u/ ăn) ǩord/

Imperfect Indicative	
ماضی استمراری	
(ما) می خوردیم	(من) می خوردم
/(mă) mi.ǩor.dim/	/(man) mi.ǩor.dam/
(شما) می خوردید	(تو) می خوردی
/(šo.mă) mi.ǩor.did/	/(to) mi.ǩor.di/
(آنها) می خوردند	(او/آن) می خورد
/(ăn.hă) mi.ǩor.dand/	/(u/ ăn) mi.ǩord/

Present Perfect	
ماضی نقلی	
(ما) خورده ایم	(من) خورده ام
/(mă) ǩor.de.im/	/(man) ǩor.de.am/
(شما) خورده اید	(تو) خورده ای
/(šo.mă) ǩor.de.id/	/(to) ǩor.de.i/
(آنها) خورده اند	(او/آن) خورده است
/(ăn.hă) ǩor.de.and/	/(u/ ăn) ǩor.de- ast/

Past Perfect	
ماضی بعید	
(ما) خورده بودیم	(من) خورده بودم
/(mă) ǩor.de- bu.dim/	/(man) ǩor.de- bu.dam/
(شما) خورده بودید	(تو) خورده بودی
/(šo.mă) ǩor.de- bu.did/	/(to) ǩor.de- bu.di/
(آنها) خورده بودند	(او/آن) خورده بود
/(ăn.hă) ǩor.de- bu.dand/	/(u/ ăn) ǩor.de- bud/

Past Subjunctive
ماضی التزامی

(ما) خورده باشیم	(من) خورده باشم
/(mă) ǩor.de- bă.šim/	/(man) ǩor.de- bă.šam/
(شما) خورده باشید	(تو) خورده باشی
/(šo.mă) ǩor.de- bă.šid/	/(to) ǩor.de- bă.ši/
(آنها) خورده باشند	(او/آن) خورده باشد
/(ăn.hă) ǩor.de- bă.šand/	/(u/ ăn) ǩor.de- bă.šad/

Past Progressive
ماضی مستمر(در جریان)

(ما) داشتیم می خوردیم	(من) داشتم می خوردم
/(mă) dăš.tim- mi.ǩor.dim/	/(man) dăš.tam- mi.ǩor.dam/
(شما) داشتید می خوردید	(تو) داشتی می خوردی
/(šo.mă) dăš.tid- mi.ǩor.did/	/(to) dăš.ti- mi.ǩor.di/
(آنها) داشتند می خوردند	(او/آن) داشت می خورد
/(ăn.hă) dăš.tand- mi.ǩor.dand/	/(u/ ăn) dăšt- mi.ǩord/

Simple Future
مستقبل (آینده ساده)

(ما) خواهیم خورد	(من) خواهم خورد
/(mă) ǩă.him- ǩord/	/(man) ǩă.ham- ǩord/
(شما) خواهید خورد	(تو) خواهی خورد
/(šo.mă) ǩă.hid- ǩord/	/(to) ǩă.hi- ǩord/
(آنها) خواهند خورد	(او/آن) خواهد خورد
/(ăn.hă) ǩă.hand- ǩord/	/(u/ ăn) ǩă.had- ǩord/

Command
امر

بخورید!	بخور!
/be.ǩo.rid/	/be.ǩor/

to empty

خالی کَردَن

/kǎ.li- kar.dan/

Plural	Singular
Simple Present مضارع اخباری(حال ساده)	
(ما) خالی می کنیم /(mǎ) kǎ.li- mi.ko.nim/	(من) خالی می کنم /(man) kǎ.li- mi.ko.nam/
(شما) خالی می کنید /(šo.mǎ) kǎ.li- mi.ko.nid/	(تو) خالی می کنی /(to) kǎ.li- mi.ko.ni/
(آنها) خالی می کنند /(ǎn.hǎ) kǎ.li- mi.ko.nand/	(او/آن) خالی می کند /(u/ ǎn) kǎ.li- mi.ko.nad/
Present Subjunctive مضارع التزامی	
(ما) خالی بکنیم /(mǎ) kǎ.li- be.ko.nim/	(من) خالی بکنم /(man) kǎ.li- be.ko.nam/
(شما) خالی بکنید /(šo.mǎ) kǎ.li- be.ko.nid/	(تو) خالی بکنی /(to) kǎ.li- be.ko.ni/
(آنها) خالی بکنند /(ǎn.hǎ) kǎ.li- be.ko.nand/	(او/آن) خالی بکند /(u/ ǎn) kǎ.li- be.ko.nad/
Present Progressive مضارع مستمر(در جریان)	
(ما) داریم خالی می کنیم /(mǎ) dǎ.rim- kǎ.li- mi.ko.nim/	(من) دارم خالی می کنم /(man) dǎ.ram- kǎ.li- mi.ko.nam/
(شما) دارید خالی می کنید /(šo.mǎ) dǎ.rid- kǎ.li- mi.ko.nid/	(تو) داری خالی می کنی /(to) dǎ.ri- kǎ.li- mi.ko.ni/
(آنها) دارند خالی می کنند /(ǎn.hǎ) dǎ.rand- kǎ.li- mi.ko.nand/	(او/آن) دارد خالی می کند /(u/ ǎn) dǎ.rad- kǎ.li- mi.ko.nad/

Simple Past
ماضی مطلق (گذشته ساده)

(ما) خالی کردیم	(من) خالی کردم
/(mă) kă.li- kar.dim/	/(man) kă.li- kar.dam/
(شما) خالی کردید	(تو) خالی کردی
/(šo.mă) kă.li- kar.did/	/(to) kă.li- kar.di/
(آنها) خالی کردند	(او/آن) خالی کرد
/(ăn.hă) kă.li- kar.dand/	/(u/ ăn) kă.li- kard/

Imperfect Indicative
ماضی استمراری

(ما) خالی می کردیم	(من) خالی می کردم
/(mă) kă.li- mi.kar.dim/	/(man) kă.li- mi.kar.dam/
(شما) خالی می کردید	(تو) خالی می کردی
/(šo.mă) kă.li- mi.kar.did/	/(to) kă.li- mi.kar.di/
(آنها) خالی می کردند	(او/آن) خالی می کرد
/(ăn.hă) kă.li- mi.kar.dand/	/(u/ ăn) kă.li- mi.kard/

Present Perfect
ماضی نقلی

(ما) خالی کرده ایم	(من) خالی کرده ام
/(mă) kă.li- kar.de.im/	/(man) kă.li- kar.de.am/
(شما) خالی کرده اید	(تو) خالی کرده ای
/(šo.mă) kă.li- kar.de.id/	/(to) kă.li- kar.de.i/
(آنها) خالی کرده اند	(او/آن) خالی کرده است
/(ăn.hă) kă.li- kar.de.and/	/(u/ ăn) kă.li- kar.de- ast/

Past Perfect
ماضی بعید

(ما) خالی کرده بودیم	(من) خالی کرده بودم
/(mă) kă.li- kar.de- bu.dim/	/(man) kă.li- kar.de- bu.dam/
(شما) خالی کرده بودید	(تو) خالی کرده بودی
/(šo.mă) kă.li- kar.de- bu.did/	/(to) kă.li- kar.de- bu.di/
(آنها) خالی کرده بودند	(او/آن) خالی کرده بود
/(ăn.hă) kă.li- kar.de- bu.dand/	/(u/ ăn) kă.li- kar.de- bud/

Past Subjunctive	
ماضی التزامی	
(ما) خالی کرده باشیم	(من) خالی کرده باشم
/(mǎ) ǩǎ.li- kar.de- bǎ.šim/	/(man) ǩǎ.li- kar.de- bǎ.šam/
(شما) خالی کرده باشید	(تو) خالی کرده باشی
/(šo.mǎ) ǩǎ.li- kar.de- bǎ.šid/	/(to) ǩǎ.li- kar.de- bǎ.ši/
(آنها) خالی کرده باشند	(او/آن) خالی کرده باشد
/(ǎn.hǎ) ǩǎ.li- kar.de- bǎ.šand/	/(u/ ǎn) ǩǎ.li- kar.de- bǎ.šad/

Past Progressive	
ماضی مستمر(در جریان)	
(ما) داشتیم خالی می کردیم	(من) داشتم خالی می کردم
/(mǎ) dǎš.tim- ǩǎ.li- mi.kar.dim/	/(man) dǎš.tam- ǩǎ.li- mi.kar.dam/
(شما) داشتید خالی می کردید	(تو) داشتی خالی می کردی
/(šo.mǎ) dǎš.tid- ǩǎ.li- mi.kar.did/	/(to) dǎš.ti- ǩǎ.li- mi.kar.di/
(آنها) داشتند خالی می کردند	(او/آن) داشت خالی می کرد
/(ǎn.hǎ) dǎš.tand- ǩǎ.li- mi.kar.dand/	/(u/ ǎn) dǎšt- ǩǎ.li- mi.kard/

Simple Future	
مستقبل (آینده ساده)	
(ما) خالی خواهیم کرد	(من) خالی خواهم کرد
/(mǎ) ǩǎ.li- ǩǎ.him- kard/	/(man) ǩǎ.li- ǩǎ.ham- kard/
(شما) خالی خواهید کرد	(تو) خالی خواهی کرد
/(šo.mǎ) ǩǎ.li- ǩǎ.hid- kard/	/(to) ǩǎ.li- ǩǎ.hi- kard/
(آنها) خالی خواهند کرد	(او/آن) خالی خواهد کرد
/(ǎn.hǎ) ǩǎ.li- ǩǎ.hand- kard/	/(u/ ǎn) ǩǎ.li- ǩǎ.had- kard/

Command	
امر	
* خالی بکنید!	* خالی بکن!
/ǩǎ.li- be.ko.nid/	/ǩǎ.li- be.kon/

* also: خالی کن!   خالی کنید!

82

to enter

وارد شُدَن

/vă.red- šo.dan/

Plural	Singular
Simple Present مضارع اخباری(حال ساده)	
(ما) وارد می شویم /(mă) vă.red- mi.ša.vim/	(من) وارد می شوم /(man) vă.red- mi.ša.vam/
(شما) وارد می شوید /(šo.mă) vă.red- mi.ša.vid/	(تو) وارد می شوی /(to) vă.red- mi.ša.vi/
(آنها) وارد می شوند /(ăn.hă) vă.red- mi.ša.vand/	(او/آن) وارد می شود /(u/ ăn) vă.red- mi.ša.vad/
Present Subjunctive مضارع التزامی	
(ما) وارد بشویم /(mă) vă.red- be.ša.vim/	(من) وارد بشوم /(man) vă.red- be.ša.vam/
(شما) وارد بشوید /(šo.mă) vă.red- be.ša.vid/	(تو) وارد بشوی /(to) vă.red- be.ša.vi/
(آنها) وارد بشوند /(ăn.hă) vă.red- be.ša.vand/	(او/آن) وارد بشود /(u/ ăn) vă.red- be.ša.vad/
Present Progressive مضارع مستمر(در جریان)	
(ما) داریم وارد می شویم /(mă) dă.rim- vă.red- mi.ša.vim/	(من) دارم وارد می شوم /(man) dă.ram- vă.red- mi.ša.vam/
(شما) دارید وارد می شوید /(šo.mă) dă.rid- vă.red- mi.ša.vid/	(تو) داری وارد می شوی /(to) dă.ri- vă.red- mi.ša.vi/
(آنها) دارند وارد می شوند /(ăn.hă) dă.rand- vă.red- mi.ša.vand/	(او/آن) دارد وارد می شود /(u/ ăn) dă.rad- vă.red- mi.ša.vad/

Simple Past	
ماضی مطلق (گذشته ساده)	
(ما) وارد شدیم	(من) وارد شدم
/(mă) vă.red- šo.dim/	/(man) vă.red- šo.dam/
(شما) وارد شدید	(تو) وارد شدی
/(šo.mă) vă.red- šo.did/	/(to) vă.red- šo.di/
(آنها) وارد شدند	(او/ آن) وارد شد
/(ăn.hă) vă.red- šo.dand/	/(u/ ăn) vă.red- šod/

Imperfect Indicative	
ماضی استمراری	
(ما) وارد می شدیم	(من) وارد می شدم
/(mă) vă.red- mi.šo.dim/	/(man) vă.red- mi.šo.dam/
(شما) وارد می شدید	(تو) وارد می شدی
/(šo.mă) vă.red- mi.šo.did/	/(to) vă.red- mi.šo.di/
(آنها) وارد می شدند	(او/ آن) وارد می شد
/(ăn.hă) vă.red- mi.šo.dand/	/(u/ ăn) vă.red- mi.šod/

Present Perfect	
ماضی نقلی	
(ما) وارد شده ایم	(من) وارد شده ام
/(mă) vă.red- šo.de.im/	/(man) vă.red- šo.de.am/
(شما) وارد شده اید	(تو) وارد شده ای
/(šo.mă) vă.red- šo.de.id/	/(to) vă.red- šo.de.i/
(آنها) وارد شده اند	(او/ آن) وارد شده است
/(ăn.hă) vă.red- šo.de.and/	/(u/ ăn) vă.red- šo.de- ast/

Past Perfect	
ماضی بعید	
(ما) وارد شده بودیم	(من) وارد شده بودم
/(mă) vă.red- šo.de- bu.dim/	/(man) vă.red- šo.de- bu.dam/
(شما) وارد شده بودید	(تو) وارد شده بودی
/(šo.mă) vă.red- šo.de- bu.did/	/(to) vă.red- šo.de- bu.di/
(آنها) وارد شده بودند	(او/ آن) وارد شده بود
/(ăn.hă) vă.red- šo.de- bu.dand/	/(u/ ăn) vă.red- šo.de- bud/

Past Subjunctive	
ماضی التزامی	
(ما) وارد شده باشیم	(من) وارد شده باشم
/(mă) vă.red- šo.de- bă.šim/	/(man) vă.red- šo.de- bă.šam/
(شما) وارد شده باشید	(تو) وارد شده باشی
/(šo.mă) vă.red- šo.de- bă.šid/	/(to) vă.red- šo.de- bă.ši/
(آنها) وارد شده باشند	(او/آن) وارد شده باشد
/(ăn.hă) vă.red- šo.de- bă.šand/	/(u/ ăn) vă.red- šo.de- bă.šad/

Past Progressive	
ماضی مستمر(در جریان)	
(ما) داشتیم وارد می شدیم	(من) داشتم وارد می شدم
/(mă) dăš.tim- vă.red- mi.šo.dim/	/(man) dăš.tam- vă.red- mi.šo.dam/
(شما) داشتید وارد می شدید	(تو) داشتی وارد می شدی
/(šo.mă) dăš.tid- vă.red- mi.šo.did/	/(to) dăš.ti- vă.red- mi.šo.di/
(آنها) داشتند وارد می شدند	(او/آن) داشت وارد می شد
/(ăn.hă) dăš.tand- vă.red- mi.šo.dand/	/(u/ ăn) dăšt- vă.red- mi.šod/

Simple Future	
مستقبل (آینده ساده)	
(ما) وارد خواهیم شد	(من) وارد خواهم شد
/(mă) vă.red- ǩă.him- šod/	/(man) vă.red- ǩă.ham- šod/
(شما) وارد خواهید شد	(تو) وارد خواهی شد
/(šo.mă) vă.red- ǩă.hid- šod/	/(to) vă.red- ǩă.hi- šod/
(آنها) وارد خواهند شد	(او/آن) وارد خواهد شد
/(ăn.hă) vă.red- ǩă.hand- šod/	/(u/ ăn) vă.red- ǩă.had- šod/

Command	
امر	
* وارد بشوید!	* وارد بشو!
/vă.red- be.ša.vid/	/vă.red- be.šo/

* also: وارد شوید!   وارد شو!

85

to exit

خارِج شُدَن

/kǎ.rej- šo.dan/

Plural	Singular
Simple Present	
مضارع اخباری(حال ساده)	
(ما) خارج می شویم	(من) خارج می شوم
/(mǎ) kǎ.rej- mi.ša.vim/	/(man) kǎ.rej- mi.ša.vam/
(شما) خارج می شوید	(تو) خارج می شوی
/(šo.mǎ) kǎ.rej- mi.ša.vid/	/(to) kǎ.rej- mi.ša.vi/
(آنها) خارج می شوند	(او/آن) خارج می شود
/(ǎn.hǎ) kǎ.rej- mi.ša.vand/	/(u/ ǎn) kǎ.rej- mi.ša.vad/

Plural	Singular
Present Subjunctive	
مضارع التزامی	
(ما) خارج بشویم	(من) خارج بشوم
/(mǎ) kǎ.rej- be.ša.vim/	/(man) kǎ.rej- be.ša.vam/
(شما) خارج بشوید	(تو) خارج بشوی
/(šo.mǎ) kǎ.rej- be.ša.vid/	/(to) kǎ.rej- be.ša.vi/
(آنها) خارج بشوند	(او/آن) خارج بشود
/(ǎn.hǎ) kǎ.rej- be.ša.vand/	/(u/ ǎn) kǎ.rej- be.ša.vad/

Plural	Singular
Present Progressive	
مضارع مستمر(در جریان)	
(ما) داریم خارج می شویم	(من) دارم خارج می شوم
/(mǎ) dǎ.rim- kǎ.rej- mi.ša.vim/	/(man) dǎ.ram- kǎ.rej- mi.ša.vam/
(شما) دارید خارج می شوید	(تو) داری خارج می شوی
/(šo.mǎ) dǎ.rid- kǎ.rej- mi.ša.vid/	/(to) dǎ.ri- kǎ.rej- mi.ša.vi/
(آنها) دارند خارج می شوند	(او/آن) دارد خارج می شود
/(ǎn.hǎ) dǎ.rand- kǎ.rej- mi.ša.vand/	/(u/ ǎn) dǎ.rad- kǎ.rej- mi.ša.vad/

Simple Past	
ماضی مطلق (گذشته ساده)	
(ما) خارج شدیم	(من) خارج شدم
/(mǎ) ǩǎ.rej- šo.dim/	/(man) ǩǎ.rej- šo.dam/
(شما) خارج شدید	(تو) خارج شدی
/(šo.mǎ) ǩǎ.rej- šo.did/	/(to) ǩǎ.rej- šo.di/
(آنها) خارج شدند	(او/آن) خارج شد
/(ǎn.hǎ) ǩǎ.rej- šo.dand/	/(u/ ǎn) ǩǎ.rej- šod/

Imperfect Indicative	
ماضی استمراری	
(ما) خارج می شدیم	(من) خارج می شدم
/(mǎ) ǩǎ.rej- mi.šo.dim/	/(man) ǩǎ.rej- mi.šo.dam/
(شما) خارج می شدید	(تو) خارج می شدی
/(šo.mǎ) ǩǎ.rej- mi.šo.did/	/(to) ǩǎ.rej- mi.šo.di/
(آنها) خارج می شدند	(او/آن) خارج می شد
/(ǎn.hǎ) ǩǎ.rej- mi.šo.dand/	/(u/ ǎn) ǩǎ.rej- mi.šod/

Present Perfect	
ماضی نقلی	
(ما) خارج شده ایم	(من) خارج شده ام
/(mǎ) ǩǎ.rej- šo.de.im/	/(man) ǩǎ.rej- šo.de.am/
(شما) خارج شده اید	(تو) خارج شده ای
/(šo.mǎ) ǩǎ.rej- šo.de.id/	/(to) ǩǎ.rej- šo.de.i/
(آنها) خارج شده اند	(او/آن) خارج شده است
/(ǎn.hǎ) ǩǎ.rej- šo.de.and/	/(u/ ǎn) ǩǎ.rej- šo.de- ast/

Past Perfect	
ماضی بعید	
(ما) خارج شده بودیم	(من) خارج شده بودم
/(mǎ) ǩǎ.rej- šo.de- bu.dim/	/(man) ǩǎ.rej- šo.de- bu.dam/
(شما) خارج شده بودید	(تو) خارج شده بودی
/(šo.mǎ) ǩǎ.rej- šo.de- bu.did/	/(to) ǩǎ.rej- šo.de- bu.di/
(آنها) خارج شده بودند	(او/آن) خارج شده بود
/(ǎn.hǎ) ǩǎ.rej- šo.de- bu.dand/	/(u/ ǎn) ǩǎ.rej- šo.de- bud/

Past Subjunctive	
ماضی التزامی	
(ما) خارج شده باشیم /(mă) ǩă.rej- šo.de- bă.šim/	(من) خارج شده باشم /(man) ǩă.rej- šo.de- bă.šam/
(شما) خارج شده باشید /(šo.mă) ǩă.rej- šo.de- bă.šid/	(تو) خارج شده باشی /(to) ǩă.rej- šo.de- bă.ši/
(آنها) خارج شده باشند /(ăn.hă) ǩă.rej- šo.de- bă.šand/	(او/ آن) خارج شده باشد /(u/ ăn) ǩă.rej- šo.de- bă.šad/

Past Progressive	
ماضی مستمر(در جریان)	
(ما) داشتیم خارج می شدیم /(mă) dăš.tim- ǩă.rej- mi.šo.dim/	(من) داشتم خارج می شدم /(man) dăš.tam- ǩă.rej- mi.šo.dam/
(شما) داشتید خارج می شدید /(šo.mă) dăš.tid- ǩă.rej- mi.šo.did/	(تو) داشتی خارج می شدی /(to) dăš.ti- ǩă.rej- mi.šo.di/
(آنها) داشتند خارج می شدند /(ăn.hă) dăš.tand- ǩă.rej- mi.šo.dand/	(او/ آن) داشت خارج می شد /(u/ ăn) dăšt- ǩă.rej- mi.šod/

Simple Future	
مستقبل (آینده ساده)	
(ما) خارج خواهیم شد /(mă) ǩă.rej- ǩă.him- šod/	(من) خارج خواهم شد /(man) ǩă.rej- ǩă.ham- šod/
(شما) خارج خواهید شد /(šo.mă) ǩă.rej- ǩă.hid- šod/	(تو) خارج خواهی شد /(to) ǩă.rej- ǩă.hi- šod/
(آنها) خارج خواهند شد /(ăn.hă) ǩă.rej- ǩă.hand- šod/	(او/ آن) خارج خواهد شد /(u/ ăn) ǩă.rej- ǩă.had- šod/

Command	
امر	
خارج بشوید! * /ǩă.rej- be.ša.vid/	خارج بشو! * /ǩă.rej- be.šo/

* also: خارج شو!   خارج شوید!

to explain

توضیح دادَن

/to.zih- dă.dan/

Plural	Singular
Simple Present <div dir="rtl">مضارع اخباری(حال ساده)</div>	
<div dir="rtl">(ما) توضیح می دهیم</div> /(mă) to.zih- mi.da.him/	<div dir="rtl">(من) توضیح می دهم</div> /(man) to.zih- mi.da.ham/
<div dir="rtl">(شما) توضیح می دهید</div> /(šo.mă) to.zih- mi.da.hid/	<div dir="rtl">(تو) توضیح می دهی</div> /(to) to.zih- mi.da.hi/
<div dir="rtl">(آنها) توضیح می دهند</div> /(ăn.hă) to.zih- mi.da.hand/	<div dir="rtl">(او/آن) توضیح می دهد</div> /(u/ ăn) to.zih- mi.da.had/
Present Subjunctive <div dir="rtl">مضارع التزامی</div>	
<div dir="rtl">(ما) توضیح بدهیم</div> /(mă) to.zih- be.da.him/	<div dir="rtl">(من) توضیح بدهم</div> /(man) to.zih- be.da.ham/
<div dir="rtl">(شما) توضیح بدهید</div> /(šo.mă) to.zih- be.da.hid/	<div dir="rtl">(تو) توضیح بدهی</div> /(to) to.zih- be.da.hi/
<div dir="rtl">(آنها) توضیح بدهند</div> /(ăn.hă) to.zih- be.da.hand/	<div dir="rtl">(او/آن) توضیح بدهد</div> /(u/ ăn) to.zih- be.da.had/
Present Progressive <div dir="rtl">مضارع مستمر(در جریان)</div>	
<div dir="rtl">(ما) داریم توضیح می دهیم</div> /(mă) dă.rim- to.zih- mi.da.him/	<div dir="rtl">(من) دارم توضیح می دهم</div> /(man) dă.ram- to.zih- mi.da.ham/
<div dir="rtl">(شما) دارید توضیح می دهید</div> /(šo.mă) dă.rid- to.zih- mi.da.hid/	<div dir="rtl">(تو) داری توضیح می دهی</div> /(to) dă.ri- to.zih- mi.da.hi/
<div dir="rtl">(آنها) دارند توضیح می دهند</div> /(ăn.hă) dă.rand- to.zih- mi.da.hand/	<div dir="rtl">(او/آن) دارد توضیح می دهد</div> /(u/ ăn) dă.rad- to.zih- mi.da.had/

Simple Past	
ماضی مطلق (گذشته ساده)	
(ما) توضیح دادیم	(من) توضیح دادم
/(mă) to.zih- dă.dim/	/(man) to.zih- dă.dam/
(شما) توضیح دادید	(تو) توضیح دادی
/(šo.mă) to.zih- dă.did/	/(to) to.zih- dă.di/
(آنها) توضیح دادند	(او/آن) توضیح داد
/(ăn.hă) to.zih- dă.dand/	/(u/ ăn) to.zih- dăd/

Imperfect Indicative	
ماضی استمراری	
(ما) توضیح می دادیم	(من) توضیح می دادم
/(mă) to.zih- mi.dă.dim/	/(man) to.zih- mi.dă.dam/
(شما) توضیح می دادید	(تو) توضیح می دادی
/(šo.mă) to.zih- mi.dă.did/	/(to) to.zih- mi.dă.di/
(آنها) توضیح می دادند	(او/آن) توضیح می داد
/(ăn.hă) to.zih- mi.dă.dand/	/(u/ ăn) to.zih- mi.dăd/

Present Perfect	
ماضی نقلی	
(ما) توضیح داده ایم	(من) توضیح داده ام
/(mă) to.zih- dă.de.im/	/(man) to.zih- dă.de.am/
(شما) توضیح داده اید	(تو) توضیح داده ای
/(šo.mă) to.zih- dă.de.id/	/(to) to.zih- dă.de.i/
(آنها) توضیح داده اند	(او/آن) توضیح داده است
/(ăn.hă) to.zih- dă.de.and/	/(u/ ăn) to.zih- dă.de- ast/

Past Perfect	
ماضی بعید	
(ما) توضیح داده بودیم	(من) توضیح داده بودم
/(mă) to.zih- da.de- bu.dim/	/(man) to.zih- da.de- bu.dam/
(شما) توضیح داده بودید	(تو) توضیح داده بودی
/(šo.mă) to.zih- da.de- bu.did/	/(to) to.zih- da.de- bu.di/
(آنها) توضیح داده بودند	(او/آن) توضیح داده بود
/(ăn.hă) to.zih- da.de- bu.dand/	/(u/ ăn) to.zih- da.de- bud/

<table>
<tr><td colspan="2" align="center">**Past Subjunctive**
ماضی التزامی</td></tr>
<tr><td>(ما) توضیح داده باشیم
/(mǎ) to.zih- dǎ.de- bǎ.šim/</td><td>(من) توضیح داده باشم
/(man) to.zih- dǎ.de- bǎ.šam/</td></tr>
<tr><td>(شما) توضیح داده باشید
/(šo.mǎ) to.zih- dǎ.de- bǎ.šid/</td><td>(تو) توضیح داده باشی
/(to) to.zih- dǎ.de- bǎ.ši/</td></tr>
<tr><td>(آنها) توضیح داده باشند
/(ǎn.hǎ) to.zih- dǎ.de- bǎ.šand/</td><td>(او/آن) توضیح داده باشد
/(u/ ǎn) to.zih- dǎ.de- bǎ.šad/</td></tr>
</table>

<table>
<tr><td colspan="2" align="center">**Past Progressive**
ماضی مستمر(در جریان)</td></tr>
<tr><td>(ما) داشتیم توضیح می دادیم
/(mǎ) dǎš.tim- to.zih- mi.dǎ.dim/</td><td>(من) داشتم توضیح می دادم
/(man) dǎš.tam- to.zih- mi.dǎ.dam/</td></tr>
<tr><td>(شما) داشتید توضیح می دادید
/(šo.mǎ) dǎš.tid- to.zih- mi.dǎ.did/</td><td>(تو) داشتی توضیح می دادی
/(to) dǎš.ti- to.zih- mi.dǎ.di/</td></tr>
<tr><td>(آنها) داشتند توضیح می دادند
/(ǎn.hǎ) dǎš.tand- to.zih- mi.dǎ.dand/</td><td>(او/آن) داشت توضیح می داد
/(u/ ǎn) dǎšt- to.zih- mi.dǎd/</td></tr>
</table>

<table>
<tr><td colspan="2" align="center">**Simple Future**
مستقبل (آینده ساده)</td></tr>
<tr><td>(ما) توضیح خواهیم داد
/(mǎ) to.zih- ǩǎ.him- dǎd/</td><td>(من) توضیح خواهم داد
/(man) to.zih- ǩǎ.ham- dǎd/</td></tr>
<tr><td>(شما) توضیح خواهید داد
/(šo.mǎ) to.zih- ǩǎ.hid- dǎd/</td><td>(تو) توضیح خواهی داد
/(to) to.zih- ǩǎ.hi- dǎd/</td></tr>
<tr><td>(آنها) توضیح خواهند داد
/(ǎn.hǎ) to.zih- ǩǎ.hand- dǎd/</td><td>(او/آن) توضیح خواهد داد
/(u/ ǎn) to.zih- ǩǎ.had- dǎd/</td></tr>
</table>

<table>
<tr><td colspan="2" align="center">**Command**
امر</td></tr>
<tr><td>توضیح بدهید!
/to.zih- be.da.hid/</td><td>توضیح بده!
/to.zih- be.de/</td></tr>
</table>

91

to feel

اِحساس کَردَن

/eh.săs- kar.dan/

Plural	Singular
Simple Present مضارع اخباری(حال ساده)	
(ما) احساس می کنیم /(mă) eh.săs- mi.ko.nim/	(من) احساس می کنم /(man) eh.săs- mi.ko.nam/
(شما) احساس می کنید /(šo.mă) eh.săs- mi.ko.nid/	(تو) احساس می کنی /(to) eh.săs- mi.ko.ni/
(آنها) احساس می کنند /(ăn.hă) eh.săs- mi.ko.nand/	(او/آن) احساس می کند /(u/ ăn) eh.săs- mi.ko.nad/
Present Subjunctive مضارع التزامی	
(ما) احساس بکنیم /(mă) eh.săs- be.ko.nim/	(من) احساس بکنم /(man) eh.săs- be.ko.nam/
(شما) احساس بکنید /(šo.mă) eh.săs- be.ko.nid/	(تو) احساس بکنی /(to) eh.săs- be.ko.ni/
(آنها) احساس بکنند /(ăn.hă) eh.săs- be.ko.nand/	(او/آن) احساس بکند /(u/ ăn) eh.săs- be.ko.nad/
Present Progressive مضارع مستمر(در جریان)	
(ما) داریم احساس می کنیم /(mă) dă.rim- eh.săs- mi.ko.nim/	(من) دارم احساس می کنم /(man) dă.ram- eh.săs- mi.ko.nam/
(شما) دارید احساس می کنید /(šo.mă) dă.rid- eh.săs- mi.ko.nid/	(تو) داری احساس می کنی /(to) dă.ri- eh.săs- mi.ko.ni/
(آنها) دارند احساس می کنند /(ăn.hă) dă.rand- eh.săs- mi.ko.nand/	(او/آن) دارد احساس می کند /(u/ ăn) dă.rad- eh.săs- mi.ko.nad/

Simple Past
ماضی مطلق (گذشته ساده)

(ما) احساس کردیم	(من) احساس کردم
/(mă) eh.săs- kar.dim/	/(man) eh.săs- kar.dam/
(شما) احساس کردید	(تو) احساس کردی
/(šo.mă) eh.săs- kar.did/	/(to) eh.săs- kar.di/
(آنها) احساس کردند	(او/آن) احساس کرد
/(ăn.hă) eh.săs- kar.dand/	/(u/ ăn) eh.săs- kard/

Imperfect Indicative
ماضی استمراری

(ما) احساس می کردیم	(من) احساس می کردم
/(mă) eh.săs- mi.kar.dim/	/(man) eh.săs- mi.kar.dam/
(شما) احساس می کردید	(تو) احساس می کردی
/(šo.mă) eh.săs- mi.kar.did/	/(to) eh.săs- mi.kar.di/
(آنها) احساس می کردند	(او/آن) احساس می کرد
/(ăn.hă) eh.săs- mi.kar.dand/	/(u/ ăn) eh.săs- mi.kard/

Present Perfect
ماضی نقلی

(ما) احساس کرده ایم	(من) احساس کرده ام
/(mă) eh.săs- kar.de.im/	/(man) eh.săs- kar.de.am/
(شما) احساس کرده اید	(تو) احساس کرده ای
/(šo.mă) eh.săs- kar.de.id/	/(to) eh.săs- kar.de.i/
(آنها) احساس کرده اند	(او/آن) احساس کرده است
/(ăn.hă) eh.săs- kar.de.and/	/(u/ ăn) eh.săs- kar.de- ast/

Past Perfect
ماضی بعید

(ما) احساس کرده بودیم	(من) احساس کرده بودم
/(mă) eh.săs- kar.de- bu.dim/	/(man) eh.săs- kar.de- bu.dam/
(شما) احساس کرده بودید	(تو) احساس کرده بودی
/(šo.mă) eh.săs- kar.de- bu.did/	/(to) eh.săs- kar.de- bu.di/
(آنها) احساس کرده بودند	(او/آن) احساس کرده بود
/(ăn.hă) eh.săs- kar.de- bu.dand/	/(u/ ăn) eh.săs- kar.de- bud/

Past Subjunctive	
ماضی التزامی	
(ما) احساس کرده باشیم	(من) احساس کرده باشم
/(mǎ) eh.sǎs- kar.de- bǎ.šim/	/(man) eh.sǎs- kar.de- bǎ.šam/
(شما) احساس کرده باشید	(تو) احساس کرده باشی
/(šo.mǎ) eh.sǎs- kar.de- bǎ.šid/	/(to) eh.sǎs- kar.de- bǎ.ši/
(آنها) احساس کرده باشند	(او/آن) احساس کرده باشد
/(ǎn.hǎ) eh.sǎs- kar.de- bǎ.šand/	/(u/ ǎn) eh.sǎs- kar.de- bǎ.šad/

Past Progressive	
ماضی مستمر(در جریان)	
(ما) داشتیم احساس می کردیم	(من) داشتم احساس می کردم
/(mǎ) dǎš.tim- eh.sǎs- mi.kar.dim/	/(man) dǎš.tam- eh.sǎs- mi.kar.dam/
(شما) داشتید احساس می کردید	(تو) داشتی احساس می کردی
/(šo.mǎ) dǎš.tid- eh.sǎs- mi.kar.did/	/(to) dǎš.ti- eh.sǎs- mi.kar.di/
(آنها) داشتند احساس می کردند	(او/آن) داشت احساس می کرد
/(ǎn.hǎ) dǎš.tand- eh.sǎs- mi.kar.dand/	/(u/ ǎn) dǎšt- eh.sǎs- mi.kard/

Simple Future	
مستقبل (آینده ساده)	
(ما) احساس خواهیم کرد	(من) احساس خواهم کرد
/(mǎ) eh.sǎs- ǩǎ.him- kard/	/(man) eh.sǎs- ǩǎ.ham- kard/
(شما) احساس خواهید کرد	(تو) احساس خواهی کرد
/(šo.mǎ) eh.sǎs- ǩǎ.hid- kard/	/(to) eh.sǎs- ǩǎ.hi- kard/
(آنها) احساس خواهند کرد	(او/آن) احساس خواهد کرد
/(ǎn.hǎ) eh.sǎs- ǩǎ.hand- kard/	/(u/ ǎn) eh.sǎs- ǩǎ.had- kard/

Command	
امر	
* احساس بکنید!	* احساس بکن!
/eh.sǎs- be.ko.nid/	/eh.sǎs- be.kon/

* also: احساس کن!   احساس کنید!

to fill

پُر گَردَن

/por- kar.dan/

Plural	Singular
Simple Present <div dir="rtl">مضارع اخباری(حال ساده)</div>	
<div dir="rtl">(ما) پر می کنیم</div> /(mă) por- mi.ko.nim/	<div dir="rtl">(من) پر می کنم</div> /(man) por- mi.ko.nam/
<div dir="rtl">(شما) پر می کنید</div> /(šo.mă) por- mi.ko.nid/	<div dir="rtl">(تو) پر می کنی</div> /(to) por- mi.ko.ni/
<div dir="rtl">(آنها) پر می کنند</div> /(ăn.hă) por- mi.ko.nand/	<div dir="rtl">(او/آن) پر می کند</div> /(u/ ăn) por- mi.ko.nad/
Present Subjunctive <div dir="rtl">مضارع التزامی</div>	
<div dir="rtl">(ما) پر بکنیم</div> /(mă) por- be.ko.nim/	<div dir="rtl">(من) پر بکنم</div> /(man) por- be.ko.nam/
<div dir="rtl">(شما) پر بکنید</div> /(šo.mă) por- be.ko.nid/	<div dir="rtl">(تو) پر بکنی</div> /(to) por- be.ko.ni/
<div dir="rtl">(آنها) پر بکنند</div> /(ăn.hă) por- be.ko.nand/	<div dir="rtl">(او/آن) پر بکند</div> /(u/ ăn) por- be.ko.nad/
Present Progressive <div dir="rtl">مضارع مستمر(در جریان)</div>	
<div dir="rtl">(ما) داریم پر می کنیم</div> /(mă) dă.rim- por- mi.ko.nim/	<div dir="rtl">(من) دارم پر می کنم</div> /(man) dă.ram- por- mi.ko.nam/
<div dir="rtl">(شما) دارید پر می کنید</div> /(šo.mă) dă.rid- por- mi.ko.nid/	<div dir="rtl">(تو) داری پر می کنی</div> /(to) dă.ri- por- mi.ko.ni/
<div dir="rtl">(آنها) دارند پر می کنند</div> /(ăn.hă) dă.rand- por- mi.ko.nand/	<div dir="rtl">(او/آن) دارد پر می کند</div> /(u/ ăn) dă.rad- por- mi.ko.nad/

Simple Past	
ماضی مطلق (گذشته ساده)	
(ما) پر کردیم /(mă) por- kar.dim/	(من) پر کردم /(man) por- kar.dam/
(شما) پر کردید /(šo.mă) por- kar-did/	(تو) پر کردی /(to) por- kar.di/
(آنها) پر کردند /(ăn.hă) por- kar.dand/	(او/آن) پر کرد /(u/ ăn) por- kard/

Imperfect Indicative	
ماضی استمراری	
(ما) پر می کردیم /(mă) por- mi.kar.dim/	(من) پر می کردم /(man) por- mi.kar.dam/
(شما) پر می کردید /(šo.mă) por- mi.kar.did/	(تو) پر می کردی /(to) por- mi.kar.di/
(آنها) پر می کردند /(ăn.hă) por- mi.kar.dand/	(او/آن) پر می کرد /(u/ ăn) por- mi.kard/

Present Perfect	
ماضی نقلی	
(ما) پر کرده ایم /(mă) por- kar.de.im/	(من) پر کرده ام /(man) por- kar.de.am/
(شما) پر کرده اید /(šo.mă) por- kar.de.id/	(تو) پر کرده ای /(to) por- kar.de.i/
(آنها) پر کرده اند /(ăn.hă) por- kar.de.and/	(او/آن) پر کرده است /(u/ ăn) por- kar.de- ast/

Past Perfect	
ماضی بعید	
(ما) پر کرده بودیم /(mă) por- kar.de- bu.dim/	(من) پر کرده بودم /(man) por- kar.de- bu.dam/
(شما) پر کرده بودید /(šo.mă) por- kar.de- bu.did/	(تو) پر کرده بودی /(to) por- kar.de- bu.di/
(آنها) پر کرده بودند /(ăn.hă) por- kar.de- bu.dand/	(او/آن) پر کرده بود /(u/ ăn) por- kar.de- bud/

Past Subjunctive ماضی التزامی	
(ما) پر کرده باشیم /(mǎ) por- kar.de- bǎ.šim/	(من) پر کرده باشم /(man) por- kar.de- bǎ.šam/
(شما) پر کرده باشید /(šo.mǎ) por- kar.de- bǎ.šid/	(تو) پر کرده باشی /(to) por- kar.de- bǎ.ši/
(آنها) پر کرده باشند /(ǎn.hǎ) por- kar.de- bǎ.šand/	(او/آن) پر کرده باشد /(u/ ǎn) por- kar.de- bǎ.šad/
Past Progressive ماضی مستمر(در جریان)	
(ما) داشتیم پر می کردیم /(mǎ) dǎš.tim- por- mi.kar.dim/	(من) داشتم پر می کردم /(man) dǎš.tam- por- mi.kar.dam/
(شما) داشتید پر می کردید /(šo.mǎ) dǎš.tid- por- mi.kar.did/	(تو) داشتی پر می کردی /(to) dǎš.ti- por- mi.kar.di/
(آنها) داشتند پر می کردند /(ǎn.hǎ) dǎš.tand- por- mi.kar.dand/	(او/آن) داشت پر می کرد /(u/ ǎn) dǎšt- por- mi.kard/
Simple Future مستقبل (آینده ساده)	
(ما) پر خواهیم کرد /(mǎ) por- ǩǎ.him- kard/	(من) پر خواهم کرد /(man) por- ǩǎ.ham- kard/
(شما) پر خواهید کرد /(šo.mǎ) por- ǩǎ.hid- kard/	(تو) پر خواهی کرد /(to) por- ǩǎ.hi- kard/
(آنها) پر خواهند کرد /(ǎn.hǎ) por- ǩǎ.hand- kard/	(او/آن) پر خواهد کرد /(u/ ǎn) por- ǩǎ.had- kard/
Command امر	
* پر بکنید! /por- be.ko.nid/	* پر بکن! /por- be.kon/

* also: پر کن! پر کنید!

to find

پیدا کَردَن

/pey.dă- kar.dan/

Plural	Singular
Simple Present <div dir="rtl">مضارع اخباری(حال ساده)</div>	
(ما) پیدا می کنیم /(mă) pey.dă- mi.ko.nim/	(من) پیدا می کنم /(man) pey.dă- mi.ko.nam/
(شما) پیدا می کنید /(šo.mă) pey.dă- mi.ko.nid/	(تو) پیدا می کنی /(to) pey.dă- mi.ko.ni/
(آنها) پیدا می کنند /(ăn.hă) pey.dă- mi.ko.nand/	(او/آن) پیدا می کند /(u/ ăn) pey.dă- mi.ko.nad/
Present Subjunctive <div dir="rtl">مضارع التزامی</div>	
(ما) پیدا بکنیم /(mă) pey.dă- be.ko.nim/	(من) پیدا بکنم /(man) pey.dă- be.ko.nam/
(شما) پیدا بکنید /(šo.mă) pey.dă- be.ko.nid/	(تو) پیدا بکنی /(to) pey.dă- be.ko.ni/
(آنها) پیدا بکنند /(ăn.hă) pey.dă- be.ko.nand/	(او/آن) پیدا بکند /(u/ ăn) pey.dă- be.ko.nad/
Present Progressive <div dir="rtl">مضارع مستمر(در جریان)</div>	
(ما) داریم پیدا می کنیم /(mă) dă.rim- pey.da- mi.ko.nim/	(من) دارم پیدا می کنم /(man) dă.ram- pey.da- mi.ko.nam/
(شما) دارید پیدا می کنید /(šo.mă) dă.rid- pey.da- mi.ko.nid/	(تو) داری پیدا می کنی /(to) dă.ri- pey.da- mi.ko.ni/
(آنها) دارند پیدا می کنند /(ăn.hă) dă.rand- pey.da- mi.ko.nand/	(او/آن) دارد پیدا می کند /(u/ ăn) dă.rad- pey.da- mi.ko.nad/

Simple Past	
ماضی مطلق (گذشته ساده)	
(ما) پیدا کردیم	(من) پیدا کردم
/(mă) pey.da- kar.dim/	/(man) pey.da- kar.dam/
(شما) پیدا کردید	(تو) پیدا کردی
/(šo.mă) pey.da- kar.did/	/(to) pey.da- kar.di/
(آنها) پیدا کردند	(او/آن) پیدا کرد
/(ăn.hă) pey.da- kar.dand/	/(u/ ăn) pey.da- kard/

Imperfect Indicative	
ماضی استمراری	
(ما) پیدا می کردیم	(من) پیدا می کردم
/(mă) pey.da- mi.kar.dim/	/(man) pey.da- mi.kar.dam/
(شما) پیدا می کردید	(تو) پیدا می کردی
/(šo.mă) pey.da- mi.kar.did/	/(to) pey.da- mi.kar.di/
(آنها) پیدا می کردند	(او/آن) پیدا می کرد
/(ăn.hă) pey.da- mi.kar.dand/	/(u/ ăn) pey.da- mi.kard/

Present Perfect	
ماضی نقلی	
(ما) پیدا کرده ایم	(من) پیدا کرده ام
/(mă) pey.da- kar.de.im/	/(man) pey.da- kar.de.am/
(شما) پیدا کرده اید	(تو) پیدا کرده ای
/(šo.mă) pey.da- kar.de.id/	/(to) pey.da- kar.de.i/
(آنها) پیدا کرده اند	(او/آن) پیدا کرده است
/(ăn.hă) pey.da- kar.de.and/	/(u/ ăn) pey.da- kar.de- ast/

Past Perfect	
ماضی بعید	
(ما) پیدا کرده بودیم	(من) پیدا کرده بودم
/(mă) pey.da- kar.de- bu.dim/	/(man) pey.da- kar.de- bu.dam/
(شما) پیدا کرده بودید	(تو) پیدا کرده بودی
/(šo.mă) pey.da- kar.de- bu.did/	/(to) pey.da- kar.de- bu.di/
(آنها) پیدا کرده بودند	(او/آن) پیدا کرده بود
/(ăn.hă) pey.da- kar.de- bu.dand/	/(u/ ăn) pey.da- kar.de- bud/

Past Subjunctive	
ماضی التزامی	
(ما) پیدا کرده باشیم	(من) پیدا کرده باشم
/(mă) pey.da- kar.de- bă.šim/	/(man) pey.da- kar.de- bă.šam/
(شما) پیدا کرده باشید	(تو) پیدا کرده باشی
/(šo.mă) pey.da- kar.de- bă.šid/	/(to) pey.da- kar.de- bă.ši/
(آنها) پیدا کرده باشند	(او/آن) پیدا کرده باشد
/(ăn.hă) pey.da- kar.de- bă.šand/	/(u/ ăn) pey.da- kar.de- bă.šad/

Past Progressive	
ماضی مستمر(در جریان)	
(ما) داشتیم پیدا می کردیم	(من) داشتم پیدا می کردم
/(mă) dăš.tim- pey.da- mi.kar.dim/	/(man) dăš.tam- pey.da- mi.kar.dam/
(شما) داشتید پیدا می کردید	(تو) داشتی پیدا می کردی
/(šo.mă) dăš.tid- pey.da- mi.kar.did/	/(to) dăš.ti- pey.da- mi.kar.di/
(آنها) داشتند پیدا می کردند	(او/آن) داشت پیدا می کرد
/(ăn.hă) dăš.tand- pey.da- mi.kar.dand/	/(u/ ăn) dăšt- pey.da- mi.kard/

Simple Future	
مستقبل (آینده ساده)	
(ما) پیدا خواهیم کرد	(من) پیدا خواهم کرد
/(mă) pey.da- kă.him- kard/	/(man) pey.da- kă.ham- kard/
(شما) پیدا خواهید کرد	(تو) پیدا خواهی کرد
/(šo.mă) pey.da- kă.hid- kard/	/(to) pey.da- kă.hi- kard/
(آنها) پیدا خواهند کرد	(او/آن) پیدا خواهد کرد
/(ăn.hă) pey.da- kă.hand- kard/	/(u/ ăn) pey.da- kă.had- kard/

Command	
امر	
پیدا بکنید! *	پیدا بکن! *
/pey.da- be.ko.nid/	/pey.da- be.kon/

* also: پیدا کن!   پیدا کنید!

to finish

تَمام کَردَن

/ta.măm- kar.dan/

Plural	Singular
Simple Present <div dir="rtl">مضارع اخباری(حال ساده)</div>	
<div dir="rtl">(ما) تمام می کنیم</div> /(mă) ta.măm- mi.ko.nim/	<div dir="rtl">(من) تمام می کنم</div> /(man) ta.măm- mi.ko.nam/
<div dir="rtl">(شما) تمام می کنید</div> /(šo.mă) ta.măm- mi.ko.nid/	<div dir="rtl">(تو) تمام می کنی</div> /(to) ta.măm- mi.ko.ni/
<div dir="rtl">(آنها) تمام می کنند</div> /(ăn.hă) ta.măm- mi.ko.nand/	<div dir="rtl">(او/آن) تمام می کند</div> /(u/ ăn) ta.măm- mi.ko.nad/
Present Subjunctive <div dir="rtl">مضارع التزامی</div>	
<div dir="rtl">(ما) تمام بکنیم</div> /(mă) ta.măm- be.ko.nim/	<div dir="rtl">(من) تمام بکنم</div> /(man) ta.măm- be.ko.nam/
<div dir="rtl">(شما) تمام بکنید</div> /(šo.mă) ta.măm- be.ko.nid/	<div dir="rtl">(تو) تمام بکنی</div> /(to) ta.măm- be.ko.ni/
<div dir="rtl">(آنها) تمام بکنند</div> /(ăn.hă) ta.măm- be.ko.nand/	<div dir="rtl">(او/آن) تمام بکند</div> /(u/ ăn) ta.măm- be.ko.nad/
Present Progressive <div dir="rtl">مضارع مستمر(در جریان)</div>	
<div dir="rtl">(ما) داریم تمام می کنیم</div> /(mă) dă.rim- ta.măm- mi.ko.nim/	<div dir="rtl">(من) دارم تمام می کنم</div> /(man) dă.ram- ta.măm- mi.ko.nam/
<div dir="rtl">(شما) دارید تمام می کنید</div> /(šo.mă) dă.rid- ta.măm- mi.ko.nid/	<div dir="rtl">(تو) داری تمام می کنی</div> /(to) dă.ri- ta.măm- mi.ko.ni/
<div dir="rtl">(آنها) دارند تمام می کنند</div> /(ăn.hă) dă.rand- ta.măm- mi.ko.nand/	<div dir="rtl">(او/آن) دارد تمام می کند</div> /(u/ ăn) dă.rad- ta.măm- mi.ko.nad/

Simple Past	
ماضی مطلق (گذشته ساده)	
(ما) تمام کردیم	(من) تمام کردم
/(mă) ta.măm- kar.dim/	/(man) ta.măm- kar.dam/
(شما) تمام کردید	(تو) تمام کردی
/(šo.mă) ta.măm- kar.did/	/(to) ta.măm- kar.di/
(آنها) تمام کردند	(او/آن) تمام کرد
/(ăn.hă) ta.măm- kar.dand/	/(u/ ăn) ta.măm- kard/

Imperfect Indicative	
ماضی استمراری	
(ما) تمام می کردیم	(من) تمام می کردم
/(mă) ta.măm- mi.kar.dim/	/(man) ta.măm- mi.kar.dam/
(شما) تمام می کردید	(تو) تمام می کردی
/(šo.mă) ta.măm- mi.kar.did/	/(to) ta.măm- mi.kar.di/
(آنها) تمام می کردند	(او/آن) تمام می کرد
/(ăn.hă) ta.măm- mi.kar.dand/	/(u/ ăn) ta.măm- mi.kard/

Present Perfect	
ماضی نقلی	
(ما) تمام کرده ایم	(من) تمام کرده ام
/(mă) ta.măm- kar.de.im/	/(man) ta.măm- kar.de.am/
(شما) تمام کرده اید	(تو) تمام کرده ای
/(šo.mă) ta.măm- kar.de.id/	/(to) ta.măm- kar.de.i/
(آنها) تمام کرده اند	(او/آن) تمام کرده است
/(ăn.hă) ta.măm- kar.de.and/	/(u/ ăn) ta.măm- kar.de- ast/

Past Perfect	
ماضی بعید	
(ما) تمام کرده بودیم	(من) تمام کرده بودم
/(mă) ta.măm- kar.de- bu.dim/	/(man) ta.măm- kar.de- bu.dam/
(شما) تمام کرده بودید	(تو) تمام کرده بودی
/(šo.mă) ta.măm- kar.de- bu.did/	/(to) ta.măm- kar.de- bu.di/
(آنها) تمام کرده بودند	(او/آن) تمام کرده بود
/(ăn.hă) ta.măm- kar.de- bu.dand/	/(u/ ăn) ta.măm- kar.de- bud/

<table>
<tr><td colspan="2" align="center">**Past Subjunctive**
ماضی التزامی</td></tr>
<tr>
<td>(ما) تمام کرده باشیم
/(mă) ta.măm- kar.de- bă.šim/</td>
<td>(من) تمام کرده باشم
/(man) ta.măm- kar.de- bă.šam/</td>
</tr>
<tr>
<td>(شما) تمام کرده باشید
/(šo.mă) ta.măm- kar.de- bă.šid/</td>
<td>(تو) تمام کرده باشی
/(to) ta.măm- kar.de- bă.ši/</td>
</tr>
<tr>
<td>(آنها) تمام کرده باشند
/(ăn.hă) ta.măm- kar.de- bă.šand/</td>
<td>(او/آن) تمام کرده باشد
/(u/ ăn) ta.măm- kar.de- bă.šad/</td>
</tr>
</table>

<table>
<tr><td colspan="2" align="center">**Past Progressive**
ماضی مستمر(در جریان)</td></tr>
<tr>
<td>(ما) داشتیم تمام می کردیم
/(mă) dăš.tim- ta.măm- mi.kar.dim/</td>
<td>(من) داشتم تمام می کردم
/(man) dăš.tam- ta.măm- mi.kar.dam/</td>
</tr>
<tr>
<td>(شما) داشتید تمام می کردید
/(šo.mă) dăš.tid- ta.măm- mi.kar.did/</td>
<td>(تو) داشتی تمام می کردی
/(to) dăš.ti- ta.măm- mi.kar.di/</td>
</tr>
<tr>
<td>(آنها) داشتند تمام می کردند
/(ăn.hă) dăš.tand- ta.măm- mi.kar.dand/</td>
<td>(او/آن) داشت تمام می کرد
/(u/ ăn) dăšt- ta. măm- mi.kard/</td>
</tr>
</table>

<table>
<tr><td colspan="2" align="center">**Simple Future**
مستقبل (آینده ساده)</td></tr>
<tr>
<td>(ما) تمام خواهیم کرد
/(mă) ta.măm- kă.him- kard/</td>
<td>(من) تمام خواهم کرد
/(man) ta.măm- kă.ham- kard/</td>
</tr>
<tr>
<td>(شما) تمام خواهید کرد
/(šo.mă) ta.măm- kă.hid- kard/</td>
<td>(تو) تمام خواهی کرد
/(to) ta.măm- kă.hi- kard/</td>
</tr>
<tr>
<td>(آنها) تمام خواهند کرد
/(ăn.hă) ta.măm- kă.hand- kard/</td>
<td>(او/آن) تمام خواهد کرد
/(u/ ăn) ta.măm- kă.had- kard/</td>
</tr>
</table>

<table>
<tr><td colspan="2" align="center">**Command**
امر</td></tr>
<tr>
<td>* تمام بکنید!
/ta.măm- be.ko.nid/</td>
<td>* تمام بکن!
/ta.măm- be.kon/</td>
</tr>
</table>

* also: تمام کن!   تمام کنید!

to fly

پَرواز کَردَن

/par.văz- kar.dan/

Plural	Singular
Simple Present مضارع اخباری(حال ساده)	
(ما) پرواز می کنیم /(mă) par.văz- mi.ko.nim/	(من) پرواز می کنم /(man) par.văz- mi.ko.nam/
(شما) پرواز می کنید /(šo.mă) par.văz- mi.ko.nid/	(تو) پرواز می کنی /(to) par.văz- mi.ko.ni/
(آنها) پرواز می کنند /(ăn.hă) par.văz- mi.ko.nand/	(او/آن) پرواز می کند /(u/ ăn) par.văz- mi.ko.nad/
Present Subjunctive مضارع التزامی	
(ما) پرواز بکنیم /(mă) par.văz- be.ko.nim/	(من) پرواز بکنم /(man) par.văz- be.ko.nam/
(شما) پرواز بکنید /(šo.mă) par.văz- be.ko.nid/	(تو) پرواز بکنی /(to) par.văz- be.ko.ni/
(آنها) پرواز بکنند /(ăn.hă) par.văz- be.ko.nand/	(او/آن) پرواز بکند /(u/ ăn) par.văz- be.ko.nad/
Present Progressive مضارع مستمر(در جریان)	
(ما) داریم پرواز می کنیم /(mă) dă.rim- par.văz- mi.ko.nim/	(من) دارم پرواز می کنم /(man) dă.ram- par.văz- mi.ko.nam/
(شما) دارید پرواز می کنید /(šo.mă) dă.rid- par.văz- mi.ko.nid/	(تو) داری پرواز می کنی /(to) dă.ri- par.văz- mi.ko.ni/
(آنها) دارند پرواز می کنند /(ăn.hă) dă.rand- par.văz- mi.ko.nand/	(او/آن) دارد پرواز می کند /(u/ ăn) dă.rad- par.văz- mi.ko.nad/

Simple Past
ماضی مطلق (گذشته ساده)

(ما) پرواز کردیم	(من) پرواز کردم
/(mă) par.văz- kar.dim/	/(man) par.văz- kar.dam/
(شما) پرواز کردید	(تو) پرواز کردی
/(šo.mă) par.văz- kar.did/	/(to) par.văz- kar.di/
(آنها) پرواز کردند	(او/آن) پرواز کرد
/(ăn.hă) par.văz- kar.dand/	/(u/ ăn) par.văz- kard/

Imperfect Indicative
ماضی استمراری

(ما) پرواز می کردیم	(من) پرواز می کردم
/(mă) par.văz- mi.kar.dim/	/(man) par.văz- mi.kar.dam/
(شما) پرواز می کردید	(تو) پرواز می کردی
/(šo.mă) par.văz- mi.kar.did/	/(to) par.văz- mi.kar.di/
(آنها) پرواز می کردند	(او/آن) پرواز می کرد
/(ăn.hă) par.văz- mi.kar.dand/	/(u/ ăn) par.văz- mi.kard/

Present Perfect
ماضی نقلی

(ما) پرواز کرده ایم	(من) پرواز کرده ام
/(mă) par.văz- kar.de.im/	/(man) par.văz- kar.de.am/
(شما) پرواز کرده اید	(تو) پرواز کرده ای
/(šo.mă) par.văz- kar.de.id/	/(to) par.văz- kar.de.i/
(آنها) پرواز کرده اند	(او/آن) پرواز کرده است
/(ăn.hă) par.văz- kar.de.and/	/(u/ ăn) par.văz- kar.de- ast/

Past Perfect
ماضی بعید

(ما) پرواز کرده بودیم	(من) پرواز کرده بودم
/(mă) par.văz- kar.de- bu.dim/	/(man) par.văz- kar.de- bu.dam/
(شما) پرواز کرده بودید	(تو) پرواز کرده بودی
/(šo.mă) par.văz- kar.de- bu.did/	/(to) par.văz- kar.de- bu.di/
(آنها) پرواز کرده بودند	(او/آن) پرواز کرده بود
/(ăn.hă) par.văz- kar.de- bu.dand/	/(u/ ăn) par.văz- kar.de- bud/

<table>
<tr><td colspan="2" align="center">**Past Subjunctive**
ماضی التزامی</td></tr>
<tr>
<td align="center">(ما) پرواز کرده باشیم
/(mǎ) par.vǎz- kar.de- bǎ.šim/</td>
<td align="center">(من) پرواز کرده باشم
/(man) par.vǎz- kar.de- bǎ.šam/</td>
</tr>
<tr>
<td align="center">(شما) پرواز کرده باشید
/(šo.mǎ) par.vǎz- kar.de- bǎ.šid/</td>
<td align="center">(تو) پرواز کرده باشی
/(to) par.vǎz- kar.de- bǎ.ši/</td>
</tr>
<tr>
<td align="center">(آنها) پرواز کرده باشند
/(ǎn.hǎ) par.vǎz- kar.de- bǎ.šand/</td>
<td align="center">(او/آن) پرواز کرده باشد
/(u/ ǎn) par.vǎz- kar.de- bǎ.šad/</td>
</tr>
</table>

<table>
<tr><td colspan="2" align="center">**Past Progressive**
ماضی مستمر(در جریان)</td></tr>
<tr>
<td align="center">(ما) داشتیم پرواز می کردیم
/(mǎ) dǎš.tim- par.vǎz- mi.kar.dim/</td>
<td align="center">(من) داشتم پرواز می کردم
/(man) dǎš.tam- par.vǎz- mi.kar.dam/</td>
</tr>
<tr>
<td align="center">(شما) داشتید پرواز می کردید
/(šo.mǎ) dǎš.tid- par.vǎz- mi.kar.did/</td>
<td align="center">(تو) داشتی پرواز می کردی
/(to) dǎš.ti- par.vǎz- mi.kar.di/</td>
</tr>
<tr>
<td align="center">(آنها) داشتند پرواز می کردند
/(ǎn.hǎ) dǎš.tand- par.vǎz- mi.kar.dand/</td>
<td align="center">(او/آن) داشت پرواز می کرد
/(u/ ǎn) dǎšt- par.vǎz- mi.kard/</td>
</tr>
</table>

<table>
<tr><td colspan="2" align="center">**Simple Future**
مستقبل (آینده ساده)</td></tr>
<tr>
<td align="center">(ما) پرواز خواهیم کرد
/(mǎ) par.vǎz- ǩǎ.him- kard/</td>
<td align="center">(من) پرواز خواهم کرد
/(man) par.vǎz- ǩǎ.ham- kard/</td>
</tr>
<tr>
<td align="center">(شما) پرواز خواهید کرد
/(šo.mǎ) par.vǎz- ǩǎ.hid- kard/</td>
<td align="center">(تو) پرواز خواهی کرد
/(to) par.vǎz- ǩǎ.hi- kard/</td>
</tr>
<tr>
<td align="center">(آنها) پرواز خواهند کرد
/(ǎn.hǎ) par.vǎz- ǩǎ.hand- kard/</td>
<td align="center">(او/آن) پرواز خواهد کرد
/(u/ ǎn) par.vǎz- ǩǎ.had- kard/</td>
</tr>
</table>

<table>
<tr><td colspan="2" align="center">**Command**
امر</td></tr>
<tr>
<td align="center">* پرواز بکنید!
/par.vǎz- be.ko.nid/</td>
<td align="center">* پرواز بکن!
/par.vǎz- be.kon/</td>
</tr>
</table>

* also: پرواز کن!   پرواز کنید!

to forget

فَراموش کَردَن

/fa.ră.muš- kar.dan/

Plural	Singular
Simple Present مضارع اخباری(حال ساده)	
(ما) فراموش می کنیم /(mă) fa.ră.muš- mi.ko.nim/	(من) فراموش می کنم /(man) fa.ră.muš- mi.ko.nam/
(شما) فراموش می کنید /(šo.mă) fa.ră.muš- mi.ko.nid/	(تو) فراموش می کنی /(to) fa.ră.muš- mi.ko.ni/
(آنها) فراموش می کنند /(ăn.hă) fa.ră.muš- mi.ko.nand/	(او/آن) فراموش می کند /(u/ ăn) fa.ră.muš- mi.ko.nad/
Present Subjunctive مضارع التزامی	
(ما) فراموش بکنیم /(mă) fa.ră.muš- be.ko.nim/	(من) فراموش بکنم /(man) fa.ră.muš- be.ko.nam/
(شما) فراموش بکنید /(šo.mă) fa.ră.muš- be.ko.nid/	(تو) فراموش بکنی /(to) fa.ră.muš- be.ko.ni/
(آنها) فراموش بکنند /(ăn.hă) fa.ră.muš- be.ko.nand/	(او/آن) فراموش بکند /(u/ ăn) fa.ră.muš- be.ko.nad/
Present Progressive مضارع مستمر(در جریان)	
(ما) داریم فراموش می کنیم /(mă) dă.rim- fa.ră.muš- mi.ko.nim/	(من) دارم فراموش می کنم /(man) dă.ram- fa.ră.muš- mi.ko.nam/
(شما) دارید فراموش می کنید /(šo.mă) dă.rid- fa.ră.muš- mi.ko.nid/	(تو) داری فراموش می کنی /(to) dă.ri- fa.ră.muš- mi.ko.ni/
(آنها) دارند فراموش می کنند /(ăn.hă) dă.rand- fa.ră.muš- mi.ko.nand/	(او/آن) دارد فراموش می کند /(u/ ăn) dă.rad- fa.ră.muš- mi.ko.nad/

107

Simple Past
ماضی مطلق (گذشته ساده)

(ما) فراموش کردیم	(من) فراموش کردم
/(mǎ) fa.rǎ.muš- kar.dim/	/(man) fa.rǎ.muš- kar.dam/
(شما) فراموش کردید	(تو) فراموش کردی
/(šo.mǎ) fa.rǎ.muš- kar.did/	/(to) fa.rǎ.muš- kar.di/
(آنها) فراموش کردند	(او/آن) فراموش کرد
/(ǎn.hǎ) fa.rǎ.muš- kar.dand/	/(u/ ǎn) fa.rǎ.muš- kard/

Imperfect Indicative
ماضی استمراری

(ما) فراموش می کردیم	(من) فراموش می کردم
/(mǎ) fa.rǎ.muš- mi.kar.dim	/(man) fa.rǎ.muš- mi.kar.dam/
(شما) فراموش می کردید	(تو) فراموش می کردی
/(šo.mǎ) fa.rǎ.muš- mi.kar.did/	/(to) fa.rǎ.muš- mi.kar.di/
(آنها) فراموش می کردند	(او/آن) فراموش می کرد
/(ǎn.hǎ) fa.rǎ.muš- mi.kar.dand/	/(u/ ǎn) fa.rǎ.muš- mi.kard

Present Perfect
ماضی نقلی

(ما) فراموش کرده ایم	(من) فراموش کرده ام
/(mǎ) fa.rǎ.muš- kar.de.im/	/(man) fa.rǎ.muš- kar.de.am/
(شما) فراموش کرده اید	(تو) فراموش کرده ای
/(šo.mǎ) fa.rǎ.muš- kar.de.id/	/(to) fa.rǎ.muš- kar.de.i/
(آنها) فراموش کرده اند	(او/آن) فراموش کرده است
/(ǎn.hǎ) fa.rǎ.muš- kar.de.and/	/(u/ ǎn) fa.rǎ.muš- kar.de- ast/

Past Perfect
ماضی بعید

(ما) فراموش کرده بودیم	(من) فراموش کرده بودم
/(mǎ) fa.rǎ.muš- kar.de- bu.dim/	/(man) fa.rǎ.muš- kar.de- bu.dam/
(شما) فراموش کرده بودید	(تو) فراموش کرده بودی
/(šo.mǎ) fa.rǎ.muš- kar.de- bu.did/	/(to) fa.rǎ.muš- kar.de- bu.di/
(آنها) فراموش کرده بودند	(او/آن) فراموش کرده بود
/(ǎn.hǎ) fa.rǎ.muš- kar.de- bu.dand/	/(u/ ǎn) fa.rǎ.muš- kar.de- bud/

	Past Subjunctive ماضی التزامی	
(ما) فراموش کرده باشیم		(من) فراموش کرده باشم
/(mă) fa.ră.muš- kar.de- bă.šim/		/(man) fa.ră.muš- kar.de- bă.šam/
(شما) فراموش کرده باشید		(تو) فراموش کرده باشی
/(šo.mă) fa.ră.muš- kar.de- bă.šid/		/(to) fa.ră.muš- kar.de- bă.ši/
(آنها) فراموش کرده باشند		(او/آن) فراموش کرده باشد
/(ăn.hă) fa.ră.muš- kar.de- bă.šand/		/(u/ ăn) fa.ră.muš- kar.de- bă.šad/

	Past Progressive ماضی مستمر (در جریان)	
(ما) داشتیم فراموش می کردیم		(من) داشتم فراموش می کردم
/(mă) dăš.tim- fa.ră.muš- mi.kar.dim/		/(man) dăš.tam- fa.ră.muš- mi.kar.dam/
(شما) داشتید فراموش می کردید		(تو) داشتی فراموش می کردی
/(šo.mă) dăš.tid- fa.ră.muš- mi.kar.did/		/(to) dăš.ti- fa.ră.muš- mi.kar.di/
(آنها) داشتند فراموش می کردند		(او/آن) داشت فراموش می کرد
/(ăn.hă) dăš.tand- fa.ră.muš- mi.kar.dand/		/(u/ ăn) dăšt- fa.ră.muš- mi.kard/

	Simple Future مستقبل (آینده ساده)	
(ما) فراموش خواهیم کرد		(من) فراموش خواهم کرد
/(mă) fa.ră.muš- ǩă.him- kard/		/(man) fa.ră.muš- ǩă.ham- kard/
(شما) فراموش خواهید کرد		(تو) فراموش خواهی کرد
/(šo.mă) fa.ră.muš- ǩă.hid- kard/		/(to) fa.ră.muš- ǩă.hi- kard/
(آنها) فراموش خواهند کرد		(او/آن) فراموش خواهد کرد
/(ăn.hă) fa.ră.muš- ǩă.hand- kard/		/(u/ ăn) fa.ră.muš- ǩă.had- kard/

	Command امر	
* فراموش بکنید!		* فراموش بکن!
/fa.ră.muš- be.ko.nid/		/fa.ră.muš- be.kon/

* also: فراموش کن!   فراموش کنید!

to give

دادَن

/dă.dan/

Plural	Singular
Simple Present مضارع اخباری(حال ساده)	
(ما) می دهیم /(mă) mi.da.him/	(من) می دهم /(man) mi.da.ham/
(شما) می دهید /(šo.mă) mi.da.hid/	(تو) می دهی /(to) mi.da.hi/
(آنها) می دهند /(ăn.hă) mi.da.hand/	(او/آن) می دهد /(u/ ăn) mi.da.had/
Present Subjunctive مضارع التزامی	
(ما) بدهیم /(mă) be.da.him/	(من) بدهم /(man) be.da.ham/
(شما) بدهید /(šo.mă) be.da.hid/	(تو) بدهی /(/to) be.da.hi/
(آنها) بدهند /(ăn.hă) be.da.hand/	(او/آن) بدهد /(u/ ăn) be.da.had/
Present Progressive مضارع مستمر(در جریان)	
(ما) داریم می دهیم /(mă) dă.rim- mi.da.him/	(من) دارم می دهم /(man) dă.ram- mi.da.ham/
(شما) دارید می دهید /(šo.mă) dă.rid- mi.da.hid/	(تو) داری می دهی /(to) dă.ri- mi.da.hi/
(آنها) دارند می دهند /(ăn.hă) dă.rand- mi.da.hand/	(او/آن) دارد می دهد /(u/ ăn) dă.rad- mi.da.had/

<table>
<tr><td colspan="2" align="center">**Simple Past**
ماضی مطلق (گذشته ساده)</td></tr>
<tr><td align="center">(ما) دادیم
/(mǎ) dǎ.dim/</td><td align="center">(من) دادم
/(man) dǎ.dam/</td></tr>
<tr><td align="center">(شما) دادید
/(šo.mǎ) dǎ.did/</td><td align="center">(تو) دادی
/(to) dǎ.di/</td></tr>
<tr><td align="center">(آنها) دادند
/(ǎn.hǎ) dǎ.dand/</td><td align="center">(او/آن) داد
/(u/ ǎn) dǎd/</td></tr>
</table>

<table>
<tr><td colspan="2" align="center">**Imperfect Indicative**
ماضی استمراری</td></tr>
<tr><td align="center">(ما) می دادیم
/(mǎ) mi.dǎ.dim/</td><td align="center">(من) می دادم
/(man) mi.dǎ.dam/</td></tr>
<tr><td align="center">(شما) می دادید
/(šo.mǎ) mi.dǎ.did/</td><td align="center">(تو) می دادی
/(to) mi.dǎ.di/</td></tr>
<tr><td align="center">(آنها) می دادند
/(ǎn.hǎ) mi.dǎ.dand/</td><td align="center">(او/آن) می داد
/(u/ ǎn) mi.dǎd/</td></tr>
</table>

<table>
<tr><td colspan="2" align="center">**Present Perfect**
ماضی نقلی</td></tr>
<tr><td align="center">(ما) داده ایم
/(mǎ) dǎ.de.im/</td><td align="center">(من) داده ام
/(man) dǎ.de.am/</td></tr>
<tr><td align="center">(شما) داده اید
/(šo.mǎ) dǎ.de.id/</td><td align="center">(تو) داده ای
/(to) dǎ.de.i/</td></tr>
<tr><td align="center">(آنها) داده اند
/(ǎn.hǎ) dǎ.de.and/</td><td align="center">(او/آن) داده است
/(u/ ǎn) dǎ.de- ast/</td></tr>
</table>

<table>
<tr><td colspan="2" align="center">**Past Perfect**
ماضی بعید</td></tr>
<tr><td align="center">(ما) داده بودیم
/(mǎ) dǎ.de- bu.dim/</td><td align="center">(من) داده بودم
/(man) dǎ.de- bu.dam/</td></tr>
<tr><td align="center">(شما) داده بودید
/(šo.mǎ) dǎ.de- bu.did/</td><td align="center">(تو) داده بودی
/(to) dǎ.de- bu.di/</td></tr>
<tr><td align="center">(آنها) داده بودند
/(ǎn.hǎ) dǎ.de- bu.dand/</td><td align="center">(او/آن) داده بود
/(u/ ǎn) dǎ.de- bud/</td></tr>
</table>

<table>
<tr><td colspan="2" align="center">**Past Subjunctive**
ماضی التزامی</td></tr>
<tr>
<td align="center">(ما) داده باشیم
/(mǎ) dǎ.de- bǎ.šim/</td>
<td align="center">(من) داده باشم
/(man) dǎ.de- bǎ.šam/</td>
</tr>
<tr>
<td align="center">(شما) داده باشید
/(šo.mǎ) dǎ.de- bǎ.šid/</td>
<td align="center">(تو) داده باشی
/(to) dǎ.de- bǎ.ši/</td>
</tr>
<tr>
<td align="center">(آنها) داده باشند
/(ǎn.hǎ) dǎ.de- bǎ.šand/</td>
<td align="center">(او/آن) داده باشد
/(u/ ǎn) dǎ.de- bǎ.šad/</td>
</tr>
</table>

<table>
<tr><td colspan="2" align="center">**Past Progressive**
ماضی مستمر(در جریان)</td></tr>
<tr>
<td align="center">(ما) داشتیم می دادیم
/(mǎ) dǎš.tim- mi.dǎ.dim/</td>
<td align="center">(من) داشتم می دادم
/(man) dǎš.tam- mi.dǎ.dam/</td>
</tr>
<tr>
<td align="center">(شما) داشتید می دادید
/(šo.mǎ) dǎš.tid- mi.dǎ.did/</td>
<td align="center">(تو) داشتی می دادی
/(to) dǎš.ti- mi.dǎ.di/</td>
</tr>
<tr>
<td align="center">(آنها) داشتند می دادند
/(ǎn.hǎ) dǎš.tand- mi.dǎ.dand/</td>
<td align="center">(او/آن) داشت می داد
/(u/ ǎn) dǎšt- mi.dǎd/</td>
</tr>
</table>

<table>
<tr><td colspan="2" align="center">**Simple Future**
مستقبل (آینده ساده)</td></tr>
<tr>
<td align="center">(ما) خواهیم داد
/(mǎ) ǩǎ.him- dǎd/</td>
<td align="center">(من) خواهم داد
/(man) ǩǎ.ham- dǎd/</td>
</tr>
<tr>
<td align="center">(شما) خواهید داد
/(šo.mǎ) ǩǎ.hid- dǎd/</td>
<td align="center">(تو) خواهی داد
/(to) ǩǎ.hi- dǎd/</td>
</tr>
<tr>
<td align="center">(آنها) خواهند داد
/(ǎn.hǎ) ǩǎ.hand- dǎd/</td>
<td align="center">(او/آن) خواهد داد
/(u/ ǎn) ǩǎ.had- dǎd/</td>
</tr>
</table>

<table>
<tr><td colspan="2" align="center">**Command**
امر</td></tr>
<tr>
<td align="center">بدهید!
/be.da.hid/</td>
<td align="center">بده!
/be.de/</td>
</tr>
</table>

to go

رَفتَن

/raf.tan/

Plural	Singular
Simple Present مضارع اخباری(حال ساده)	
(ما) می رویم /(mă) mi.ra.vim/	(من) می روم /(man) mi.ra.vam/
(شما) می روید /(šo.mă) mi.ra.vid/	(تو) می روی /(to) mi.ra.vi/
(آنها) می روند /(ăn.hă) mi.ra.vand/	(او/آن) می رود /(u/ ăn) mi.ra.vad/
Present Subjunctive مضارع التزامی	
(ما) برویم /(mă) be.ra.vim/	(من) بروم /(man) be.ra.vam/
(شما) بروید /(šo.mă) be.ra.vid/	(تو) بروی /(to) be.ra.vi/
(آنها) بروند /(ăn.hă) be.ra.vand/	(او/آن) برود /(u/ ăn) be.ra.vad/
Present Progressive مضارع مستمر(در جریان)	
(ما) داریم می رویم /(mă) dă.rim- mi.ra.vim/	(من) دارم می روم /(man) dă.ram- mi.ra.vam/
(شما) دارید می روید /(šo.mă) dă.rid- mi.ra.vid/	(تو) داری می روی /(to) dă.ri- mi.ra.vi/
(آنها) دارند می روند /(ăn.hă) dă.rand- mi.ra.vand/	(او/آن) دارد می رود /(u/ ăn) dă.rad- mi.ra.vad/

Simple Past
ماضی مطلق (گذشته ساده)

(ما) رفتیم	(من) رفتم
/(mǎ) raf.tim/	/(man) raf.tam/
(شما) رفتید	(تو) رفتی
/(šo.mǎ) raf.tid/	/(to) raf.ti/
(آنها) رفتند	(او/آن) رفت
/(ǎn.hǎ) raf.tand/	/(u/ ǎn) raft/

Imperfect Indicative
ماضی استمراری

(ما) می رفتیم	(من) می رفتم
/(mǎ) mi.raf.tim/	/(man) mi.raf.tam/
(شما) می رفتید	(تو) می رفتی
/(šo.mǎ) mi.raf.tid/	/(to) mi.raf.ti/
(آنها) می رفتند	(او/آن) می رفت
/(ǎn.hǎ) mi.raf.tand/	/(u/ ǎn) mi.raft/

Present Perfect
ماضی نقلی

(ما) رفته ایم	(من) رفته ام
/(mǎ) raf.te.im/	/(man) raf.te.am/
(شما) رفته اید	(تو) رفته ای
/(šo.mǎ) raf.te.id/	/(to) raf.te.i/
(آنها) رفته اند	(او/آن) رفته است
/(ǎn.hǎ) raf.te.and/	/(u/ ǎn) raf.te- ast/

Past Perfect
ماضی بعید

(ما) رفته بودیم	(من) رفته بودم
/(mǎ) raf.te- bu.dim/	/(man) raf.te- bu.dam/
(شما) رفته بودید	(تو) رفته بودی
/(šo.mǎ) raf.te- bu.did/	/(to) raf.te- bu.di/
(آنها) رفته بودند	(او/آن) رفته بود
/(ǎn.hǎ) raf.te- bu.dand/	/(u/ ǎn) raf.te- bud/

<table>
<tr><td colspan="2" align="center">**Past Subjunctive**
ماضی التزامی</td></tr>
<tr>
<td align="center">(ما) رفته باشیم
/(mă) raf.te- bă.šim/</td>
<td align="center">(من) رفته باشم
/(man) raf.te- bă.šam/</td>
</tr>
<tr>
<td align="center">(شما) رفته باشید
/(šo.mă) raf.te- bă.šid/</td>
<td align="center">(تو) رفته باشی
/(to) raf.te- bă.ši/</td>
</tr>
<tr>
<td align="center">(آنها) رفته باشند
/(ăn.hă) raf.te- bă.šand/</td>
<td align="center">(او/ آن) رفته باشد
/(u/ ăn) raf.te- bă.šad/</td>
</tr>
</table>

<table>
<tr><td colspan="2" align="center">**Past Progressive**
ماضی مستمر(در جریان)</td></tr>
<tr>
<td align="center">(ما) داشتیم می رفتیم
/(mă) dăš.tim- mi.raf.tim/</td>
<td align="center">(من) داشتم می رفتم
/(man) dăš.tam- mi.raf.tam/</td>
</tr>
<tr>
<td align="center">(شما) داشتید می رفتید
/(šo.mă) dăš.tid- mi.raf.tid/</td>
<td align="center">(تو) داشتی می رفتی
/(to) dăš.ti- mi.raf.ti/</td>
</tr>
<tr>
<td align="center">(آنها) داشتند می رفتند
/(ăn.hă) dăš.tand- mi.raf.tand/</td>
<td align="center">(او/آن) داشت می رفت
/(u/ ăn) dăšt- mi.raft/</td>
</tr>
</table>

<table>
<tr><td colspan="2" align="center">**Simple Future**
مستقبل (آینده ساده)</td></tr>
<tr>
<td align="center">(ما) خواهیم رفت
/(mă) kă.him- raft/</td>
<td align="center">(من) خواهم رفت
/(man) kă.ham- raft/</td>
</tr>
<tr>
<td align="center">(شما) خواهید رفت
/(šo.mă) kă.hid- raft/</td>
<td align="center">(تو) خواهی رفت
/(to) kă.hi- raft/</td>
</tr>
<tr>
<td align="center">(آنها) خواهند رفت
/(ăn.hă) kă.hand- raft/</td>
<td align="center">(او/آن) خواهد رفت
/(u/ ăn) kă.had- raft/</td>
</tr>
</table>

<table>
<tr><td colspan="2" align="center">**Command**
امر</td></tr>
<tr>
<td align="center">بروید!
/be.ra.vid/</td>
<td align="center">برو!
/bo.ro/</td>
</tr>
</table>

to happen

اِتّفاق اُفتادَن

/et.te.fãğ- of.tă.dan/

Plural	Singular
Simple Present مضارع اخباری(حال ساده)	
(ما) اتّفاق می افتیم /(mă) et.te.fãğ- mi.of.tim/	(من) اتّفاق می افتم /(man) et.te.fãğ- mi.of.tam/
(شما) اتّفاق می افتید /(šo.mă) et.te.fãğ- mi.of.tid/	(تو) اتّفاق می افتی /(to) et.te.fãğ- mi.of.ti/
(آنها) اتّفاق می افتند /(ăn.hă) et.te.fãğ- mi.of.tand/	(او/آن) اتّفاق می افتد /(u/ ăn) et.te.fãğ- mi.of.tad/
Present Subjunctive مضارع التزامی	
(ما) اتّفاق بیفتیم /(mă) et.te.fãğ- bi.yof.tim/	(من) اتّفاق بیفتم /(man) et.te.fãğ- bi.yof.tam/
(شما) اتّفاق بیفتید /(šo.mă) et.te.fãğ- bi.yof.tid/	(تو) اتّفاق بیفتی /(to) et.te.fãğ- bi.yof.ti/
(آنها) اتّفاق بیفتند /(ăn.hă) et.te.fãğ- bi.yof.tand/	(او/آن) اتّفاق بیفتد /(u/ ăn) et.te.fãğ- bi.yof.tad/
Present Progressive مضارع مستمر(در جریان)	
(ما) داریم اتّفاق می افتیم /(mă) dă.rim- et.te.fãğ- mi.of.tim/	(من) دارم اتّفاق می افتم /(man) dă.ram- et.te.fãğ- mi.of.tam/
(شما) دارید اتّفاق می افتید /(šo.mă) dă.rid- et.te.fãğ- mi.of.tid/	(تو) داری اتّفاق می افتی /(to) dă.ri- et.te.fãğ- mi.of.ti/
(آنها) دارند اتّفاق می افتند /(ăn.hă) dă.rand- et.te.fãğ- mi.of.tand/	(او/آن) دارد اتّفاق می افتد /(u/ ăn) dă.rad- et.te.fãğ- mi.of.tad/

Simple Past	
ماضی مطلق (گذشته ساده)	
(ما) اتّفاق افتادیم	(من) اتّفاق افتادم
/(mă) et.te.făğ- of.tă.dim/	/(man) et.te.făğ- of.tă.dam/
(شما) اتّفاق افتادید	(تو) اتّفاق افتادی
/(šo.mă) et.te.făğ- of.tă.did/	/(to) et.te.făğ- of.tă.di/
(آنها) اتّفاق افتادند	(او/ آن) اتّفاق افتاد
/(ăn.hă) et.te.făğ- of.tă.dand/	/(u/ ăn) et.te.făğ- of.tăd/

Imperfect Indicative	
ماضی استمراری	
(ما) اتّفاق می افتادیم	(من) اتّفاق می افتادم
/(mă) et.te.făğ- mi.of.tă.dim/	/(man) et.te.făğ- mi.of.tă.dam/
(شما) اتّفاق می افتادید	(تو) اتّفاق می افتادی
/(šo.mă) et.te.făğ- mi.of.tă.did/	/(to) et.te.făğ- mi.of.tă.di/
(آنها) اتّفاق می افتادند	(او/ آن) اتّفاق می افتاد
/(ăn.hă) et.te.făğ- mi.of.tă.dand/	/(u/ ăn) et.te.făğ- mi.of.tăd/

Present Perfect	
ماضی نقلی	
(ما) اتّفاق افتاده ایم	(من) اتّفاق افتاده ام
/(mă) et.te.făğ- of.tă.de.im/	/(man) et.te.făğ- of.tă.de.am/
(شما) اتّفاق افتاده اید	(تو) اتّفاق افتاده ای
/(šo.mă) et.te.făğ- of.tă.de.id/	/(to) et.te.făğ- of.tă.de.i/
(آنها) اتّفاق افتاده اند	(او/ آن) اتّفاق افتاده است
/(ăn.hă) et.te.făğ- of.tă.de.and/	/(u/ ăn) et.te.făğ- of.tă.de- ast/

Past Perfect	
ماضی بعید	
(ما) اتّفاق افتاده بودیم	(من) اتّفاق افتاده بودم
/(mă) et.te.făğ- of.tă.de- bu.dim/	/(man) et.te.făğ- of.tă.de- bu.dam/
(شما) اتّفاق افتاده بودید	(تو) اتّفاق افتاده بودی
/(šo.mă) et.te.făğ- of.tă.de- bu.did/	/(to) et.te.făğ- of.tă.de- bu.di/
(آنها) اتّفاق افتاده بودند	(او/ آن) اتّفاق افتاده بود
/(ăn.hă) et.te.făğ- of.tă.de- bu.dand/	/(u/ ăn) et.te.făğ- of.tă.de- bud/

117

Past Subjunctive	
ماضی التزامی	
(ما) اتّفاق افتاده باشیم /(mǎ) et.te.fǎğ- of.tǎ.de- bǎ.šim/	(من) اتّفاق افتاده باشم /(man) et.te.fǎğ- of.tǎ.de- bǎ.šam/
(شما) اتّفاق افتاده باشید /(šo.mǎ) et.te.fǎğ- of.tǎ.de- bǎ.šid/	(تو) اتّفاق افتاده باشی /(to) et.te.fǎğ- of.tǎ.de- bǎ.ši/
(آنها) اتّفاق افتاده باشند /(ǎn.hǎ) et.te.fǎğ- of.tǎ.de- bǎ.šand/	(او/ آن) اتّفاق افتاده باشد /(u/ ǎn) et.te.fǎğ- of.tǎ.de- bǎ.šad/

Past Progressive	
ماضی مستمر(در جریان)	
(ما) داشتیم اتّفاق می افتادیم /(mǎ) dǎš.tim- et.te.fǎğ- mi.of.tǎ.dim/	(من) داشتم اتّفاق می افتادم /(man) dǎš.tam- et.te.fǎğ- mi.of.tǎ.dam/
(شما) داشتید اتّفاق می افتادید /(šo.mǎ) dǎš.tid- et.te.fǎğ- mi.of.tǎ.did/	(تو) داشتی اتّفاق می افتادی /(to) dǎš.ti- et.te.fǎğ- mi.of.tǎ.di/
(آنها) داشتند اتّفاق می افتادند /(ǎn.hǎ) dǎš.tand- et.te.fǎğ- mi.of.tǎ.dand/	(او/ آن) داشت اتّفاق می افتاد /(u/ ǎn) dǎšt- et.te.fǎğ- mi.of.tǎd/

Simple Future	
مستقبل (آینده ساده)	
(ما) اتّفاق خواهیم افتاد /(mǎ) et.te.fǎğ- ǩǎ.him- of.tǎd/	(من) اتّفاق خواهم افتاد /(man) et.te.fǎğ- ǩǎ.ham- of.tǎd/
(شما) اتّفاق خواهید افتاد /(šo.mǎ) et.te.fǎğ- ǩǎ.hid- of.tǎd/	(تو) اتّفاق خواهی افتاد /(to) et.te.fǎğ- ǩǎ.hi- of.tǎd/
(آنها) اتّفاق خواهند افتاد /(ǎn.hǎ) et.te.fǎğ- ǩǎ.hand- of.tǎd/	(او/ آن) اتّفاق خواهد افتاد /(u/ ǎn) et.te.fǎğ- ǩǎ.had- of.tǎd/

Command	
امر	
اتّفاق بیفتید! /et.te.fǎğ- bi.yof.tid/	اتّفاق بیفت! /et.te.fǎğ- bi.yoft/

to have

داشتَن

/dăš.tan/

Plural	Singular
Simple Present	
مضارع اخباری(حال ساده)	
(ما) داریم	(من) دارم
/(mă) dă.rim/	/(man) dă.ram/
(شما) دارید	(تو) داری
/(šo.mă) dă.rid/	/(to) dă.ri/
(آنها) دارند	(او/آن) دارد
/(ăn.hă) dă.rand/	/(u/ ăn) dă.rad/
Present Subjunctive	
مضارع التزامی	
(ما) بداریم	(من) بدارم
/(mă) be.dă.rim/	/(man) be.dă.ram/
(شما) بدارید	(تو) بداری
/(šo.mă) be.dă.rid/	/(to) be.dă.ri/
(آنها) بدارند	(او/آن) بدارد
/(ăn.hă) be.dă.rand/	/(u/ ăn) be.dă.rad/
Present Progressive	
مضارع مستمر(در جریان)	
(ما) داریم می داریم	(من) دارم می دارم
/(mă) dă.rim- mi.dă.rim/	/(man) dă.ram- mi.dă.ram/
(شما) دارید می دارید	(تو) داری می داری
/(šo.mă) dă.rid- mi.dă.rid/	/(to) dă.ri- mi.dă.ri/
(آنها) دارند می دارند	(او/آن) دارد می دارد
/(ăn.hă) dă.rand- mi.dă.rand/	/(u/ ăn) dă.rad- mi.dă.rad/

Simple Past	
ماضی مطلق (گذشته ساده)	
(ما) داشتیم	(من) داشتم
/(mă) dăš.tim/	/(man) dăš.tam/
(شما) داشتید	(تو) داشتی
/(šo.mă) dăš.tid/	/(to) dăš.ti/
(آنها) داشتند	(او/ آن) داشت
/(ăn.hă) dăš.tand/	/(u/ ăn) dăšt/

Imperfect Indicative	
ماضی استمراری	
(ما) می داشتیم	(من) می داشتم
/(mă) mi.dăš.tim/	/(man) mi.dăš.tam/
(شما) می داشتید	(تو) می داشتی
/(šo.mă) mi.dăš.tid/	/(to) mi.dăš.ti/
(آنها) می داشتند	(او/ آن) می داشت
/(ăn.hă) mi.dăš.tand/	/(u/ ăn) mi.dăšt/

Present Perfect	
ماضی نقلی	
(ما) داشته ایم	(من) داشته ام
/(mă) dăš.te.im/	/(man) dăš.te.am/
(شما) داشته اید	(تو) داشته ای
/(šo.mă) dăš.te.id/	/(to) dăš.te.i/
(آنها) داشته اند	(او/ آن) داشته است
/(ăn.hă) dăš.te.and/	/(u/ ăn) dăš.te- ast/

Past Perfect	
ماضی بعید	
(ما) داشته بودیم	(من) داشته بودم
/(mă) dăš.te- bu.dim/	/(man) dăš.te- bu.dam/
(شما) داشته بودید	(تو) داشته بودی
/(šo.mă) dăš.te- bu.did	/(to) dăš.te- bu.di/
(آنها) داشته بودند	(او/ آن) داشته بود
/(ăn.hă) dăš.te- bu.dand/	/(u/ ăn) dăš.te- bud/

<table>
<tr><td colspan="2" align="center">**Past Subjunctive**
ماضی التزامی</td></tr>
<tr><td align="center">(ما) داشته باشیم
/(mǎ) dǎš.te- bǎ.šim/</td><td align="center">(من) داشته باشم
/(man) dǎš.te- bǎ.šam/</td></tr>
<tr><td align="center">(شما) داشته باشید
/(šo.mǎ) dǎš.te- bǎ.šid/</td><td align="center">(تو) داشته باشی
/(to) dǎš.te- bǎ.ši/</td></tr>
<tr><td align="center">(آنها) داشته باشند
/(ǎn.hǎ) dǎš.te- bǎ.šand/</td><td align="center">(او/آن) داشته باشد
/(u/ ǎn) dǎš.te- bǎ.šad/</td></tr>
</table>

<table>
<tr><td colspan="2" align="center">**Past Progressive**
ماضی مستمر(در جریان)</td></tr>
<tr><td align="center">(ما) داشتیم می داشتیم
/(mǎ) dǎš.tim- mi.dǎš.tim/</td><td align="center">(من) داشتم می داشتم
/(man) dǎš.tam- mi.dǎš.tam/</td></tr>
<tr><td align="center">(شما) داشتید می داشتید
/(šo.mǎ) dǎš.tid- mi.dǎš.tid/</td><td align="center">(تو) داشتی می داشتی
/(to) dǎš.ti- mi.dǎš.ti/</td></tr>
<tr><td align="center">(آنها) داشتند می داشتند
/(ǎn.hǎ) dǎš.tand- mi.dǎš.tand/</td><td align="center">(او/آن) داشت می داشت
/(u/ ǎn) dǎšt- mi.dǎšt/</td></tr>
</table>

<table>
<tr><td colspan="2" align="center">**Simple Future**
مستقبل (آینده ساده)</td></tr>
<tr><td align="center">(ما) خواهیم داشت
/(mǎ) ǩǎ.him- dǎšt/</td><td align="center">(من) خواهم داشت
/(man) ǩǎ.ham- dǎšt/</td></tr>
<tr><td align="center">(شما) خواهید داشت
/(šo.mǎ) ǩǎ.hid- dǎšt/</td><td align="center">(تو) خواهی داشت
/(to) ǩǎ.hi- dǎšt/</td></tr>
<tr><td align="center">(آنها) خواهند داشت
/(ǎn.hǎ) ǩǎ.hand- dǎšt/</td><td align="center">(او/آن) خواهد داشت
/(u/ ǎn) ǩǎ.had- dǎšt/</td></tr>
</table>

<table>
<tr><td colspan="2" align="center">**Command**
امر</td></tr>
<tr><td align="center">بدارید! *
/be.dǎ.rid/</td><td align="center">بدار! *
/be.dǎr/</td></tr>
</table>

* also: داشته باشید!   داشته باش!

to hear

/še.ni.dan/

Plural	Singular
Simple Present	
مضارع اخباری(حال ساده)	
(ما) می شنویم	(من) می شنوم
/(mǎ) mi.še.na.vim/	/(man) mi.še.na.vam/
(شما) می شنوید	(تو) می شنوی
/(šo.mǎ) mi.še.na.vid/	/(to) mi.še.na.vi/
(آنها) می شنوند	(او/آن) می شنود
/(ǎn.hǎ) mi.še.na.vand/	/(u/ ǎn) mi.še.na.vad/
Present Subjunctive	
مضارع التزامی	
(ما) بشنویم	(من) بشنوم
/(mǎ) be.še.na.vim/	/(man) be.še.na.vam/
(شما) بشنوید	(تو) بشنوی
/(šo.mǎ) be.še.na.vid/	/(to) be.še.na.vi/
(آنها) بشنوند	(او/آن) بشنود
/(ǎn.hǎ) be.še.na.vand/	/(u/ ǎn) be.še.na.vad/
Present Progressive	
مضارع مستمر(در جریان)	
(ما) داریم می شنویم	(من) دارم می شنوم
/(mǎ) dǎ.rim- mi.še.na.vim/	/(man) dǎ.ram- mi.še.na.vam/
(شما) دارید می شنوید	(تو) داری می شنوی
/(šo.mǎ) dǎ.rid- mi.še.na.vid/	/(to) dǎ.ri- mi.še.na.vi/
(آنها) دارند می شنوند	(او/آن) دارد می شنود
/(ǎn.hǎ) dǎ.rand- mi.še.na.vand/	/(u/ ǎn) dǎ.rad- mi.še.na.vad/

Simple Past
ماضی مطلق (گذشته ساده)

(ما) شنیدیم	(من) شنیدم
/(mă) še.ni.dim/	/(man) še.ni.dam/
(شما) شنیدید	(تو) شنیدی
/(šo.mă) še.ni.did/	/(to) še.ni.di/
(آنها) شنیدند	(او/آن) شنید
/(ăn.hă) še.ni.dand/	/(u/ ăn) še.nid/

Imperfect Indicative
ماضی استمراری

(ما) می شنیدیم	(من) می شنیدم
/(mă) mi.še.ni.dim/	/(man) mi.še.ni.dam/
(شما) می شنیدید	(تو) می شنیدی
/(šo.mă) mi.še.ni.did/	/(to) mi.še.ni.di/
(آنها) می شنیدند	(او/آن) می شنید
/(ăn.hă) mi.še.ni.dand/	/(u/ ăn) mi.še.nid/

Present Perfect
ماضی نقلی

(ما) شنیده ایم	(من) شنیده ام
/(mă) še.ni.de.im/	/(man) še.ni.de.am/
(شما) شنیده اید	(تو) شنیده ای
/(šo.mă) še.ni.de.id/	/(to) še.ni.de.i/
(آنها) شنیده اند	(او/آن) شنیده است
/(ăn.hă) še.ni.de.and/	/(u/ ăn) še.ni.de- ast/

Past Perfect
ماضی بعید

(ما) شنیده بودیم	(من) شنیده بودم
/(mă) še.ni.de- bu.dim/	/(man) še.ni.de- bu.dam/
(شما) شنیده بودید	(تو) شنیده بودی
/(šo.mă) še.ni.de- bu.did/	/(to) še.ni.de- bu.di/
(آنها) شنیده بودند	(او/آن) شنیده بود
/(ăn.hă) še.ni.de- bu.dand/	/(u/ ăn) še.ni.de- bud/

123

Past Subjunctive	
ماضی التزامی	
(ما) شنیده باشیم /(mă) še.ni.de- bă.šim/	(من) شنیده باشم /(man) še.ni.de- bă.šam/
(شما) شنیده باشید /(šo.mă) še.ni.de- bă.šid/	(تو) شنیده باشی /(to) še.ni.de- bă.ši/
(آنها) شنیده باشند /(ăn.hă) še.ni.de- bă.šand/	(او/آن) شنیده باشد /(u/ ăn) še.ni.de- bă.šad/

Past Progressive	
ماضی مستمر(در جریان)	
(ما) داشتیم می شنیدیم /(mă) dăš.tim- mi.še.ni.dim/	(من) داشتم می شنیدم /(man) dăš.tam- mi.še.ni.dam/
(شما) داشتید می شنیدید /(šo.mă) dăš.tid- mi.še.ni.did/	(تو) داشتی می شنیدی /(to) dăš.ti- mi.še.ni.di/
(آنها) داشتند می شنیدند /(ăn.hă) dăš.tand- mi.še.ni.dand/	(او/آن) داشت می شنید /(u/ ăn) dăšt- mi.še.nid/

Simple Future	
مستقبل (آینده ساده)	
(ما) خواهیم شنید /(mă) kă.him- še.nid/	(من) خواهم شنید /(man) kă.ham- še.nid/
(شما) خواهید شنید /(šo.mă) kă.hid- še.nid/	(تو) خواهی شنید /(to) kă.hi- še.nid/
(آنها) خواهند شنید /(ăn.hă) kă.hand- še.nid/	(او/آن) خواهد شنید /(u/ ăn) kă.had- še.nid/

Command	
امر	
بشنوید! /be.še.na.vid/	بشنو! /be.še.no/

to increase

زیاد کَردَن

/zi.yăd- kar.dan/

Plural	Singular
Simple Present <div dir="rtl">مضارع اخباری(حال ساده)</div>	
<div dir="rtl">(ما) زیاد می کنیم</div> /(mă) zi.yăd- mi.ko.nim/	<div dir="rtl">(من) زیاد می کنم</div> /(man) zi.yăd- mi.ko.nam/
<div dir="rtl">(شما) زیاد می کنید</div> /(šo.mă) zi.yăd- mi.ko.nid/	<div dir="rtl">(تو) زیاد می کنی</div> /(to) zi.yăd- mi.ko.ni/
<div dir="rtl">(آنها) زیاد می کنند</div> /(ăn.hă) zi.yăd- mi.ko.nand/	<div dir="rtl">(او/آن) زیاد می کند</div> /(u/ ăn) zi.yăd- mi.ko.nad/
Present Subjunctive <div dir="rtl">مضارع التزامی</div>	
<div dir="rtl">(ما) زیاد بکنیم</div> /(mă) zi.yăd- be.ko.nim/	<div dir="rtl">(من) زیاد بکنم</div> /(man) zi.yăd- be.ko.nam/
<div dir="rtl">(شما) زیاد بکنید</div> /(šo.mă) zi.yăd- be.ko.nid/	<div dir="rtl">(تو) زیاد بکنی</div> /(to) zi.yăd- be.ko.ni/
<div dir="rtl">(آنها) زیاد بکنند</div> /(ăn.hă) zi.yăd- be.ko.nand/	<div dir="rtl">(او/آن) زیاد بکند</div> /(u/ ăn) zi.yăd- be.ko.nad/
Present Progressive <div dir="rtl">مضارع مستمر(در جریان)</div>	
<div dir="rtl">(ما) داریم زیاد می کنیم</div> /(mă) dă.rim- zi.yăd- mi.ko.nim/	<div dir="rtl">(من) دارم زیاد می کنم</div> /(man) dă.ram- zi.yăd- mi.ko.nam/
<div dir="rtl">(شما) دارید زیاد می کنید</div> /(šo.mă) dă.rid- zi.yăd- mi.ko.nid/	<div dir="rtl">(تو) داری زیاد می کنی</div> /(to) dă.ri- zi.yăd- mi.ko.ni/
<div dir="rtl">(آنها) دارند زیاد می کنند</div> /(ăn.hă) dă.rand- zi.yăd- mi.ko.nand/	<div dir="rtl">(او/آن) دارد زیاد می کند</div> /(u/ ăn) dă.rad- zi.yăd- mi.ko.nad/

	Simple Past	
	ماضی مطلق (گذشته ساده)	
(ما) زیاد کردیم		(من) زیاد کردم
/(mǎ) zi.yǎd- kar.dim/		/(man) zi.yǎd- kar.dam/
(شما) زیاد کردید		(تو) زیاد کردی
/(šo.mǎ) zi.yǎd- kar.did/		/(to) zi.yǎd- kar.di/
(آنها) زیاد کردند		(او/آن) زیاد کرد
/(ǎn.hǎ) zi.yǎd- kar.dand/		/(u/ ǎn) zi.yǎd- kard/

	Imperfect Indicative	
	ماضی استمراری	
(ما) زیاد می کردیم		(من) زیاد می کردم
/(mǎ) zi.yǎd- mi.kar.dim/		/(man) zi.yǎd- mi.kar.dam/
(شما) زیاد می کردید		(تو) زیاد می کردی
/(šo.mǎ) zi.yǎd- mi.kar.did/		/(to) zi.yǎd- mi.kar.di/
(آنها) زیاد می کردند		(او/آن) زیاد می کرد
/(ǎn.hǎ) zi.yǎd- mi.kar.dand/		/(u/ ǎn) zi.yǎd- mi.kard/

	Present Perfect	
	ماضی نقلی	
(ما) زیاد کرده ایم		(من) زیاد کرده ام
/(mǎ) zi.yǎd- kar.de.im/		/(man) zi.yǎd- kar.de.am/
(شما) زیاد کرده اید		(تو) زیاد کرده ای
/(šo.mǎ) zi.yǎd- kar.de.id/		/(to) zi.yǎd- kar.de.i/
(آنها) زیاد کرده اند		(او/آن) زیاد کرده است
/(ǎn.hǎ) zi.yǎd- kar.de.and/		/(u/ ǎn) zi.yǎd- kar.de- ast/

	Past Perfect	
	ماضی بعید	
(ما) زیاد کرده بودیم		(من) زیاد کرده بودم
/(mǎ) zi.yǎd- kar.de- bu.dim/		/(man) zi.yǎd- kar.de- bu.dam/
(شما) زیاد کرده بودید		(تو) زیاد کرده بودی
/(šo.mǎ) zi.yǎd- kar.de- bu.did/		/(to) zi.yǎd- kar.de- bu.di/
(آنها) زیاد کرده بودند		(او/آن) زیاد کرده بود
/(ǎn.hǎ) zi.yǎd- kar.de- bu.dand/		/(u/ ǎn) zi.yǎd- kar.de- bud/

126

<table>
<tr><td colspan="2" align="center">Past Subjunctive
ماضی التزامی</td></tr>
</table>

(ما) زیاد کرده باشیم /(mǎ) zi.yǎd- kar.de- bǎ.šim/	(من) زیاد کرده باشم /(man) zi.yǎd- kar.de- bǎ.šam/
(شما) زیاد کرده باشید /(šo.mǎ) zi.yǎd- kar.de- bǎ.šid/	(تو) زیاد کرده باشی /(to) zi.yǎd- kar.de- bǎ.ši/
(آنها) زیاد کرده باشند /(ǎn.hǎ) zi.yǎd- kar.de- bǎ.šand/	(او/آن) زیاد کرده باشد /(u/ ǎn) zi.yǎd- kar.de- bǎ.šad/

<table>
<tr><td colspan="2" align="center">Past Progressive
ماضی مستمر(در جریان)</td></tr>
</table>

(ما) داشتیم زیاد می کردیم /(mǎ) dǎš.tim- zi.yǎd- mi.kar.dim/	(من) داشتم زیاد می کردم /(man) dǎš.tam- zi.yǎd- mi.kar.dam/
(شما) داشتید زیاد می کردید /(šo.mǎ) dǎš.tid- zi.yǎd- mi.kar.did/	(تو) داشتی زیاد می کردی /(to) dǎš.ti- zi.yǎd- mi.kar.di/
(آنها) داشتند زیاد می کردند /(ǎn.hǎ) dǎš.tand- zi.yǎd- mi.kar.dand/	(او/آن) داشت زیاد می کرد /(u/ ǎn) dǎšt- zi.yǎd- mi.kard/

<table>
<tr><td colspan="2" align="center">Simple Future
مستقبل (آینده ساده)</td></tr>
</table>

(ما) زیاد خواهیم کرد /(mǎ) zi.yǎd- ǩǎ.him- kard/	(من) زیاد خواهم کرد /(man) zi.yǎd- ǩǎ.ham- kard/
(شما) زیاد خواهید کرد /(šo.mǎ) zi.yǎd- ǩǎ.hid- kard/	(تو) زیاد خواهی کرد /(to) zi.yǎd- ǩǎ.hi- kard/
(آنها) زیاد خواهند کرد /(ǎn.hǎ) zi.yǎd- ǩǎ.hand- kard/	(او/آن) زیاد خواهد کرد /(u/ ǎn) zi.yǎd- ǩǎ.had- kard/

<table>
<tr><td colspan="2" align="center">Command
امر</td></tr>
</table>

* زیاد بکنید! /zi.yǎd- be.ko.nid/	* زیاد بکن! /zi.yǎd- be.kon/

* also: زیاد کن!   زیاد کنید!

to introduce

مُعَرِفی کَردَن

/mo.ʿa.re.fi- kar.dan/

Plural	Singular
Simple Present مضارع اخباری(حال ساده)	
(ما) معرفی می کنیم /(mǎ) mo.ʿa.re.fi- mi.ko.nim/	(من) معرفی می کنم /(man) mo.ʿa.re.fi- mi.ko.nam/
(شما) معرفی می کنید /(šo.mǎ) mo.ʿa.re.fi- mi.ko.nid/	(تو) معرفی می کنی /(to) mo.ʿa.re.fi- mi.ko.ni/
(آنها) معرفی می کنند /(ǎn.hǎ) mo.ʿa.re.fi- mi.ko.nand/	(او/آن) معرفی می کند /(u/ ǎn) mo.ʿa.re.fi- mi.ko.nad/
Present Subjunctive مضارع التزامی	
(ما) معرفی بکنیم /(mǎ) mo.ʿa.re.fi- be.ko.nim/	(من) معرفی بکنم /(man) mo.ʿa.re.fi- be.ko.nam/
(شما) معرفی بکنید /(šo.mǎ) mo.ʿa.re.fi- be.ko.nid/	(تو) معرفی بکنی /(to) mo.ʿa.re.fi- be.ko.ni/
(آنها) معرفی بکنند /(ǎn.hǎ) mo.ʿa.re.fi- be.ko.nand/	(او/آن) معرفی بکند /(u/ ǎn) mo.ʿa.re.fi- be.ko.nad/
Present Progressive مضارع مستمر(در جریان)	
(ما) داریم معرفی می کنیم /(mǎ) dǎ.rim- mo.ʿa.re.fi- mi.ko.nim/	(من) دارم معرفی می کنم /(man) dǎ.ram- mo.ʿa.re.fi- mi.ko.nam/
(شما) دارید معرفی می کنید /(šo.mǎ) dǎ.rid- mo.ʿa.re.fi- mi.ko.nid/	(تو) داری معرفی می کنی /(to) dǎ.ri- mo.ʿa.re.fi- mi.ko.ni/
(آنها) دارند معرفی می کنند /(ǎn.hǎ) dǎ.rand- mo.ʿa.re.fi- mi.ko.nand/	(او/آن) دارد معرفی می کند /(u/ ǎn) dǎ.rad- mo.ʿa.re.fi- mi.ko.nad/

Simple Past
ماضی مطلق (گذشته ساده)

(ما) معرفی کردیم	(من) معرفی کردم
/(mǎ) mo.ʿa.re.fi- kar.dim/	/(man) mo.ʿa.re.fi- kar.dam/
(شما) معرفی کردید	(تو) معرفی کردی
/(šo.mǎ) mo.ʿa.re.fi- kar.did/	/(to) mo.ʿa.re.fi- kar.di/
(آنها) معرفی کردند	(او/آن) معرفی کرد
/(ǎn.hǎ) mo.ʿa.re.fi- kar.dand/	/(u/ ǎn) mo.ʿa.re.fi- kard/

Imperfect Indicative
ماضی استمراری

(ما) معرفی می کردیم	(من) معرفی می کردم
/(mǎ) mo.ʿa.re.fi- mi.kar.dim/	/(man) mo.ʿa.re.fi- mi.kar.dam/
(شما) معرفی می کردید	(تو) معرفی می کردی
/(šo.mǎ) mo.ʿa.re.fi- mi.kar.did/	/(to) mo.ʿa.re.fi- mi.kar.di/
(آنها) معرفی می کردند	(او/آن) معرفی می کرد
/(ǎn.hǎ) mo.ʿa.re.fi- mi.kar.dand/	/(u/ ǎn) mo.ʿa.re.fi- mi.kard/

Present Perfect
ماضی نقلی

(ما) معرفی کرده ایم	(من) معرفی کرده ام
/(mǎ) mo.ʿa.re.fi- kar.de.im/	/(man) mo.ʿa.re.fi- kar.de.am/
(شما) معرفی کرده اید	(تو) معرفی کرده ای
/(šo.mǎ) mo.ʿa.re.fi- kar.de.id/	/(to) mo.ʿa.re.fi- kar.de.i/
(آنها) معرفی کرده اند	(او/آن) معرفی کرده است
/(ǎn.hǎ) mo.ʿa.re.fi- kar.de.and/	/(u/ ǎn) mo.ʿa.re.fi- kar.de- ast/

Past Perfect
ماضی بعید

(ما) معرفی کرده بودیم	(من) معرفی کرده بودم
/(mǎ) mo.ʿa.re.fi- kar.de- bu.dim/	/(man) mo.ʿa.re.fi- kar.de- bu.dam/
(شما) معرفی کرده بودید	(تو) معرفی کرده بودی
/(šo.mǎ) mo.ʿa.re.fi- kar.de- bu.did/	/(to) mo.ʿa.re.fi- kar.de- bu.di/
(آنها) معرفی کرده بودند	(او/آن) معرفی کرده بود
/(ǎn.hǎ) mo.ʿa.re.fi- kar.de- bu.dand/	/(u/ ǎn) mo.ʿa.re.fi- kar.de- bud/

<table>
<tr><td colspan="2" align="center">**Past Subjunctive**
ماضی التزامی</td></tr>
<tr>
<td align="center">(ما) معرفی کرده باشیم
/(mǎ) mo.ʿa.re.fi- kar.de- bǎ.šim/</td>
<td align="center">(من) معرفی کرده باشم
/(man) mo.ʿa.re.fi- kar.de- bǎ.šam/</td>
</tr>
<tr>
<td align="center">(شما) معرفی کرده باشید
/(šo.mǎ) mo.ʿa.re.fi- kar.de- bǎ.šid/</td>
<td align="center">(تو) معرفی کرده باشی
/(to) mo.ʿa.re.fi- kar.de- bǎ.ši/</td>
</tr>
<tr>
<td align="center">(آنها) معرفی کرده باشند
/(ǎn.hǎ) mo.ʿa.re.fi- kar.de- bǎ.šand/</td>
<td align="center">(او/ آن) معرفی کرده باشد
/(u/ ǎn) mo.ʿa.re.fi- kar.de- bǎ.šad/</td>
</tr>
</table>

<table>
<tr><td colspan="2" align="center">**Past Progressive**
ماضی مستمر(در جریان)</td></tr>
<tr>
<td align="center">(ما) داشتیم معرفی می کردیم
/(mǎ) dǎš.tim- mo.ʿa.re.fi- mi.kar.dim/</td>
<td align="center">(من) داشتم معرفی می کردم
/(man) dǎš.tam- mo.ʿa.re.fi- mi.kar.dam/</td>
</tr>
<tr>
<td align="center">(شما) داشتید معرفی می کردید
/(šo.mǎ) dǎš.tid- mo.ʿa.re.fi- mi.kar.did/</td>
<td align="center">(تو) داشتی معرفی می کردی
/(to) dǎš.ti- mo.ʿa.re.fi- mi.kar.di/</td>
</tr>
<tr>
<td align="center">(آنها) داشتند معرفی می کردند
/(ǎn.hǎ) dǎš.tand- mo.ʿa.re.fi- mi.kar.dand/</td>
<td align="center">(او/آن) داشت معرفی می کرد
/(u/ ǎn) dǎšt- mo.ʿa.re.fi- mi.kard/</td>
</tr>
</table>

<table>
<tr><td colspan="2" align="center">**Simple Future**
مستقبل (آینده ساده)</td></tr>
<tr>
<td align="center">(ما) معرفی خواهیم کرد
/(mǎ) mo.ʿa.re.fi- ǩǎ.him- kard/</td>
<td align="center">(من) معرفی خواهم کرد
/(man) mo.ʿa.re.fi- ǩǎ.ham- kard/</td>
</tr>
<tr>
<td align="center">(شما) معرفی خواهید کرد
/(šo.mǎ) mo.ʿa.re.fi- ǩǎ.hid- kard/</td>
<td align="center">(تو) معرفی خواهی کرد
/(to) mo.ʿa.re.fi- ǩǎ.hi- kard/</td>
</tr>
<tr>
<td align="center">(آنها) معرفی خواهند کرد
/(ǎn.hǎ) mo.ʿa.re.fi- ǩǎ.hand- kard/</td>
<td align="center">(او/آن) معرفی خواهد کرد
/(u/ ǎn) mo.ʿa.re.fi- ǩǎ.had- kard/</td>
</tr>
</table>

<table>
<tr><td colspan="2" align="center">**Command**
امر</td></tr>
<tr>
<td align="center">* معرفی بکنید!
/mo.ʿa.re.fi- be.ko.nid/</td>
<td align="center">* معرفی بکن!
/mo.ʿa.re.fi- be.kon/</td>
</tr>
</table>

* also: معرفی کن!   معرفی کنید!

to invite

دَعوَت کَردَن

/daʿ.vat- kar.dan/

Plural	Singular
Simple Present <div dir="rtl">مضارع اخباری(حال ساده)</div>	
(ما) دعوت می کنیم /(mǎ) daʿ.vat- mi.ko.nim/	(من) دعوت می کنم /(man) daʿ.vat- mi.ko.nam/
(شما) دعوت می کنید /(šo.mǎ) daʿ.vat- mi.ko.nid/	(تو) دعوت می کنی /(to) daʿ.vat- mi.ko.ni/
(آنها) دعوت می کنند /(ǎn.hǎ) daʿ.vat- mi.ko.nand/	(او/آن) دعوت می کند /(u/ ǎn) daʿ.vat- mi.ko.nad/
Present Subjunctive <div dir="rtl">مضارع التزامی</div>	
(ما) دعوت بکنیم /(mǎ) daʿ.vat- be.ko.nim/	(من) دعوت بکنم /(man) daʿ.vat- be.ko.nam/
(شما) دعوت بکنید /(šo.mǎ) daʿ.vat- be.ko.nid/	(تو) دعوت بکنی /(to) daʿ.vat- be.ko.ni/
(آنها) دعوت بکنند /(ǎn.hǎ) daʿ.vat- be.ko.nand/	(او/آن) دعوت بکند /(u/ ǎn) daʿ.vat- be.ko.nad/
Present Progressive <div dir="rtl">مضارع مستمر(در جریان)</div>	
(ما) داریم دعوت می کنیم /(mǎ) dǎ.rim- daʿ.vat- mi.ko.nim/	(من) دارم دعوت می کنم /(man) dǎ.ram- daʿ.vat- mi.ko.nam/
(شما) دارید دعوت می کنید /(šo.mǎ) dǎ.rid- daʿ.vat- mi.ko.nid/	(تو) داری دعوت می کنی /(to) dǎ.ri- daʿ.vat- mi.ko.ni/
(آنها) دارند دعوت می کنند /(ǎn.hǎ) dǎ.rand- daʿ.vat- mi.ko.nand	(او/آن) دارد دعوت می کند /(u/ ǎn) dǎ.rad- daʿ.vat- mi.ko.nad/

131

Simple Past
ماضی مطلق (گذشته ساده)

(ما) دعوت کردیم	(من) دعوت کردم
/(mă) da'.vat- kar.dim/	/(man) da'.vat- kar.dam/
(شما) دعوت کردید	(تو) دعوت کردی
/(šo.mă) da'.vat- kar.did/	/(to) da'.vat- kar.di/
(آنها) دعوت کردند	(او/آن) دعوت کرد
/(ăn.hă) da'.vat- kar.dand/	/(u/ ăn) da'.vat- kard/

Imperfect Indicative
ماضی استمراری

(ما) دعوت می کردیم	(من) دعوت می کردم
/(mă) da'.vat- mi.kar.dim/	/(man) da'.vat- mi.kar.dam/
(شما) دعوت می کردید	(تو) دعوت می کردی
/(šo.mă) da'.vat- mi.kar.did/	/(to) da'.vat- mi.kar.di/
(آنها) دعوت می کردند	(او/آن) دعوت می کرد
/(ăn.hă) da'.vat- mi.kar.dand/	/(u/ ăn) da'.vat- mi.kard/

Present Perfect
ماضی نقلی

(ما) دعوت کرده ایم	(من) دعوت کرده ام
/(mă) da'.vat- kar.de.im/	/(man) da'.vat- kar.de.am/
(شما) دعوت کرده اید	(تو) دعوت کرده ای
/(šo.mă) da'.vat- kar.de.id/	/(to) da'.vat- kar.de.i/
(آنها) دعوت کرده اند	(او/آن) دعوت کرده است
/(ăn.hă) da'.vat- kar.de.and/	/(u/ ăn) da'.vat- kar.de- ast/

Past Perfect
ماضی بعید

(ما) دعوت کرده بودیم	(من) دعوت کرده بودم
/(mă) da'.vat- kar.de- bu.dim/	/(man) da'.vat- kar.de- bu.dam/
(شما) دعوت کرده بودید	(تو) دعوت کرده بودی
/(šo.mă) da'.vat- kar.de- bu.did/	/(to) da'.vat- kar.de- bu.di/
(آنها) دعوت کرده بودند	(او/آن) دعوت کرده بود
/(ăn.hă) da'.vat- kar.de- bu.dand/	/(u/ ăn) da'.vat- kar.de- bud/

<table>
<tr><td colspan="2" align="center">**Past Subjunctive**
ماضی التزامی</td></tr>
<tr>
<td>(ما) دعوت کرده باشیم

/(mǎ) da'.vat- kar.de- bǎ.šim/</td>
<td>(من) دعوت کرده باشم

/(man) da'.vat- kar.de- bǎ.šam/</td>
</tr>
<tr>
<td>(شما) دعوت کرده باشید

/(šo.mǎ) da'.vat- kar.de- bǎ.šid/</td>
<td>(تو) دعوت کرده باشی

/(to) da'.vat- kar.de- bǎ.ši/</td>
</tr>
<tr>
<td>(آنها) دعوت کرده باشند

/(ǎn.hǎ) da'.vat- kar.de- bǎ.šand/</td>
<td>(او/آن) دعوت کرده باشد

/(u/ ǎn) da'.vat- kar.de- bǎ.šad/</td>
</tr>
</table>

<table>
<tr><td colspan="2" align="center">**Past Progressive**
ماضی مستمر(در جریان)</td></tr>
<tr>
<td>(ما) داشتیم دعوت می کردیم

/(mǎ) dǎš.tim- da'.vat- mi.kar.dim/</td>
<td>(من) داشتم دعوت می کردم

/(man) dǎš.tam- da'.vat- mi.kar.dam/</td>
</tr>
<tr>
<td>(شما) داشتید دعوت می کردید

/(šo.mǎ) dǎš.tid- da'.vat- mi.kar.did/</td>
<td>(تو) داشتی دعوت می کردی

/(to) dǎš.ti- da'.vat- mi.kar.di/</td>
</tr>
<tr>
<td>(آنها) داشتند دعوت می کردند

/(ǎn.hǎ) dǎš.tand- da'.vat- mi.kar.dand/</td>
<td>(او/آن) داشت دعوت می کرد

/(u/ ǎn) dǎšt- da'.vat- mi.kard/</td>
</tr>
</table>

<table>
<tr><td colspan="2" align="center">**Simple Future**
مستقبل (آینده ساده)</td></tr>
<tr>
<td>(ما) دعوت خواهیم کرد

/(mǎ) da'.vat- ǩǎ.him- kard/</td>
<td>(من) دعوت خواهم کرد

/(man) da'.vat- ǩǎ.ham- kard/</td>
</tr>
<tr>
<td>(شما) دعوت خواهید کرد

/(šo.mǎ) da'.vat- ǩǎ.hid- kard/</td>
<td>(تو) دعوت خواهی کرد

/(to) da'.vat- ǩǎ.hi- kard/</td>
</tr>
<tr>
<td>(آنها) دعوت خواهند کرد

/(ǎn.hǎ) da'.vat- ǩǎ.hand- kard/</td>
<td>(او/آن) دعوت خواهد کرد

/(u/ ǎn) da'.vat - ǩǎ.had- kard/</td>
</tr>
</table>

<table>
<tr><td colspan="2" align="center">**Command**
امر</td></tr>
<tr>
<td>* دعوت بکنید!

/da'.vat- be.ko.nid/</td>
<td>* دعوت بکن!

/da'.vat- be.kon/</td>
</tr>
</table>

* also: دعوت کنید!   دعوت کن!

to kiss

بوسیدَن

/bu.si.dan/

Plural	Singular
Simple Present مضارع اخباری(حال ساده)	
(ما) می بوسیم /(mă) mi.bu.sim/	(من) می بوسم /(man) mi.bu.sam/
(شما) می بوسید /(šo.mă) mi.bu.sid/	(تو) می بوسی /(to) mi.bu.si/
(آنها) می بوسند /(ăn.hă) mi.bu.sand/	(او/آن) می بوسد /(u/ ăn) mi.bu.sad/
Present Subjunctive مضارع التزامی	
(ما) ببوسیم /(mă) be.bu.sim/	(من) ببوسم /(man) be.bu.sam/
(شما) ببوسید /(šo.mă) be.bu.sid/	(تو) ببوسی /(to) be.bu.si/
(آنها) ببوسند /(ăn.hă) be.bu.sand/	(او/آن) ببوسد /(u/ ăn) be.bu.sad/
Present Progressive مضارع مستمر(در جریان)	
(ما) داریم می بوسیم /(mă) dă.rim- mi.bu.sim/	(من) دارم می بوسم /(man) dă.ram- mi.bu.sam/
(شما) دارید می بوسید /(šo.mă) dă.rid- mi.bu.sid/	(تو) داری می بوسی /(to) dă.ri- mi.bu.si/
(آنها) دارند می بوسند /(ăn.hă) dă.rand- mi.bu.sand/	(او/آن) دارد می بوسد /(u/ ăn) dă.rad- mi.bu.sad/

<table>
<tr><td colspan="2" align="center">Simple Past
ماضی مطلق (گذشته ساده)</td></tr>
<tr><td align="center">(ما) بوسیدیم
/(mă) bu.si.dim/</td><td align="center">(من) بوسیدم
/(man) bu.si.dam/</td></tr>
<tr><td align="center">(شما) بوسیدید
/(šo.mă) bu.si.did/</td><td align="center">(تو) بوسیدی
/(to) bu.si.di/</td></tr>
<tr><td align="center">(آنها) بوسیدند
/(ăn.hă) bu.si.dand/</td><td align="center">(او/آن) بوسید
/(u/ ăn) bu.sid/</td></tr>
</table>

<table>
<tr><td colspan="2" align="center">Imperfect Indicative
ماضی استمراری</td></tr>
<tr><td align="center">(ما) می بوسیدیم
/(mă) mi.bu.si.dim/</td><td align="center">(من) می بوسیدم
/(man) mi.bu.si.dam/</td></tr>
<tr><td align="center">(شما) می بوسیدید
/(šo.mă) mi.bu.si.did/</td><td align="center">(تو) می بوسیدی
/(to) mi.bu.si.di/</td></tr>
<tr><td align="center">(آنها) می بوسیدند
/(ăn.hă) mi.bu.si.dand/</td><td align="center">(او/آن) می بوسید
/(u/ ăn) mi.bu.sid/</td></tr>
</table>

<table>
<tr><td colspan="2" align="center">Present Perfect
ماضی نقلی</td></tr>
<tr><td align="center">(ما) بوسیده ایم
/(mă) bu.si.de.im/</td><td align="center">(من) بوسیده ام
/(man) bu.si.de.am/</td></tr>
<tr><td align="center">(شما) بوسیده اید
/(šo.mă) bu.si.de.id/</td><td align="center">(تو) بوسیده ای
/(to) bu.si.de.i/</td></tr>
<tr><td align="center">(آنها) بوسیده اند
/(ăn.hă) bu.si.de.and/</td><td align="center">(او/آن) بوسیده است
/(u/ ăn) bu.si.de- ast/</td></tr>
</table>

<table>
<tr><td colspan="2" align="center">Past Perfect
ماضی بعید</td></tr>
<tr><td align="center">(ما) بوسیده بودیم
/(mă) bu.si.de- bu.dim/</td><td align="center">(من) بوسیده بودم
/(man) bu.si.de- bu.dam/</td></tr>
<tr><td align="center">(شما) بوسیده بودید
/(šo.mă) bu.si.de- bu.did/</td><td align="center">(تو) بوسیده بودی
/(to) bu.si.de- bu.di/</td></tr>
<tr><td align="center">(آنها) بوسیده بودند
/(ăn.hă) bu.si.de- bu.dand/</td><td align="center">(او/آن) بوسیده بود
/(u/ ăn) bu.si.de- bud/</td></tr>
</table>

<table>
<tr><td colspan="2" align="center">**Past Subjunctive**
ماضی التزامی،</td></tr>
<tr>
<td align="center">(ما) بوسیده باشیم
/(mă) bu.si.de- bǎ.šim/</td>
<td align="center">(من) بوسیده باشم
/(man) bu.si.de- bǎ.šam/</td>
</tr>
<tr>
<td align="center">(شما) بوسیده باشید
/(šo.mǎ) bu.si.de- bǎ.šid/</td>
<td align="center">(تو) بوسیده باشی
/(to) bu.si.de- bǎ.ši/</td>
</tr>
<tr>
<td align="center">(آنها) بوسیده باشند
/(ǎn.hǎ) bu.si.de- bǎ.šand/</td>
<td align="center">(او/آن) بوسیده باشد
/(u/ ǎn) bu.si.de- bǎ.šad/</td>
</tr>
</table>

<table>
<tr><td colspan="2" align="center">**Past Progressive**
ماضی مستمر(در جریان)</td></tr>
<tr>
<td align="center">(ما) داشتیم می بوسیدیم
/(mǎ) dǎš.tim- mi.bu.si.dim/</td>
<td align="center">(من) داشتم می بوسیدم
/(man) dǎš.tam- mi.bu.si.dam/</td>
</tr>
<tr>
<td align="center">(شما) داشتید می بوسیدید
/(šo.mǎ) dǎš.tid- mi.bu.si.did/</td>
<td align="center">(تو) داشتی می بوسیدی
/(to) dǎš.ti- mi.bu.si.di/</td>
</tr>
<tr>
<td align="center">(آنها) داشتند می بوسیدند
/(ǎn.hǎ) dǎš.tand- mi.bu.si.dand/</td>
<td align="center">(او/آن) داشت می بوسید
/(u/ ǎn) dǎšt- mi.bu.sid/</td>
</tr>
</table>

<table>
<tr><td colspan="2" align="center">**Simple Future**
مستقبل (آینده ساده)</td></tr>
<tr>
<td align="center">(ما) خواهیم بوسید
/(mǎ) kǎ.him- bu.sid/</td>
<td align="center">(من) خواهم بوسید
/(man) kǎ.ham- bu.sid/</td>
</tr>
<tr>
<td align="center">(شما) خواهید بوسید
/(šo.mǎ) kǎ.hid- bu.sid/</td>
<td align="center">(تو) خواهی بوسید
/(to) kǎ.hi- bu.sid/</td>
</tr>
<tr>
<td align="center">(آنها) خواهند بوسید
/(ǎn.hǎ) kǎ.hand- bu.sid/</td>
<td align="center">(او/آن) خواهد بوسید
/(u/ ǎn) kǎ.had- bu.sid/</td>
</tr>
</table>

<table>
<tr><td colspan="2" align="center">**Command**
امر</td></tr>
<tr>
<td align="center">ببوسید!
/be.bu.sid/</td>
<td align="center">ببوس!
/be.bus/</td>
</tr>
</table>

to know

دانِستَن

/dă.nes.tan/

Plural	*Singular*
Simple Present <div dir="rtl">مضارع اخباری(حال ساده)</div>	
<div dir="rtl">(ما) می دانیم</div> /(mă) mi.dă.nim/	<div dir="rtl">(من) می دانم</div> /(man) mi.dă.nam/
<div dir="rtl">(شما) می دانید</div> /(šo.mă) mi.dă.nid/	<div dir="rtl">(تو) می دانی</div> /(to) mi.dă.ni/
<div dir="rtl">(آنها) می دانند</div> /(ăn.hă) mi.dă.nand/	<div dir="rtl">(او/آن) می داند</div> /(u/ ăn) mi.dă.nad/
Present Subjunctive <div dir="rtl">مضارع التزامی</div>	
<div dir="rtl">(ما) بدانیم</div> /(mă) be.dă.nim/	<div dir="rtl">(من) بدانم</div> /(man) be.dă.nam/
<div dir="rtl">(شما) بدانید</div> /(šo.mă) be.dă.nid/	<div dir="rtl">(تو) بدانی</div> /(to) be.dă.ni/
<div dir="rtl">(آنها) بدانند</div> /(ăn.hă) be.dă.nand/	<div dir="rtl">(او/آن) بداند</div> /(u/ ăn) be.dă.nad/
Present Progressive <div dir="rtl">مضارع مستمر(در جریان)</div>	
<div dir="rtl">(ما) داریم می دانیم</div> /(mă) dă.rim- mi.dă.nim/	<div dir="rtl">(من) دارم می دانم</div> /(man) dă.ram- mi.dă.nam/
<div dir="rtl">(شما) دارید می دانید</div> /(šo.mă) dă.rid- mi.dă.nid/	<div dir="rtl">(تو) داری می دانی</div> /(to) dă.ri- mi.dă.ni/
<div dir="rtl">(آنها) دارند می دانند</div> /(ăn.hă) dă.rand- mi.dă.nand/	<div dir="rtl">(او/آن) دارد می داند</div> /(u/ ăn) dă.rad- mi.dă.nad/

Simple Past
ماضی مطلق (گذشته ساده)

(ما) دانستیم	(من) دانستم
/(mǎ) dǎ.nes.tim/	/(man) dǎ.nes.tam/
(شما) دانستید	(تو) دانستی
/(šo.mǎ) dǎ.nes.tid/	/(to) dǎ.nes.ti/
(آنها) دانستند	(او/آن) دانست
/(ǎn.hǎ) dǎ.nes.tand/	/(u/ ǎn) dǎ.nest/

Imperfect Indicative
ماضی استمراری

(ما) می دانستیم	(من) می دانستم
/(mǎ) mi.dǎ.nes.tim/	/(man) mi.dǎ.nes.tam/
(شما) می دانستید	(تو) می دانستی
/(šo.mǎ) mi.dǎ.nes.tid/	/(to) mi.dǎ.nes.ti/
(آنها) می دانستند	(او/آن) می دانست
/(ǎn.hǎ) mi.dǎ.nes.tand/	/(u/ ǎn) mi.dǎ.nest/

Present Perfect
ماضی نقلی

(ما) دانسته ایم	(من) دانسته ام
/(mǎ) dǎ.nes.te.im/	/(man) dǎ.nes.te.am/
(شما) دانسته اید	(تو) دانسته ای
/(šo.mǎ) dǎ.nes.te.id/	/(to) dǎ.nes.te.i/
(آنها) دانسته اند	(او/آن) دانسته است
/(ǎn.hǎ) dǎ.nes.te.and/	/(u/ ǎn) dǎ.nes.te- ast/

Past Perfect
ماضی بعید

(ما) دانسته بودیم	(من) دانسته بودم
/(mǎ) dǎ.nes.te- bu.dim/	/(man) dǎ.nes.te- bu.dam/
(شما) دانسته بودید	(تو) دانسته بودی
/(šo.mǎ) dǎ.nes.te- bu.did/	/(to) dǎ.nes.te- bu.di/
(آنها) دانسته بودند	(او/آن) دانسته بود
/(ǎn.hǎ) dǎ.nes.te- bu.dand/	/(u/ ǎn) dǎ.nes.te- bud/

<table>
<tr><td colspan="2" align="center">**Past Subjunctive**
ماضی التزامی</td></tr>
<tr><td align="center">(ما) دانسته باشیم
/(mǎ) dǎ.nes.te- bǎ.šim/</td><td align="center">(من) دانسته باشم
/(man) dǎ.nes.te- bǎ.šam/</td></tr>
<tr><td align="center">(شما) دانسته باشید
/(šo.mǎ) dǎ.nes.te- bǎ.šid/</td><td align="center">(تو) دانسته باشی
/(to) dǎ.nes.te- bǎ.ši/</td></tr>
<tr><td align="center">(آنها) دانسته باشند
/(ǎn.hǎ) dǎ.nes.te- bǎ.šand/</td><td align="center">(او/آن) دانسته باشد
/(u/ ǎn) dǎ.nes.te- bǎ.šad/</td></tr>
<tr><td colspan="2" align="center">**Past Progressive**
ماضی مستمر(در جریان)</td></tr>
<tr><td align="center">(ما) داشتیم می دانستیم
/(mǎ) dǎš.tim- mi.dǎ.nes.tim/</td><td align="center">(من) داشتم می دانستم
/(man) dǎš.tam- mi.dǎ.nes.tam/</td></tr>
<tr><td align="center">(شما) داشتید می دانستید
/(šo.mǎ) dǎš.tid- mi.dǎ.nes.tid/</td><td align="center">(تو) داشتی می دانستی
/(to) dǎš.ti- mi.dǎ.nes.ti/</td></tr>
<tr><td align="center">(آنها) داشتند می دانستند
/(ǎn.hǎ) dǎš.tand- mi.dǎ.nes.tand/</td><td align="center">(او/آن) داشت می دانست
/(u/ ǎn) dǎšt- mi.dǎ.nest/</td></tr>
<tr><td colspan="2" align="center">**Simple Future**
مستقبل (آینده ساده)</td></tr>
<tr><td align="center">(ما) خواهیم دانست
/(mǎ) kǎ.him- dǎ.nest/</td><td align="center">(من) خواهم دانست
/(man) kǎ.ham- dǎ.nest/</td></tr>
<tr><td align="center">(شما) خواهید دانست
/(šo.mǎ) kǎ.hid- dǎ.nest/</td><td align="center">(تو) خواهی دانست
/(to) kǎ.hi- dǎ.nest/</td></tr>
<tr><td align="center">(آنها) خواهند دانست
/(ǎn.hǎ) kǎ.hand- dǎ.nest/</td><td align="center">(او/آن) خواهد دانست
/(u/ ǎn) kǎ.had- dǎ.nest/</td></tr>
<tr><td colspan="2" align="center">**Command**
امر</td></tr>
<tr><td align="center">بدانید!
/be.dǎ.nid/</td><td align="center">بدان!
/be.dǎn/</td></tr>
</table>

139

to laugh

خَندیدَن

/ǩan.di.dan/

Plural	Singular
Simple Present مضارع اخباری(حال ساده)	
(ما) می خندیم /(mǎ) mi.ǩan.dim/	(من) می خندم /(man) mi.ǩan.dam/
(شما) می خندید /(šo.mǎ) mi.ǩan.did/	(تو) می خندی /(to) mi.ǩan.di/
(آنها) می خندند /(ǎn.hǎ) mi.ǩan.dand/	(او/آن) می خندد /(u/ ǎn) mi.ǩan.dad/
Present Subjunctive مضارع التزامی	
(ما) بخندیم /(mǎ) be.ǩan.dim/	(من) بخندم /(man) be.ǩan.dam/
(شما) بخندید /(šo.mǎ) be.ǩan.did/	(تو) بخندی /(to) be.ǩan.di/
(آنها) بخندند /(ǎn.hǎ) be.ǩan.dand/	(او/آن) بخندد /(u/ ǎn) be.ǩan.dad/
Present Progressive مضارع مستمر(در جریان)	
(ما) داریم می خندیم /(mǎ) dǎ.rim- mi.ǩan.dim/	(من) دارم می خندم /(man) dǎ.ram- mi.ǩan.dam/
(شما) دارید می خندید /(šo.mǎ) dǎ.rid- mi.ǩan.did/	(تو) داری می خندی /(to) dǎ.ri- mi.ǩan.di/
(آنها) دارند می خندند /(ǎn.hǎ) dǎ.rand- mi.ǩan.dand/	(او/آن) دارد می خندد /(u/ ǎn) dǎ.rad- mi.ǩan.dad/

<table>
<tr><td colspan="2" align="center">Simple Past
ماضی مطلق (گذشته ساده)</td></tr>
<tr><td align="center">(ما) خندیدیم
/(mă) ǩan.di.dim/</td><td align="center">(من) خندیدم
/(man) ǩan.di.dam/</td></tr>
<tr><td align="center">(شما) خندیدید
/(šo.mă) ǩan.di.did/</td><td align="center">(تو) خندیدی
/(to) ǩan.di.di/</td></tr>
<tr><td align="center">(آنها) خندیدند
/(ăn.hă) ǩan.di.dand/</td><td align="center">(او/آن) خندید
/(u/ ăn) ǩan.did/</td></tr>
</table>

<table>
<tr><td colspan="2" align="center">Imperfect Indicative
ماضی استمراری</td></tr>
<tr><td align="center">(ما) می خندیدیم
/(mă) mi.ǩan.di.dim/</td><td align="center">(من) می خندیدم
/(man) mi.ǩan.di.dam/</td></tr>
<tr><td align="center">(شما) می خندیدید
/(šo.mă) mi.ǩan.di.did/</td><td align="center">(تو) می خندیدی
/(to) mi.ǩan.di.di/</td></tr>
<tr><td align="center">(آنها) می خندیدند
/(ăn.hă) mi.ǩan.di.dand/</td><td align="center">(او/آن) می خندید
/(u/ ăn) mi.ǩan.did/</td></tr>
</table>

<table>
<tr><td colspan="2" align="center">Present Perfect
ماضی نقلی</td></tr>
<tr><td align="center">(ما) خندیده ایم
/(mă) ǩan.di.de.im/</td><td align="center">(من) خندیده ام
/(man) ǩan.di.de.am/</td></tr>
<tr><td align="center">(شما) خندیده اید
/(šo.mă) ǩan.di.de.id/</td><td align="center">(تو) خندیده ای
/(to) ǩan.di.de.i/</td></tr>
<tr><td align="center">(آنها) خندیده اند
/(ăn.hă) ǩan.di.de.and/</td><td align="center">(او/آن) خندیده است
/(u/ ăn) ǩan.di.de- ast/</td></tr>
</table>

<table>
<tr><td colspan="2" align="center">Past Perfect
ماضی بعید</td></tr>
<tr><td align="center">(ما) خندیده بودیم
/(mă) ǩan.di.de- bu.dim/</td><td align="center">(من) خندیده بودم
/(man) ǩan.di.de- bu.dam/</td></tr>
<tr><td align="center">(شما) خندیده بودید
/(šo.mă) ǩan.di.de- bu.did/</td><td align="center">(تو) خندیده بودی
/(to) ǩan.di.de- bu.di/</td></tr>
<tr><td align="center">(آنها) خندیده بودند
/(ăn.hă) ǩan.di.de- bu.dand/</td><td align="center">(او/آن) خندیده بود
/(u/ ăn) ǩan.di.de- bud/</td></tr>
</table>

Past Subjunctive
ماضی التزامی

(ما) خندیده باشیم	(من) خندیده باشم
/(mǎ) ǩan.di.de- bǎ.šim/	/(man) ǩan.di.de- bǎ.šam/
(شما) خندیده باشید	(تو) خندیده باشی
/(šo.mǎ) ǩan.di.de- bǎ.šid/	/(to) ǩan.di.de- bǎ.ši/
(آنها) خندیده باشند	(او/آن) خندیده باشد
/(ǎn.hǎ) ǩan.di.de- bǎ.šand/	/(u/ ǎn) ǩan.di.de- bǎ.šad/

Past Progressive
ماضی مستمر(در جریان)

(ما) داشتیم می خندیدیم	(من) داشتم می خندیدم
/(mǎ) dǎš.tim- mi.ǩan.di.dim/	/(man) dǎš.tam- mi.ǩan.di.dam/
(شما) داشتید می خندیدید	(تو) داشتی می خندیدی
/(šo.mǎ) dǎš.tid- mi.ǩan.di.did/	/(to) dǎš.ti- mi.ǩan.di.di/
(آنها) داشتند می خندیدند	(او/آن) داشت می خندید
/(ǎn.hǎ) dǎš.tand- mi.ǩan.di.dand/	/(u/ ǎn) dǎšt- mi.ǩan.did/

Simple Future
مستقبل (آینده ساده)

(ما) خواهیم خندید	(من) خواهم خندید
/(mǎ) ǩǎ.him- ǩan.did/	/(man) ǩǎ.ham- ǩan.did/
(شما) خواهید خندید	(تو) خواهی خندید
/(šo.mǎ) ǩǎ.hid- ǩan.did/	/(to) ǩǎ.hi- ǩan.did/
(آنها) خواهند خندید	(او/آن) خواهد خندید
/(ǎn.hǎ) ǩǎ.hand- ǩan.did/	/(u/ ǎn) ǩǎ.had- ǩan.did/

Command
امر

بخندید!	بخند!
/be.ǩan.did/	/be.ǩand/

142

to learn

یاد گِرِفتَن

/yăd- ge.ref.tan/

Plural	Singular
Simple Present مضارع اخباری(حال ساده)	
(ما) یاد می گیریم /(mă) yăd- mi.gi.rim/	(من) یاد می گیرم /(man) yăd- mi.gi.ram/
(شما) یاد می گیرید /(šo.mă) yăd- mi.gi.rid/	(تو) یاد می گیری /(to) yăd- mi.gi.ri/
(آنها) یاد می گیرند /(ăn.hă) yăd- mi.gi.rand/	(او/آن) یاد می گیرد /(u/ ăn) yăd- mi.gi.rad/
Present Subjunctive مضارع التزامی	
(ما) یاد بگیریم /(mă) yăd- be.gi.rim/	(من) یاد بگیرم /(man) yăd- be.gi.ram/
(شما) یاد بگیرید /(šo.mă) yăd- be.gi.rid/	(تو) یاد بگیری /(to) yăd- be.gi.ri/
(آنها) یاد بگیرند /(ăn.hă) yăd- be.gi.rand/	(او/آن) یاد بگیرد /(u/ ăn) yăd- be.gi.rad/
Present Progressive مضارع مستمر(در جریان)	
(ما) داریم یاد می گیریم /(mă) dă.rim- yăd- mi.gi.rim/	(من) دارم یاد می گیرم /(man) dă.ram- yăd- mi.gi.ram/
(شما) دارید یاد می گیرید /(šo.mă) dă.rid- yăd- mi.gi.rid/	(تو) داری یاد می گیری /(to) dă.ri- yăd- mi.gi.ri/
(آنها) دارند یاد می گیرند /(ăn.hă) dă.rand- yăd- mi.gi.rand/	(او/آن) دارد یاد می گیرد /(u/ ăn) dă.rad- yăd- mi.gi.rad/

Simple Past	
ماضی مطلق (گذشته ساده)	
(ما) یاد گرفتیم /(mǎ) yǎd- ge.ref.tim/	(من) یاد گرفتم /(man) yǎd- ge.ref.tam/
(شما) یاد گرفتید /(šo.mǎ) yǎd- ge.ref.tid/	(تو) یاد گرفتی /(to) yǎd- ge.ref.ti/
(آنها) یاد گرفتند /(ǎn.hǎ) yǎd- ge.ref.tand/	(او/آن) یاد گرفت /(u/ ǎn) yǎd- ge.reft/

Imperfect Indicative	
ماضی استمراری	
(ما) یاد می گرفتیم /(mǎ) yǎd- mi.ge.ref.tim/	(من) یاد می گرفتم /(man) yǎd- mi.ge.ref.tam/
(شما) یاد می گرفتید /(šo.mǎ) yǎd- mi.ge.ref.tid/	(تو) یاد می گرفتی /(to) yǎd- mi.ge.ref.ti/
(آنها) یاد می گرفتند /(ǎn.hǎ) yǎd- mi.ge.ref.tand/	(او/آن) یاد می گرفت /(u/ ǎn) yǎd- mi.ge.reft/

Present Perfect	
ماضی نقلی	
(ما) یاد گرفته ایم /(mǎ) yǎd- ge.ref.te.im/	(من) یاد گرفته ام /(man) yǎd- ge.ref.te.am/
(شما) یاد گرفته اید /(šo.mǎ) yǎd- ge.ref.te.id/	(تو) یاد گرفته ای /(to) yǎd- ge.ref.te.i/
(آنها) یاد گرفته اند /(ǎn.hǎ) yǎd- ge.ref.te.and/	(او/آن) یاد گرفته است /(u/ ǎn) yǎd- ge.ref.te- ast/

Past Perfect	
ماضی بعید	
(ما) یاد گرفته بودیم /(mǎ) yǎd- ge.ref.te- bu.dim/	(من) یاد گرفته بودم /(man) yǎd- ge.ref.te- bu.dam/
(شما) یاد گرفته بودید /(šo.mǎ) yǎd- ge.ref.te- bu.did/	(تو) یاد گرفته بودی /(to) yǎd- ge.ref.te- bu.di/
(آنها) یاد گرفته بودند /(ǎn.hǎ) yǎd- ge.ref.te- bu.dand/	(او/آن) یاد گرفته بود /(u/ ǎn) yǎd- ge.ref.te- bud/

144

Past Subjunctive	
ماضی التزامی	
(ما) یاد گرفته باشیم	(من) یاد گرفته باشم
/(mǎ) yǎd- ge.ref.te- bǎ.šim/	/(man) yǎd- ge.ref.te- bǎ.šam/
(شما) یاد گرفته باشید	(تو) یاد گرفته باشی
/(šo.mǎ) yǎd- ge.ref.te- bǎ.šid/	/(to) yǎd- ge.ref.te- bǎ.ši/
(آنها) یاد گرفته باشند	(او/آن) یاد گرفته باشد
/(ǎn.hǎ) yǎd- ge.ref.te- bǎ.šand/	/(u/ ǎn) yǎd- ge.ref.te- bǎ.šad/

Past Progressive	
ماضی مستمر(در جریان)	
(ما) داشتیم یاد می گرفتیم	(من) داشتم یاد می گرفتم
/(mǎ) dǎš.tim- yǎd- mi.ge.ref.tim/	/(man) dǎš.tam- yǎd- mi.ge.ref.tam/
(شما) داشتید یاد می گرفتید	(تو) داشتی یاد می گرفتی
/(šo.mǎ) dǎš.tid- yǎd- mi.ge.ref.tid/	/(to) dǎš.ti- yǎd- mi.ge.ref.ti/
(آنها) داشتند یاد می گرفتند	(او/آن) داشت یاد می گرفت
/(ǎn.hǎ) dǎš.tand- yǎd- mi.ge.ref.tand/	/(u/ ǎn) dǎšt- yǎd- mi.ge.reft/

Simple Future	
مستقبل (آینده ساده)	
(ما) یاد خواهیم گرفت	(من) یاد خواهم گرفت
/(mǎ) yǎd- ǩǎ.him- ge.reft/	/(man) yǎd- ǩǎ.ham- ge.reft/
(شما) یاد خواهید گرفت	(تو) یاد خواهی گرفت
/(šo.mǎ) yǎd- ǩǎ.hid- ge.reft/	/(to) yǎd- ǩǎ.hi- ge.reft/
(آنها) یاد خواهند گرفت	(او/آن) یاد خواهد گرفت
/(ǎn.hǎ) yǎd- ǩǎ.hand- ge.reft/	/(u/ ǎn) yǎd- ǩǎ.had- ge.reft/

Command	
امر	
یاد بگیرید!	یاد بگیر!
/yǎd- be.gi.rid/	/yǎd- be.gir/

to listen

گوش دادَن

/guš- dǎ.dan/

Plural	Singular
Simple Present <div dir="rtl">مضارع اخباری(حال ساده)</div>	
(ما) گوش می دهیم /(mǎ) guš- mi.da.him/	(من) گوش می دهم /(man) guš- mi.da.ham/
(شما) گوش می دهید /(šo.mǎ) guš- mi.da.hid/	(تو) گوش می دهی /(to) guš- mi.da.hi/
(آنها) گوش می دهند /(ǎn.hǎ) guš- mi.da.hand/	(او/آن) گوش می دهد /(u/ ǎn) guš- mi.da.had/
Present Subjunctive <div dir="rtl">مضارع التزامی</div>	
(ما) گوش بدهیم /(mǎ) guš- be.da.him/	(من) گوش بدهم /(man) guš- be.da.ham/
(شما) گوش بدهید /(šo.mǎ) guš- be.da.hid/	(تو) گوش بدهی /(to) guš- be.da.hi/
(آنها) گوش بدهند /(ǎn.hǎ) guš- be.da.hand/	(او/آن) گوش بدهد /(u/ ǎn) guš- be.da.had/
Present Progressive <div dir="rtl">مضارع مستمر(در جریان)</div>	
(ما) داریم گوش می دهیم /(mǎ) dǎ.rim- guš- mi.da.him/	(من) دارم گوش می دهم /(man) dǎ.ram- guš- mi.da.ham/
(شما) دارید گوش می دهید /(šo.mǎ) dǎ.rid- guš- mi.da.hid/	(تو) داری گوش می دهی /(to) dǎ.ri- guš- mi.da.hi/
(آنها) دارند گوش می دهند /(ǎn.hǎ) dǎ.rand- guš- mi.da.hand/	(او/آن) دارد گوش می دهد /(u/ ǎn) dǎ.rad- guš- mi.da.had/

Simple Past
ماضی مطلق (گذشته ساده)

(ما) گوش دادیم	(من) گوش دادم
/(mă) guš- dă.dim/	/(man) guš- dă.dam/
(شما) گوش دادید	(تو) گوش دادی
/(šo.mă) guš- dă.did/	/(to) guš- dă.di/
(آنها) گوش دادند	(او/آن) گوش داد
/(ăn.hă) guš- dă.dand/	/(u/ ăn) guš- dăd/

Imperfect Indicative
ماضی استمراری

(ما) گوش می دادیم	(من) گوش می دادم
/(mă) guš- mi.dă.dim/	/(man) guš- mi.dă.dam/
(شما) گوش می دادید	(تو) گوش می دادی
/(šo.mă) guš- mi.dă.did/	/(to) guš- mi.dă.di/
(آنها) گوش می دادند	(او/آن) گوش می داد
/(ăn.hă) guš- mi.dă.dand/	/(u/ ăn) guš- mi.dăd/

Present Perfect
ماضی نقلی

(ما) گوش داده ایم	(من) گوش داده ام
/(mă) guš- dă.de.im/	/(man) guš- dă.de.am/
(شما) گوش داده اید	(تو) گوش داده ای
/(šo.mă) guš- dă.de.id/	/(to) guš- dă.de.i/
(آنها) گوش داده اند	(او/آن) گوش داده است
/(ăn.hă) guš- dă.de.and/	/(u/ ăn) guš- dă.de- ast/

Past Perfect
ماضی بعید

(ما) گوش داده بودیم	(من) گوش داده بودم
/(mă) guš- dă.de- bu.dim/	/(man) guš- dă.de- bu.dam/
(شما) گوش داده بودید	(تو) گوش داده بودی
/(šo.mă) guš- dă.de- bu.did/	/(to) guš- dă.de- bu.di/
(آنها) گوش داده بودند	(او/آن) گوش داده بود
/(ăn.hă) guš- dă.de- bu.dand/	/(u/ ăn) guš- dă.de- bud/

<table>
<tr><td colspan="2" align="center">**Past Subjunctive**
ماضی التزامی</td></tr>
<tr>
<td align="center">(ما) گوش داده باشیم
/(mă) guš- dă.de- bă.šim/</td>
<td align="center">(من) گوش داده باشم
/(man) guš- dă.de- bă.šam/</td>
</tr>
<tr>
<td align="center">(شما) گوش داده باشید
/(šo.mă) guš- dă.de- bă.šid/</td>
<td align="center">(تو) گوش داده باشی
/(to) guš- dă.de- bă.ši/</td>
</tr>
<tr>
<td align="center">(آنها) گوش داده باشند
/(ăn.hă) guš- dă.de- bă.šand/</td>
<td align="center">(او/آن) گوش داده باشد
/(u/ ăn) guš- dă.de- bă.šad/</td>
</tr>
</table>

<table>
<tr><td colspan="2" align="center">**Past Progressive**
ماضی مستمر(در جریان)</td></tr>
<tr>
<td align="center">(ما) داشتیم گوش می دادیم
/(mă) dăš.tim- guš- mi.dă.dim/</td>
<td align="center">(من) داشتم گوش می دادم
/(man) dăš.tam- guš- mi.dă.dam/</td>
</tr>
<tr>
<td align="center">(شما) داشتید گوش می دادید
/(šo.mă) dăš.tid- guš- mi.dă.did/</td>
<td align="center">(تو) داشتی گوش می دادی
/(to) dăš.ti- guš- mi.dă.di/</td>
</tr>
<tr>
<td align="center">(آنها) داشتند گوش می دادند
/(ăn.hă) dăš.tand- guš- mi.dă.dand/</td>
<td align="center">(او/آن) داشت گوش می داد
/(u/ ăn) dăšt- guš- mi.dăd/</td>
</tr>
</table>

<table>
<tr><td colspan="2" align="center">**Simple Future**
مستقبل (آینده ساده)</td></tr>
<tr>
<td align="center">(ما) گوش خواهیم داد
/(mă) guš- kă.him- dăd/</td>
<td align="center">(من) گوش خواهم داد
/(man) guš- kă.ham- dăd/</td>
</tr>
<tr>
<td align="center">(شما) گوش خواهید داد
/(šo.mă) guš- kă.hid- dăd/</td>
<td align="center">(تو) گوش خواهی داد
/(to) guš- kă.hi- dăd/</td>
</tr>
<tr>
<td align="center">(آنها) گوش خواهند داد
/(ăn.hă) guš- kă.hand- dăd/</td>
<td align="center">(او/آن) گوش خواهد داد
/(u/ ăn) guš- kă.had- dăd/</td>
</tr>
</table>

<table>
<tr><td colspan="2" align="center">**Command**
امر</td></tr>
<tr>
<td align="center">گوش بدهید!
/guš- be.da.hid/</td>
<td align="center">گوش بده!
/guš- be.de/</td>
</tr>
</table>

148

to live

زِندِگی کَردَن

/ze.de.gi- kar.dan/

Plural	Singular
Simple Present <div dir="rtl">مضارع اخباری(حال ساده)</div>	
<div dir="rtl">(ما) زندگی می کنیم</div> /(mǎ) zen.de.gi- mi.ko.nim/	<div dir="rtl">(من) زندگی می کنم</div> /(man) zen.de.gi- mi.ko.nam/
<div dir="rtl">(شما) زندگی می کنید</div> /(šo.mǎ) zen.de.gi- mi.ko.nid/	<div dir="rtl">(تو) زندگی می کنی</div> /(to) zen.de.gi- mi.ko.ni/
<div dir="rtl">(آنها) زندگی می کنند</div> /(ǎn.hǎ) zen.de.gi- mi.ko.nand/	<div dir="rtl">(او/آن) زندگی می کند</div> /(u/ ǎn) zen.de.gi- mi.ko.nad/
Present Subjunctive <div dir="rtl">مضارع التزامی</div>	
<div dir="rtl">(ما) زندگی بکنیم</div> /(mǎ) zen.de.gi- be.ko.nim/	<div dir="rtl">(من) زندگی بکنم</div> /(man) zen.de.gi- be.ko.nam/
<div dir="rtl">(شما) زندگی بکنید</div> /(šo.mǎ) zen.de.gi- be.ko.nid/	<div dir="rtl">(تو) زندگی بکنی</div> /(to) zen.de.gi- be.ko.ni/
<div dir="rtl">(آنها) زندگی بکنند</div> /(ǎn.hǎ) zen.de.gi- be.ko.nand/	<div dir="rtl">(او/آن) زندگی بکند</div> /(u/ ǎn) zen.de.gi- be.ko.nad/
Present Progressive <div dir="rtl">مضارع مستمر(در جریان)</div>	
<div dir="rtl">(ما) داریم زندگی می کنیم</div> /(mǎ) dǎ.rim- zen.de.gi- mi.ko.nim/	<div dir="rtl">(من) دارم زندگی می کنم</div> /(man) dǎ.ram- zen.de.gi- mi.ko.nam/
<div dir="rtl">(شما) دارید زندگی می کنید</div> /(šo.mǎ) dǎ.rid- zen.de.gi- mi.ko.nid/	<div dir="rtl">(تو) داری زندگی می کنی</div> /(to) dǎ.ri- zen.de.gi- mi.ko.ni/
<div dir="rtl">(آنها) دارند زندگی می کنند</div> /(ǎn.hǎ) dǎ.rand- zen.de.gi- mi.ko.nand/	<div dir="rtl">(او/آن) دارد زندگی می کند</div> /(u/ ǎn) dǎ.rad- zen.de.gi- mi.ko.nad/

Simple Past
ماضی مطلق (گذشته ساده)

(ما) زندگی کردیم	(من) زندگی کردم
/(mǎ) zen.de.gi- kar.dim/	/(man) zen.de.gi- kar.dam/
(شما) زندگی کردید	(تو) زندگی کردی
/(šo.mǎ) zen.de.gi- kar.did/	/(to) zen.de.gi- kar.di/
(آنها) زندگی کردند	(او/آن) زندگی کرد
/(ǎn.hǎ) zen.de.gi- kar.dand/	/(u/ ǎn) zen.de.gi- kard/

Imperfect Indicative
ماضی استمراری

(ما) زندگی می کردیم	(من) زندگی می کردم
/(mǎ) zen.de.gi- mi.kar.dim/	/(man) zen.de.gi- mi.kar.dam/
(شما) زندگی می کردید	(تو) زندگی می کردی
/(šo.mǎ) zen.de.gi- mi.kar.did/	/(to) zen.de.gi- mi.kar.di/
(آنها) زندگی می کردند	(او/آن) زندگی می کرد
/(ǎn.hǎ) zen.de.gi- mi.kar.dand/	/(u/ ǎn) zen.de.gi- mi.kard/

Present Perfect
ماضی نقلی

(ما) زندگی کرده ایم	(من) زندگی کرده ام
/(mǎ) zen.de.gi- kar.de.im/	/(man) zen.de.gi- kar.de.am/
(شما) زندگی کرده اید	(تو) زندگی کرده ای
/(šo.mǎ) zen.de.gi- kar.de.id/	/(to) zen.de.gi- kar.de.i/
(آنها) زندگی کرده اند	(او/آن) زندگی کرده است
/(ǎn.hǎ) zen.de.gi- kar.de.and/	/(u/ ǎn) zen.de.gi- kar.de- ast/

Past Perfect
ماضی بعید

(ما) زندگی کرده بودیم	(من) زندگی کرده بودم
/(mǎ) zen.de.gi- kar.de- bu.dim/	/(man) zen.de.gi- kar.de- bu.dam/
(شما) زندگی کرده بودید	(تو) زندگی کرده بودی
/(šo.mǎ) zen.de.gi- kar.de- bu.did/	/(to) zen.de.gi- kar.de- bu.di/
(آنها) زندگی کرده بودند	(او/آن) زندگی کرده بود
/(ǎn.hǎ) zen.de.gi- kar.de- bu.dand/	/(u/ ǎn) zen.de.gi- kar.de- bud/

<table>
<tr><td colspan="2" align="center">**Past Subjunctive**
ماضی التزامی</td></tr>
<tr>
<td align="center">(ما) زندگی کرده باشیم
/(mă) zen.de.gi- kar.de- bă.šim/</td>
<td align="center">(من) زندگی کرده باشم
/(man) zen.de.gi- kar.de- bă.šam/</td>
</tr>
<tr>
<td align="center">(شما) زندگی کرده باشید
/(šo.mă) zen.de.gi- kar.de- bă.šid/</td>
<td align="center">(تو) زندگی کرده باشی
/(to) zen.de.gi- kar.de- bă.ši/</td>
</tr>
<tr>
<td align="center">(آنها) زندگی کرده باشند
/(ăn.hă) zen.de.gi- kar.de- bă.šand/</td>
<td align="center">(او/آن) زندگی کرده باشد
/(u/ ăn) zen.de.gi- kar.de- bă.šad/</td>
</tr>
</table>

<table>
<tr><td colspan="2" align="center">**Past Progressive**
ماضی مستمر(در جریان)</td></tr>
<tr>
<td align="center">(ما) داشتیم زندگی می کردیم
/(mă) dăš.tim- zen.de.gi- mi.kar.dim/</td>
<td align="center">(من) داشتم زندگی می کردم
/(man) dăš.tam- zen.de.gi- mi.kar.dam/</td>
</tr>
<tr>
<td align="center">(شما) داشتید زندگی می کردید
/(šo.mă) dăš.tid- zen.de.gi- mi.kar.did/</td>
<td align="center">(تو) داشتی زندگی می کردی
/(to) dăš.ti- zen.de.gi- mi.kar.di/</td>
</tr>
<tr>
<td align="center">(آنها) داشتند زندگی می کردند
/(ăn.hă) dăš.tand- zen.de.gi- mi.kar.dand/</td>
<td align="center">(او/آن) داشت زندگی می کرد
/(u/ ăn) dăšt- zen.de.gi- mi.kard/</td>
</tr>
</table>

<table>
<tr><td colspan="2" align="center">**Simple Future**
مستقبل (آینده ساده)</td></tr>
<tr>
<td align="center">(ما) زندگی خواهیم کرد
/(mă) zen.de.gi- kă.him- kard/</td>
<td align="center">(من) زندگی خواهم کرد
/(man) zen.de.gi- kă.ham- kard/</td>
</tr>
<tr>
<td align="center">(شما) زندگی خواهید کرد
/(šo.mă) zen.de.gi- kă.hid- kard/</td>
<td align="center">(تو) زندگی خواهی کرد
/(to) zen.de.gi- kă.hi- kard/</td>
</tr>
<tr>
<td align="center">(آنها) زندگی خواهند کرد
/(ăn.hă) zen.de.gi- kă.hand- kard/</td>
<td align="center">(او/آن) زندگی خواهد کرد
/(u/ ăn) zen.de.gi- kă.had- kard/</td>
</tr>
</table>

<table>
<tr><td colspan="2" align="center">**Command**
امر</td></tr>
<tr>
<td align="center">* زندگی بکنید!
/zen.de.gi- be.ko.nid/</td>
<td align="center">* زندگی بکن!
/zen.de.gi- be.kon/</td>
</tr>
</table>

* also: زندگی کن!   زندگی کنید!

to lose

گُم کَردَن

/gom- kar.dan/

Plural	Singular
Simple Present <div dir="rtl">مضارع اخباری(حال ساده)</div>	
<div dir="rtl">(ما) گم می کنیم</div> /(mǎ) gom- mi.ko.nim/	<div dir="rtl">(من) گم می کنم</div> /(man) gom- mi.ko.nam/
<div dir="rtl">(شما) گم می کنید</div> /(šo.mǎ) gom- mi.ko.nid/	<div dir="rtl">(تو) گم می کنی</div> /(to) gom- mi.ko.ni/
<div dir="rtl">(آنها) گم می کنند</div> /(ǎn.hǎ) gom- mi.ko.nand/	<div dir="rtl">(او/آن) گم می کند</div> /(u/ ǎn) gom- mi.ko.nad/
Present Subjunctive <div dir="rtl">مضارع التزامی</div>	
<div dir="rtl">(ما) گم بکنیم</div> /(mǎ) gom- be.ko.nim/	<div dir="rtl">(من) گم بکنم</div> /(man) gom- be.ko.nam/
<div dir="rtl">(شما) گم بکنید</div> /(šo.mǎ) gom- be.ko.nid/	<div dir="rtl">(تو) گم بکنی</div> /(to) gom- be.ko.ni/
<div dir="rtl">(آنها) گم بکنند</div> /(ǎn.hǎ) gom- be.ko.nand/	<div dir="rtl">(او/آن) گم بکند</div> /(u/ ǎn) gom- be.ko.nad/
Present Progressive <div dir="rtl">مضارع مستمر(در جریان)</div>	
<div dir="rtl">(ما) داریم گم می کنیم</div> /(mǎ) dǎ.rim- gom- mi.ko.nim/	<div dir="rtl">(من) دارم گم می کنم</div> /(man) dǎ.ram- gom- mi.ko.nam/
<div dir="rtl">(شما) دارید گم می کنید</div> /(šo.mǎ) dǎ.rid- gom- mi.ko.nid/	<div dir="rtl">(تو) داری گم می کنی</div> /(to) dǎ.ri- gom- mi.ko.ni/
<div dir="rtl">(آنها) دارند گم می کنند</div> /(ǎn.hǎ) dǎ.rand- gom- mi.ko.nand/	<div dir="rtl">(او/آن) دارد گم می کند</div> /(u/ ǎn) dǎ.rad- gom- mi.ko.nad/

<table>
<tr><td colspan="2" align="center">**Simple Past**
ماضی مطلق (گذشته ساده)</td></tr>
<tr><td align="center">(ما) گم کردیم
/(mǎ) gom- kar.dim/</td><td align="center">(من) گم کردم
/(man) gom- kar.dam/</td></tr>
<tr><td align="center">(شما) گم کردید
/(šo.mǎ) gom- kar.did/</td><td align="center">(تو) گم کردی
/(to) gom- kar.di/</td></tr>
<tr><td align="center">(آنها) گم کردند
/(ǎn.hǎ) gom- kar.dand/</td><td align="center">(او/آن) گم کرد
/(u/ ǎn) gom- kard/</td></tr>
</table>

<table>
<tr><td colspan="2" align="center">**Imperfect Indicative**
ماضی استمراری</td></tr>
<tr><td align="center">(ما) گم می کردیم
/(mǎ) gom- mi.kar.dim/</td><td align="center">(من) گم می کردم
/(man) gom- mi.kar.dam/</td></tr>
<tr><td align="center">(شما) گم می کردید
/(šo.mǎ) gom- mi.kar.did/</td><td align="center">(تو) گم می کردی
/(to) gom- mi.kar.di/</td></tr>
<tr><td align="center">(آنها) گم می کردند
/(ǎn.hǎ) gom- mi.kar.dand/</td><td align="center">(او/آن) گم می کرد
/(u/ ǎn) gom- mi.kard/</td></tr>
</table>

<table>
<tr><td colspan="2" align="center">**Present Perfect**
ماضی نقلی</td></tr>
<tr><td align="center">(ما) گم کرده ایم
/(mǎ) gom- kar.de.im/</td><td align="center">(من) گم کرده ام
/(man) gom- kar.de.am/</td></tr>
<tr><td align="center">(شما) گم کرده اید
/(šo.mǎ) gom- kar.de.id/</td><td align="center">(تو) گم کرده ای
/(to) gom- kar.de.i/</td></tr>
<tr><td align="center">(آنها) گم کرده اند
/(ǎn.hǎ) gom- kar.de.and/</td><td align="center">(او/آن) گم کرده است
/(u/ ǎn) gom- kar.de- ast/</td></tr>
</table>

<table>
<tr><td colspan="2" align="center">**Past Perfect**
ماضی بعید</td></tr>
<tr><td align="center">(ما) گم کرده بودیم
/(mǎ) gom- kar.de- bu.dim/</td><td align="center">(من) گم کرده بودم
/(man) gom- kar.de- bu.dam/</td></tr>
<tr><td align="center">(شما) گم کرده بودید
/(šo.mǎ) gom- kar.de- bu.did/</td><td align="center">(تو) گم کرده بودی
/(to) gom- kar.de- bu.di/</td></tr>
<tr><td align="center">(آنها) گم کرده بودند
/(ǎn.hǎ) gom- kar.de- bu.dand/</td><td align="center">(او/آن) گم کرده بود
/(u/ ǎn) gom- kar.de- bud/</td></tr>
</table>

<table>
<tr><th colspan="2">Past Subjunctive
ماضی التزامی</th></tr>
</table>

(ما) گم کرده باشیم	(من) گم کرده باشم
/(mă) gom- kar.de- bă.šim/	/(man) gom- kar.de- bă.šam/
(شما) گم کرده باشید	(تو) گم کرده باشی
/(šo.mă) gom- kar.de- bă.šid/	/(to) gom- kar.de- bă.ši/
(آنها) گم کرده باشند	(او/آن) گم کرده باشد
/(ăn.hă) gom- kar.de- bă.šand/	/(u/ ăn) gom- kar.de- bă.šad/

<table>
<tr><th colspan="2">Past Progressive
ماضی مستمر(در جریان)</th></tr>
</table>

(ما) داشتیم گم می کردیم	(من) داشتم گم می کردم
/(mă) dăš.tim- gom- mi.kar.dim/	/(man) dăš.tam- gom- mi.kar.dam/
(شما) داشتید گم می کردید	(تو) داشتی گم می کردی
/(šo.mă) dăš.tid- gom- mi.kar.did/	/(to) dăš.ti- gom- mi.kar.di/
(آنها) داشتند گم می کردند	(او/آن) داشت گم می کرد
/(ăn.hă) dăš.tand- gom- mi.kar.dand/	/(u/ ăn) dăšt- gom- mi.kard/

<table>
<tr><th colspan="2">Simple Future
مستقبل (آینده ساده)</th></tr>
</table>

(ما) گم خواهیم کرد	(من) گم خواهم کرد
/(mă) gom- kă.him- kard/	/(man) gom- kă.ham- kard/
(شما) گم خواهید کرد	(تو) گم خواهی کرد
/(šo.mă) gom- kă.hid- kard	/(to) gom- kă.hi- kard/
(آنها) گم خواهند کرد	(او/آن) گم خواهد کرد
/(ăn.hă) gom- kă.hand- kard/	/(u/ ăn) gom- kă.had- kard/

<table>
<tr><th colspan="2">Command
امر</th></tr>
</table>

* گم بکنید!	* گم بکن!
/gom- be.ko.nid/	/gom- be.kon/

* also: گم کنید!   گم کن!

to love

دوست داشتَن

/dust- dăš.tan/

Plural	Singular
Simple Present مضارع اخباری(حال ساده)	
(ما) دوست داریم /(mă) dust- dă.rim/	(من) دوست دارم /(man) dust- dă.ram/
(شما) دوست دارید /(šo.mă) dust- dă.rid/	(تو) دوست داری /(to) dust- dă.ri/
(آنها) دوست دارند /(ăn.hă) dust- dă.rand/	(او/آن) دوست دارد /(u/ ăn) dust- dă.rad/

Plural	Singular
Present Subjunctive مضارع التزامی	
(ما) دوست بداریم /(mă) dust- be.dă.rim/	(من) دوست بدارم /(man) dust- be.dă.ram/
(شما) دوست بدارید /(šo.mă) dust- be.dă.rid/	(تو) دوست بداری /(to) dust- be.dă.ri/
(آنها) دوست بدارند /(ăn.hă) dust- be.dă.rand/	(او/آن) دوست بدارد /(u/ ăn) dust- be.dă.rad/

Plural	Singular
Present Progressive مضارع مستمر(در جریان)	
(ما) داریم دوست می داریم /(mă) dă.rim- dust- mi.dă.rim/	(من) دارم دوست می دارم /(man) dă.ram- dust- mi.dă.ram/
(شما) دارید دوست می دارید /(šo.mă) dă.rid- dust- mi.dă.rid/	(تو) داری دوست می داری /(to) dă.ri- dust- mi.dă.ri/
(آنها) دارند دوست می دارند /(ăn.hă) dă.rand- dust- mi.dă.rand/	(او/آن) دارد دوست می دارد /(u/ ăn) dă.rad- dust- mi.dă.rad/

Simple Past
ماضی مطلق (گذشته ساده)

(ما) دوست داشتیم	(من) دوست داشتم
/(mă) dust- dăš.tim/	/(man) dust- dăš.tam/
(شما) دوست داشتید	(تو) دوست داشتی
/(šo.mă) dust- dăš.tid/	/(to) dust- dăš.ti/
(آنها) دوست داشتند	(او/آن) دوست داشت
/(ăn.hă) dust- dăš.tand/	/(u/ ăn) dust- dăšt/

Imperfect Indicative
ماضی استمراری

(ما) دوست می داشتیم	(من) دوست می داشتم
/(mă) dust- mi.dăš.tim/	/(man) dust- mi.dăš.tam/
(شما) دوست می داشتید	(تو) دوست می داشتی
/(šo.mă) dust- mi.dăš.tid/	/(to) dust- mi.dăš.ti/
(آنها) دوست می داشتند	(او/آن) دوست می داشت
/(ăn.hă) dust- mi.dăš.tand/	/(u/ ăn) dust- mi.dăšt/

Present Perfect
ماضی نقلی

(ما) دوست داشته ایم	(من) دوست داشته ام
/(mă) dust- dăš.te.im/	/(man) dust- dăš.te.am/
(شما) دوست داشته اید	(تو) دوست داشته ای
/(šo.mă) dust- dăš.te.id/	/(to) dust- dăš.te.i/
(آنها) دوست داشته اند	(او/آن) دوست داشته است
/(ăn.hă) dust- dăš.te.and/	/(u/ ăn) dust- dăš.te- ast/

Past Perfect
ماضی بعید

(ما) دوست داشته بودیم	(من) دوست داشته بودم
/(mă) dust- dăš.te- bu.dim/	/(man) dust- dăš.te- bu.dam/
(شما) دوست داشته بودید	(تو) دوست داشته بودی
/(šo.mă) dust- dăš.te- bu.did/	/(to) dust- dăš.te- bu.di/
(آنها) دوست داشته بودند	(او/آن) دوست داشته بود
/(ăn.hă) dust- dăš.te- bu.dand/	/(u/ ăn) dust- dăš.te- bud/

<table>
<tr><td colspan="2" align="center">**Past Subjunctive**
ماضی التزامی</td></tr>
<tr>
<td align="center">(ما) دوست داشته باشیم
/(mǎ) dust- dǎš.te- bǎ.šim/</td>
<td align="center">(من) دوست داشته باشم
/(man) dust- dǎš.te- bǎ.šam/</td>
</tr>
<tr>
<td align="center">(شما) دوست داشته باشید
/(šo.mǎ) dust- dǎš.te- bǎ.šid/</td>
<td align="center">(تو) دوست داشته باشی
/(to) dust- dǎš.te- bǎ.ši/</td>
</tr>
<tr>
<td align="center">(آنها) دوست داشته باشند
/(ǎn.hǎ) dust- dǎš.te- bǎ.šand/</td>
<td align="center">(او/آن) دوست داشته باشد
/(u/ ǎn) dust- dǎš.te- bǎ.šad/</td>
</tr>
</table>

<table>
<tr><td colspan="2" align="center">**Past Progressive**
ماضی مستمر(در جریان)</td></tr>
<tr>
<td align="center">(ما) داشتیم دوست می داشتیم
/(mǎ) dǎš.tim- dust- mi.dǎš.tim/</td>
<td align="center">(من) داشتم دوست می داشتم
/(man) dǎš.tam- dust- mi.dǎš.tam/</td>
</tr>
<tr>
<td align="center">(شما) داشتید دوست می داشتید
/(šo.mǎ) dǎš.tid- dust- mi.dǎš.tid/</td>
<td align="center">(تو) داشتی دوست می داشتی
/(to) dǎš.ti- dust- mi.dǎš.ti/</td>
</tr>
<tr>
<td align="center">(آنها) داشتند دوست می داشتند
/(ǎn.hǎ) dǎš.tand- dust- mi.dǎš.tand/</td>
<td align="center">(او/آن) داشت دوست می داشت
/(u/ ǎn) dǎšt- dust- mi.dǎšt/</td>
</tr>
</table>

<table>
<tr><td colspan="2" align="center">**Simple Future**
مستقبل (آینده ساده)</td></tr>
<tr>
<td align="center">(ما) دوست خواهیم داشت
/(mǎ) dust- ǩǎ.him- dǎšt/</td>
<td align="center">(من) دوست خواهم داشت
/(man) dust- ǩǎ.ham- dǎšt/</td>
</tr>
<tr>
<td align="center">(شما) دوست خواهید داشت
/(šo.mǎ) dust- ǩǎ.hid- dǎšt/</td>
<td align="center">(تو) دوست خواهی داشت
/(to) dust- ǩǎ.hi- dǎšt/</td>
</tr>
<tr>
<td align="center">(آنها) دوست خواهند داشت
/(ǎn.hǎ) dust- ǩǎ.hand- dǎšt/</td>
<td align="center">(او/آن) دوست خواهد داشت
/(u/ ǎn) dust- ǩǎ.had- dǎšt/</td>
</tr>
</table>

<table>
<tr><td colspan="2" align="center">**Command**
امر</td></tr>
<tr>
<td align="center">* دوست بدارید!
/dust- be.dǎ.rid/</td>
<td align="center">* دوست بدار!
/dust- be.dǎr/</td>
</tr>
</table>

* also: دوست داشته باشید!   دوست داشته باش!

to measure

اَندازه گِرفتَن

/an.dă.ze- ge.ref.tan/

Plural	Singular
Simple Present مضارع اخباری(حال ساده)	
(ما) اندازه می گیریم /(mă) an.dă.ze- mi.gi.rim/	(من) اندازه می گیرم /(man) an.dă.ze- mi.gi.ram/
(شما) اندازه می گیرید /(šo.mă) an.dă.ze- mi.gi.rid/	(تو) اندازه می گیری /(to) an.dă.ze- mi.gi.ri/
(آنها) اندازه می گیرند /(ăn.hă) an.dă.ze- mi.gi.rand/	(او/آن) اندازه می گیرد /(u/ ăn) an.dă.ze- mi.gi.rad/
Present Subjunctive مضارع التزامی	
(ما) اندازه بگیریم /(mă) an.dă.ze- be.gi.rim/	(من) اندازه بگیرم /(man) an.dă.ze- be.gi.ram/
(شما) اندازه بگیرید /(šo.mă) an.dă.ze- be.gi.rid/	(تو) اندازه بگیری /(to) an.dă.ze- be.gi.ri/
(آنها) اندازه بگیرند /(ăn.hă) an.dă.ze- be.gi.rand/	(او/آن) اندازه بگیرد /(u/ ăn) an.dă.ze- be.gi.rad/
Present Progressive مضارع مستمر(در جریان)	
(ما) داریم اندازه می گیریم /(mă) dă.rim- an.dă.ze- mi.gi.rim/	(من) دارم اندازه می گیرم /(man) dă.ram- an.dă.ze- mi.gi.ram/
(شما) دارید اندازه می گیرید /(šo.mă) dă.rid- an.dă.ze- mi.gi.rid/	(تو) داری اندازه می گیری /(to) dă.ri- an.dă.ze- mi.gi.ri/
(آنها) دارند اندازه می گیرند /(ăn.hă) dă.rand- an.dă.ze- mi.gi.rand/	(او/آن) دارد اندازه می گیرد /(u/ ăn) dă.rad- an.dă.ze- mi.gi.rad/

<table>
<tr><td colspan="2" align="center">**Simple Past**
ماضی مطلق (گذشته ساده)</td></tr>
<tr>
<td align="center">(ما) اندازه گرفتیم
/(mǎ) an.dǎ.ze- ge.ref.tim/</td>
<td align="center">(من) اندازه گرفتم
/(man) an.dǎ.ze- ge.ref.tam/</td>
</tr>
<tr>
<td align="center">(شما) اندازه گرفتید
/(šo.mǎ) an.dǎ.ze- ge.ref.tid/</td>
<td align="center">(تو) اندازه گرفتی
/(to) an.dǎ.ze- ge.ref.ti/</td>
</tr>
<tr>
<td align="center">(آنها) اندازه گرفتند
/(ǎn.hǎ) an.dǎ.ze- ge.ref.tand/</td>
<td align="center">(او/ آن) اندازه گرفت
/(u/ ǎn) an.dǎ.ze- ge.reft/</td>
</tr>
</table>

<table>
<tr><td colspan="2" align="center">**Imperfect Indicative**
ماضی استمراری</td></tr>
<tr>
<td align="center">(ما) اندازه می گرفتیم
/(mǎ) an.dǎ.ze- mi.ge.ref.tim/</td>
<td align="center">(من) اندازه می گرفتم
/(man) an.dǎ.ze- mi.ge.ref.tam/</td>
</tr>
<tr>
<td align="center">(شما) اندازه می گرفتید
/(šo.mǎ) an.dǎ.ze- mi.ge.ref.tid/</td>
<td align="center">(تو) اندازه می گرفتی
/(to) an.dǎ.ze- mi.ge.ref.ti/</td>
</tr>
<tr>
<td align="center">(آنها) اندازه می گرفتند
/(ǎn.hǎ) an.dǎ.ze- mi.ge.ref.tand/</td>
<td align="center">(او/آن) اندازه می گرفت
/(u/ ǎn) an.dǎ.ze- mi.ge.reft/</td>
</tr>
</table>

<table>
<tr><td colspan="2" align="center">**Present Perfect**
ماضی نقلی</td></tr>
<tr>
<td align="center">(ما) اندازه گرفته ایم
/(mǎ) an.dǎ.ze- ge.ref.te.im/</td>
<td align="center">(من) اندازه گرفته ام
/(man) an.dǎ.ze- ge.ref.te.am/</td>
</tr>
<tr>
<td align="center">(شما) اندازه گرفته اید
/(šo.mǎ) an.dǎ.ze- ge.ref.te.id/</td>
<td align="center">(تو) اندازه گرفته ای
/(to) an.dǎ.ze- ge.ref.te.i/</td>
</tr>
<tr>
<td align="center">(آنها) اندازه گرفته اند
/(ǎn.hǎ) an.dǎ.ze- ge.ref.te.and/</td>
<td align="center">(او/ آن) اندازه گرفته است
/(u/ ǎn) an.dǎ.ze- ge.ref.te- ast/</td>
</tr>
</table>

<table>
<tr><td colspan="2" align="center">**Past Perfect**
ماضی بعید</td></tr>
<tr>
<td align="center">(ما) اندازه گرفته بودیم
/(mǎ) an.dǎ.ze- ge.ref.te- bu.dim/</td>
<td align="center">(من) اندازه گرفته بودم
/(man) an.dǎ.ze- ge.ref.te- bu.dam/</td>
</tr>
<tr>
<td align="center">(شما) اندازه گرفته بودید
/(šo.mǎ) an.dǎ.ze- ge.ref.te- bu.did/</td>
<td align="center">(تو) اندازه گرفته بودی
/(to) an.dǎ.ze- ge.ref.te- bu.di/</td>
</tr>
<tr>
<td align="center">(آنها) اندازه گرفته بودند
/(ǎn.hǎ) an.dǎ.ze- ge.ref.te- bu.dand/</td>
<td align="center">(او/ آن) اندازه گرفته بود
/(u/ ǎn) an.dǎ.ze- ge.ref.te- bud/</td>
</tr>
</table>

<table>
<tr><th colspan="2">Past Subjunctive
ماضی التزامی</th></tr>
<tr>
<td>(ما) اندازه گرفته باشیم
/(mǎ) an.dǎ.ze- ge.ref.te- bǎ.šim/</td>
<td>(من) اندازه گرفته باشم
/(man) an.dǎ.ze- ge.ref.te- bǎ.šam/</td>
</tr>
<tr>
<td>(شما) اندازه گرفته باشید
/(šo.mǎ) an.dǎ.ze- ge.ref.te- bǎ.šid/</td>
<td>(تو) اندازه گرفته باشی
/(to) an.dǎ.ze- ge.ref.te- bǎ.ši/</td>
</tr>
<tr>
<td>(آنها) اندازه گرفته باشند
/(ǎn.hǎ) an.dǎ.ze- ge.ref.te- bǎ.šand/</td>
<td>(او/ آن) اندازه گرفته باشد
/(u/ ǎn) an.dǎ.ze- ge.ref.te- bǎ.šad/</td>
</tr>
</table>

<table>
<tr><th colspan="2">Past Progressive
ماضی مستمر(در جریان)</th></tr>
<tr>
<td>(ما) داشتیم اندازه می گرفتیم
/(mǎ) dǎš.tim- an.dǎ.ze- mi.ge.ref.tim/</td>
<td>(من) داشتم اندازه می گرفتم
/(man) dǎš.tam- an.dǎ.ze- mi.ge.ref.tam/</td>
</tr>
<tr>
<td>(شما) داشتید اندازه می گرفتید
/(šo.mǎ) dǎš.tid- an.dǎ.ze- mi.ge.ref.tid/</td>
<td>(تو) داشتی اندازه می گرفتی
/(to) dǎš.ti- an.dǎ.ze- mi.ge.ref.ti/</td>
</tr>
<tr>
<td>(آنها) داشتند اندازه می گرفتند
/(ǎn.hǎ) dǎš.tand- an.dǎ.ze- mi.ge.ref.tand/</td>
<td>(او/آن) داشت اندازه می گرفت
/(u/ ǎn) dǎšt- an.dǎ.ze- mi.ge.reft/</td>
</tr>
</table>

<table>
<tr><th colspan="2">Simple Future
مستقبل (آینده ساده)</th></tr>
<tr>
<td>(ما) اندازه خواهیم گرفت
/(mǎ) an.dǎ.ze- ǩǎ.him- ge.reft/</td>
<td>(من) اندازه خواهم گرفت
/(man) an.dǎ.ze- ǩǎ.ham- ge.reft/</td>
</tr>
<tr>
<td>(شما) اندازه خواهید گرفت
/(šo.mǎ) an.dǎ.ze- ǩǎ.hid- ge.reft/</td>
<td>(تو) اندازه خواهی گرفت
/(to) an.dǎ.ze- ǩǎ.hi- ge.reft/</td>
</tr>
<tr>
<td>(آنها) اندازه خواهند گرفت
/(ǎn.hǎ) an.dǎ.ze- ǩǎ.hand- ge.reft/</td>
<td>(او/آن) اندازه خواهد گرفت
/(u/ ǎn) an.dǎ.ze- ǩǎ.had- ge.reft/</td>
</tr>
</table>

<table>
<tr><th colspan="2">Command
امر</th></tr>
<tr>
<td>اندازه بگیرید!
/an.dǎ.ze- be.gi.rid/</td>
<td>اندازه بگیر!
/an.dǎ.ze- be.gir/</td>
</tr>
</table>

to meet

آشِنا شُدَن

/ăš.nă- šo.dan/

Plural	Singular
Simple Present مضارع اخباری(حال ساده)	
(ما) آشنا می شویم /(mă) ăš.nă- mi.ša.vim/	(من) آشنا می شوم /(man) ăš.nă- mi.ša.vam/
(شما) آشنا می شوید /(šo.mă) ăš.nă- mi.ša.vid/	(تو) آشنا می شوی /(to) ăš.nă- mi.ša.vi/
(آنها) آشنا می شوند /(ăn.hă) ăš.nă- mi.ša.vand/	(او/ آن) آشنا می شود /(u/ ăn) ăš.nă- mi.ša.vad/
Present Subjunctive مضارع التزامی	
(ما) آشنا بشویم /(mă) ăš.nă- be.ša.vim/	(من) آشنا بشوم /(man) ăš.nă- be.ša.vam/
(شما) آشنا بشوید /(šo.mă) ăš.nă- be.ša.vid/	(تو) آشنا بشوی /(to) ăš.nă- be.ša.vi/
(آنها) آشنا بشوند /(ăn.hă) ăš.nă- be.ša.vand/	(او/آن) آشنا بشود /(u/ ăn) ăš.nă- be.ša.vad/
Present Progressive مضارع مستمر(در جریان)	
(ما) داریم آشنا می شویم /(mă) dă.rim- ăš.nă- mi.ša.vim/	(من) دارم آشنا می شوم /(man) dă.ram- ăš.nă- mi.ša.vam/
(شما) دارید آشنا می شوید /(šo.mă) dă.rid- ăš.nă- mi.ša.vid/	(تو) داری آشنا می شوی /(to) dă.ri- ăš.nă- mi.ša.vi/
(آنها) دارند آشنا می شوند /(ăn.hă) dă.rand- ăš.nă- mi.ša.vand/	(او/آن) دارد آشنا می شود /(u/ ăn) dă.rad- ăš.nă- mi.ša.vad/

Simple Past	
ماضی مطلق (گذشته ساده)	
(ما) آشنا شدیم	(من) آشنا شدم
/(mă) ăš.nă- šo.dim/	/(man) ăš.nă- šo.dam/
(شما) آشنا شدید	(تو) آشنا شدی
/(šo.mă) ăš.nă- šo.did/	/(to) ăš.nă- šo.di/
(آنها) آشنا شدند	(او/آن) آشنا شد
/(ăn.hă) ăš.nă- šo.dand/	/(u/ ăn) ăš.nă- šod/

Imperfect Indicative	
ماضی استمراری	
(ما) آشنا می شدیم	(من) آشنا می شدم
/(mă) ăš.nă- mi.šo.dim/	/(man) ăš.nă- mi.šo.dam/
(شما) آشنا می شدید	(تو) آشنا می شدی
/(šo.mă) ăš.nă- mi.šo.did/	/(to) ăš.nă- mi.šo.di/
(آنها) آشنا می شدند	(او/آن) آشنا می شد
/(ăn.hă) ăš.nă- mi.šo.dand/	/(u/ ăn) ăš.nă- mi.šod/

Present Perfect	
ماضی نقلی	
(ما) آشنا شده ایم	(من) آشنا شده ام
/(mă) ăš.nă- šo.de.im/	/(man) ăš.nă- šo.de.am/
(شما) آشنا شده اید	(تو) آشنا شده ای
/(šo.mă) ăš.nă- šo.de.id/	/(to) ăš.nă- šo.de.i/
(آنها) آشنا شده اند	(او/آن) آشنا شده است
/(ăn.hă) ăš.nă- šo.de.and/	/(u/ ăn) ăš.nă- šo.de- ast/

Past Perfect	
ماضی بعید	
(ما) آشنا شده بودیم	(من) آشنا شده بودم
/(mă) ăš.nă- šo.de- bu.dim/	/(man) ăš.nă- šo.de- bu.dam/
(شما) آشنا شده بودید	(تو) آشنا شده بودی
/(šo.mă) ăš.nă- šo.de- bu.did/	/(to) ăš.nă- šo.de- bu.di/
(آنها) آشنا شده بودند	(او/آن) آشنا شده بود
/(ăn.hă) ăš.nă- šo.de- bu.dand/	/(u/ ăn) ăš.nă- šo.de- bud/

<table>
<tr><td colspan="2" align="center">**Past Subjunctive**
ماضی التزامی</td></tr>
<tr>
<td align="center">(ما) آشنا شده باشیم
/(mă) ăš.nă- šo.de- bă.šim/</td>
<td align="center">(من) آشنا شده باشم
/(man) ăš.nă- šo.de- bă.šam/</td>
</tr>
<tr>
<td align="center">(شما) آشنا شده باشید
/(šo.mă) ăš.nă- šo.de- bă.šid/</td>
<td align="center">(تو) آشنا شده باشی
/(to) ăš.nă- šo.de- bă.ši/</td>
</tr>
<tr>
<td align="center">(آنها) آشنا شده باشند
/(ăn.hă) ăš.nă- šo.de- bă.šand/</td>
<td align="center">(او/ آن) آشنا شده باشد
/(u/ ăn) ăš.nă- šo.de- bă.šad/</td>
</tr>
</table>

<table>
<tr><td colspan="2" align="center">**Past Progressive**
ماضی مستمر(در جریان)</td></tr>
<tr>
<td align="center">(ما) داشتیم آشنا می شدیم
/(mă) dăš.tim- ăš.nă- mi.šo.dim/</td>
<td align="center">(من) داشتم آشنا می شدم
/(man) dăš.tam- ăš.nă- mi.šo.dam/</td>
</tr>
<tr>
<td align="center">(شما) داشتید آشنا می شدید
/(šo.mă) dăš.tid- ăš.nă- mi.šo.did/</td>
<td align="center">(تو) داشتی آشنا می شدی
/(to) dăš.ti- ăš.nă- mi.šo.di/</td>
</tr>
<tr>
<td align="center">(آنها) داشتند آشنا می شدند
/(ăn.hă) dăš.tand- ăš.nă- mi.šo.dand/</td>
<td align="center">(او/آن) داشت آشنا می شد
/(u/ ăn) dăšt- ăš.nă- mi.šod/</td>
</tr>
</table>

<table>
<tr><td colspan="2" align="center">**Simple Future**
مستقبل (آینده ساده)</td></tr>
<tr>
<td align="center">(ما) آشنا خواهیم شد
/(mă) ăš.nă- ǩă.him- šod/</td>
<td align="center">(من) آشنا خواهم شد
/(man) ăš.nă- ǩă.ham- šod/</td>
</tr>
<tr>
<td align="center">(شما) آشنا خواهید شد
/(šo.mă) ăš.nă- ǩă.hid- šod/</td>
<td align="center">(تو) آشنا خواهی شد
/(to) ăš.nă- ǩă.hi- šod/</td>
</tr>
<tr>
<td align="center">(آنها) آشنا خواهند شد
/(ăn.hă) ăš.nă- ǩă.hand- šod/</td>
<td align="center">(او/آن) آشنا خواهد شد
/(u/ ăn) ăš.nă- ǩă.had- šod/</td>
</tr>
</table>

<table>
<tr><td colspan="2" align="center">**Command**
امر</td></tr>
<tr>
<td align="center">* آشنا بشوید!
/ăš.nă- be.ša.vid/</td>
<td align="center">* آشنا بشو!
/ăš.nă- be.šo/</td>
</tr>
</table>

* also: آشنا شو!   آشنا شوید!

to need

اِحتیاج داشتَن

/eh.ti.yǎj- dǎš.tan/

Plural	Singular
Simple Present	
مضارع اخباری(حال ساده)	
(ما) احتیاج داریم	(من) احتیاج دارم
/(mǎ) eh.ti.yǎj - dǎ.rim/	/(man) eh.ti.yǎj- dǎ.ram/
(شما) احتیاج دارید	(تو) احتیاج داری
/(šo.mǎ) eh.ti.yǎj- dǎ.rid/	/(to) eh.ti.yǎj- dǎ.ri/
(آنها) احتیاج دارند	(او/آن) احتیاج دارد
/(ǎn.hǎ) eh.ti.yǎj- dǎ.rand/	/(u/ ǎn) eh.ti.yǎj- dǎ.rad/
Present Subjunctive	
مضارع التزامی	
(ما) احتیاج بداریم	(من) احتیاج بدارم
/(mǎ) eh.ti.yǎj- be.dǎ.rim/	/(man) eh.ti.yǎj- be.dǎ.ram/
(شما) احتیاج بدارید	(تو) احتیاج بداری
/(šo.mǎ) eh.ti.yǎj- be.dǎ.rid/	/(to) eh.ti.yǎj- be.dǎ.ri/
(آنها) احتیاج بدارند	(او/آن) احتیاج بدارد
/(ǎn.hǎ) eh.ti.yǎj- be.dǎ.rand/	/(u/ ǎn) eh.ti.yǎj- be.dǎ.rad/
Present Progressive	
مضارع مستمر(در جریان)	
(ما) داریم احتیاج می داریم	(من) دارم احتیاج می دارم
/(mǎ) dǎ.rim- eh.ti.yǎj- mi.dǎ.rim/	/(man) dǎ.ram- eh.ti.yǎj- mi.dǎ.ram/
(شما) دارید احتیاج می دارید	(تو) داری احتیاج می داری
/(šo.mǎ) dǎ.rid- eh.ti.yǎj- mi.dǎ.rid/	/(to) dǎ.ri- eh.ti.yǎj- mi.dǎ.ri/
(آنها) دارند احتیاج می دارند	(او/آن) دارد احتیاج می دارد
/(ǎn.hǎ) dǎ.rand- eh.ti.yǎj- mi.dǎ.rand/	/(u/ ǎn) dǎ.rad- eh.ti.yǎj- mi.dǎ.rad/

Simple Past	
ماضی مطلق (گذشته ساده)	
(ما) احتیاج داشتیم	(من) احتیاج داشتم
/(mǎ) eh.ti.yǎj- dǎš.tim/	/(man) eh.ti.yǎj- dǎš.tam/
(شما) احتیاج داشتید	(تو) احتیاج داشتی
/(šo.mǎ) eh.ti.yǎj- dǎš.tid/	/(to) eh.ti.yǎj- dǎš.ti/
(آنها) احتیاج داشتند	(او/ آن) احتیاج داشت
/(ǎn.hǎ) eh.ti.yǎj- dǎš.tand/	/(u/ ǎn) eh.ti.yǎj- dǎšt/

Imperfect Indicative	
ماضی استمراری	
(ما) احتیاج می داشتیم	(من) احتیاج می داشتم
/(mǎ) eh.ti.yǎj- mi.dǎš.tim/	/(man) eh.ti.yǎj- mi.dǎš.tam/
(شما) احتیاج می داشتید	(تو) احتیاج می داشتی
/(šo.mǎ) eh.ti.yǎj- mi.dǎš.tid/	/(to) eh.ti.yǎj- mi.dǎš.ti/
(آنها) احتیاج می داشتند	(او/ آن) احتیاج می داشت
/(ǎn.hǎ) eh.ti.yǎj- mi.dǎš.tand/	/(u/ ǎn) eh.ti.yǎj- mi.dǎšt/

Present Perfect	
ماضی نقلی	
(ما) احتیاج داشته ایم	(من) احتیاج داشته ام
/(mǎ) eh.ti.yǎj- dǎš.te.im/	/(man) eh.ti.yǎj- dǎš.te.am/
(شما) احتیاج داشته اید	(تو) احتیاج داشته ای
/(šo.mǎ) eh.ti.yǎj- dǎš.te.id/	/(to) eh.ti.yǎj- dǎš.te.i/
(آنها) احتیاج داشته اند	(او/ آن) احتیاج داشته است
/(ǎn.hǎ) eh.ti.yǎj- dǎš.te.and/	/(u/ ǎn) eh.ti.yǎj- dǎš.te- ast/

Past Perfect	
ماضی بعید	
(ما) احتیاج داشته بودیم	(من) احتیاج داشته بودم
/(mǎ) eh.ti.yǎj- dǎš.te- bu.dim/	/(man) eh.ti.yǎj- dǎš.te- bu.dam/
(شما) احتیاج داشته بودید	(تو) احتیاج داشته بودی
/(šo.mǎ) eh.ti.yǎj- dǎš.te- bu.did/	/(to) eh.ti.yǎj- dǎš.te- bu.di/
(آنها) احتیاج داشته بودند	(او/ آن) احتیاج داشته بود
/(ǎn.hǎ) eh.ti.yǎj- dǎš.te- bu.dand/	/(u/ ǎn) eh.ti.yǎj- dǎš.te- bud/

<table>
<tr><td colspan="2" align="center">**Past Subjunctive**
ماضی التزامی</td></tr>
<tr>
<td align="center">(ما) احتیاج داشته باشیم
/(mă) eh.ti.yăj- dăš.te- bă.šim/</td>
<td align="center">(من) احتیاج داشته باشم
/(man) eh.ti.yăj- dăš.te- bă.šam/</td>
</tr>
<tr>
<td align="center">(شما) احتیاج داشته باشید
/(šo.mă) eh.ti.yăj- dăš.te- bă.šid/</td>
<td align="center">(تو) احتیاج داشته باشی
/(to) eh.ti.yăj- dăš.te- bă.ši/</td>
</tr>
<tr>
<td align="center">(آنها) احتیاج داشته باشند
/(ăn.hă) eh.ti.yăj- dăš.te- bă.šand/</td>
<td align="center">(او/آن) احتیاج داشته باشد
/(u/ ăn) eh.ti.yăj- dăš.te- bă.šad/</td>
</tr>
</table>

<table>
<tr><td colspan="2" align="center">**Past Progressive**
ماضی مستمر(در جریان)</td></tr>
<tr>
<td align="center">(ما) داشتیم احتیاج می داشتیم
/(mă) dăš.tim- eh.ti.yăj- mi.dăš.tim/</td>
<td align="center">(من) داشتم احتیاج می داشتم
/(man) dăš.tam- eh.ti.yăj- mi.dăš.tam/</td>
</tr>
<tr>
<td align="center">(شما) داشتید احتیاج می داشتید
/(šo.mă) dăš.tid- eh.ti.yăj- mi.dăš.tid/</td>
<td align="center">(تو) داشتی احتیاج می داشتی
/(to) dăš.ti- eh.ti.yăj- mi.dăš.ti/</td>
</tr>
<tr>
<td align="center">(آنها) داشتند احتیاج می داشتند
/(ăn.hă) dăš.tand- eh.ti.yăj- mi.dăš.tand/</td>
<td align="center">(او/آن) داشت احتیاج می داشت
/(u/ ăn) dăšt- eh.ti.yăj- mi.dăšt/</td>
</tr>
</table>

<table>
<tr><td colspan="2" align="center">**Simple Future**
مستقبل (آینده ساده)</td></tr>
<tr>
<td align="center">(ما) احتیاج خواهیم داشت
/(mă) eh.ti.yăj- ǩă.him- dăšt/</td>
<td align="center">(من) احتیاج خواهم داشت
/(man) eh.ti.yăj- ǩă.ham- dăšt/</td>
</tr>
<tr>
<td align="center">(شما) احتیاج خواهید داشت
/(šo.mă) eh.ti.yăj- ǩă.hid- dăšt/</td>
<td align="center">(تو) احتیاج خواهی داشت
/(to) eh.ti.yăj- ǩă.hi- dăšt/</td>
</tr>
<tr>
<td align="center">(آنها) احتیاج خواهند داشت
/(ăn.hă) eh.ti.yăj- ǩă.hand- dăšt/</td>
<td align="center">(او/آن) احتیاج خواهد داشت
/(u/ ăn) eh.ti.yăj- ǩă.had- dăšt/</td>
</tr>
</table>

<table>
<tr><td colspan="2" align="center">**Command**
امر</td></tr>
<tr>
<td align="center">* احتیاج بدارید!
/eh.ti.yăj- be.dăr/</td>
<td align="center">* احتیاج بدار!
/eh.ti.yăj- be.dă.rid/</td>
</tr>
</table>

* also: احتیاج داشته باشید!   احتیاج داشته باش!

to open

باز کَردَن

/băz- kar.dan/

Plural	Singular
Simple Present <div dir="rtl">مضارع اخباری(حال ساده)</div>	
<div dir="rtl">(ما) باز می کنیم</div> /(mă) băz- mi.ko.nim/	<div dir="rtl">(من) باز می کنم</div> /(man) băz- mi.ko.nam/
<div dir="rtl">(شما) باز می کنید</div> /(šo.mă) băz- mi.ko.nid/	<div dir="rtl">(تو) باز می کنی</div> /(to) băz- mi.ko.ni/
<div dir="rtl">(آنها) باز می کنند</div> /(ăn.hă) băz- mi.ko.nand/	<div dir="rtl">(او/آن) باز می کند</div> /(u/ ăn) băz- mi.ko.nad/
Present Subjunctive <div dir="rtl">مضارع التزامی</div>	
<div dir="rtl">(ما) باز بکنیم</div> /(mă) băz- be.ko.nim/	<div dir="rtl">(من) باز بکنم</div> /(man) băz- be.ko.nam/
<div dir="rtl">(شما) باز بکنید</div> /(šo.mă) băz- be.ko.nid/	<div dir="rtl">(تو) باز بکنی</div> /(to) băz- be.ko.ni/
<div dir="rtl">(آنها) باز بکنند</div> /(ăn.hă) băz- be.ko.nand/	<div dir="rtl">(او/آن) باز بکند</div> /(u/ ăn) băz- be.ko.nad/
Present Progressive <div dir="rtl">مضارع مستمر(در جریان)</div>	
<div dir="rtl">(ما) داریم باز می کنیم</div> /(mă) dă.rim- băz- mi.ko.nim/	<div dir="rtl">(من) دارم باز می کنم</div> /(man) dă.ram- băz- mi.ko.nam/
<div dir="rtl">(شما) دارید باز می کنید</div> /(šo.mă) dă.rid- băz- mi.ko.nid/	<div dir="rtl">(تو) داری باز می کنی</div> /(to) dă.ri- băz- mi.ko.ni/
<div dir="rtl">(آنها) دارند باز می کنند</div> /(ăn.hă) dă.rand- băz- mi.ko.nand/	<div dir="rtl">(او/آن) دارد باز می کند</div> /(u/ ăn) dă.rad- băz- mi.ko.nad/

	Simple Past
ماضی مطلق (گذشته ساده)	
(ما) باز کردیم	(من) باز کردم
/(mǎ) bǎz- kar.dim/	/(man) bǎz- kar.dam/
(شما) باز کردید	(تو) باز کردی
/(šo.mǎ) bǎz- kar.did/	/(to) bǎz- kar.di/
(آنها) باز کردند	(او/ آن) باز کرد
/(ǎn.hǎ) bǎz- kar.dand/	/(u/ ǎn) bǎz- kard/

	Imperfect Indicative
ماضی استمراری	
(ما) باز می کردیم	(من) باز می کردم
/(mǎ) bǎz- mi.kar.dim/	/(man) bǎz- mi.kar.dam/
(شما) باز می کردید	(تو) باز می کردی
/(šo.mǎ) bǎz- mi.kar.did/	/(to) bǎz- mi.kar.di/
(آنها) باز می کردند	(او/ آن) باز می کرد
/(ǎn.hǎ) bǎz- mi.kar.dand/	/(u/ ǎn) bǎz- mi.kard/

	Present Perfect
ماضی نقلی	
(ما) باز کرده ایم	(من) باز کرده ام
/(mǎ) bǎz- kar.de.im/	/(man) bǎz- kar.de.am/
(شما) باز کرده اید	(تو) باز کرده ای
/(šo.mǎ) bǎz- kar.de.id/	/(to) bǎz- kar.de.i/
(آنها) باز کرده اند	(او/ آن) باز کرده است
/(ǎn.hǎ) bǎz- kar.de.and/	/(u/ ǎn) bǎz- kar.de- ast/

	Past Perfect
ماضی بعید	
(ما) باز کرده بودیم	(من) باز کرده بودم
/(mǎ) bǎz- kar.de- bu.dim/	/(man) bǎz- kar.de- bu.dam/
(شما) باز کرده بودید	(تو) باز کرده بودی
/(šo.mǎ) bǎz- kar.de- bu.did/	/(to) bǎz- kar.de- bu.di/
(آنها) باز کرده بودند	(او/ آن) باز کرده بود
/(ǎn.hǎ) bǎz- kar.de- bu.dand/	/(u/ ǎn) bǎz- kar.de- bud/

<table>
<tr><td colspan="2" align="center">**Past Subjunctive**
ماضی التزامی</td></tr>
<tr>
<td align="center">(ما) باز کرده باشیم
/(mǎ) bǎz- kar.de- bǎ.šim/</td>
<td align="center">(من) باز کرده باشم
/(man) bǎz- kar.de- bǎ.šam/</td>
</tr>
<tr>
<td align="center">(شما) باز کرده باشید
/(šo.mǎ) bǎz- kar.de- bǎ.šid/</td>
<td align="center">(تو) باز کرده باشی
/(to) bǎz- kar.de- bǎ.ši/</td>
</tr>
<tr>
<td align="center">(آنها) باز کرده باشند
/(ǎn.hǎ) bǎz- kar.de- bǎ.šand/</td>
<td align="center">(او/آن) باز کرده باشد
/(u/ ǎn) bǎz- kar.de- bǎ.šad/</td>
</tr>
</table>

<table>
<tr><td colspan="2" align="center">**Past Progressive**
ماضی مستمر (در جریان)</td></tr>
<tr>
<td align="center">(ما) داشتیم باز می کردیم
/(mǎ) dǎš.tim- bǎz- mi.kar.dim/</td>
<td align="center">(من) داشتم باز می کردم
/(man) dǎš.tam- bǎz- mi.kar.dam/</td>
</tr>
<tr>
<td align="center">(شما) داشتید باز می کردید
/(šo.mǎ) dǎš.tid- bǎz- mi.kar.did/</td>
<td align="center">(تو) داشتی باز می کردی
/(to) dǎš.ti- bǎz- mi.kar.di/</td>
</tr>
<tr>
<td align="center">(آنها) داشتند باز می کردند
/(ǎn.hǎ) dǎš.tand- bǎz- mi.kar.dand/</td>
<td align="center">(او/آن) داشت باز می کرد
/(u/ ǎn) dǎšt- bǎz- mi.kard/</td>
</tr>
</table>

<table>
<tr><td colspan="2" align="center">**Simple Future**
مستقبل (آینده ساده)</td></tr>
<tr>
<td align="center">(ما) باز خواهیم کرد
/(mǎ) bǎz- ǩǎ.him- kard/</td>
<td align="center">(من) باز خواهم کرد
/(man) bǎz- ǩǎ.ham- kard/</td>
</tr>
<tr>
<td align="center">(شما) باز خواهید کرد
/(šo.mǎ) bǎz- ǩǎ.hid- kard/</td>
<td align="center">(تو) باز خواهی کرد
/(to) bǎz- ǩǎ.hi- kard/</td>
</tr>
<tr>
<td align="center">(آنها) باز خواهند کرد
/(ǎn.hǎ) bǎz- ǩǎ.hand- kard/</td>
<td align="center">(او/آن) باز خواهد کرد
/(u/ ǎn) bǎz- ǩǎ.had- kard/</td>
</tr>
</table>

<table>
<tr><td colspan="2" align="center">**Command**
امر</td></tr>
<tr>
<td align="center">* باز بکنید!
/bǎz- be.ko.nid/</td>
<td align="center">* باز بکن!
/bǎz- be.kon/</td>
</tr>
</table>

* also: باز کن!   باز کنید!

169

to pick up

بَرداشتَن

/bar.dăš.tan/

Plural	Singular
Simple Present <div dir="rtl">مضارع اخباری(حال ساده)</div>	
(ما) برمی داریم /(mă) bar.mi.dă.rim/	(من) برمی دارم /(man) bar.mi.dă.ram/
(شما) برمی دارید /(šo.mă) bar.mi.dă.rid/	(تو) برمی داری /(to) bar.mi.dă.ri/
(آنها) برمی دارند /(ăn.hă) bar.mi.dă.rand/	(او/آن) برمی دارد /(u/ ăn) bar.mi.dă.rad/
Present Subjunctive <div dir="rtl">مضارع التزامی</div>	
(ما) برداریم /(mă) bar.dă.rim/	(من) بردارم /(man) bar.dă.ram/
(شما) بردارید /(šo.mă) bar.dă.rid/	(تو) برداری /(to) bar.dă.ri/
(آنها) بردارند /(ăn.hă) bar.dă.rand/	(او/آن) بردارد /(u/ ăn) bar.dă.rad/
Present Progressive <div dir="rtl">مضارع مستمر(در جریان)</div>	
(ما) داریم بر می داریم /(mă) dă.rim- bar.mi.dă.rim/	(من) دارم بر می دارم /(man) dă.ram- bar.mi.dă.ram/
(شما) دارید بر می دارید /(šo.mă) dă.rid- bar.mi.dă.rid/	(تو) داری بر می داری /(to) dă.ri- bar.mi.dă.ri/
(آنها) دارند بر می دارند /(ăn.hă) dă.rand- bar.mi.dă.rand/	(او/آن) دارد بر می دارد /(u/ ăn) dă.rad- bar.mi.dă.rad/

Simple Past
ماضی مطلق (گذشته ساده)

(ما) برداشتیم	(من) برداشتم
/(mǎ) bar.dǎš.tim/	/(man) bar.dǎš.tam/
(شما) برداشتید	(تو) برداشتی
/(šo.mǎ) bar.dǎš.tid/	/(to) bar.dǎš.ti/
(آنها) برداشتند	(او/ آن) برداشت
/(ǎn.hǎ) bar.dǎš.tand/	/(u/ ǎn) bar.dǎšt/

Imperfect Indicative
ماضی استمراری

(ما) برمی داشتیم	(من) برمی داشتم
/(mǎ) bar.mi.dǎš.tim/	/(man) bar.mi.dǎš.tam/
(شما) برمی داشتید	(تو) برمی داشتی
/(šo.mǎ) bar.mi.dǎš.tid/	/(to) bar.mi.dǎš.ti/
(آنها) برمی داشتند	(او/ آن) بر می داشت
/(ǎn.hǎ) bar.mi.dǎš.tand/	/(u/ ǎn) bar.mi.dǎšt/

Present Perfect
ماضی نقلی

(ما) برداشته ایم	(من) برداشته ام
/(mǎ) bar.dǎš.te.im/	/(man) bar.dǎš.te.am/
(شما) برداشته اید	(تو) برداشته ای
/(šo.mǎ) bar.dǎš.te.id/	/(to) bar.dǎš.te.i/
(آنها) برداشته اند	(او/ آن) برداشته است
/(ǎn.hǎ) bar.dǎš.te.and/	/(u/ ǎn) bar.dǎš.te- ast/

Past Perfect
ماضی بعید

(ما) برداشته بودیم	(من) برداشته بودم
/(mǎ) bar.dǎš.te- bu.dim/	/(man) bar.dǎš.te- bu.dam/
(شما) برداشته بودید	(تو) برداشته بودی
/(šo.mǎ) bar.dǎš.te- bu.did/	/(to) bar.dǎš.te- bu.di/
(آنها) برداشته بودند	(او/ آن) برداشته بود
/(ǎn.hǎ) bar.dǎš.te- bu.dand/	/(u/ ǎn) bar.dǎš.te- bud/

Past Subjunctive	
ماضی التزامی	
(ما) برداشته باشیم	(من) برداشته باشم
/(mǎ) bar.dǎš.te- bǎ.šim/	/(man) bar.dǎš.te- bǎ.šam/
(شما) برداشته باشید	(تو) برداشته باشی
/(šo.mǎ) bar.dǎš.te- bǎ.šid/	/(to) bar.dǎš.te- bǎ.ši/
(آنها) برداشته باشند	(او/ آن) برداشته باشد
/(ǎn.hǎ) bar.dǎš.te- bǎ.šand/	/(u/ ǎn) bar.dǎš.te- bǎ.šad/

Past Progressive	
ماضی مستمر(در جریان)	
(ما) داشتیم برمی داشتیم	(من) داشتم برمی داشتم
/(mǎ) dǎš.tim- bar.mi.dǎš.tim/	/(man) dǎš.tam- bar.mi.dǎš.tam/
(شما) داشتید برمی داشتید	(تو) داشتی برمی داشتی
/(šo.mǎ) dǎš.tid- bar.mi.dǎš.tid/	/(to) dǎš.ti- bar.mi.dǎš.ti/
(آنها) داشتند برمی داشتند	(او/آن) داشت برمی داشت
/(ǎn.hǎ) dǎš.tand- bar.mi.dǎš.tand/	/(u/ ǎn) dǎšt- bar.mi.dǎšt/

Simple Future	
مستقبل (آینده ساده)	
(ما) برخواهیم داشت	(من) برخواهم داشت
/(mǎ) bar.kǎ.him- dǎšt/	/(man) bar.kǎ.ham- dǎšt/
(شما) برخواهید داشت	(تو) برخواهی داشت
/(šo.mǎ) bar.kǎ.hid- dǎšt/	/(to) bar.kǎ.hi- dǎšt/
(آنها) برخواهند داشت	(او/آن) برخواهد داشت
/(ǎn.hǎ) bar.kǎ.hand- dǎšt/	/(u/ ǎn) bar.kǎ.had- dǎšt/

Command	
امر	
بردارید!	بردار!
/bar.dǎ.rid/	/bar.dǎr/

to play

بازی کَردَن

/bǎ.zi- kar.dan/

Plural	*Singular*
Simple Present	
مضارع اخباری(حال ساده)	
(ما) بازی می کنیم	(من) بازی می کنم
/(mǎ) bǎ.zi- mi.ko.nim/	/(man) bǎ.zi- mi.ko.nam/
(شما) بازی می کنید	(تو) بازی می کنی
/(šo.mǎ) bǎ.zi- mi.ko.nid/	/(to) bǎ.zi- mi.ko.ni/
(آنها) بازی می کنند	(او/آن) بازی می کند
/(ǎn.hǎ) bǎ.zi- mi.ko.nand/	/(u/ ǎn) bǎ.zi- mi.ko.nad/

Present Subjunctive	
مضارع التزامی	
(ما) بازی بکنیم	(من) بازی بکنم
/(mǎ) bǎ.zi- be.ko.nim/	/(man) bǎ.zi- be.ko.nam/
(شما) بازی بکنید	(تو) بازی بکنی
/(šo.mǎ) bǎ.zi- be.ko.nid/	/(to) bǎ.zi- be.ko.ni/
(آنها) بازی بکنند	(او/آن) بازی بکند
/(ǎn.hǎ) bǎ.zi- be.ko.nand/	/(u/ ǎn) bǎ.zi- be.ko.nad/

Present Progressive	
مضارع مستمر(در جریان)	
(ما) داریم بازی می کنیم	(من) دارم بازی می کنم
/(mǎ) dǎ.rim- bǎ.zi- mi.ko.nim/	/(man) dǎ.ram- bǎ.zi- mi.ko.nam/
(شما) دارید بازی می کنید	(تو) داری بازی می کنی
/(šo.mǎ) dǎ.rid- bǎ.zi- mi.ko.nid/	/(to) dǎ.ri- bǎ.zi- mi.ko.ni/
(آنها) دارند بازی می کنند	(او/آن) دارد بازی می کند
/(ǎn.hǎ) dǎ.rand- bǎ.zi- mi.ko.nand/	/(u/ ǎn) dǎ.rad- bǎ.zi- mi.ko.nad/

Simple Past
ماضی مطلق (گذشته ساده)

(ما) بازی کردیم	(من) بازی کردم
/(mǎ) bǎ.zi- kar.dim/	/(man) bǎ.zi- kar.dam/
(شما) بازی کردید	(تو) بازی کردی
/(šo.mǎ) bǎ.zi- kar.did/	/(to) bǎ.zi- kar.di/
(آنها) بازی کردند	(او/ آن) بازی کرد
/(ǎn.hǎ) bǎ.zi- kar.dand/	/(u/ ǎn) bǎ.zi- kard/

Imperfect Indicative
ماضی استمراری

(ما) بازی می کردیم	(من) بازی می کردم
/(mǎ) bǎ.zi- mi.kar.dim/	/(man) bǎ.zi- mi.kar.dam/
(شما) بازی می کردید	(تو) بازی می کردی
/(šo.mǎ) bǎ.zi- mi.kar.did/	/(to) bǎ.zi- mi.kar.di/
(آنها) بازی می کردند	(او/ آن) بازی می کرد
/(ǎn.hǎ) bǎ.zi- mi.kar.dand/	/(u/ ǎn) bǎ.zi- mi.kard/

Present Perfect
ماضی نقلی

(ما) بازی کرده ایم	(من) بازی کرده ام
/(mǎ) bǎ.zi- kar.de.im/	/(man) bǎ.zi- kar.de.am/
(شما) بازی کرده اید	(تو) بازی کرده ای
/(šo.mǎ) bǎ.zi- kar.de.id/	/(to) bǎ.zi- kar.de.i/
(آنها) بازی کرده اند	(او/ آن) بازی کرده است
/(ǎn.hǎ) bǎ.zi- kar.de.and/	/(u/ ǎn) bǎ.zi- kar.de- ast/

Past Perfect
ماضی بعید

(ما) بازی کرده بودیم	(من) بازی کرده بودم
/(mǎ) bǎ.zi- kar.de- bu.dim/	/(man) bǎ.zi- kar.de- bu.dam/
(شما) بازی کرده بودید	(تو) بازی کرده بودی
/(šo.mǎ) bǎ.zi- kar.de- bu.did/	/(to) bǎ.zi- kar.de- bu.di/
(آنها) بازی کرده بودند	(او/ آن) بازی کرده بود
/(ǎn.hǎ) bǎ.zi- kar.de- bu.dand/	/(u/ ǎn) bǎ.zi- kar.de- bud/

<table>
<tr><td colspan="2" align="center">Past Subjunctive
ماضی التزامی</td></tr>
<tr>
<td align="center">(ما) بازی کرده باشیم
/(mǎ) bǎ.zi- kar.de- bǎ.šim/</td>
<td align="center">(من) بازی کرده باشم
/(man) bǎ.zi- kar.de- bǎ.šam/</td>
</tr>
<tr>
<td align="center">(شما) بازی کرده باشید
/(šo.mǎ) bǎ.zi- kar.de- bǎ.šid/</td>
<td align="center">(تو) بازی کرده باشی
/(to) bǎ.zi- kar.de- bǎ.ši/</td>
</tr>
<tr>
<td align="center">(آنها) بازی کرده باشند
/(ǎn.hǎ) bǎ.zi- kar.de- bǎ.šand/</td>
<td align="center">(او/آن) بازی کرده باشد
/(u/ ǎn) bǎ.zi- kar.de- bǎ.šad/</td>
</tr>
</table>

<table>
<tr><td colspan="2" align="center">Past Progressive
ماضی مستمر(در جریان)</td></tr>
<tr>
<td align="center">(ما) داشتیم بازی می کردیم
/(mǎ) dǎš.tim- bǎ.zi- mi.kar.dim/</td>
<td align="center">(من) داشتم بازی می کردم
/(man) dǎš.tam- bǎ.zi- mi.kar.dam/</td>
</tr>
<tr>
<td align="center">(شما) داشتید بازی می کردید
/(šo.mǎ) dǎš.tid- bǎ.zi- mi.kar.did/</td>
<td align="center">(تو) داشتی بازی می کردی
/(to) dǎš.ti- bǎ.zi- mi.kar.di/</td>
</tr>
<tr>
<td align="center">(آنها) داشتند بازی می کردند
/(ǎn.hǎ) dǎš.tand- bǎ.zi- mi.kar.dand/</td>
<td align="center">(او/آن) داشت بازی می کرد
/(u/ ǎn) dǎšt- bǎ.zi- mi.kard/</td>
</tr>
</table>

<table>
<tr><td colspan="2" align="center">Simple Future
مستقبل (آینده ساده)</td></tr>
<tr>
<td align="center">(ما) بازی خواهیم کرد
/(mǎ) bǎ.zi- ǩǎ.him- kard/</td>
<td align="center">(من) بازی خواهم کرد
/(man) bǎ.zi- ǩǎ.ham- kard/</td>
</tr>
<tr>
<td align="center">(شما) بازی خواهید کرد
/(šo.mǎ) bǎ.zi- ǩǎ.hid- kard/</td>
<td align="center">(تو) بازی خواهی کرد
/(to) bǎ.zi- ǩǎ.hi- kard/</td>
</tr>
<tr>
<td align="center">(آنها) بازی خواهند کرد
/(ǎn.hǎ) bǎ.zi- ǩǎ.hand- kard/</td>
<td align="center">(او/آن) بازی خواهد کرد
/(u/ ǎn) bǎ.zi- ǩǎ.had- kard/</td>
</tr>
</table>

<table>
<tr><td colspan="2" align="center">Command
امر</td></tr>
<tr>
<td align="center">* بازی بکنید!
/bǎ.zi- be.ko.nid/</td>
<td align="center">* بازی بکن!
/bǎ.zi- be.kon/</td>
</tr>
</table>

* also: بازی کن!   بازی کنید!

to practice

تَمرین کَردَن

/tam.rin- kar.dan/

Plural	Singular
Simple Present مضارع اخباری(حال ساده)	
(ما) تمرین می کنیم /(mă) tam.rin- mi.ko.nim/	(من) تمرین می کنم /(man) tam.rin- mi.ko.nam/
(شما) تمرین می کنید /(šo.mă) tam.rin- mi.ko.nid/	(تو) تمرین می کنی /(to) tam.rin- mi.ko.ni/
(آنها) تمرین می کنند /(ăn.hă) tam.rin- mi.ko.nand/	(او/آن) تمرین می کند /(u/ ăn) tam.rin- mi.ko.nad/
Present Subjunctive مضارع التزامی	
(ما) تمرین بکنیم /(mă) tam.rin- be.ko.nim/	(من) تمرین بکنم /(man) tam.rin- be.ko.nam/
(شما) تمرین بکنید /(šo.mă) tam.rin- be.ko.nid/	(تو) تمرین بکنی /(to) tam.rin- be.ko.ni/
(آنها) تمرین بکنند /(ăn.hă) tam.rin- be.ko.nand/	(او/آن) تمرین بکند /(u/ ăn) tam.rin- be.ko.nad/
Present Progressive مضارع مستمر(در جریان)	
(ما) داریم تمرین می کنیم /(mă) dă.rim- tam.rin- mi.ko.nim/	(من) دارم تمرین می کنم /(man) dă.ram- tam.rin- mi.ko.nam/
(شما) دارید تمرین می کنید /(šo.mă) dă.rid- tam.rin- mi.ko.nid/	(تو) داری تمرین می کنی /(to) dă.ri- tam.rin- mi.ko.ni/
(آنها) دارند تمرین می کنند /(ăn.hă) dă.rand- tam.rin- mi.ko.nand/	(او/آن) دارد تمرین می کند /(u/ ăn) dă.rad- tam.rin- mi.ko.nad/

176

Simple Past
ماضی مطلق (گذشته ساده)

(ما) تمرین کردیم	(من) تمرین کردم
/(mǎ) tam.rin- kar.dim/	/(man) tam.rin- kar.dam/
(شما) تمرین کردید	(تو) تمرین کردی
/(šo.mǎ) tam.rin- kar.did/	/(to) tam.rin- kar.di/
(آنها) تمرین کردند	(او/آن) تمرین کرد
/(ǎn.hǎ) tam.rin- kar.dand/	/(u/ ǎn) tam.rin- kard/

Imperfect Indicative
ماضی استمراری

(ما) تمرین می کردیم	(من) تمرین می کردم
/(mǎ) tam.rin- mi.kar.dim/	/(man) tam.rin- mi.kar.dam/
(شما) تمرین می کردید	(تو) تمرین می کردی
/(šo.mǎ) tam.rin- mi.kar.did/	/(to) tam.rin- mi.kar.di/
(آنها) تمرین می کردند	(او/آن) تمرین می کرد
/(ǎn.hǎ) tam.rin- mi.kar.dand/	/(u/ ǎn) tam.rin- mi.kard/

Present Perfect
ماضی نقلی

(ما) تمرین کرده ایم	(من) تمرین کرده ام
/(mǎ) tam.rin- kar.de.im/	/(man) tam.rin- kar.de.am/
(شما) تمرین کرده اید	(تو) تمرین کرده ای
/(šo.mǎ) tam.rin- kar.de.id/	/(to) tam.rin- kar.de.i/
(آنها) تمرین کرده اند	(او/آن) تمرین کرده است
/(ǎn.hǎ) tam.rin- kar.de.and/	/(u/ ǎn) tam.rin- kar.de- ast/

Past Perfect
ماضی بعید

(ما) تمرین کرده بودیم	(من) تمرین کرده بودم
/(mǎ) tam.rin- kar.de- bu.dim/	/(man) tam.rin- kar.de- bu.dam/
(شما) تمرین کرده بودید	(تو) تمرین کرده بودی
/(šo.mǎ) tam.rin- kar.de- bu.did/	/(to) tam.rin- kar.de- bu.di/
(آنها) تمرین کرده بودند	(او/آن) تمرین کرده بود
/(ǎn.hǎ) tam.rin- kar.de- bu.dand/	/(u/ ǎn) tam.rin- kar.de- bud/

<table>
<tr><td colspan="2" align="center">

Past Subjunctive

ماضی التزامی

</td></tr>
<tr>
<td align="center">

(ما) تمرین کرده باشیم

/(mǎ) tam.rin- kar.de- bǎ.šim/

</td>
<td align="center">

(من) تمرین کرده باشم

/(man) tam.rin- kar.de- bǎ.šam/

</td>
</tr>
<tr>
<td align="center">

(شما) تمرین کرده باشید

/(šo.mǎ) tam.rin- kar.de- bǎ.šid/

</td>
<td align="center">

(تو) تمرین کرده باشی

/(to) tam.rin- kar.de- bǎ.ši/

</td>
</tr>
<tr>
<td align="center">

(آنها) تمرین کرده باشند

/(ǎn.hǎ) tam.rin- kar.de- bǎ.šand/

</td>
<td align="center">

(او/آن) تمرین کرده باشد

/(u/ ǎn) tam.rin- kar.de- bǎ.šad/

</td>
</tr>
</table>

<table>
<tr><td colspan="2" align="center">

Past Progressive

ماضی مستمر(در جریان)

</td></tr>
<tr>
<td align="center">

(ما) داشتیم تمرین می کردیم

/(mǎ) dǎš.tim- tam.rin- mi.kar.dim/

</td>
<td align="center">

(من) داشتم تمرین می کردم

/(man) dǎš.tam- tam.rin- mi.kar.dam/

</td>
</tr>
<tr>
<td align="center">

(شما) داشتید تمرین می کردید

/(šo.mǎ) dǎš.tid- tam.rin- mi.kar.did/

</td>
<td align="center">

(تو) داشتی تمرین می کردی

/(to) dǎš.ti- tam.rin- mi.kar.di/

</td>
</tr>
<tr>
<td align="center">

(آنها) داشتند تمرین می کردند

/(ǎn.hǎ) dǎš.tand- tam.rin- mi.kar.dand/

</td>
<td align="center">

(او/آن) داشت تمرین می کرد

/(u/ ǎn) dǎšt- tam.rin- mi.kard/

</td>
</tr>
</table>

<table>
<tr><td colspan="2" align="center">

Simple Future

مستقبل (آینده ساده)

</td></tr>
<tr>
<td align="center">

(ما) تمرین خواهیم کرد

/(mǎ) tam.rin- ǩǎ.him- kard/

</td>
<td align="center">

(من) تمرین خواهم کرد

/(man) tam.rin- ǩǎ.ham- kard/

</td>
</tr>
<tr>
<td align="center">

(شما) تمرین خواهید کرد

/(šo.mǎ) tam.rin- ǩǎ.hid- kard/

</td>
<td align="center">

(تو) تمرین خواهی کرد

/(to) tam.rin- ǩǎ.hi- kard/

</td>
</tr>
<tr>
<td align="center">

(آنها) تمرین خواهند کرد

/(ǎn.hǎ) tam.rin- ǩǎ.hand- kard/

</td>
<td align="center">

(او/آن) تمرین خواهد کرد

/(u/ ǎn) tam.rin- ǩǎ.had- kard/

</td>
</tr>
</table>

<table>
<tr><td colspan="2" align="center">

Command

امر

</td></tr>
<tr>
<td align="center">

تمرین بکنید! *

/tam.rin- be.ko.nid/

</td>
<td align="center">

تمرین بکن! *

/tam.rin- be.kon/

</td>
</tr>
</table>

* also: تمرین کن!   تمرین کنید!

178

to prepare

آماده کَردَن

/ă.mă.de- kar.dan/

Plural	*Singular*
Simple Present مضارع اخباری(حال ساده)	
(ما) آماده می کنیم /(mă) ă.mă.de- mi.ko.nim/	(من) آماده می کنم /(man) ă.mă.de- mi.ko.nam/
(شما) آماده می کنید /(šo.mă) ă.mă.dc- mi.ko.nid/	(تو) آماده می کنی /(to) ă.mă.de- mi.ko.ni/
(آنها) آماده می کنند /(ăn.hă) ă.mă.de- mi.ko.nand/	(او/آن) آماده می کند /(u/ ăn) ă.mă.de- mi.ko.nad/
Present Subjunctive مضارع التزامی	
(ما) آماده بکنیم /(mă) ă.mă.de- be.ko.nim/	(من) آماده بکنم /(man) ă.mă.de- be.ko.nam/
(شما) آماده بکنید /(šo.mă) ă.mă.de- be.ko.nid/	(تو) آماده بکنی /(to) ă.mă.de- be.ko.ni/
(آنها) آماده بکنند /(ăn.hă) ă.mă.de- be.ko.nand/	(او/آن) آماده بکند /(u/ ăn) ă.mă.de- be.ko.nad/
Present Progressive مضارع مستمر(در جریان)	
(ما) داریم آماده می کنیم /(mă) dă.rim- ă.mă.de- mi.ko.nim/	(من) دارم آماده می کنم /(man) dă.ram- ă.mă.de- mi.ko.nam/
(شما) دارید آماده می کنید /(šo.mă) dă.rid- ă.mă.de- mi.ko.nid/	(تو) داری آماده می کنی /(to) dă.ri- ă.mă.de- mi.ko.ni/
(آنها) دارند آماده می کنند /(ăn.hă) dă.rand- ă.mă.de- mi.ko.nand/	(او/آن) دارد آماده می کند /(u/ ăn) dă.rad- ă.mă.de- mi.ko.nad/

Simple Past	
ماضی مطلق (گذشته ساده)	
(ما) آماده کردیم	(من) آماده کردم
/(mă) ă.mă.de- kar.dim/	/(man) ă.mă.de- kar.dam/
(شما) آماده کردید	(تو) آماده کردی
/(šo.mă) ă.mă.de- kar.did/	/(to) ă.mă.de- kar.di/
(آنها) آماده کردند	(او/آن) آماده کرد
/(ăn.hă) ă.mă.de- kar.dand/	/(u/ ăn) ă.mă.de- kard/

Imperfect Indicative	
ماضی استمراری	
(ما) آماده می کردیم	(من) آماده می کردم
/(mă) ă.mă.de- mi.kar.dim/	/(man) ă.mă.de- mi.kar.dam/
(شما) آماده می کردید	(تو) آماده می کردی
/(šo.mă) ă.mă.de- mi.kar.did/	/(to) ă.mă.de- mi.kar.di/
(آنها) آماده می کردند	(او/آن) آماده می کرد
/(ăn.hă) ă.mă.de- kar.dand/	/(u/ ăn) ă.mă.de- mi.kard/

Present Perfect	
ماضی نقلی	
(ما) آماده کرده ایم	(من) آماده کرده ام
/(mă) ă.mă.de- kar.de.im/	/(man) ă.mă.de- kar.de.am/
(شما) آماده کرده اید	(تو) آماده کرده ای
/(šo.mă) ă.mă.de- kar.de.id/	/(to) ă.mă.de- kar.de.i/
(آنها) آماده کرده اند	(او/آن) آماده کرده است
/(ăn.hă) ă.mă.de- kar.de.and/	/(u/ ăn) ă.mă.de- kar.de- ast/

Past Perfect	
ماضی بعید	
(ما) آماده کرده بودیم	(من) آماده کرده بودم
/(mă) ă.mă.de- kar.de- bu.dim/	/(man) ă.mă.de- kar.de- bu.dam/
(شما) آماده کرده بودید	(تو) آماده کرده بودی
/(šo.mă) ă.mă.de- kar.de- bu.did/	/(to) ă.mă.de- kar.de- bu.di/
(آنها) آماده کرده بودند	(او/آن) آماده کرده بود
/(ăn.hă) ă.mă.de- kar.de- bu.dand/	/(u/ ăn) ă.mă.de- kar.de- bud/

<table>
<tr><th colspan="2" align="center">Past Subjunctive
ماضی التزامی</th></tr>
<tr>
<td align="center">(ما) آماده کرده باشیم
/(mă) ă.mă.de- kar.de- bă.šim/</td>
<td align="center">(من) آماده کرده باشم
/(man) ă.mă.de- kar.de- bă.šam/</td>
</tr>
<tr>
<td align="center">(شما) آماده کرده باشید
/(šo.mă) ă.mă.de- kar.de- bă.šid/</td>
<td align="center">(تو) آماده کرده باشی
/(to) ă.mă.de- kar.de- bă.ši/</td>
</tr>
<tr>
<td align="center">(آنها) آماده کرده باشند
/(ăn.hă) ă.mă.de- kar.de- bă.šand/</td>
<td align="center">(او/ آن) آماده کرده باشد
/(u/ ăn) ă.mă.de- kar.de- bă.šad/</td>
</tr>
</table>

<table>
<tr><th colspan="2" align="center">Past Progressive
ماضی مستمر(در جریان)</th></tr>
<tr>
<td align="center">(ما) داشتیم آماده می کردیم
/(mă) dăš.tim- ă.mă.de- mi.kar.dim/</td>
<td align="center">(من) داشتم آماده می کردم
/(man) dăš.tam- ă.mă.de- mi.kar.dam/</td>
</tr>
<tr>
<td align="center">(شما) داشتید آماده می کردید
/(šo.mă) dăš.tid- ă.mă.de- mi.kar.did/</td>
<td align="center">(تو) داشتی آماده می کردی
/(to) dăš.ti- ă.mă.de- mi.kar.di/</td>
</tr>
<tr>
<td align="center">(آنها) داشتند آماده می کردند
/(ăn.hă) dăš.tand- ă.mă.de- mi.kar.dand/</td>
<td align="center">(او/ آن) داشت آماده می کرد
/(u/ ăn) dăšt- ă.mă.de- mi.kard/</td>
</tr>
</table>

<table>
<tr><th colspan="2" align="center">Simple Future
مستقبل (آینده ساده)</th></tr>
<tr>
<td align="center">(ما) آماده خواهیم کرد
/(mă) ă.mă.de- ǩă.him- kard/</td>
<td align="center">(من) آماده خواهم کرد
/(man) ă.mă.de- ǩă.ham- kard/</td>
</tr>
<tr>
<td align="center">(شما) آماده خواهید کرد
/(šo.mă) ă.mă.de- ǩă.hid- kard/</td>
<td align="center">(تو) آماده خواهی کرد
/(to) ă.mă.de- ǩă.hi- kard/</td>
</tr>
<tr>
<td align="center">(آنها) آماده خواهند کرد
/(ăn.hă) ă.mă.de- ǩă.hand- kard/</td>
<td align="center">(او/ آن) آماده خواهد کرد
/(u/ ăn) ă.mă.de- ǩă.had- kard/</td>
</tr>
</table>

<table>
<tr><th colspan="2" align="center">Command
امر</th></tr>
<tr>
<td align="center">* آماده بکنید!
/ă.mă.de- be.ko.nid/</td>
<td align="center">* آماده بکن!
/ă.mă.de- be.kon/</td>
</tr>
</table>

* also: آماده کن!   آماده کنید!

to put

گُذاشتَن

/go.zǎš.tan/

Plural	Singular
Simple Present مضارع اخباری(حال ساده)	
(ما) می گذاریم /(mǎ) mi.go.zǎ.rim/	(من) می گذارم /(man) mi.go.zǎ.ram/
(شما) می گذارید /(šo.mǎ) mi.go.zǎ.rid/	(تو) می گذاری /(to) mi.go.zǎ.ri/
(آنها) می گذارند /(ǎn.hǎ) mi.go.zǎ.rand/	(او/آن) می گذارد /(u/ ǎn) mi.go.zǎ.rad/
Present Subjunctive مضارع التزامی	
(ما) بگذاریم /(mǎ) be.go.zǎ.rim/	(من) بگذارم /(man) be.go.zǎ.ram/
(شما) بگذارید /(šo.mǎ) be.go.zǎ.rid/	(تو) بگذاری /(to) be.go.zǎ.ri/
(آنها) بگذارند /(ǎn.hǎ) be.go.zǎ.rand/	(او/آن) بگذارد /(u/ ǎn) be.go.zǎ.rad/
Present Progressive مضارع مستمر(در جریان)	
(ما) داریم می گذاریم /(mǎ) dǎ.rim- mi.go.zǎ.rim/	(من) دارم می گذارم /(man) dǎ.ram- mi.go.zǎ.ram/
(شما) دارید می گذارید /(šo.mǎ) dǎ.rid- mi.go.zǎ.rid/	(تو) داری می گذاری /(to) dǎ.ri- mi.go.zǎ.ri/
(آنها) دارند می گذارند /(ǎn.hǎ) dǎ.rand- mi.go.zǎ.rand/	(او/آن) دارد می گذارد /(u/ ǎn) dǎ.rad- mi.go.zǎ.rad/

182

Simple Past
ماضی مطلق (گذشته ساده)

(ما) گذاشتیم	(من) گذاشتم
/(mǎ) go.zǎš.tim/	/(man) go.zǎš.tam/
(شما) گذاشتید	(تو) گذاشتی
/(šo.mǎ) go.zǎš.tid/	/(to) go.zǎš.ti/
(آنها) گذاشتند	(او/آن) گذاشت
/(ǎn.hǎ) go.zǎš.tand/	/(u/ ǎn) go.zǎšt/

Imperfect Indicative
ماضی استمراری

(ما) می گذاشتیم	(من) می گذاشتم
/(mǎ) mi.go.zǎš.tim/	/(man) mi.go.zǎš.tam/
(شما) می گذاشتید	(تو) می گذاشتی
/(šo.mǎ) mi.go.zǎš.tid/	/(to) mi.go.zǎš.ti/
(آنها) می گذاشتند	(او/آن) می گذاشت
/(ǎn.hǎ) mi.go.zǎš.tand/	/(u/ ǎn) mi.go.zǎšt/

Present Perfect
ماضی نقلی

(ما) گذاشته ایم	(من) گذاشته ام
/(mǎ) go.zǎš.te.im/	/(man) go.zǎš.te.am/
(شما) گذاشته اید	(تو) گذاشته ای
/(šo.mǎ) go.zǎš.te.id/	/(to) go.zǎš.te.i/
(آنها) گذاشته اند	(او/آن) گذاشته است
/(ǎn.hǎ) go.zǎš.te.and/	/(u/ ǎn) go.zǎš.te- ast/

Past Perfect
ماضی بعید

(ما) گذاشته بودیم	(من) گذاشته بودم
/(mǎ) go.zǎš.te- bu.dim/	/(man) go.zǎš.te- bu.dam/
(شما) گذاشته بودید	(تو) گذاشته بودی
/(šo.mǎ) go.zǎš.te- bu.did/	/(to) go.zǎš.te- bu.di/
(آنها) گذاشته بودند	(او/آن) گذاشته بود
/(ǎn.hǎ) go.zǎš.te- bu.dand/	/(u/ ǎn) go.zǎš.te- bud/

Past Subjunctive	
ماضی التزامی	
(ما) گذاشته باشیم	(من) گذاشته باشم
/(mǎ) go.zǎš.te- bǎ.šim/	/(man) go.zǎš.te- bǎ.šam/
(شما) گذاشته باشید	(تو) گذاشته باشی
/(šo.mǎ) go.zǎš.te- bǎ.šid/	/(to) go.zǎš.te- bǎ.ši/
(آنها) گذاشته باشند	(او/ آن) گذاشته باشد
/(ǎn.hǎ) go.zǎš.te- bǎ.šand/	/(u/ ǎn) go.zǎš.te- bǎ.šad/

Past Progressive	
ماضی مستمر(در جریان)	
(ما) داشتیم می گذاشتیم	(من) داشتم می گذاشتم
/(mǎ) dǎš.tim- mi.go.zǎš.tim/	/(man) dǎš.tam- mi.go.zǎš.tam/
(شما) داشتید می گذاشتید	(تو) داشتی می گذاشتی
/(šo.mǎ) dǎš.tid- mi.go.zǎš.tid/	/(to) dǎš.ti- mi.go.zǎš.ti/
(آنها) داشتند می گذاشتند	(او/ آن) داشت می گذاشت
/(ǎn.hǎ) dǎš.tand- mi.go.zǎš.tand/	/(u/ ǎn) dǎšt- mi.go.zǎšt/

Simple Future	
مستقبل (آینده ساده)	
(ما) خواهیم گذاشت	(من) خواهم گذاشت
/(mǎ) kǎ.him- go.zǎšt/	/(man) kǎ.ham- go.zǎšt/
(شما) خواهید گذاشت	(تو) خواهی گذاشت
/(šo.mǎ) kǎ.hid- go.zǎšt/	/(to) kǎ.hi- go.zǎšt/
(آنها) خواهند گذاشت	(او/ آن) خواهد گذاشت
/(ǎn.hǎ) kǎ.hand- go.zǎšt/	/(u/ ǎn) kǎ.had- go.zǎšt/

Command	
امر	
بگذارید!	بگذار!
/be.go.zǎ.rid/	/be.go.zǎr/

to read

خواندَن

/kăn.dan/

Plural	*Singular*
Simple Present	
مضارع اخباری(حال ساده)	
(ما) می خوانیم	(من) می خوانم
/(mă) mi.kă.nim/	/(man) mi.kă.nam/
(شما) می خوانید	(تو) می خوانی
/(šo.mă) mi.kă.nid/	/(to) mi.kă.ni/
(آنها) می خوانند	(او/آن) می خواند
/(ăn.hă) mi.kă.nand/	/(u/ ăn) mi.kă.nad/

Plural	*Singular*
Present Subjunctive	
مضارع التزامی	
(ما) بخوانیم	(من) بخوانم
/(mă) be.kă.nim/	/(man) be.kă.nam/
(شما) بخوانید	(تو) بخوانی
/(šo.mă) be.kă.nid/	/(to) be.kă.ni/
(آنها) بخوانند	(او/آن) بخواند
/(ăn.hă) be.kă.nand/	/(u/ ăn) be.kă.nad/

Plural	*Singular*
Present Progressive	
مضارع مستمر(در جریان)	
(ما) داریم می خوانیم	(من) دارم می خوانم
/(mă) dă.rim- mi.kă.nim/	/(man) dă.ram- mi.kă.nam/
(شما) دارید می خوانید	(تو) داری می خوانی
/(šo.mă) dă.rid- mi.kă.nid/	/(to) dă.ri- mi.kă.ni/
(آنها) دارند می خوانند	(او/آن) دارد می خواند
/(ăn.hă) dă.rand- mi.kă.nand/	/(u/ ăn) dă.rad- mi.kă.nad/

<table>
<tr><td colspan="2" align="center">Simple Past
ماضی مطلق (گذشته ساده)</td></tr>
<tr><td align="center">(ما) خواندیم
/(mă) ǩăn.dim/</td><td align="center">(من) خواندم
/(man) ǩăn.dam/</td></tr>
<tr><td align="center">(شما) خواندید
/(šo.mă) ǩăn.did/</td><td align="center">(تو) خواندی
/(to) ǩăn.di/</td></tr>
<tr><td align="center">(آنها) خواندند
/(ăn.hă) ǩăn.dand/</td><td align="center">(او/آن) خواند
/(u/ ăn) ǩănd/</td></tr>
</table>

<table>
<tr><td colspan="2" align="center">Imperfect Indicative
ماضی استمراری</td></tr>
<tr><td align="center">(ما) می خواندیم
/(mă) mi.ǩăn.dim/</td><td align="center">(من) می خواندم
/(man) mi.ǩăn.dam/</td></tr>
<tr><td align="center">(شما) می خواندید
/(šo.mă) mi.ǩăn.did/</td><td align="center">(تو) می خواندی
/(to) mi.ǩăn.di/</td></tr>
<tr><td align="center">(آنها) می خواندند
/(ăn.hă) mi.ǩăn.dand/</td><td align="center">(او/آن) می خواند
/(u/ ăn) mi.ǩănd/</td></tr>
</table>

<table>
<tr><td colspan="2" align="center">Present Perfect
ماضی نقلی</td></tr>
<tr><td align="center">(ما) خوانده ایم
/(mă) ǩăn.de.im/</td><td align="center">(من) خوانده ام
/(man) ǩăn.de.am/</td></tr>
<tr><td align="center">(شما) خوانده اید
/(šo.mă) ǩăn.de.id/</td><td align="center">(تو) خوانده ای
/(to) ǩăn.de.i/</td></tr>
<tr><td align="center">(آنها) خوانده اند
/(ăn.hă) ǩăn.de.and/</td><td align="center">(او/آن) خوانده است
/(u/ ăn) ǩăn.de- ast/</td></tr>
</table>

<table>
<tr><td colspan="2" align="center">Past Perfect
ماضی بعید</td></tr>
<tr><td align="center">(ما) خوانده بودیم
/(mă) ǩăn.de- bu.dim/</td><td align="center">(من) خوانده بودم
/(man) ǩăn.de- bu.dam/</td></tr>
<tr><td align="center">(شما) خوانده بودید
/(šo.mă) ǩăn.de- bu.did/</td><td align="center">(تو) خوانده بودی
/(to) ǩăn.de- bu.di/</td></tr>
<tr><td align="center">(آنها) خوانده بودند
/(ăn.hă) ǩăn.de- bu.dand/</td><td align="center">(او/آن) خوانده بود
/(u/ ăn) ǩăn.de- bud/</td></tr>
</table>

<table>
<tr><td colspan="2" align="center">**Past Subjunctive**
ماضی التزامی</td></tr>
<tr>
<td align="center">(ما) خوانده باشیم
/(mǎ) ǩǎn.de- bǎ.šim/</td>
<td align="center">(من) خوانده باشم
/(man) ǩǎn.de- bǎ.šam/</td>
</tr>
<tr>
<td align="center">(شما) خوانده باشید
/(šo.mǎ) ǩǎn.de- bǎ.šid/</td>
<td align="center">(تو) خوانده باشی
/(to) ǩǎn.de- bǎ.ši/</td>
</tr>
<tr>
<td align="center">(آنها) خوانده باشند
/(ǎn.hǎ) ǩǎn.de- bǎ.šand/</td>
<td align="center">(او/آن) خوانده باشد
/(u/ ǎn) ǩǎn.de- bǎ.šad/</td>
</tr>
</table>

<table>
<tr><td colspan="2" align="center">**Past Progressive**
ماضی مستمر(در جریان)</td></tr>
<tr>
<td align="center">(ما) داشتیم می خواندیم
/(mǎ) dǎš.tim- mi.ǩǎn.dim/</td>
<td align="center">(من) داشتم می خواندم
/(man) dǎš.tam- mi.ǩǎn.dam/</td>
</tr>
<tr>
<td align="center">(شما) داشتید می خواندید
/(šo.mǎ) dǎš.tid- mi.ǩǎn.did/</td>
<td align="center">(تو) داشتی می خواندی
/(to) dǎš.ti- mi.ǩǎn.di/</td>
</tr>
<tr>
<td align="center">(آنها) داشتند می خواندند
/(ǎn.hǎ) dǎš.tand- mi.ǩǎn.dand/</td>
<td align="center">(او/آن) داشت می خواند
/(u/ ǎn) dǎšt- mi.ǩǎnd/</td>
</tr>
</table>

<table>
<tr><td colspan="2" align="center">**Simple Future**
مستقبل (آینده ساده)</td></tr>
<tr>
<td align="center">(ما) خواهیم خواند
/(mǎ) ǩǎ.him- ǩǎnd/</td>
<td align="center">(من) خواهم خواند
/(man) ǩǎ.ham- ǩǎnd/</td>
</tr>
<tr>
<td align="center">(شما) خواهید خواند
/(šo.mǎ) ǩǎ.hid- ǩǎnd/</td>
<td align="center">(تو) خواهی خواند
/(to) ǩǎ.hi- ǩǎnd/</td>
</tr>
<tr>
<td align="center">(آنها) خواهند خواند
/(ǎn.hǎ) ǩǎ.hand- ǩǎnd/</td>
<td align="center">(او/آن) خواهد خواند
/(u/ ǎn) ǩǎ.had- ǩǎnd/</td>
</tr>
</table>

<table>
<tr><td colspan="2" align="center">**Command**
امر</td></tr>
<tr>
<td align="center">بخوانید!
/be.ǩǎ.nid/</td>
<td align="center">بخوان!
/be.ǩǎn/</td>
</tr>
</table>

to remember

به یاد آوَردَن

/be- yăd- ă.var.dan/

Plural	Singular
Simple Present مضارع اخباری(حال ساده)	
(ما) به یاد می آوریم /(mă) be- yăd- mi.ă.va.rim/	(من) به یاد می آورم /(man) be- yăd- mi.ă.va.ram/
(شما) به یاد می آورید /(šo.mă) be- yăd- mi.ă.va.rid/	(تو) به یاد می آوری /(to) be- yăd- mi.ă.va.ri/
(آنها) به یاد می آورند /(ăn.hă) be- yăd- mi.ă.va.rand/	(او/آن) به یاد می آورد /(u/ ăn) be- yăd- mi.ă.va.rad/
Present Subjunctive مضارع التزامی	
(ما) به یاد بیاوریم /(mă) be- yăd- bi.yă.va.rim/	(من) به یاد بیاورم /(man) be- yăd- bi.yă.va.ram/
(شما) به یاد بیاورید /(šo.mă) be- yăd- bi.yă.va.rid/	(تو) به یاد بیاوری /(to) be- yăd- bi.yă.va.ri/
(آنها) به یاد بیاورند /(ăn.hă) be- yăd- bi.yă.va.rand/	(او/آن) به یاد بیاورد /(u/ ăn) be- yăd- bi.yă.va.rad/
Present Progressive مضارع مستمر(در جریان)	
(ما) داریم به یاد می آوریم /(mă) dă.rim- be- yăd- mi.ă.va.rim/	(من) دارم به یاد می آورم /(man) dă.ram- be- yăd- mi.ă.va.ram/
(شما) دارید به یاد می آورید /(šo.mă) dă.rid- be- yăd- mi.ă.va.rid/	(تو) داری به یاد می آوری /(to) dă.ri- be- yăd- mi.ă.va.ri/
(آنها) دارند به یاد می آورند /(ăn.hă) dă.rand- be- yăd- mi.ă.va.rand/	(او/آن) دارد به یاد می آورد /(u/ ăn) dă.rad- be- yăd- mi.ă.va.rad/

	Simple Past
	ماضی مطلق (گذشته ساده)
(ما) به یاد آوردیم	(من) به یاد آوردم
/(mă) be- yăd- ă.var.dim/	/(man) be- yăd- ă.var.dam/
(شما) به یاد آوردید	(تو) به یاد آوردی
/(šo.mă) be- yăd- ă.var.did/	/(to) be- yăd- ă.var.di/
(آنها) به یاد آوردند	(او/آن) به یاد آورد
/(ăn.hă) be- yăd- ă.var.dand/	/(u/ ăn) be- yăd- ă.vard/

	Imperfect Indicative
	ماضی استمراری
(ما) به یاد می آوردیم	(من) به یاد می آوردم
/(mă) be- yăd- mi.ă.var.dim/	/(man) be- yăd- mi.ă.var.dam/
(شما) به یاد می آوردید	(تو) به یاد می آوردی
/(šo.mă) be- yăd- mi.ă.var.did/	/(to) be- yăd- mi.ă.var.di/
(آنها) به یاد می آوردند	(او/آن) به یاد می آورد
/(ăn.hă) be- yăd- mi.ă.var.dand/	/(u/ ăn) be- yăd- mi.ă.vard/

	Present Perfect
	ماضی نقلی
(ما) به یاد آورده ایم	(من) به یاد آورده ام
/(mă) be- yăd- ă.var.de.im/	/(man) be- yăd- ă.var.de.am/
(شما) به یاد آورده اید	(تو) به یاد آورده ای
/(šo.mă) be- yăd- ă.var.de.id/	/(to) be- yăd- ă.var.de.i/
(آنها) به یاد آورده اند	(او/آن) به یاد آورده است
/(ăn.hă) be- yăd- ă.var.de.and/	/(u/ ăn) be- yăd- ă.var.de- ast/

	Past Perfect
	ماضی بعید
(ما) به یاد آورده بودیم	(من) به یاد آورده بودم
/(mă) be- yăd- ă.var.de- bu.dim/	/(man) be- yăd- ă.var.de- bu.dam/
(شما) به یاد آورده بودید	(تو) به یاد آورده بودی
/(šo.mă) be- yăd- ă.var.de- bu.did/	/(to) be- yăd- ă.var.de- bu.di/
(آنها) به یاد آورده بودند	(او/آن) به یاد آورده بود
/(ăn.hă) be- yăd- ă.var.de- bu.dand/	/(u/ ăn) be- yăd- ă.var.de- bud/

<table>
<tr><th colspan="2" align="center">Past Subjunctive
ماضی التزامی</th></tr>
<tr>
<td align="center">(ما) به یاد آورده باشیم
/(mă) be- yăd- ă.var.de- bă.šim/</td>
<td align="center">(من) به یاد آورده باشم
/(man) be- yăd- ă.var.de- bă.šam/</td>
</tr>
<tr>
<td align="center">(شما) به یاد آورده باشید
/(šo.mă) be- yăd- ă.var.de- bă.šid/</td>
<td align="center">(تو) به یاد آورده باشی
/(to) be- yăd- ă.var.de- bă.ši/</td>
</tr>
<tr>
<td align="center">(آنها) به یاد آورده باشند
/(ăn.hă) be- yăd- ă.var.de- bă.šand/</td>
<td align="center">(او/آن) به یاد آورده باشد
/(u/ ăn) be- yăd- ă.var.de- bă.šad/</td>
</tr>
</table>

<table>
<tr><th colspan="2" align="center">Past Progressive
ماضی مستمر(در جریان)</th></tr>
<tr>
<td align="center">(ما) داشتیم به یاد می آوردیم
/(mă) dăš.tim- be- yăd- mi.ă.var.dim/</td>
<td align="center">(من) داشتم به یاد می آوردم
/(man) dăš.tam- be- yăd- mi.ă.var.dam/</td>
</tr>
<tr>
<td align="center">(شما) داشتید به یاد می آوردید
/(šo.mă) dăš.tid- be- yăd- mi.ă.var.did/</td>
<td align="center">(تو) داشتی به یاد می آوردی
/(to) dăš.ti- be- yăd- mi.ă.var.di/</td>
</tr>
<tr>
<td align="center">(آنها) داشتند به یاد می آوردند
/(ăn.hă) dăš.tand- be- yăd- mi.ă.var.dand/</td>
<td align="center">(او/آن) داشت به یاد می آورد
/(u/ ăn) dăšt- be- yăd- mi.ă.vard/</td>
</tr>
</table>

<table>
<tr><th colspan="2" align="center">Simple Future
مستقبل (آینده ساده)</th></tr>
<tr>
<td align="center">(ما) به یاد خواهیم آورد
/(mă) be- yăd- ǩă.him- ă.vard/</td>
<td align="center">(من) به یاد خواهم آورد
/(man) be- yăd- ǩă.ham- ă.vard/</td>
</tr>
<tr>
<td align="center">(شما) به یاد خواهید آورد
/(šo.mă) be- yăd- ǩă.hid- ă.vard/</td>
<td align="center">(تو) به یاد خواهی آورد
/(to) be- yăd- ǩă.hi- ă.vard/</td>
</tr>
<tr>
<td align="center">(آنها) به یاد خواهند آورد
/(ăn.hă) be- yăd- ǩă.hand- ă.vard/</td>
<td align="center">(او/آن) به یاد خواهد آورد
/(u/ ăn) be- yăd- ǩă.had- ă.vard/</td>
</tr>
</table>

<table>
<tr><th colspan="2" align="center">Command
امر</th></tr>
<tr>
<td align="center">به یاد بیاورید!
/be- yăd- bi.yă.va.rid/</td>
<td align="center">به یاد بیاور!
/be- yăd- bi.yă.var/</td>
</tr>
</table>

to repeat

تِکرار گَردَن

/tek.rǎr- kar.dan/

Plural	*Singular*
Simple Present مضارع اخباری(حال ساده)	
(ما) تکرار می کنیم /(mǎ) tek.rǎr- mi.ko.nim/	(من) تکرار می کنم /(man) tek.rǎr- mi.ko.nam/
(شما) تکرار می کنید /(šo.mǎ) tek.rǎr- mi.ko.nid/	(تو) تکرار می کنی /(to) tek.rǎr- mi.ko.ni/
(آنها) تکرار می کنند /(ǎn.hǎ) tek.rǎr- mi.ko.nand/	(او/آن) تکرار می کند /(u/ ǎn) tek.rǎr- mi.ko.nad/
Present Subjunctive مضارع التزامی	
(ما) تکرار بکنیم /(mǎ) tek.rǎr- be.ko.nim/	(من) تکرار بکنم /(man) tek.rǎr- be.ko.nam/
(شما) تکرار بکنید /(šo.mǎ) tek.rǎr- be.ko.nid/	(تو) تکرار بکنی /(to) tek.rǎr- be.ko.ni/
(آنها) تکرار بکنند /(ǎn.hǎ) tek.rǎr- be.ko.nand/	(او/آن) تکرار بکند /(u/ ǎn) tek.rǎr- be.ko.nad/
Present Progressive مضارع مستمر(در جریان)	
(ما) داریم تکرار می کنیم /(mǎ) dǎ.rim- tek.rǎr- mi.ko.nim/	(من) دارم تکرار می کنم /(man) dǎ.ram- tek.rǎr- mi.ko.nam/
(شما) دارید تکرار می کنید /(šo.mǎ) dǎ.rid- tek.rǎr- mi.ko.nid/	(تو) داری تکرار می کنی /(to) dǎ.ri- tek.rǎr- mi.ko.ni/
(آنها) دارند تکرار می کنند /(ǎn.hǎ) dǎ.rand- tek.rǎr- mi.ko.nand/	(او/آن) دارد تکرار می کند /(u/ ǎn) dǎ.rad- tek.rǎr- mi.ko.nad/

Simple Past
ماضی مطلق (گذشته ساده)

(ما) تکرار کردیم	(من) تکرا رکردم
/(mǎ) tek.rǎr- kar.dim/	/(man) tek.rǎr- kar.dam/
(شما) تکرار کردید	(تو) تکرار کردی
/(šo.mǎ) tek.rǎr- kar.did/	/(to) tek.rǎr- kar.di/
(آنها) تکرار کردند	(او/آن) تکرار کرد
/(ǎn.hǎ) tek.rǎr- kar.dand/	/(u/ ǎn) tek.rǎr- kard/

Imperfect Indicative
ماضی استمراری

(ما) تکرار می کردیم	(من) تکرار می کردم
/(mǎ) tek.rǎr- mi.kar.dim/	/(man) tek.rǎr- mi.kar.dam/
(شما) تکرار می کردید	(تو) تکرار می کردی
/(šo.mǎ) tek.rǎr- mi.kar.did/	/(to) tek.rǎr- mi.kar.di/
(آنها) تکرار می کردند	(او/آن) تکرا ر می کرد
/(ǎn.hǎ) tek.rǎr- mi.kar.dand/	/(u/ ǎn) tek.rǎr- mi.kard/

Present Perfect
ماضی نقلی

(ما) تکرار کرده ایم	(من) تکرار کرده ام
/(mǎ) tek.rǎr- kar.de.im/	/(man) tek.rǎr- kar.de.am/
(شما) تکرار کرده اید	(تو) تکرار کرده ای
/(šo.mǎ) tek.rǎr- kar.de.id/	/(to) tek.rǎr- kar.de.i/
(آنها) تکرار کرده اند	(او/آن) تکرار کرده است
/(ǎn.hǎ) tek.rǎr- kar.de.and/	/(u/ ǎn) tek.rǎr- kar.de- ast/

Past Perfect
ماضی بعید

(ما) تکرار کرده بودیم	(من) تکرار کرده بودم
/(mǎ) tek.rǎr- kar.de- bu.dim/	/(man) tek.rǎr- kar.de- bu.dam/
(شما) تکرارکرده بودید	(تو) تکرار کرده بودی
/(šo.mǎ) tek.rǎr- kar.de- bu.did/	/(to) tek.rǎr- kar.de- bu.di/
(آنها) تکرار کرده بودند	(او/آن) تکرارکرده بود
/(ǎn.hǎ) tek.rǎr- kar.de- bu.dand/	/(u/ ǎn) tek.rǎr- kar.de- bud/

<table>
<tr><td colspan="2" align="center">**Past Subjunctive**
ماضی التزامی</td></tr>
<tr><td align="center">(م) تکرار کرده باشیم
/(mă) tek.răr- kar.de- bă.šim/</td><td align="center">(من) تکرار کرده باشم
/(man) tek.răr- kar.de- bă.šam/</td></tr>
<tr><td align="center">(شما) تکرار کرده باشید
/(šo.mă) tek.răr- kar.de- bă.šid/</td><td align="center">(تو) تکرار کرده باشی
/(to) tek.răr- kar.de- bă.ši/</td></tr>
<tr><td align="center">(آنها) تکرار کرده باشند
/(ăn.hă) tek.răr- kar.de- bă.šand/</td><td align="center">(او/آن) تکرار کرده باشد
/(u/ ăn) tek.răr- kar.de- bă.šad/</td></tr>
</table>

<table>
<tr><td colspan="2" align="center">**Past Progressive**
ماضی مستمر(در جریان)</td></tr>
<tr><td align="center">(ما) داشتیم تکرار می کردیم
/(mă) dăš.tim- tek.răr- mi.kar.dim/</td><td align="center">(من) داشتم تکرار می کردم
/(man) dăš.tam- tek.răr- mi.kar.dam/</td></tr>
<tr><td align="center">(شما) داشتید تکرار می کردید
/(šo.mă) dăš.tid- tek.răr- mi.kar.did/</td><td align="center">(تو) داشتی تکرار می کردی
/(to) dăš.ti- tek.răr- mi.kar.di/</td></tr>
<tr><td align="center">(آنها) داشتند تکرار می کردند
/(ăn.hă) dăš.tand- tek.răr- mi.kar.dand/</td><td align="center">(او/آن) داشت تکرار می کرد
/(u/ ăn) dăšt- tek.răr- mi.kard/</td></tr>
</table>

<table>
<tr><td colspan="2" align="center">**Simple Future**
مستقبل (آینده ساده)</td></tr>
<tr><td align="center">(ما) تکرار خواهیم کرد
/(mă) tek.răr- ǩă.him- kard/</td><td align="center">(من) تکرار خواهم کرد
/(man) tek.răr- ǩă.ham- kard/</td></tr>
<tr><td align="center">(شما) تکرار خواهید کرد
/(šo.mă) tek.răr- ǩă.hid- kard/</td><td align="center">(تو) تکرار خواهی کرد
/(to) tek.răr- ǩă.hi- kard/</td></tr>
<tr><td align="center">(آنها) تکرار خواهند کرد
/(ăn.hă) tek.răr- ǩă.hand- kard/</td><td align="center">(او/آن) تکرار خواهد کرد
/(u/ ăn) tek.răr- ǩă.had- kard/</td></tr>
</table>

<table>
<tr><td colspan="2" align="center">**Command**
امر</td></tr>
<tr><td align="center">* تکرار بکنید!
/tek.răr- be.ko.nid/</td><td align="center">* تکرار بکن!
/tek.răr- be.kon/</td></tr>
</table>

* also: تکرار کن! تکرار کنید!

to return

بَرگَشتَن

/bar.gaš.tan/

Plural	Singular
Simple Present مضارع اخباری(حال ساده)	
(ما) برمی گردیم /(mǎ) bar.mi gar.dim/	(من) برمی گردم /(man) bar.mi.gar.dam/
(شما) برمی گردید /(šo.mǎ) bar.mi gar.did/	(تو) برمی گردی /(to) bar.mi gar.di/
(آنها) برمی گردند /(ǎn.hǎ) bar.mi gar.dand/	(او/آن) برمی گردد /(u/ ǎn) bar.mi gar.dad/
Present Subjunctive مضارع التزامی	
(ما) برگردیم /(mǎ) bar.gar.dim/	(من) برگردم /(man) bar.gar.dam/
(شما) برگردید /(šo.mǎ) bar.gar.did/	(تو) برگردی /(to) bar.gar.di/
(آنها) برگردند /(ǎn.hǎ) bar.gar.dand/	(او/آن) برگردد /(u/ ǎn) bar.gar.dad/
Present Progressive مضارع مستمر(در جریان)	
(ما) داریم برمی گردیم /(mǎ) dǎ.rim- bar.mi.gar.dim/	(من) دارم برمی گردم /(man) dǎ.ram- bar.mi.gar.dam/
(شما) دارید برمی گردید /(šo.mǎ) dǎ.rid- bar.mi.gar.did/	(تو) داری برمی گردی /(to) dǎ.ri- bar.mi.gar.di/
(آنها) دارند برمی گردند /(ǎn.hǎ) dǎ.rand- bar.mi.gar.dand/	(او/آن) دارد برمی گردد /(u/ ǎn) dǎ.rad- bar.mi.gar.dad/

<table>
<tr><td colspan="2" align="center">**Simple Past**
ماضی مطلق (گذشته ساده)</td></tr>
<tr><td align="center">(ما) برگشتیم
/(mă) bar.gaš.tim/</td><td align="center">(من) برگشتم
/(man) bar.gaš.tam/</td></tr>
<tr><td align="center">(شما) برگشتید
/(šo.mă) bar.gaš.tid/</td><td align="center">(تو) برگشتی
/(to) bar.gaš.ti/</td></tr>
<tr><td align="center">(آنها) برگشتند
/(ăn.hă) bar.gaš.tand/</td><td align="center">(او/آن) برگشت
/(u/ ăn) bar.gašt/</td></tr>
</table>

<table>
<tr><td colspan="2" align="center">**Imperfect Indicative**
ماضی استمراری</td></tr>
<tr><td align="center">(ما) برمی گشتیم
/(mă) bar.mi.gaš.tim/</td><td align="center">(من) برمی گشتم
/(man) bar.mi.gaš.tam/</td></tr>
<tr><td align="center">(شما) برمی گشتید
/(šo.mă) bar.mi.gaš.tid/</td><td align="center">(تو) برمی گشتی
/(to) bar.mi.gaš.ti/</td></tr>
<tr><td align="center">(آنها) برمی گشتند
/(ăn.hă) bar.mi.gaš.tand/</td><td align="center">(او/آن) برمی گشت
/(u/ ăn) bar.mi.gašt/</td></tr>
</table>

<table>
<tr><td colspan="2" align="center">**Present Perfect**
ماضی نقلی</td></tr>
<tr><td align="center">(ما) برگشته ایم
/(mă) bar.gaš.te.im/</td><td align="center">(من) برگشته ام
/(man) bar.gaš.te.am/</td></tr>
<tr><td align="center">(شما) برگشته اید
/(šo.mă) bar.gaš.te.id/</td><td align="center">(تو) برگشته ای
/(to) bar.gaš.te.i/</td></tr>
<tr><td align="center">(آنها) برگشته اند
/(ăn.hă) bar.gaš.te.and/</td><td align="center">(او/آن) برگشته است
/(u/ ăn) bar.gaš.te- ast/</td></tr>
</table>

<table>
<tr><td colspan="2" align="center">**Past Perfect**
ماضی بعید</td></tr>
<tr><td align="center">(ما) برگشته بودیم
/(mă) bar.gaš.te- bu.dim/</td><td align="center">(من) برگشته بودم
/(man) bar.gaš.te- bu.dam/</td></tr>
<tr><td align="center">(شما) برگشته بودید
/(šo.mă) bar.gaš.te- bu.did/</td><td align="center">(تو) برگشته بودی
/(to) bar.gaš.te- bu.di/</td></tr>
<tr><td align="center">(آنها) برگشته بودند
/(ăn.hă) bar.gaš.te- bu.dand/</td><td align="center">(او/آن) برگشته بود
/(u/ ăn) bar.gaš.te- bud/</td></tr>
</table>

<table>
<tr><td colspan="2" align="center">

Past Subjunctive

ماضی التزامی
</td></tr>
</table>

(ما) برگشته باشیم	(من) برگشته باشم
/(mǎ) bar.gaš.te- bǎ.šim/	/(man) bar.gaš.te- bǎ.šam/
(شما) برگشته باشید	(تو) برگشته باشی
/(šo.mǎ) bar.gaš.te- bǎ.šid/	/(to) bar.gaš.te- bǎ.ši/
(آنها) برگشته باشند	(او/آن) برگشته باشد
/(ǎn.hǎ) bar.gaš.te- bǎ.šand/	/(u/ ǎn) bar.gaš.te- bǎ.šad/

<table>
<tr><td colspan="2" align="center">

Past Progressive

ماضی مستمر(در جریان)
</td></tr>
</table>

(ما) داشتیم برمی گشتیم	(من) داشتم برمی گشتم
/(mǎ) dǎš.tim- bar.mi.gaš.tim/	/(man) dǎš.tam- bar.mi.gaš.tam/
(شما) داشتید برمی گشتید	(تو) داشتی برمی گشتی
/(šo.mǎ) dǎš.tid- bar.mi.gaš.tid/	/(to) dǎš.ti- bar.mi.gaš.ti/
(آنها) داشتند برمی گشتند	(او/آن) داشت برمی گشت
/(ǎn.hǎ) dǎš.tand- bar.mi.gaš.tand/	/(u/ ǎn) dǎšt- bar.mi.gašt/

<table>
<tr><td colspan="2" align="center">

Simple Future

مستقبل (آینده ساده)
</td></tr>
</table>

(ما) برخواهیم گشت	(من) برخواهم گشت
/(mǎ) bar.ǩǎ.him- gašt/	/(man) bar.ǩǎ.ham- gašt/
(شما) برخواهید گشت	(تو) برخواهی گشت
/(šo.mǎ) bar.ǩǎ.hid- gašt/	/(to) bar.ǩǎ.hi- gašt/
(آنها) برخواهند گشت	(او/آن) برخواهد گشت
/(ǎn.hǎ) bar.ǩǎ.hand- gašt/	/(u/ ǎn) bar.ǩǎ.had- gašt/

<table>
<tr><td colspan="2" align="center">

Command

امر
</td></tr>
</table>

برگردید!	برگرد!
/bar.gar.did/	/bar.gard/

to run

دَویدَن

/da.vi.dan/

Plural	Singular
Simple Present مضارع اخباری(حال ساده)	
(ما) می دویم /(mǎ) mi.da.vim/	(من) می دوم /(man) mi.da.vam/
(شما) می دوید /(šo.mǎ) mi.da.vid/	(تو) می دوی /(to) mi.da.vi/
(آنها) می دوند /(ǎn.hǎ) mi.da.vand/	(او/آن) می دود /(u/ ǎn) mi.da.vad/
Present Subjunctive مضارع التزامی	
(ما) بدویم /(mǎ) be.da.vim/	(من) بدوم /(man) be.da.vam/
(شما) بدوید /(šo.mǎ) be.da.vid/	(تو) بدوی /(to) be.da.vi/
(آنها) بدوند /(ǎn.hǎ) be.da.vand/	(او/آن) بدود /(u/ ǎn) be.da.vad/
Present Progressive مضارع مستمر(در جریان)	
(ما) داریم می دویم /(mǎ) dǎ.rim- mi.da.vim/	(من) دارم می دوم /(man) dǎ.ram- mi.da.vam/
(شما) دارید می دوید /(šo.mǎ) dǎ.rid- mi.da.vid/	(تو) داری می دوی /(to) dǎ.ri- mi.da.vi/
(آنها) دارند می دوند /(ǎn.hǎ) dǎ.rand- mi.da.vand/	(او/آن) دارد می دود /(u/ ǎn) dǎ.rad- mi.da.vad/

Simple Past
ماضی مطلق (گذشته ساده)

(ما) دویدیم	(من) دویدم
/(mǎ) da.vi.dim/	/(man) da.vi.dam/
(شما) دویدید	(تو) دویدی
/(šo.mǎ) da.vi.did/	/(to) da.vi.di/
(آنها) دویدند	(او/آن) دوید
/(ǎn.hǎ) da.vi.dand/	/(u/ ǎn) da.vid/

Imperfect Indicative
ماضی استمراری

(ما) می دویدیم	(من) می دویدم
/(mǎ) mi.da.vi.dim/	/(man) mi.da.vi.dam/
(شما) می دویدید	(تو) می دویدی
/(šo.mǎ) mi.da.vi.did/	/(to) mi.da.vi.di/
(آنها) می دویدند	(او/آن) می دوید
/(ǎn.hǎ) mi.da.vi.dand/	/(u/ ǎn) mi.da.vid/

Present Perfect
ماضی نقلی

(ما) دویده ایم	(من) دویده ام
/(mǎ) da.vi.de.im/	/(man) da.vi.de.am/
(شما) دویده اید	(تو) دویده ای
/(šo.mǎ) da.vi.de.id/	/(to) da.vi.de.i/
(آنها) دویده اند	(او/آن) دویده است
/(ǎn.hǎ) da.vi.de.and/	/(u/ ǎn) da.vi.de- ast/

Past Perfect
ماضی بعید

(ما) دویده بودیم	(من) دویده بودم
/(mǎ) da.vi.de- bu.dim/	/(man) da.vi.de- bu.dam/
(شما) دویده بودید	(تو) دویده بودی
/(šo.mǎ) da.vi.de- bu.did/	/(to) da.vi.de- bu.di/
(آنها) دویده بودند	(او/آن) دویده بود
/(ǎn.hǎ) da.vi.de- bu.dand/	/(u/ ǎn) da.vi.de- bud/

<table>
<tr><td colspan="2" align="center">**Past Subjunctive**
ماضی التزامی</td></tr>
<tr>
<td align="center">(ما) دویده باشیم
/(mă) da.vi.de- bă.šim/</td>
<td align="center">(من) دویده باشم
/(man) da.vi.de- bă.šam/</td>
</tr>
<tr>
<td align="center">(شما) دویده باشید
/(šo.mă) da.vi.de- bă.šid/</td>
<td align="center">(تو) دویده باشی
/(to) da.vi.de- bă.ši/</td>
</tr>
<tr>
<td align="center">(آنها) دویده باشند
/(ăn.hă) da.vi.de- bă.šand/</td>
<td align="center">(او/آن) دویده باشد
/(u/ ăn) da.vi.de- bă.šad/</td>
</tr>
</table>

<table>
<tr><td colspan="2" align="center">**Past Progressive**
ماضی مستمر(در جریان)</td></tr>
<tr>
<td align="center">(ما) داشتیم می دویدیم
/(mă) dăš.tim- mi.da.vi.dim/</td>
<td align="center">(من) داشتم می دویدم
/(man) dăš.tam- mi.da.vi.dam/</td>
</tr>
<tr>
<td align="center">(شما) داشتید می دویدید
/(šo.mă) dăš.tid- mi.da.vi.did/</td>
<td align="center">(تو) داشتی می دویدی
/(to) dăš.ti- mi.da.vi.di/</td>
</tr>
<tr>
<td align="center">(آنها) داشتند می دویدند
/(ăn.hă) dăš.tand- mi.da.vi.dand/</td>
<td align="center">(او/آن) داشت می دوید
/(u/ ăn) dăšt- mi.da.vid/</td>
</tr>
</table>

<table>
<tr><td colspan="2" align="center">**Simple Future**
مستقبل (آینده ساده)</td></tr>
<tr>
<td align="center">(ما) خواهیم دوید
/(mă) kă.him- da.vid/</td>
<td align="center">(من) خواهم دوید
/(man) kă.ham- da.vid/</td>
</tr>
<tr>
<td align="center">(شما) خواهید دوید
/(šo.mă) kă.hid- da.vid/</td>
<td align="center">(تو) خواهی دوید
/(to) kă.hi- da.vid/</td>
</tr>
<tr>
<td align="center">(آنها) خواهند دوید
/(ăn.hă) kă.hand- da.vid/</td>
<td align="center">(او/آن) خواهد دوید
/(u/ ăn) kă.had- da.vid/</td>
</tr>
</table>

<table>
<tr><td colspan="2" align="center">**Command**
امر</td></tr>
<tr>
<td align="center">بدوید!
/be.da.vid/</td>
<td align="center">بدو!
/be.do/</td>
</tr>
</table>

to say

گُفتَن

/gof.tan/

Plural	Singular
Simple Present مضارع اخباری(حال ساده)	
(ما) می گوییم /(mǎ) mi.gu.yim/	(من) می گویم /(man) mi.gu.yam/
(شما) می گویید /(šo.mǎ) mi.gu.yid/	(تو) می گویی /(to) mi.gu.yi/
(آنها) می گویند /(ǎn.hǎ) mi.gu.yand/	(او/آن) می گوید /(u/ ǎn) mi.gu.yad/
Present Subjunctive مضارع التزامی	
(ما) بگوییم /(mǎ) be.gu.yim/	(من) بگویم /(man) be.gu.yam/
(شما) بگویید /(šo.mǎ) be.gu.yid/	(تو) بگویی /(to) be.gu.yi/
(آنها) بگویند /(ǎn.hǎ) be.gu.yand/	(او/آن) بگوید /(u/ ǎn) be.gu.yad/
Present Progressive مضارع مستمر(در جریان)	
(ما) داریم می گوییم /(mǎ) dǎ.rim- mi.gu.yim/	(من) دارم می گویم /(man) dǎ.ram- mi.gu.yam/
(شما) دارید می گویید /(šo.mǎ) dǎ.rid- mi.gu.yid/	(تو) داری می گویی /(to) dǎ.ri- mi.gu.yi/
(آنها) دارند می گویند /(ǎn.hǎ) dǎ.rand- mi.gu.yand/	(او/آن) دارد می گوید /(u/ ǎn) dǎ.rad- mi.gu.yad/

Simple Past
ماضی مطلق (گذشته ساده)

(ما) گفتیم	(من) گفتم
/(mǎ) gof.tim/	/(man) gof.tam/
(شما) گفتید	(تو) گفتی
/(šo.mǎ) gof.tid/	/(to) gof.ti/
(آنها) گفتند	(او/آن) گفت
/(ǎn.hǎ) gof.tand/	/(u/ ǎn) goft/

Imperfect Indicative
ماضی استمراری

(ما) می گفتیم	(من) می گفتم
/(mǎ) mi.gof.tim/	/(man) mi.gof.tam/
(شما) می گفتید	(تو) می گفتی
/(šo.mǎ) mi.gof.tid/	/(to) mi.gof.ti/
(آنها) می گفتند	(او/آن) می گفت
/(ǎn.hǎ) mi.gof.tand/	/(u/ ǎn) mi.goft/

Present Perfect
ماضی نقلی

(ما) گفته ایم	(من) گفته ام
/(mǎ) gof.te.im/	/(man) gof.te.am/
(شما) گفته اید	(تو) گفته ای
/(šo.mǎ) gof.te.id/	/(to) gof.te.i/
(آنها) گفته اند	(او/آن) گفته است
/(ǎn.hǎ) gof.te.and/	/(u/ ǎn) gof.te- ast/

Past Perfect
ماضی بعید

(ما) گفته بودیم	(من) گفته بودم
/(mǎ) gof.te- bu.dim/	/(man) gof.te- bu.dam/
(شما) گفته بودید	(تو) گفته بودی
/(šo.mǎ) gof.te- bu.did/	/(to) gof.te- bu.di/
(آنها) گفته بودند	(او/آن) گفته بود
/(ǎn.hǎ) gof.te- bu.dand/	/(u/ ǎn) gof.te- bud/

Past Subjunctive
ماضی التزامی

(ما) گفته باشیم	(من) گفته باشم
/(mǎ) gof.te- bǎ.šim/	/(man) gof.te- bǎ.šam/
(شما) گفته باشید	(تو) گفته باشی
/(šo.mǎ) gof.te- bǎ.šid/	/(to) gof.te- bǎ.ši/
(آنها) گفته باشند	(او/آن) گفته باشد
/(ǎn.hǎ) gof.te- bǎ.šand/	/(u/ ǎn) gof.te- bǎ.šad/

Past Progressive
ماضی مستمر(در جریان)

(ما) داشتیم می گفتیم	(من) داشتم می گفتم
/(mǎ) dǎš.tim- mi.gof.tim/	/(man) dǎš.tam- mi.gof.tam/
(شما) داشتید می گفتید	(تو) داشتی می گفتی
/(šo.mǎ) dǎš.tid- mi.gof.tid/	/(to) dǎš.ti- mi.gof.ti/
(آنها) داشتند می گفتند	(او/آن) داشت می گفت
/(ǎn.hǎ) dǎš.tand- mi.gof.tand/	/(u/ ǎn) dǎšt- mi.goft/

Simple Future
مستقبل (آینده ساده)

(ما) خواهیم گفت	(من) خواهم گفت
/(mǎ) ǩǎ.him- goft/	/(man) ǩǎ.ham- goft/
(شما) خواهید گفت	(تو) خواهی گفت
/(šo.mǎ) ǩǎ.hid- goft/	/(to) ǩǎ.hi- goft/
(آنها) خواهند گفت	(او /آن) خواهد گفت
/(ǎn.hǎ) ǩǎ.hand- goft/	/(u/ ǎn) ǩǎ.had- goft/

Command
امر

بگویید!	بگو!
/be.gu.yid/	/be.gu/

202

to say good bye

خُداحافِظی کَردَن

/ko.dă.hă.fe.zi- kar.dan/

Plural	Singular
Simple Present	
مضارع اخباری(حال ساده)	
(ما) خداحافظی می کنیم	(من) خداحافظی می کنم
/(mă) ko.dă.hă.fe.zi- mi.ko.nim/	/(man) ko.dă.hă.fe.zi- mi.ko.nam/
(شما) خداحافظی می کنید	(تو) خداحافظی می کنی
/(šo.mă) ko.dă.hă.fe.zi- mi.ko.nid/	/(to) ko.dă.hă.fe.zi- mi.ko.ni/
(آنها) خداحافظی می کنند	(او/آن) خداحافظی می کند
/(ăn.hă) ko.dă.hă.fe.zi- mi.ko.nand/	/(u/ ăn) ko.dă.hă.fe.zi- mi.ko.nad/
Present Subjunctive	
مضارع التزامی	
(ما) خداحافظی بکنیم	(من) خداحافظی بکنم
/(mă) ko.dă.hă.fe.zi- be.ko.nim/	/(man) ko.dă.hă.fe.zi- be.ko.nam/
(شما) خداحافظی بکنید	(تو) خداحافظی بکنی
/(šo.mă) ko.dă.hă.fe.zi- be.ko.nid/	/(to) ko.dă.hă.fe.zi- be.ko.ni/
(آنها) خداحافظی بکنند	(او/آن) خداحافظی بکند
/(ăn.hă) ko.dă.hă.fe.zi- be.ko.nand/	/(u/ ăn) ko.dă.hă.fe.zi- be.ko.nad/
Present Progressive	
مضارع مستمر(در جریان)	
(ما) داریم خداحافظی می کنیم	(من) دارم خداحافظی می کنم
/(mă) dă.rim- ko.dă.hă.fe.zi- mi.ko.nim/	/(man) dă.ram- ko.dă.hă.fe.zi- mi.ko.nam/
(شما) دارید خداحافظی می کنید	(تو) داری خداحافظی می کنی
/(šo.mă) dă.rid- ko.dă.hă.fe.zi- mi.ko.nid/	/(to) dă.ri- ko.dă.hă.fe.zi- mi.ko.ni/
(آنها) دارند خداحافظی می کنند	(او/آن) دارد خداحافظی می کند
/(ăn.hă) dă.rand- ko.dă.hă.fe.zi- mi.ko.nand/	/(u/ ăn) dă.rad- ko.dă.hă.fe.zi- mi.ko.nad/

<table>
<tr><td colspan="2" align="center">**Simple Past**
ماضی مطلق (گذشته ساده)</td></tr>
<tr>
<td>(ما) خداحافظی کردیم
/(mă) ǩo.dă.hă.fe.zi- kar.dim/</td>
<td>(من) خداحافظی کردم
/(man) ǩo.dă.hă.fe.zi- kar.dam/</td>
</tr>
<tr>
<td>(شما) خداحافظی کردید
/(šo.mă) ǩo.dă.hă.fe.zi- kar.did/</td>
<td>(تو) خداحافظی کردی
/(to) ǩo.dă.hă.fe.zi- kar.di/</td>
</tr>
<tr>
<td>(آنها) خداحافظی کردند
/(ăn.hă) ǩo.dă.hă.fe.zi- kar.dand/</td>
<td>(او/آن) خداحافظی کرد
/(u/ ăn) ǩo.dă.hă.fe.zi- kard/</td>
</tr>
</table>

<table>
<tr><td colspan="2" align="center">**Imperfect Indicative**
ماضی استمراری</td></tr>
<tr>
<td>(ما) خداحافظی می کردیم
/(mă) ǩo.dă.hă.fe.zi- mi.kar.dim/</td>
<td>(من) خداحافظی می کردم
/(man) ǩo.dă.hă.fe.zi- mi.kar.dam/</td>
</tr>
<tr>
<td>(شما) خداحافظی می کردید
/(šo.mă) ǩo.dă.hă.fe.zi- mi.kar.did/</td>
<td>(تو) خداحافظی می کردی
/(to) ǩo.dă.hă.fe.zi- mi.kar.di/</td>
</tr>
<tr>
<td>(آنها) خداحافظی می کردند
/(ăn.hă) ǩo.dă.hă.fe.zi- mi.kar.dand/</td>
<td>(او/آن) خداحافظی می کرد
/(u/ ăn) ǩo.dă.hă.fe.zi- mi.kard/</td>
</tr>
</table>

<table>
<tr><td colspan="2" align="center">**Present Perfect**
ماضی نقلی</td></tr>
<tr>
<td>(ما) خداحافظی کرده ایم
/(mă) ǩo.dă.hă.fe.zi- kar.de.im/</td>
<td>(من) خداحافظی کرده ام
/(man) ǩo.dă.hă.fe.zi- kar.de.am/</td>
</tr>
<tr>
<td>(شما) خداحافظی کرده اید
/(šo.mă) ǩo.dă.hă.fe.zi- kar.de.id/</td>
<td>(تو) خداحافظی کرده ای
/(to) ǩo.dă.hă.fe.zi- kar.de.i/</td>
</tr>
<tr>
<td>(آنها) خداحافظی کرده اند
/(ăn.hă) ǩo.dă.hă.fe.zi- kar.de.and/</td>
<td>(او/آن) خداحافظی کرده است
/(u/ ăn) ǩo.dă.hă.fe.zi- kar.de- ast/</td>
</tr>
</table>

<table>
<tr><td colspan="2" align="center">**Past Perfect**
ماضی بعید</td></tr>
<tr>
<td>(ما) خداحافظی کرده بودیم
/(mă) ǩo.dă.hă.fe.zi- kar.de- bu.dim/</td>
<td>(من) خداحافظی کرده بودم
/(man) ǩo.dă.hă.fe.zi- kar.de- bu.dam/</td>
</tr>
<tr>
<td>(شما) خداحافظی کرده بودید
/(šo.mă) ǩo.dă.hă.fe.zi- kar.de- bu.did/</td>
<td>(تو) خداحافظی کرده بودی
/(to) ǩo.dă.hă.fe.zi- kar.de- bu.di/</td>
</tr>
<tr>
<td>(آنها) خداحافظی کرده بودند
/(ăn.hă) ǩo.dă.hă.fe.zi- kar.de- bu.dand/</td>
<td>(او/آن) خداحافظی کرده بود
/(u/ ăn) ǩo.dă.hă.fe.zi- kar.de- bud/</td>
</tr>
</table>

	Past Subjunctive
	ماضی التزامی
(ما) خداحافظی کرده باشیم	(من) خداحافظی کرده باشم
/(mă) ǩo.dă.hă.fe.zi- kar.de- bă.šim/	/(man) ǩo.dă.hă.fe.zi- kar.de- bă.šam/
(شما) خداحافظی کرده باشید	(تو) خداحافظی کرده باشی
/(šo.mă) ǩo.dă.hă.fe.zi- kar.de- bă.šid/	/(to) ǩo.dă.hă.fe.zi- kar.de- bă.ši/
(آنها) خداحافظی کرده باشند	(او/آن) خداحافظی کرده باشد
/(ăn.hă) ǩo.dă.hă.fe.zi- kar.de- bă.šand/	/(u/ ăn) ǩo.dă.hă.fe.zi- kar.de- bă.šad/

	Past Progressive
	ماضی مستمر(در جریان)
(ما) داشتیم خداحافظی می کردیم	(من) داشتم خداحافظی می کردم
/(mă) dăš.tim- ǩo.dă.hă.fe.zi- mi.kar.dim/	/(man) dăš.tam- ǩo.dă.hă.fe.zi- mi.kar.dam/
(شما) داشتید خداحافظی می کردید	(تو) داشتی خداحافظی می کردی
/(šo.mă) dăš.tid- ǩo.dă.hă.fe.zi- mi.kar.did/	/(to) dăš.ti- ǩo.dă.hă.fe.zi- mi.kar.di/
(آنها) داشتند خداحافظی می کردند	(او/ آن) داشت خداحافظی می کرد
/(ăn.hă) dăš.tand- ǩo.dă.hă.fe.zi- mi.kar.dand/	/(u/ ăn) dăšt- ǩo.dă.hă.fe.zi- mi.kard/

	Simple Future
	مستقبل (آینده ساده)
(ما) خداحافظی خواهیم کرد	(من) خداحافظی خواهم کرد
/(mă) ǩo.dă.hă.fe.zi- ǩă.him- kard/	/(man) ǩo.dă.hă.fe.zi- ǩă.ham- kard/
(شما) خداحافظی خواهید کرد	(تو) خداحافظی خواهی کرد
/(šo.mă) ǩo.dă.hă.fe.zi- ǩă.hid- kard/	/(to) ǩo.dă.hă.fe.zi- ǩă.hi- kard/
(آنها) خداحافظی خواهند کرد	(او/آن) خداحافظی خواهد کرد
/(ăn.hă) ǩo.dă.hă.fe.zi- ǩă.hand- kard/	/(u/ ăn) ǩo.dă.hă.fe.zi- ǩă.had- kard/

	Command
	امر
خداحافظی بکنید! *	خداحافظی بکن! *
/ǩo.dă.hă.fe.zi- be.ko.nid/	/ǩo.dă.hă.fe.zi- be.kon/

* also: خداحافظی کنید!   خداحافظی کن!

to say hello

سَلام کَردَن

/sa.lăm- kar.dan/

Plural	*Singular*
Simple Present مضارع اخباری(حال ساده)	
(ما) سلام می کنیم /(mă) sa.lăm- mi.ko.nim/	(من) سلام می کنم /(man) sa.lăm- mi.ko.nam/
(شما) سلام می کنید /(šo.mă) sa.lăm- mi.ko.nid/	(تو) سلام می کنی /(to) sa.lăm- mi.ko.ni/
(آنها) سلام می کنند /(ăn.hă) sa.lăm- mi.ko.nand/	(او/آن) سلام می کند /(u/ ăn) sa.lăm- mi.ko.nad/
Present Subjunctive مضارع التزامی	
(ما) سلام بکنیم /(mă) sa.lăm- be.ko.nim/	(من) سلام بکنم /(man) sa.lăm- be.ko.nam/
(شما) سلام بکنید /(šo.mă) sa.lăm- be.ko.nid/	(تو) سلام بکنی /(to) sa.lăm- be.ko.ni/
(آنها) سلام بکنند /(ăn.hă) sa.lăm- be.ko.nand/	(او/آن) سلام بکند /(u/ ăn) sa.lăm- be.ko.nad/
Present Progressive مضارع مستمر(در جریان)	
(ما) داریم سلام می کنیم /(mă) dă.rim- sa.lăm- mi.ko.nim/	(من) دارم سلام می کنم /(man) dă.ram- sa.lăm- mi.ko.nam/
(شما) دارید سلام می کنید /(šo.mă) dă.rid- sa.lăm- mi.ko.nid/	(تو) داری سلام می کنی /(to) dă.ri- sa.lăm- mi.ko.ni/
(آنها) دارند سلام می کنند /(ăn.hă) dă.rand- sa.lăm- mi.ko.nand/	(او/آن) دارد سلام می کند /(u/ ăn) dă.rad- sa.lăm- mi.ko.nad/

206

<table>
<tr><td colspan="2" align="center">**Simple Past**
ماضی مطلق (گذشته ساده)</td></tr>
<tr>
<td align="center">(ما) سلام کردیم
/(mă) sa.lăm- kar.dim/</td>
<td align="center">(من) سلام کردم
/(man) sa.lăm- kar.dam/</td>
</tr>
<tr>
<td align="center">(شما) سلام کردید
/(šo.mă) sa.lăm- kar.did/</td>
<td align="center">(تو) سلام کردی
/(to) sa.lăm- kar.di/</td>
</tr>
<tr>
<td align="center">(آنها) سلام کردند
/(ăn.hă) sa.lăm- kar.dand/</td>
<td align="center">(او/آن) سلام کرد
/(u/ ăn) sa.lăm- kard/</td>
</tr>
</table>

<table>
<tr><td colspan="2" align="center">**Imperfect Indicative**
ماضی استمراری</td></tr>
<tr>
<td align="center">(ما) سلام می کردیم
/(mă) sa.lăm- mi.kar.dim/</td>
<td align="center">(من) سلام می کردم
/(man) sa.lăm- mi.kar.dam/</td>
</tr>
<tr>
<td align="center">(شما) سلام می کردید
/(šo.mă) sa.lăm- mi.kar.did/</td>
<td align="center">(تو) سلام می کردی
/(to) sa.lăm- mi.kar.di/</td>
</tr>
<tr>
<td align="center">(آنها) سلام می کردند
/(ăn.hă) sa.lăm- mi.kar.dand/</td>
<td align="center">(او/آن) سلام می کرد
/(u/ ăn) sa.lăm- mi.kard/</td>
</tr>
</table>

<table>
<tr><td colspan="2" align="center">**Present Perfect**
ماضی نقلی</td></tr>
<tr>
<td align="center">(ما) سلام کرده ایم
/(mă) sa.lăm- kar.de.im/</td>
<td align="center">(من) سلام کرده ام
/(man) sa.lăm- kar.de.am/</td>
</tr>
<tr>
<td align="center">(شما) سلام کرده اید
/(šo.mă) sa.lăm- kar.de.id/</td>
<td align="center">(تو) سلام کرده ای
/(to) sa.lăm- kar.de.i/</td>
</tr>
<tr>
<td align="center">(آنها) سلام کرده اند
/(ăn.hă) sa.lăm- kar.de.and/</td>
<td align="center">(او/آن) سلام کرده است
/(u/ ăn) sa.lăm- kar.de-ast/</td>
</tr>
</table>

<table>
<tr><td colspan="2" align="center">**Past Perfect**
ماضی بعید</td></tr>
<tr>
<td align="center">(ما) سلام کرده بودیم
/(mă) sa.lăm- kar.de- bu.dim/</td>
<td align="center">(من) سلام کرده بودم
/(man) sa.lăm- kar.de- bu.dam/</td>
</tr>
<tr>
<td align="center">(شما) سلام کرده بودید
/(šo.mă) sa.lăm- kar.de- bu.did/</td>
<td align="center">(تو) سلام کرده بودی
/(to) sa.lăm- kar.de- bu.di/</td>
</tr>
<tr>
<td align="center">(آنها) سلام کرده بودند
/(ăn.hă) sa.lăm- kar.de- bu.dand/</td>
<td align="center">(او/آن) سلام کرده بود
/(u/ ăn) sa.lăm- kar.de- bud/</td>
</tr>
</table>

Past Subjunctive
ماضی التزامی

(ما) سلام کرده باشیم	(من) سلام کرده باشم
/(mă) sa.lăm- kar.de- bă.šim/	/(man) sa.lăm- kar.de- bă.šam/
(شما) سلام کرده باشید	(تو) سلام کرده باشی
/(šo.mă) sa.lăm- kar.de- bă.šid/	/(to) sa.lăm- kar.de- bă.ši/
(آنها) سلام کرده باشند	(او/آن) سلام کرده باشد
/(ăn.hă) sa.lăm- kar.de- bă.šand/	/(u/ ăn) sa.lăm- kar.de- bă.šad/

Past Progressive
ماضی مستمر(در جریان)

(ما) داشتیم سلام می کردیم	(من) داشتم سلام می کردم
/(mă) dăš.tim- sa.lăm- mi.kar.dim/	/(man) dăš.tam- sa.lăm- mi.kar.dam/
(شما) داشتید سلام می کردید	(تو) داشتی سلام می کردی
/(šo.mă) dăš.tid- sa.lăm- mi.kar.did/	/(to) dăš.ti- sa.lăm- mi.kar.di/
(آنها) داشتند سلام می کردند	(او/آن) داشت سلام می کرد
/(ăn.hă) dăš.tand- sa.lăm- mi.kar.dand/	/(u/ ăn) dăšt- sa.lăm- mi.kard/

Simple Future
مستقبل (آینده ساده)

(ما) سلام خواهیم کرد	(من) سلام خواهم کرد
/(mă) sa.lăm- ǩă.him- kard/	/(man) sa.lăm- ǩă.ham- kard/
(شما) سلام خواهید کرد	(تو) سلام خواهی کرد
/(šo.mă) sa.lăm- ǩă.hid- kard/	/(to) sa.lăm- ǩă.hi- kard/
(آنها) سلام خواهند کرد	(او/آن) سلام خواهد کرد
/(ăn.hă) sa.lăm- ǩă.hand- kard/	/(u/ ăn) sa.lăm- ǩă.had- kard/

Command
امر

* سلام بکنید!	* سلام بکن!
/sa.lăm- be.ko.nid/	/sa.lăm- be.kon/

* also: سلام کن!   سلام کنید!

208

to scream

فَریاد زَدَن

/far.yǎd- za.dan/

Plural	Singular
Simple Present مضارع اخباری(حال ساده)	
(ما) فریاد می زنیم /(mǎ) far.yǎd- mi.za.nim/	(من) فریاد می زنم /(man) far.yǎd- mi.za.nam/
(شما) فریاد می زنید /(šo.mǎ) far.yǎd- mi.za.nid/	(تو) فریاد می زنی /(to) far.yǎd- mi.za.ni/
(آنها) فریاد می زنند /(ǎn.hǎ) far.yǎd- mi.za.nand/	(او/آن) فریاد می زند /(u/ ǎn) far.yǎd- mi.za.nad/
Present Subjunctive مضارع التزامی	
(ما) فریاد بزنیم /(mǎ) far.yǎd- be.za.nim/	(من) فریاد بزنم /(man) far.yǎd- be.za.nam/
(شما) فریاد بزنید /(šo.mǎ) far.yǎd- be.za.nid/	(تو) فریاد بزنی /(to) far.yǎd- be.za.ni/
(آنها) فریاد بزنند /(ǎn.hǎ) far.yǎd- be.za.nand/	(او/آن) فریاد بزند /(u/ ǎn) far.yǎd- be.za.nad/
Present Progressive مضارع مستمر(در جریان)	
(ما) داریم فریاد می زنیم /(mǎ) dǎ.rim- far.yǎd- mi.za.nim/	(من) دارم فریاد می زنم /(man) dǎ.ram- far.yǎd- mi.za.nam/
(شما) دارید فریاد می زنید /(šo.mǎ) dǎ.rid- far.yǎd- mi.za.nid/	(تو) داری فریاد می زنی /(to) dǎ.ri- far.yǎd- mi.za.ni/
(آنها) دارند فریاد می زنند /(ǎn.hǎ) dǎ.rand- far.yǎd- mi.za.nand/	(او/آن) دارد فریاد می زند /(u/ ǎn) dǎ.rad- far.yǎd- mi.za.nad/

<table>
<tr><td colspan="2" align="center">**Simple Past**
ماضی مطلق (گذشته ساده)</td></tr>
<tr>
<td align="center">(ما) فریاد زدیم
/(mă) far.yăd- za.dim/</td>
<td align="center">(من) فریاد زدم
/(man) far.yăd- za.dam/</td>
</tr>
<tr>
<td align="center">(شما) فریاد زدید
/(šo.mă) far.yăd- za.did/</td>
<td align="center">(تو) فریاد زدی
/(to) far.yăd- za.di/</td>
</tr>
<tr>
<td align="center">(آنها) فریاد زدند
/(ăn.hă) far.yăd- za.dand/</td>
<td align="center">(او/آن) فریاد زد
/(u/ ăn) far.yăd- zad/</td>
</tr>
</table>

<table>
<tr><td colspan="2" align="center">**Imperfect Indicative**
ماضی استمراری</td></tr>
<tr>
<td align="center">(ما) فریاد می زدیم
/(mă) far.yăd- mi.za.dim/</td>
<td align="center">(من) فریاد می زدم
/(man) far.yăd- mi.za.dam/</td>
</tr>
<tr>
<td align="center">(شما) فریاد می زدید
/(šo.mă) far.yăd- mi.za.did/</td>
<td align="center">(تو) فریاد می زدی
/(to) far.yăd- mi.za.di/</td>
</tr>
<tr>
<td align="center">(آنها) فریاد می زدند
/(ăn.hă) far.yăd- mi.za.dand/</td>
<td align="center">(او/آن) فریاد می زد
/(u/ ăn) far.yăd- mi.zad/</td>
</tr>
</table>

<table>
<tr><td colspan="2" align="center">**Present Perfect**
ماضی نقلی</td></tr>
<tr>
<td align="center">(ما) فریاد زده ایم
/(mă) far.yăd- za.de.im/</td>
<td align="center">(من) فریاد زده ام
/(man) far.yăd- za.de.am/</td>
</tr>
<tr>
<td align="center">(شما) فریاد زده اید
/(šo.mă) far.yăd- za.de.id/</td>
<td align="center">(تو) فریاد زده ای
/(to) far.yăd- za.de.i/</td>
</tr>
<tr>
<td align="center">(آنها) فریاد زده اند
/(ăn.hă) far.yăd- za.de.and/</td>
<td align="center">(او/آن) فریاد زده است
/(u/ ăn) far.yăd- za.de- ast/</td>
</tr>
</table>

<table>
<tr><td colspan="2" align="center">**Past Perfect**
ماضی بعید</td></tr>
<tr>
<td align="center">(ما) فریاد زده بودیم
/(mă) far.yăd- za.de- bu.dim/</td>
<td align="center">(من) فریاد زده بودم
/(man) far.yăd- za.de- bu.dam/</td>
</tr>
<tr>
<td align="center">(شما) فریاد زده بودید
/(šo.mă) far.yăd- za.de- bu.did/</td>
<td align="center">(تو) فریاد زده بودی
/(to) far.yăd- za.de- bu.di/</td>
</tr>
<tr>
<td align="center">(آنها) فریاد زده بودند
/(ăn.hă) far.yăd- za.de- bu.dand/</td>
<td align="center">(او/آن) فریاد زده بود
/(u/ ăn) far.yăd- za.de- bud/</td>
</tr>
</table>

<table>
<tr><td colspan="2" align="center">**Past Subjunctive**
ماضی التزامی</td></tr>
<tr>
<td align="center">(ما) فریاد زده باشیم
/(mǎ) far.yǎd- za.de- bǎ.šim/</td>
<td align="center">(من) فریاد زده باشم
/(man) far.yǎd- za.de- bǎ.šam/</td>
</tr>
<tr>
<td align="center">(شما) فریاد زده باشید
/(šo.mǎ) far.yǎd- za.de- bǎ.šid/</td>
<td align="center">(تو) فریاد زده باشی
/(to) far.yǎd- za.de- bǎ.ši/</td>
</tr>
<tr>
<td align="center">(آنها) فریاد زده باشند
/(ǎn.hǎ) far.yǎd- za.de- bǎ.šand/</td>
<td align="center">(او/آن) فریاد زده باشد
/(u/ ǎn) far.yǎd- za.de- bǎ.šad/</td>
</tr>
</table>

<table>
<tr><td colspan="2" align="center">**Past Progressive**
ماضی مستمر(در جریان)</td></tr>
<tr>
<td align="center">(ما) داشتیم فریاد می زدیم
/(mǎ) dǎš.tim- far.yǎd- mi.za.dim/</td>
<td align="center">(من) داشتم فریاد می زدم
/(man) dǎš.tam- far.yǎd- mi.za.dam/</td>
</tr>
<tr>
<td align="center">(شما) داشتید فریاد می زدید
/(šo.mǎ) dǎš.tid- far.yǎd- mi.za.did/</td>
<td align="center">(تو) داشتی فریاد می زدی
/(to) dǎš.ti- far.yǎd- mi.za.di/</td>
</tr>
<tr>
<td align="center">(آنها) داشتند فریاد می زدند
/(ǎn.hǎ) dǎš.tand- far.yǎd- mi.za.dand/</td>
<td align="center">(او/آن) داشت فریاد می زد
/(u/ ǎn) dǎšt- far.yǎd- mi.zad/</td>
</tr>
</table>

<table>
<tr><td colspan="2" align="center">**Simple Future**
مستقبل (آینده ساده)</td></tr>
<tr>
<td align="center">(ما) فریاد خواهیم زد
/(mǎ) far.yǎd- ǩǎ.him- zad/</td>
<td align="center">(من) فریاد خواهم زد
/(man) far.yǎd- ǩǎ.ham- zad/</td>
</tr>
<tr>
<td align="center">(شما) فریاد خواهید زد
/(šo.mǎ) far.yǎd- ǩǎ.hid- zad/</td>
<td align="center">(تو) فریاد خواهی زد
/(to) far.yǎd- ǩǎ.hi- zad/</td>
</tr>
<tr>
<td align="center">(آنها) فریاد خواهند زد
/(ǎn.hǎ) far.yǎd- ǩǎ.hand- zad/</td>
<td align="center">(او/آن) فریاد خواهد زد
/(u/ ǎn) far.yǎd- ǩǎ.had- zad/</td>
</tr>
</table>

<table>
<tr><td colspan="2" align="center">**Command**
امر</td></tr>
<tr>
<td align="center">فریاد بزنید!
/far.yǎd- be.za.nid/</td>
<td align="center">فریاد بزن!
/far.yǎd- be.zan/</td>
</tr>
</table>

to see

دیدَن

/di.dan/

Plural	Singular
Simple Present مضارع اخباری(حال ساده)	
(ما) می بینیم /(mǎ) mi.bi.nim/	(من) می بینم /(man) mi.bi.nam/
(شما) می بینید /(šo.mǎ) mi.bi.nid/	(تو) می بینی /(to) mi.bi.ni/
(آنها) می بینند /(ǎn.hǎ) mi.bi.nand/	(او/آن) می بیند /(u/ ǎn) mi.bi.nad/
Present Subjunctive مضارع التزامی	
(ما) ببینیم /(mǎ) be.bi.nim/	(من) ببینم /(man) be.bi.nam/
(شما) ببینید /(šo.mǎ) be.bi.nid/	(تو) ببینی /(to) be.bi.ni/
(آنها) ببینند /(ǎn.hǎ) be.bi.nand/	(او/آن) ببیند /(u/ ǎn) be.bi.nad/
Present Progressive مضارع مستمر(در جریان)	
(ما) داریم می بینیم /(mǎ) dǎ.rim- mi.bi.nim/	(من) دارم می بینم /(man) dǎ.ram- mi.bi.nam/
(شما) دارید می بینید /(šo.mǎ) dǎ.rid- mi.bi.nid/	(تو) داری می بینی /(to) dǎ.ri- mi.bi.ni/
(آنها) دارند می بینند /(ǎn.hǎ) dǎ.rand- mi.bi.nand/	(او/ آن) دارد می بیند /(u/ ǎn) dǎ.rad- mi.bi.nad/

Simple Past	
ماضی مطلق (گذشته ساده)	
(ما) دیدیم	(من) دیدم
/(mă) di.dim/	/(man) di.dam/
(شما) دیدید	(تو) دیدی
/(šo.mă) di.did/	/(to) di.di/
(آنها) دیدند	(او/آن) دید
/(ăn.hă) di.dand/	/(u/ ăn) did/

Imperfect Indicative	
ماضی استمراری	
(ما) می دیدیم	(من) می دیدم
/(mă) mi.di.dim/	/(man) mi.di.dam/
(شما) می دیدید	(تو) می دیدی
/(šo.mă) mi.di.did/	/(to) mi.di.di/
(آنها) می دیدند	(او/آن) می دید
/(ăn.hă) mi.di.dand/	/(u/ ăn) mi.did/

Present Perfect	
ماضی نقلی	
(ما) دیده ایم	(من) دیده ام
/(mă) de.de.im/	/(man) di.de.am/
(شما) دیده اید	(تو) دیده ای
/(šo.mă) di.de.id/	/(to) di.de.i/
(آنها) دیده اند	(او/آن) دیده است
/(ăn.hă) di.de.and/	/(u/ ăn) di.de- ast/

Past Perfect	
ماضی بعید	
(ما) دیده بودیم	(من) دیده بودم
/(mă) di.de- bu.dim/	/(man) di.de- bu.dam/
(شما) دیده بودید	(تو) دیده بودی
/(šo.mă) di.de- bu.did/	/(to) di.de- bu.di/
(آنها) دیده بودند	(او/آن) دیده بود
/(ăn.hă) di.de- bu.dand/	/(u/ ăn) di.de- bud/

Past Subjunctive	
ماضی التزامی	
(ما) دیده باشیم /(mǎ) di.de- bǎ.šim/	(من) دیده باشم /(man) di.de- bǎ.šam/
(شما) دیده باشید /(šo.mǎ) di.de- bǎ.šid/	(تو) دیده باشی /(to) di.de- bǎ.ši/
(آنها) دیده باشند /(ǎn.hǎ) di.de- bǎ.šand/	(او/آن) دیده باشد /(u/ ǎn) di.de- bǎ.šad/

Past Progressive	
ماضی مستمر(در جریان)	
(ما) داشتیم می دیدیم /(mǎ) dǎš.tim- mi.di.dim/	(من) داشتم می دیدم /(man) dǎš.tam- mi.di.dam/
(شما) داشتید می دیدید /(šo.mǎ) dǎš.tid- mi.di.did/	(تو) داشتی می دیدی /(to) dǎš.ti- mi.di.di/
(آنها) داشتند می دیدند /(ǎn.hǎ) dǎš.tand- mi.di.dand/	(او/آن) داشت می دید /(u/ ǎn) dǎšt- mi.did/

Simple Future	
مستقبل (آینده ساده)	
(ما) خواهیم دید /(mǎ) ǩǎ.him- did/	(من) خواهم دید /(man) ǩǎ.ham- did/
(شما) خواهید دید /(šo.mǎ) ǩǎ.hid- did/	(تو) خواهی دید /(to) ǩǎ.hi- did/
(آنها) خواهند دید /(ǎn.hǎ) ǩǎ.hand- did/	(او/آن) خواهد دید /(u/ ǎn) ǩǎ.had- did/

Command	
امر	
ببینید! /be.bi.nid/	ببین ! /be.bin/

to sell

فُروختَن

/fo.ruǩ.tan/

Plural	Singular
Simple Present مضارع اخباری(حال ساده)	
(ما) می فروشیم /(mǎ) mi.fo.ru.šim/	(من) می فروشم /(man) mi.fo.ru.šam/
(شما) می فروشید /(šo.mǎ) mi.fo.ru.šid/	(تو) می فروشی /(to) mi.fo.ru.ši/
(آنها) می فروشند /(ǎn.hǎ) mi.fo.ru.šand/	(او/آن) می فروشد /(u/ ǎn) mi.fo.ru.šad/

Plural	Singular
Present Subjunctive مضارع التزامی	
(ما) بفروشیم /(mǎ) be.fo.ru.šim/	(من) بفروشم /(man) be.fo.ru.šam/
(شما) بفروشید /(šo.mǎ) be.fo.ru.šid/	(تو) بفروشی /(to) be.fo.ru.ši/
(آنها) بفروشند /(ǎn.hǎ) be.fo.ru.šand/	(او/آن) بفروشد /(u/ ǎn) be.fo.ru.šad/

Plural	Singular
Present Progressive مضارع مستمر(در جریان)	
(ما) داریم می فروشیم /(mǎ) dǎ.rim- mi.fo.ru.šim/	(من) دارم می فروشم /(man) dǎ.ram- mi.fo.ru.šam/
(شما) دارید می فروشید /(šo.mǎ) dǎ.rid- mi.fo.ru.šid/	(تو) داری می فروشی /(to) dǎ.ri- mi.fo.ru.ši/
(آنها) دارند می فروشند /(ǎn.hǎ) dǎ.rand- mi.fo.ru.šand/	(او/آن) دارد می فروشد /(u/ ǎn) dǎ.rad- mi.fo.ru.šad/

Simple Past
ماضی مطلق (گذشته ساده)

(ما) فروختیم	(من) فروختم
/(mǎ) fo.ruǩ.tim/	/(man) fo.ruǩ.tam/
(شما) فروختید	(تو) فروختی
/(šo.mǎ) fo.ruǩ.tid/	/(to) fo.ruǩ.ti/
(آنها) فروختند	(او/آن) فروخت
/(ǎn.hǎ) fo.ruǩ.tand/	/(u/ ǎn) fo.ruǩt/

Imperfect Indicative
ماضی استمراری

(ما) می فروختیم	(من) می فروختم
/(mǎ) mi.fo.ruǩ.tim/	/(man) mi.fo.ruǩ.tam/
(شما) می فروختید	(تو) می فروختی
/(šo.mǎ) mi.fo.ruǩ.tid/	/(to) mi.fo.ruǩ.ti/
(آنها) می فروختند	(او/آن) می فروخت
/(ǎn.hǎ) mi.fo.ruǩ.tand/	/(u/ ǎn) mi.fo.ruǩt/

Present Perfect
ماضی نقلی

(ما) فروخته ایم	(من) فروخته ام
/(mǎ) fo.ruǩ.te.im/	/(man) fo.ruǩ.te.am/
(شما) فروخته اید	(تو) فروخته ای
/(šo.mǎ) fo.ruǩ.te.id/	/(to) fo.ruǩ.te.i/
(آنها) فروخته اند	(او/آن) فروخته است
/(ǎn.hǎ) fo.ruǩ.te.and/	/(u/ ǎn) fo.ruǩ.te- ast/

Past Perfect
ماضی بعید

(ما) فروخته بودیم	(من) فروخته بودم
/(mǎ) fo.ruǩ.te- bu.dim/	/(man) fo.ruǩ.te- bu.dam/
(شما) فروخته بودید	(تو) فروخته بودی
/(šo.mǎ) fo.ruǩ.te- bu.did/	/(to) fo.ruǩ.te- bu.di/
(آنها) فروخته بودند	(او/آن) فروخته بود
/(ǎn.hǎ) fo.ruǩ.te- bu.dand/	/(u/ ǎn) fo.ruǩ.te- bud/

Past Subjunctive	
ماضی التزامی	
(ما) فروخته باشیم	(من) فروخته باشم
/(mǎ) fo.ruǩ.te- bǎ.šim/	/(man) fo.ruǩ.te- bǎ.šam/
(شما) فروخته باشید	(تو) فروخته باشی
/(šo.mǎ) fo.ruǩ.te- bǎ.šid/	/(to) fo.ruǩ.te- bǎ.ši/
(آنها) فروخته باشند	(او/آن) فروخته باشد
/(ǎn.hǎ) fo.ruǩ.te- bǎ.šand/	/(u/ ǎn) fo.ruǩ.te- bǎ.šad/

Past Progressive	
ماضی مستمر(در جریان)	
(ما) داشتیم می فروختیم	(من) داشتم می فروختم
/(mǎ) dǎš.tim- mi.fo.ruǩ.tim/	/(man) dǎš.tam- mi.fo.ruǩ.tam/
(شما) داشتید می فروختید	(تو) داشتی می فروختی
/(šo.mǎ) dǎš.tid- mi.fo.ruǩ.tid/	/(to) dǎš.ti- mi.fo.ruǩ.ti/
(آنها) داشتند می فروختند	(او/آن) داشت می فروخت
/(ǎn.hǎ) dǎš.tand- mi.fo.ruǩ.tand/	/(u/ ǎn) dǎšt- mi.fo.ruǩt/

Simple Future	
مستقبل (آینده ساده)	
(ما) خواهیم فروخت	(من) خواهم فروخت
/(mǎ) ǩǎ.him- fo.ruǩt/	/(man) ǩǎ.ham- fo.ruǩt/
(شما) خواهید فروخت	(تو) خواهی فروخت
/(šo.mǎ) ǩǎ.hid- fo.ruǩt/	/(to) ǩǎ.hi- fo.ruǩt/
(آنها) خواهند فروخت	(او/آن) خواهد فروخت
/(ǎn.hǎ) ǩǎ.hand- fo.ruǩt/	/(u/ ǎn) ǩǎ.had- fo.ruǩt/

Command	
امر	
بفروشید!	بفروش!
/be.fo.ru.šid/	/be.fo.ruš/

to send

فِرِستادَن

/fe.res.tă.dan/

Plural	Singular
Simple Present مضارع اخباری(حال ساده)	
(ما) می فرستیم /(mă) mi.fe.res.tim/	(من) می فرستم /(man) mi.fe.res.tam/
(شما) می فرستید /(šo.mă) mi.fe.res.tid/	(تو) می فرستی /(to) mi.fe.res.ti/
(آنها) می فرستند /(ăn.hă) mi.fe.res.tand/	(او/آن) می فرستد /(u/ ăn) mi.fe.res.tad/
Present Subjunctive مضارع التزامی	
(ما) بفرستیم /(mă) be.fe.res.tim/	(من) بفرستم /(man) be.fe.res.tam/
(شما) بفرستید /(šo.mă) be.fe.res.tid/	(تو) بفرستی /(to) be.fe.res.ti/
(آنها) بفرستند /(ăn.hă) be.fe.res.tand/	(او/آن) بفرستد /(u/ ăn) be.fe.res.tad/
Present Progressive مضارع مستمر(در جریان)	
(ما) داریم می فرستیم /(mă) dă.rim- mi.fe.res.tim/	(من) دارم می فرستم /(man) dă.ram- mi.fe.res.tam/
(شما) دارید می فرستید /(šo.mă) dă.rid- mi.fe.res.tid/	(تو) داری می فرستی /(to) dă.ri- mi.fe.res.ti/
(آنها) دارند می فرستند /(ăn.hă) dă.rand- mi.fe.res.tand/	(او/آن) دارد می فرستد /(u/ ăn) dă.rad- mi.fe.res.tad/

Simple Past
ماضی مطلق (گذشته ساده)

(ما) فرستادیم	(من) فرستادم
/(mă) fe.res.tă.dim/	/(man) fe.res.tă.dam/
(شما) فرستادید	(تو) فرستادی
/(šo.mă) fe.res.tă.did/	/(to) fe.res.tă.di/
(آنها) فرستادند	(او/آن) فرستاد
/(ăn.hă) fe.res.tă.dand/	/(u/ ăn) fe.res.tăd/

Imperfect Indicative
ماضی استمراری

(ما) می فرستادیم	(من) می فرستادم
/(mă) mi.fe.res.tă.dim/	/(man) mi.fe.res.tă.dam/
(شما) می فرستادید	(تو) می فرستادی
/(šo.mă) mi.fe.res.tă.did/	/(to) mi.fe.res.tă.di/
(آنها) می فرستادند	(او/آن) می فرستاد
/(ăn.hă) mi.fe.res.tă.dand/	/(u/ ăn) mi.fe.res.tăd/

Present Perfect
ماضی نقلی

(ما) فرستاده ایم	(من) فرستاده ام
/(mă) fe.res.tă.de.im/	/(man) fe.res.tă.de.am/
(شما) فرستاده اید	(تو) فرستاده ای
/(šo.mă) fe.res.tă.de.id/	/(to) fe.res.tă.de.i/
(آنها) فرستاده اند	(او/آن) فرستاده است
/(ăn.hă) fe.res.tă.de.and/	/(u/ ăn) fe.res.tă.de- ast/

Past Perfect
ماضی بعید

(ما) فرستاده بودیم	(من) فرستاده بودم
/(mă) fe.res.tă.de- bu.dim/	/(man) fe.res.tă.de- bu.dam/
(شما) فرستاده بودید	(تو) فرستاده بودی
/(šo.mă) fe.res.tă.de- bu.did/	/(to) fe.res.tă.de- bu.di/
(آنها) فرستاده بودند	(او/آن) فرستاده بود
/(ăn.hă) fe.res.tă.de- bu.dand/	/(u/ ăn) fe.res.tă.de- bud/

<table>
<tr><td colspan="2" align="center">

Past Subjunctive

ماضی التزامی

</td></tr>
<tr>
<td align="center">

(ما) فرستاده باشیم

/(mă) fe.res.tă.de- bă.šim/

</td>
<td align="center">

(من) فرستاده باشم

/(man) fe.res.tă.de- bă.šam/

</td>
</tr>
<tr>
<td align="center">

(شما) فرستاده باشید

/(šo.mă) fe.res.tă.de- bă.šid/

</td>
<td align="center">

(تو) فرستاده باشی

/(to) fe.res.tă.de- bă.ši/

</td>
</tr>
<tr>
<td align="center">

(آنها) فرستاده باشند

/(ăn.hă) fe.res.tă.de- bă.šand/

</td>
<td align="center">

(او/آن) فرستاده باشد

/(u/ ăn) fe.res.tă.de- bă.šad/

</td>
</tr>
</table>

<table>
<tr><td colspan="2" align="center">

Past Progressive

ماضی مستمر(در جریان)

</td></tr>
<tr>
<td align="center">

(ما) داشتیم می فرستادیم

/(mă) dăš.tim- mi.fe.res.tă.dim/

</td>
<td align="center">

(من) داشتم می فرستادم

/(man) dăš.tam- mi.fe.res.tă.dam/

</td>
</tr>
<tr>
<td align="center">

(شما) داشتید می فرستادید

/(šo.mă) dăš.tid- mi.fe.res.tă.did/

</td>
<td align="center">

(تو) داشتی می فرستادی

/(to) dăš.ti- mi.fe.res.tă.di/

</td>
</tr>
<tr>
<td align="center">

(آنها) داشتند می فرستادند

/(ăn.hă) dăš.tand- mi.fe.res.tă.dand/

</td>
<td align="center">

(او/آن) داشت می فرستاد

/(u/ ăn) dăšt- mi.fe.res.tăd/

</td>
</tr>
</table>

<table>
<tr><td colspan="2" align="center">

Simple Future

مستقبل (آینده ساده)

</td></tr>
<tr>
<td align="center">

(ما) خواهیم فرستاد

/(mă) kǎ.him- fe.res.tăd/

</td>
<td align="center">

(من) خواهم فرستاد

/(man) kǎ.ham- fe.res.tăd/

</td>
</tr>
<tr>
<td align="center">

(شما) خواهید فرستاد

/(šo.mă) kǎ.hid- fe.res.tăd/

</td>
<td align="center">

(تو) خواهی فرستاد

/(to) kǎ.hi- fe.res.tăd/

</td>
</tr>
<tr>
<td align="center">

(آنها) خواهند فرستاد

/(ăn.hă) kǎ.hand- fe.res.tăd/

</td>
<td align="center">

(او/آن) خواهد فرستاد

/(u/ ăn) kǎ.had- fe.res.tăd/

</td>
</tr>
</table>

<table>
<tr><td colspan="2" align="center">

Command

امر

</td></tr>
<tr>
<td align="center">

بفرستید!

/be.fe.res.tid/

</td>
<td align="center">

بفرست!

/be.fe.rest/

</td>
</tr>
</table>

to show

نِشان دادَن

/ne.šăn- dă.dan/

Plural	*Singular*
Simple Present مضارع اخباری(حال ساده)	
(ما) نشان می دهیم /(mă) ne.šăn- mi.da.him/	(من) نشان می دهم /(man) ne.šăn- mi.da.ham/
(شما) نشان می دهید /(šo.mă) ne.šăn- mi.da.hid/	(تو) نشان می دهی /(to) ne.šăn- mi.da.hi/
(آنها) نشان می دهند /(ăn.hă) ne.šăn- mi.da.hand/	(او/آن) نشان می دهد /(u/ ăn) ne.šăn- mi.da.had/
Present Subjunctive مضارع التزامی	
(ما) نشان بدهیم /(mă) ne.šăn- be.da.him/	(من) نشان بدهم /(man) ne.šăn- be.da.ham/
(شما) نشان بدهید /(šo.mă) ne.šăn- be.da.hid/	(تو) نشان بدهی /(to) ne.šăn- be.da.hi/
(آنها) نشان بدهند /(ăn.hă) ne.šăn- be.da.hand/	(او/آن) نشان بدهد /(u/ ăn) ne.šăn- be.da.had/
Present Progressive مضارع مستمر(در جریان)	
(ما) داریم نشان می دهیم /(mă) dă.rim- ne.šăn- mi.da.him/	(من) دارم نشان می دهم /(man) dă.ram- ne.šăn- mi.da.ham/
(شما) دارید نشان می دهید /(šo.mă) dă.rid- ne.šăn- mi.da.hid/	(تو) داری نشان می دهی /(to) dă.ri- ne.šăn- mi.da.hi/
(آنها) دارند نشان می دهند /(ăn.hă) dă.rand- ne.šăn- mi.da.hand/	(او/آن) دارد نشان می دهد /(u/ ăn) dă.rad- ne.šăn- mi.da.had/

Simple Past
ماضی مطلق (گذشته ساده)

(ما) نشان دادیم	(من) نشان دادم
/(mǎ) ne.šǎn- dǎ.dim/	/(man) ne.šǎn- dǎ.dam/
(شما) نشان دادید	(تو) نشان دادی
/(šo.mǎ) ne.šǎn- dǎ.did/	/(to) ne.šǎn- dǎ.di/
(آنها) نشان دادند	(او/آن) نشان داد
/(ǎn.hǎ) ne.šǎn- dǎ.dand/	/(u/ ǎn) ne.šǎn- dǎd/

Imperfect Indicative
ماضی استمراری

(ما) نشان می دادیم	(من) نشان می دادم
/(mǎ) ne.šǎn- mi.dǎ.dim/	/(man) ne.šǎn- mi.dǎ.dam/
(شما) نشان می دادید	(تو) نشان می دادی
/(šo.mǎ) ne.šǎn- mi.dǎ.did/	/(to) ne.šǎn- mi.dǎ.di/
(آنها) نشان می دادند	(او/آن) نشان می داد
/(ǎn.hǎ) ne.šǎn- mi.dǎ.dand/	/(u/ ǎn) ne.šǎn- mi.dǎd/

Present Perfect
ماضی نقلی

(ما) نشان داده ایم	(من) نشان داده ام
/(mǎ) ne.šǎn- dǎ.de.im/	/(man) ne.šǎn- dǎ.de.am/
(شما) نشان داده اید	(تو) نشان داده ای
/(šo.mǎ) ne.šǎn- dǎ.de.id/	/(to) ne.šǎn- dǎ.de.i/
(آنها) نشان داده اند	(او/آن) نشان داده است
/(ǎn.hǎ) ne.šǎn- dǎ.de.and/	/(u/ ǎn) ne.šǎn- dǎ.de- ast/

Past Perfect
ماضی بعید

(ما) نشان داده بودیم	(من) نشان داده بودم
/(mǎ) ne.šǎn- dǎ.de- bu.dim/	/(man) ne.šǎn- dǎ.de- bu.dam/
(شما) نشان داده بودید	(تو) نشان داده بودی
/(šo.mǎ) ne.šǎn- dǎ.de- bu.did/	/(to) ne.šǎn- dǎ.de- bu.di/
(آنها) نشان داده بودند	(او/آن) نشان داده بود
/(ǎn.hǎ) ne.šǎn- dǎ.de- bu.dand/	/(u/ ǎn) ne.šǎn- dǎ.de- bud/

<table>
<tr><td colspan="2" align="center">Past Subjunctive
ماضی التزامی</td></tr>
<tr>
<td align="center">(ما) نشان داده باشیم
/(mă) ne.šăn- dă.de- bă.šim/</td>
<td align="center">(من) نشان داده باشم
/(man) ne.šăn- dă.de- bă.šam/</td>
</tr>
<tr>
<td align="center">(شما) نشان داده باشید
/(šo.mă) ne.šăn- dă.de- bă.šid/</td>
<td align="center">(تو) نشان داده باشی
/(to) ne.šăn- dă.de- bă.ši/</td>
</tr>
<tr>
<td align="center">(آنها) نشان داده باشند
/(ăn.hă) ne.šăn- dă.de- bă.šand/</td>
<td align="center">(او/آن) نشان داده باشد
/(u/ ăn) ne.šăn- dă.de- bă.šad/</td>
</tr>
</table>

<table>
<tr><td colspan="2" align="center">Past Progressive
ماضی مستمر(در جریان)</td></tr>
<tr>
<td align="center">(ما) داشتیم نشان می دادیم
/(mă) dăš.tim- ne.šăn- mi.dă.dim/</td>
<td align="center">(من) داشتم نشان می دادم
/(man) dăš.tam- ne.šăn- mi.dă.dam/</td>
</tr>
<tr>
<td align="center">(شما) داشتید نشان می دادید
/(šo.mă) dăš.tid- ne.šăn- mi.dă.did/</td>
<td align="center">(تو) داشتی نشان می دادی
/(to) dăš.ti- ne.šăn- mi.dă.di/</td>
</tr>
<tr>
<td align="center">(آنها) داشتند نشان می دادند
/(ăn.hă) dăš.tand- ne.šăn- mi.dă.dand/</td>
<td align="center">(او/آن) داشت نشان می داد
/(u/ ăn) dăšt- ne.šăn- mi.dăd/</td>
</tr>
</table>

<table>
<tr><td colspan="2" align="center">Simple Future
مستقبل (آینده ساده)</td></tr>
<tr>
<td align="center">(ما) نشان خواهیم داد
/(mă) ne.šăn- ǩă.him- dăd/</td>
<td align="center">(من) نشان خواهم داد
/(man) ne.šăn- ǩă.ham- dăd/</td>
</tr>
<tr>
<td align="center">(شما) نشان خواهید داد
/(šo.mă) ne.šăn- ǩă.hid- dăd/</td>
<td align="center">(تو) نشان خواهی داد
/(to) ne.šăn- ǩă.hi- dăd/</td>
</tr>
<tr>
<td align="center">(آنها) نشان خواهند داد
/(ăn.hă) ne.šăn- ǩă.hand- dăd/</td>
<td align="center">(او/ آن) نشان خواهد داد
/(u/ ăn) ne.šăn- ǩă.had- dăd/</td>
</tr>
</table>

<table>
<tr><td colspan="2" align="center">Command
امر</td></tr>
<tr>
<td align="center">نشان بدهید!
/ne.šăn- be.da.hid/</td>
<td align="center">نشان بده!
/ne.šăn- be.de/</td>
</tr>
</table>

223

to sing

آواز خواندَن

/ǎ.vǎz- ǩǎn.dan/

Plural	Singular
Simple Present مضارع اخباری(حال ساده)	
(ما) آواز می خوانیم /(mǎ) ǎ.vǎz- mi.ǩǎ.nim/	(من) آواز می خوانم /(man) ǎ.vǎz- mi.ǩǎ.nam/
(شما) آواز می خوانید /(šo.mǎ) ǎ.vǎz- mi.ǩǎ.nid/	(تو) آواز می خوانی /(to) ǎ.vǎz- mi.ǩǎ.ni/
(آنها) آواز می خوانند /(ǎn.hǎ) ǎ.vǎz- mi.ǩǎ.nand/	(او/آن) آواز می خواند /(u/ ǎn) ǎ.vǎz- mi.ǩǎ.nad/
Present Subjunctive مضارع التزامی	
(ما) آواز بخوانیم /(mǎ) ǎ.vǎz- be.ǩǎ.nim/	(من) آواز بخوانم /(man) ǎ.vǎz- be.ǩǎ.nam/
(شما) آواز بخوانید /(šo.mǎ) ǎ.vǎz- be.ǩǎ.nid/	(تو) آواز بخوانی /(to) ǎ.vǎz- be.ǩǎ.ni/
(آنها) آواز بخوانند /(ǎn.hǎ) ǎ.vǎz- be.ǩǎ.nand/	(او/آن) آواز بخواند /(u/ ǎn) ǎ.vǎz- be.ǩǎ.nad/
Present Progressive مضارع مستمر(در جریان)	
(ما) داریم آواز می خوانیم /(mǎ) dǎ.rim- ǎ.vǎz- mi.ǩǎ.nim/	(من) دارم آواز می خوانم /(man) dǎ.ram- ǎ.vǎz- mi.ǩǎ.nam/
(شما) دارید آواز می خوانید /(šo.mǎ) dǎ.rid- ǎ.vǎz- mi.ǩǎ.nid/	(تو) داری آواز می خوانی /(to) dǎ.ri- ǎ.vǎz- mi.ǩǎ.ni/
(آنها) دارند آواز می خوانند /(ǎn.hǎ) dǎ.rand- ǎ.vǎz- mi.ǩǎ.nand/	(او/آن) دارد آواز می خواند /(u/ ǎn) dǎ.rad- ǎ.vǎz- mi.ǩǎ.nad/

<table>
<tr><td colspan="2" align="center">**Simple Past**
ماضی مطلق (گذشته ساده)</td></tr>
</table>

(ما) آواز خواندیم /(mă) ă.văz- ǩăn.dim/	(من) آواز خواندم /(man) ă.văz- ǩăn.dam/
(شما) آواز خواندید /(šo.mă) ă.văz- ǩăn.did/	(تو) آواز خواندی /(to) ă.văz- ǩăn.di/
(آنها) آواز خواندند /(ăn.hă) ă.văz- ǩăn.dand/	(او/آن) آواز خواند /(u/ ăn) ă.văz- ǩănd/

<table>
<tr><td colspan="2" align="center">**Imperfect Indicative**
ماضی استمراری</td></tr>
</table>

(ما) آواز می خواندیم /(mă) ă.văz- mi.ǩăn.dim/	(من) آواز می خواندم /(man) ă.văz- mi.ǩăn.dam/
(شما) آواز می خواندید /(šo.mă) ă.văz- mi.ǩăn.did/	(تو) آواز می خواندی /(to) ă.văz- mi.ǩăn.di/
(آنها) آواز می خواندند /(ăn.hă) ă.văz- mi.ǩăn.dand/	(او/آن) آواز می خواند /(u/ ăn) ă.văz- mi.ǩănd/

<table>
<tr><td colspan="2" align="center">**Present Perfect**
ماضی نقلی</td></tr>
</table>

(ما) آواز خوانده ایم /(mă) ă.văz- ǩăn.de.im/	(من) آواز خوانده ام /(man) ă.văz- ǩăn.de.am/
(شما) آواز خوانده اید /(šo.mă) ă.văz- ǩăn.de.id/	(تو) آواز خوانده ای /(to) ă.văz- ǩăn.de.i/
(آنها) آواز خوانده اند /(ăn.hă) ă.văz- ǩăn.de.and/	(او/آن) آواز خوانده است /(u/ ăn) ă.văz- ǩăn.de- ast/

<table>
<tr><td colspan="2" align="center">**Past Perfect**
ماضی بعید</td></tr>
</table>

(ما) آواز خوانده بودیم /(mă) ă.văz- ǩăn.de- bu.dim/	(من) آواز خوانده بودم /(man) ă.văz- ǩăn.de- bu.dam/
(شما) آواز خوانده بودید /(šo.mă) ă.văz- ǩăn.de- bu.did/	(تو) آواز خوانده بودی /(to) ă.văz- ǩăn.de- bu.di/
(آنها) آواز خوانده بودند /(ăn.hă) ă.văz- ǩăn.de- bu.dand/	(او/آن) آواز خوانده بود /(u/ ăn) ă.văz- ǩăn.de- bud/

<table>
<tr><th colspan="2">Past Subjunctive
ماضی التزامی</th></tr>
<tr>
<td>(ما) آواز خوانده باشیم
/(mă) ă.văz- ǩăn.de- bă.šim/</td>
<td>(من) آواز خوانده باشم
/(man) ă.văz- ǩăn.de- bă.šam/</td>
</tr>
<tr>
<td>(شما) آواز خوانده باشید
/(šo.mă) ă.văz- ǩăn.de- bă.šid/</td>
<td>(تو) آواز خوانده باشی
/(to) ă.văz- ǩăn.de- bă.ši/</td>
</tr>
<tr>
<td>(آنها) آواز خوانده باشند
/(ăn.hă) ă.văz- ǩăn.de- bă.šand/</td>
<td>(او/آن) آواز خوانده باشد
/(u/ ăn) ă.văz- ǩăn.de- bă.šad/</td>
</tr>
</table>

<table>
<tr><th colspan="2">Past Progressive
ماضی مستمر(در جریان)</th></tr>
<tr>
<td>(ما) داشتیم آواز می خواندیم
/(mă) dăš.tim- ă.văz- mi.ǩăn.dim/</td>
<td>(من) داشتم آواز می خواندم
/(man) dăš.tam- ă.văz- mi.ǩăn.dam/</td>
</tr>
<tr>
<td>(شما) داشتید آواز می خواندید
/(šo.mă) dăš.tid- ă.văz- mi.ǩăn.did/</td>
<td>(تو) داشتی آواز می خواندی
/(to) dăš.ti- ă.văz- mi.ǩăn.di/</td>
</tr>
<tr>
<td>(آنها) داشتند آواز می خواندند
/(ăn.hă) dăš.tand- ă.văz- mi.ǩăn.dand/</td>
<td>(او/آن) داشت آواز می خواند
/(u/ ăn) dăšt- ă.văz- mi.ǩănd/</td>
</tr>
</table>

<table>
<tr><th colspan="2">Simple Future
مستقبل (آینده ساده)</th></tr>
<tr>
<td>(ما) آواز خواهیم خواند
/(mă) ă.văz- ǩă.him- ǩănd/</td>
<td>(من) آواز خواهم خواند
/(man) ă.văz- ǩă.ham- ǩănd/</td>
</tr>
<tr>
<td>(شما) آواز خواهید خواند
/(šo.mă) ă.văz- ǩă.hid- ǩănd/</td>
<td>(تو) آواز خواهی خواند
/(to) ă.văz- ǩă.hi- ǩănd/</td>
</tr>
<tr>
<td>(آنها) آواز خواهند خواند
/(ăn.hă) ă.văz- ǩă.hand- ǩănd/</td>
<td>(او/آن) آواز خواهد خواند
/(u/ ăn) ă.văz- ǩă.had- ǩănd/</td>
</tr>
</table>

<table>
<tr><th colspan="2">Command
امر</th></tr>
<tr>
<td>آواز بخوانید!
/ă.văz- be.ǩă.nid/</td>
<td>آواز بخوان!
/ă.văz- be.ǩăn/</td>
</tr>
</table>

to sit

نِشَستَن

/ne.šas.tan/

Plural	Singular
Simple Present مضارع اخباری(حال ساده)	
(ما) می نشینیم /(mǎ) mi.ne.ši.nim/	(من) می نشینم /(man) mi.ne.ši.nam/
(شما) می نشینید /(šo.mǎ) mi.ne.ši.nid/	(تو) می نشینی /(to) mi.ne.ši.ni/
(آنها) می نشینند /(ǎn.hǎ) mi.ne.ši.nand/	(او/آن) می نشیند /(u/ ǎn) mi.ne.ši.nad/
Present Subjunctive مضارع التزامی	
(ما) بنشینیم /(mǎ) be.ne.ši.nim/	(من) بنشینم /(man) be.ne.ši.nam/
(شما) بنشینید /(šo.mǎ) be.ne.ši.nid/	(تو) بنشینی /(to) be.ne.ši.ni/
(آنها) بنشینند /(ǎn.hǎ) be.ne.ši.nand/	(او/آن) بنشیند /(u/ ǎn) be.ne.ši.nad/
Present Progressive مضارع مستمر(در جریان)	
(ما) داریم می نشینیم /(mǎ) dǎ.rim- mi.ne.ši.nim/	(من) دارم می نشینم /(man) dǎ.ram- mi.ne.ši.nam/
(شما) دارید می نشینید /(šo.mǎ) dǎ.rid- mi.ne.ši.nid/	(تو) داری می نشینی /(to) dǎ.ri- mi.ne.ši.ni/
(آنها) دارند می نشینند /(ǎn.hǎ) dǎ.rand- mi.ne.ši.nand/	(او/آن) دارد می نشیند /(u/ ǎn) dǎ.rad- mi.ne.ši.nad/

<table>
<tr><td colspan="2">Simple Past
ماضی مطلق (گذشته ساده)</td></tr>
<tr><td>(ما) نشستیم
/(mǎ) ne.šas.tim/</td><td>(من) نشستم
/(man) ne.šas.tam/</td></tr>
<tr><td>(شما) نشستید
/(šo.mǎ) ne.šas.tid/</td><td>(تو) نشستی
/(to) ne.šas.ti/</td></tr>
<tr><td>(آنها) نشستند
/(ǎn.hǎ) ne.šas.tand/</td><td>(او/آن) نشست
/(u/ ǎn) ne.šast/</td></tr>
</table>

<table>
<tr><td colspan="2">Imperfect Indicative
ماضی استمراری</td></tr>
<tr><td>(ما) می نشستیم
/(mǎ) mi.ne.šas.tim/</td><td>(من) می نشستم
/(man) mi.ne.šas.tam/</td></tr>
<tr><td>(شما) می نشستید
/(šo.mǎ) mi.ne.šas.tid/</td><td>(تو) می نشستی
/(to) mi.ne.šas.ti/</td></tr>
<tr><td>(آنها) می نشستند
/(ǎn.hǎ) mi.ne.šas.tand/</td><td>(او/آن) می نشست
/(u/ ǎn) mi.ne.šast/</td></tr>
</table>

<table>
<tr><td colspan="2">Present Perfect
ماضی نقلی</td></tr>
<tr><td>(ما) نشسته ایم
/(mǎ) ne.šas.te.im/</td><td>(من) نشسته ام
/(man) ne.šas.te.am/</td></tr>
<tr><td>(شما) نشسته اید
/(šo.mǎ) ne.šas.te.id/</td><td>(تو) نشسته ای
/(to) ne.šas.te.i/</td></tr>
<tr><td>(آنها) نشسته اند
/(ǎn.hǎ) ne.šas.te.and/</td><td>(او/آن) نشسته است
/(u/ ǎn) ne.šas.te- ast/</td></tr>
</table>

<table>
<tr><td colspan="2">Past Perfect
ماضی بعید</td></tr>
<tr><td>(ما) نشسته بودیم
/(mǎ) ne.šas.te- bu.dim/</td><td>(من) نشسته بودم
/(man) ne.šas.te- bu.dam/</td></tr>
<tr><td>(شما) نشسته بودید
/(šo.mǎ) ne.šas.te- bu.did/</td><td>(تو) نشسته بودی
/(to) ne.šas.te- bu.di/</td></tr>
<tr><td>(آنها) نشسته بودند
/(ǎn.hǎ) ne.šas.te- bu.dand/</td><td>(او/آن) نشسته بود
/(u/ ǎn) ne.šas.te- bud/</td></tr>
</table>

<table>
<tr><td colspan="2" align="center">**Past Subjunctive**
ماضی التزامی</td></tr>
<tr>
<td align="center">(ما) نشسته باشیم
/(mǎ) ne.šas.te- bǎ.šim/</td>
<td align="center">(من) نشسته باشم
/(man) ne.šas.te- bǎ.šam/</td>
</tr>
<tr>
<td align="center">(شما) نشسته باشید
/(šo.mǎ) ne.šas.te- bǎ.šid/</td>
<td align="center">(تو) نشسته باشی
/(to) ne.šas.te- bǎ.ši/</td>
</tr>
<tr>
<td align="center">(آنها) نشسته باشند
/(ǎn.hǎ) ne.šas.te- bǎ.šand/</td>
<td align="center">(او/آن) نشسته باشد
/(u/ ǎn) ne.šas.te- bǎ.šad/</td>
</tr>
</table>

<table>
<tr><td colspan="2" align="center">**Past Progressive**
ماضی مستمر(در جریان)</td></tr>
<tr>
<td align="center">(ما) داشتیم می نشستیم
/(mǎ) dǎš.tim- mi.ne.šas.tim/</td>
<td align="center">(من) داشتم می نشستم
/(man) dǎš.tam- mi.ne.šas.tam/</td>
</tr>
<tr>
<td align="center">(شما) داشتید می نشستید
/(šo.mǎ) dǎš.tid- mi.ne.šas.tid/</td>
<td align="center">(تو) داشتی می نشستی
/(to) dǎš.ti- mi.ne.šas.ti/</td>
</tr>
<tr>
<td align="center">(آنها) داشتند می نشستند
/(ǎn.hǎ) dǎš.tand- mi.ne.šas.tand/</td>
<td align="center">(او/آن) داشت می نشست
/(u/ ǎn) dǎšt- mi.ne.šast/</td>
</tr>
</table>

<table>
<tr><td colspan="2" align="center">**Simple Future**
مستقبل (آینده ساده)</td></tr>
<tr>
<td align="center">(ما) خواهیم نشست
/(mǎ) kǎ.him- ne.šast/</td>
<td align="center">(من) خواهم نشست
/(man) kǎ.ham- ne.šast/</td>
</tr>
<tr>
<td align="center">(شما) خواهید نشست
/(šo.mǎ) kǎ.hid- ne.šast/</td>
<td align="center">(تو) خواهی نشست
/(to) kǎ.hi- ne.šast/</td>
</tr>
<tr>
<td align="center">(آنها) خواهند نشست
/(ǎn.hǎ) kǎ.hand- ne.šast/</td>
<td align="center">(او/آن) خواهد نشست
/(u/ ǎn) kǎ.had- ne.šast/</td>
</tr>
</table>

<table>
<tr><td colspan="2" align="center">**Command**
امر</td></tr>
<tr>
<td align="center">بنشینید !
/be.ne.ši.nid/</td>
<td align="center">بنشین !
/be.ne.šin/</td>
</tr>
</table>

to sleep

خوابیدَن

/kǎ.bi.dan/

Plural	Singular
Simple Present <div dir="rtl">مضارع اخباری(حال ساده)</div>	
<div dir="rtl">(ما) می خوابیم</div> /(mǎ) mi.kǎ.bim/	<div dir="rtl">(من) می خوابم</div> /(man) mi.kǎ.bam/
<div dir="rtl">(شما) می خوابید</div> /(šo.mǎ) mi.kǎ.bid/	<div dir="rtl">(تو) می خوابی</div> /(to) mi.kǎ.bi/
<div dir="rtl">(آنها) می خوابند</div> /(ǎn.hǎ) mi.kǎ.band/	<div dir="rtl">(او/آن) می خوابد</div> /(u/ ǎn) mi.kǎ.bad/
Present Subjunctive <div dir="rtl">مضارع التزامی</div>	
<div dir="rtl">(ما) بخوابیم</div> /(mǎ) be.kǎ.bim/	<div dir="rtl">(من) بخوابم</div> /(man) be.kǎ.bam/
<div dir="rtl">(شما) بخوابید</div> /(šo.mǎ) be.kǎ.bid/	<div dir="rtl">(تو) بخوابی</div> /(to) be.kǎ.bi/
<div dir="rtl">(آنها) بخوابند</div> /(ǎn.hǎ) be.kǎ.band/	<div dir="rtl">(او/آن) بخوابد</div> /(u/ ǎn) be.kǎ.bad/
Present Progressive <div dir="rtl">مضارع مستمر(در جریان)</div>	
<div dir="rtl">(ما) داریم می خوابیم</div> /(mǎ) dǎ.rim- mi.kǎ.bim/	<div dir="rtl">(من) دارم می خوابم</div> /(man) dǎ.ram- mi.kǎ.bam/
<div dir="rtl">(شما) دارید می خوابید</div> /(šo.mǎ) dǎ.rid- mi.kǎ.bid/	<div dir="rtl">(تو) داری می خوابی</div> /(to) dǎ.ri- mi.kǎ.bi/
<div dir="rtl">(آنها) دارند می خوابند</div> /(ǎn.hǎ) dǎ.rand- mi.kǎ.band/	<div dir="rtl">(او/آن) دارد می خوابد</div> /(u/ ǎn) dǎ.rad- mi.kǎ.bad/

<table>
<tr><td colspan="2" align="center">**Simple Past**
ماضی مطلق (گذشته ساده)</td></tr>
<tr><td align="center">(ما) خوابیدیم
/(mǎ) ǩǎ.bi.dim/</td><td align="center">(من) خوابیدم
/(man) ǩǎ.bi.dam/</td></tr>
<tr><td align="center">(شما) خوابیدید
/(šo.mǎ) ǩǎ.bi.did/</td><td align="center">(تو) خوابیدی
/(to) ǩǎ.bi.di/</td></tr>
<tr><td align="center">(آنها) خوابیدند
/(ǎn.hǎ) ǩǎ.bi.dand/</td><td align="center">(او/ آن) خوابید
/(u/ ǎn) ǩǎ.bid/</td></tr>
</table>

<table>
<tr><td colspan="2" align="center">**Imperfect Indicative**
ماضی استمراری</td></tr>
<tr><td align="center">(ما) می خوابیدیم
/(mǎ) mi.ǩǎ.bi.dim/</td><td align="center">(من) می خوابیدم
/(man) mi.ǩǎ.bi.dam/</td></tr>
<tr><td align="center">(شما) می خوابیدید
/(šo.mǎ) mi.ǩǎ.bi.did/</td><td align="center">(تو) می خوابیدی
/(to) mi.ǩǎ.bi.di/</td></tr>
<tr><td align="center">(آنها) می خوابیدند
/(ǎn.hǎ) mi.ǩǎ.bi.dand/</td><td align="center">(او/آن) می خوابید
/(u/ ǎn) mi.ǩǎ.bid/</td></tr>
</table>

<table>
<tr><td colspan="2" align="center">**Present Perfect**
ماضی نقلی</td></tr>
<tr><td align="center">(ما) خوابیده ایم
/(mǎ) ǩǎ.bi.de.im/</td><td align="center">(من) خوابیده ام
/(man) ǩǎ.bi.de.am/</td></tr>
<tr><td align="center">(شما) خوابیده اید
/(šo.mǎ) ǩǎ.bi.de.id/</td><td align="center">(تو) خوابیده ای
/(to) ǩǎ.bi.de.i/</td></tr>
<tr><td align="center">(آنها) خوابیده اند
/(ǎn.hǎ) ǩǎ.bi.de.and/</td><td align="center">(او/آن) خوابیده است
/(u/ ǎn) ǩǎ.bi.de- ast/</td></tr>
</table>

<table>
<tr><td colspan="2" align="center">**Past Perfect**
ماضی بعید</td></tr>
<tr><td align="center">(ما) خوابیده بودیم
/(mǎ) ǩǎ.bi.de- bu.dim/</td><td align="center">(من) خوابیده بودم
/(man) ǩǎ.bi.de- bu.dam/</td></tr>
<tr><td align="center">(شما) خوابیده بودید
/(šo.mǎ) ǩǎ.bi.de- bu.did/</td><td align="center">(تو) خوابیده بودی
/(to) ǩǎ.bi.de- bu.di/</td></tr>
<tr><td align="center">(آنها) خوابیده بودند
/(ǎn.hǎ) ǩǎ.bi.de- bu.dand/</td><td align="center">(او/ آن) خوابیده بود
/(u/ ǎn) ǩǎ.bi.de- bud/</td></tr>
</table>

<table>
<tr><td colspan="2" align="center">**Past Subjunctive**
ماضی التزامی</td></tr>
<tr>
<td align="center">(ما) خوابیده باشیم
/(mǎ) ǩǎ.bi.de- bǎ.šim/</td>
<td align="center">(من) خوابیده باشم
/(man) ǩǎ.bi.de- bǎ.šam/</td>
</tr>
<tr>
<td align="center">(شما) خوابیده باشید
/(šo.mǎ) ǩǎ.bi.de- bǎ.šid/</td>
<td align="center">(تو) خوابیده باشی
/(to) ǩǎ.bi.de- bǎ.ši/</td>
</tr>
<tr>
<td align="center">(آنها) خوابیده باشند
/(ǎn.hǎ) ǩǎ.bi.de- bǎ.šand/</td>
<td align="center">(او/آن) خوابیده باشد
/(u/ ǎn) ǩǎ.bi.de- bǎ.šad/</td>
</tr>
</table>

<table>
<tr><td colspan="2" align="center">**Past Progressive**
ماضی مستمر(در جریان)</td></tr>
<tr>
<td align="center">(ما) داشتیم می خوابیدیم
/(mǎ) dǎš.tim- mi.ǩǎ.bi.dim/</td>
<td align="center">(من) داشتم می خوابیدم
/(man) dǎš.tam- mi.ǩǎ.bi.dam/</td>
</tr>
<tr>
<td align="center">(شما) داشتید می خوابیدید
/(šo.mǎ) dǎš.tid- mi.ǩǎ.bi.did/</td>
<td align="center">(تو) داشتی می خوابیدی
/(to) dǎš.ti- mi.ǩǎ.bi.di/</td>
</tr>
<tr>
<td align="center">(آنها) داشتند می خوابیدند
/(ǎn.hǎ) dǎš.tand- mi.ǩǎ.bi.dand/</td>
<td align="center">(او/آن) داشت می خوابید
/(u/ ǎn) dǎšt- mi.ǩǎ.bid/</td>
</tr>
</table>

<table>
<tr><td colspan="2" align="center">**Simple Future**
مستقبل (آینده ساده)</td></tr>
<tr>
<td align="center">(ما) خواهیم خوابید
/(mǎ) ǩǎ.him- ǩǎ.bid/</td>
<td align="center">(من) خواهم خوابید
/(man) ǩǎ.ham- ǩǎ.bid/</td>
</tr>
<tr>
<td align="center">(شما) خواهید خوابید
/(šo.mǎ) ǩǎ.hid- ǩǎ.bid/</td>
<td align="center">(تو) خواهی خوابید
/(to) ǩǎ.hi- ǩǎ.bid/</td>
</tr>
<tr>
<td align="center">(آنها) خواهند خوابید
/(ǎn.hǎ) ǩǎ.hand- ǩǎ.bid/</td>
<td align="center">(او/آن) خواهد خوابید
/(u/ ǎn) ǩǎ.had- ǩǎ.bid/</td>
</tr>
</table>

<table>
<tr><td colspan="2" align="center">**Command**
امر</td></tr>
<tr>
<td align="center">بخوابید !
/be.ǩǎ.bid/</td>
<td align="center">بخواب !
/be.ǩǎb/</td>
</tr>
</table>

to smell

بوییدَن

/bu.yi.dan/

Plural	Singular
Simple Present مضارع اخباری(حال ساده)	
(ما) می بوییم /(mǎ) mi.bu.yim/	(من) می بویم /(man) mi.bu.yam/
(شما) می بویید /(šo.mǎ) mi.bu.yid/	(تو) می بویی /(to) mi.bu.yi/
(آنها) می بویند /(ǎn.hǎ) mi.bu.yand/	(او/آن) می بوید /(u/ ǎn) mi.bu.yad/
Present Subjunctive مضارع التزامی	
(ما) ببوییم /(mǎ) be.bu.yim/	(من) ببویم /(man) be.bu.yam/
(شما) ببویید /(šo.mǎ) be.bu.yid/	(تو) ببویی /(to) be.bu.yi/
(آنها) ببویند /(ǎn.hǎ) be.bu.yand/	(او/آن) ببوید /(u/ ǎn) be.bu.yad/
Present Progressive مضارع مستمر(در جریان)	
(ما) داریم می بوییم /(mǎ) dǎ.rim- mi.bu.yim/	(من) دارم می بویم /(man) dǎ.ram- mi.bu.yam/
(شما) دارید می بویید /(šo.mǎ) dǎ.rid- mi.bu.yid/	(تو) داری می بویی /(to) dǎ.ri- mi.bu.yi/
(آنها) دارند می بویند /(ǎn.hǎ) dǎ.rand- mi.bu.yand/	(او/آن) دارد می بوید /(u/ ǎn) dǎ.rad- mi.bu.yad/

<table>
<tr><td colspan="2" align="center">**Simple Past**
ماضی مطلق (گذشته ساده)</td></tr>
<tr>
<td align="center">(ما) بوییدیم
/(mǎ) bu.yi.dim/</td>
<td align="center">(من) بوییدم
/(man) bu.yi.dam/</td>
</tr>
<tr>
<td align="center">(شما) بوییدید
/(šo.mǎ) bu.yi.did/</td>
<td align="center">(تو) بوییدی
/(to) bu.yi.di/</td>
</tr>
<tr>
<td align="center">(آنها) بوییدند
/(ǎn.hǎ) bu.yi.dand/</td>
<td align="center">(او/آن) بویید
/(u/ ǎn) bu.yid/</td>
</tr>
</table>

<table>
<tr><td colspan="2" align="center">**Imperfect Indicative**
ماضی استمراری</td></tr>
<tr>
<td align="center">(ما) می بوییدیم
/(mǎ) mi.bu.yi.dim/</td>
<td align="center">(من) می بوییدم
/(man) mi.bu.yi.dam/</td>
</tr>
<tr>
<td align="center">(شما) می بوییدید
/(šo.mǎ) mi.bu.yi.did/</td>
<td align="center">(تو) می بوییدی
/(to) mi.bu.yi.di/</td>
</tr>
<tr>
<td align="center">(آنها) می بوییدند
/(ǎn.hǎ) mi.bu.yi.dand/</td>
<td align="center">(او/آن) می بویید
/(u/ ǎn) mi.bu.yid/</td>
</tr>
</table>

<table>
<tr><td colspan="2" align="center">**Present Perfect**
ماضی نقلی</td></tr>
<tr>
<td align="center">(ما) بوییده ایم
/(mǎ) bu.yi.de.im/</td>
<td align="center">(من) بوییده ام
/(man) bu.yi.de.am/</td>
</tr>
<tr>
<td align="center">(شما) بوییده اید
/(šo.mǎ) bu.yi.de.id/</td>
<td align="center">(تو) بوییده ای
/(to) bu.yi.de.i/</td>
</tr>
<tr>
<td align="center">(آنها) بوییده اند
/(ǎn.hǎ) bu.yi.de.and/</td>
<td align="center">(او/آن) بوییده است
/(u/ ǎn) bu.yi.de- ast/</td>
</tr>
</table>

<table>
<tr><td colspan="2" align="center">**Past Perfect**
ماضی بعید</td></tr>
<tr>
<td align="center">(ما) بوییده بودیم
/(mǎ) bu.yi.de- bu.dim/</td>
<td align="center">(من) بوییده بودم
/(man) bu.yi.de- bu.dam/</td>
</tr>
<tr>
<td align="center">(شما) بوییده بودید
/(šo.mǎ) bu.yi.de- bu.did/</td>
<td align="center">(تو) بوییده بودی
/(to) bu.yi.de- bu.di/</td>
</tr>
<tr>
<td align="center">(آنها) بوییده بودند
/(ǎn.hǎ) bu.yi.de- bu.dand/</td>
<td align="center">(او/آن) بوییده بود
/(u/ ǎn) bu.yi.de- bud/</td>
</tr>
</table>

Past Subjunctive	
ماضی التزامی	
(ما) بوییده باشیم	(من) بوییده باشم
/(mǎ) bu.yi.de- bǎ.šim/	/(man) bu.yi.de- bǎ.šam/
(شما) بوییده باشید	(تو) بوییده باشی
/(šo.mǎ) bu.yi.de- bǎ.šid/	/(to) bu.yi.de- bǎ.ši/
(آنها) بوییده باشند	(او/آن) بوییده باشد
/(ǎn.hǎ) bu.yi.de- bǎ.šand/	/(u/ ǎn) bu.yi.de- bǎ.šad/

Past Progressive	
ماضی مستمر(در جریان)	
(ما) داشتیم می بوییدیم	(من) داشتم می بوییدم
/(mǎ) dǎš.tim- mi.bu.yi.dim/	/(man) dǎš.tam- mi.bu.yi.dam/
(شما) داشتید می بوییدید	(تو) داشتی می بوییدی
/(šo.mǎ) dǎš.tid- mi.bu.yi.did/	/(to) dǎš.ti- mi.bu.yi.di/
(آنها) داشتند می بوییدند	(او/آن) داشت می بویید
/(ǎn.hǎ) dǎš.tand- mi.bu.yi.dand/	/(u/ ǎn) dǎšt- mi.bu.yid/

Simple Future	
مستقبل (آینده ساده)	
(ما) خواهیم بویید	(من) خواهم بویید
/(mǎ) kǎ.him- bu.yid/	/(man) kǎ.ham- bu.yid/
(شما) خواهید بویید	(تو) خواهی بویید
/(šo.mǎ) kǎ.hid- bu.yid/	/(to) kǎ.hi- bu.yid/
(آنها) خواهند بویید	(او/آن) خواهد بویید
/(ǎn.hǎ) kǎ.hand- bu.yid/	/(u/ ǎn) kǎ.had- bu.yid/

Command	
امر	
ببویید!	ببوی!
/be.bu.yid/	/be.buy/

to smile

لَبخَند زَدَن

/lab.ǩand- za.dan/

Plural	Singular
Simple Present مضارع اخباری(حال ساده)	
(ما) لبخند می زنیم /(mǎ) lab.ǩand- mi.za.nim/	(من) لبخند می زنم /(man) lab.ǩand- mi.za.nam/
(شما) لبخند می زنید /(šo.mǎ) lab.ǩand- mi.za.nid/	(تو) لبخند می زنی /(to) lab.ǩand- mi.za.ni/
(آنها) لبخند می زنند /(ǎn.hǎ) lab.ǩand- mi.za.nand/	(او/آن) لبخند می زند /(u/ ǎn) lab.ǩand- mi.za.nad/
Present Subjunctive مضارع التزامی	
(ما) لبخند بزنیم /(mǎ) lab.ǩand- be.za.nim/	(من) لبخند بزنم /(man) lab.ǩand- be.za.nam/
(شما) لبخند بزنید /(šo.mǎ) lab.ǩand- be.za.nid/	(تو) لبخند بزنی /(to) lab.ǩand- be.za.ni/
(آنها) لبخند بزنند /(ǎn.hǎ) lab.ǩand- be.za.nand/	(او/آن) لبخند بزند /(u/ ǎn) lab.ǩand- be.za.nad/
Present Progressive مضارع مستمر(در جریان)	
(ما) داریم لبخند می زنیم /(mǎ) dǎ.rim- lab.ǩand- mi.za.nim/	(من) دارم لبخند می زنم /(man) dǎ.ram- lab.ǩand- mi.za.nam/
(شما) دارید لبخند می زنید /(šo.mǎ) dǎ.rid- lab.ǩand- mi.za.nid/	(تو) داری لبخند می زنی /(to) dǎ.ri- lab.ǩand- mi.za.ni/
(آنها) دارند لبخند می زنند /(ǎn.hǎ) dǎ.rand- lab.ǩand- mi.za.nand/	(او/آن) دارد لبخند می زند /(u/ ǎn) dǎ.rad- lab.ǩand- mi.za.nad/

	Simple Past
	ماضی مطلق (گذشته ساده)
(ما) لبخند زدیم	(من) لبخند زدم
/(mǎ) lab.ǩand- za.dim/	/(man) lab.ǩand- za.dam/
(شما) لبخند زدید	(تو) لبخند زدی
/(šo.mǎ) lab.ǩand- za.did/	/(to) lab.ǩand- za.di/
(آنها) لبخند زدند	(او/آن) لبخند زد
/(ǎn.hǎ) lab.ǩand- za.dand/	/(u/ ǎn) lab.ǩand- zad/

	Imperfect Indicative
	ماضی استمراری
(ما) لبخند می زدیم	(من) لبخند می زدم
/(mǎ) lab.ǩand- mi.za.dim/	/(man) lab.ǩand- mi.za.dam/
(شما) لبخند می زدید	(تو) لبخند می زدی
/(šo.mǎ) lab.ǩand- mi.za.did/	/(to) lab.ǩand- mi.za.di/
(آنها) لبخند می زدند	(او/آن) لبخند می زد
/(ǎn.hǎ) lab.ǩand- mi.za.dand/	/(u/ ǎn) lab.ǩand- mi.zad/

	Present Perfect
	ماضی نقلی
(ما) لبخند زده ایم	(من) لبخند زده ام
/(mǎ) lab.ǩand- za.de.im/	/(man) lab.ǩand- za.de.am/
(شما) لبخند زده اید	(تو) لبخند زده ای
/(šo.mǎ) lab.ǩand- za.de.id/	/(to) lab.ǩand- za.de.i/
(آنها) لبخند زده اند	(او/آن) لبخند زده است
/(ǎn.hǎ) lab.ǩand- za.de.and/	/(u/ ǎn) lab.ǩand- za.de- ast/

	Past Perfect
	ماضی بعید
(ما) لبخند زده بودیم	(من) لبخند زده بودم
/(mǎ) lab.ǩand- za.de- bu.dim/	/(man) lab.ǩand- za.de- bu.dam/
(شما) لبخند زده بودید	(تو) لبخند زده بودی
/(šo.mǎ) lab.ǩand- za.de- bu.did/	/(to) lab.ǩand- za.de- bu.di/
(آنها) لبخند زده بودند	(او/آن) لبخند زده بود
/(ǎn.hǎ) lab.ǩand- za.de- bu.dand/	/(u/ ǎn) lab.ǩand- za.de- bud/

<table>
<tr><td colspan="2" align="center">**Past Subjunctive**
ماضی التزامی</td></tr>
<tr>
<td align="center">(ما) لبخند زده باشیم
/(mă) lab.ǩand- za.de- bă.šim/</td>
<td align="center">(من) لبخند زده باشم
/(man) lab.ǩand- za.de- bă.šam/</td>
</tr>
<tr>
<td align="center">(شما) لبخند زده باشید
/(šo.mă) lab.ǩand- za.de- bă.šid/</td>
<td align="center">(تو) لبخند زده باشی
/(to) lab.ǩand- za.de- bă.ši/</td>
</tr>
<tr>
<td align="center">(آنها) لبخند زده باشند
/(ăn.hă) lab.ǩand- za.de- bă.šand/</td>
<td align="center">(او/آن) لبخند زده باشد
/(u/ ăn) lab.ǩand- za.de- bă.šad/</td>
</tr>
</table>

<table>
<tr><td colspan="2" align="center">**Past Progressive**
ماضی مستمر(در جریان)</td></tr>
<tr>
<td align="center">(ما) داشتیم لبخند می زدیم
/(mă) dăš.tim- lab.ǩand- mi.za.dim/</td>
<td align="center">(من) داشتم لبخند می زدم
/(man) dăš.tam- lab.ǩand- mi.za.dam/</td>
</tr>
<tr>
<td align="center">(شما) داشتید لبخند می زدید
/(šo.mă) dăš.tid- lab.ǩand- mi.za.did/</td>
<td align="center">(تو) داشتی لبخند می زدی
/(to) dăš.ti- lab.ǩand- mi.za.di/</td>
</tr>
<tr>
<td align="center">(آنها) داشتند لبخند می زدند
/(ăn.hă) dăš.tand- lab.ǩand- mi.za.dand/</td>
<td align="center">(او/آن) داشت لبخند می زد
/(u/ ăn) dăšt- lab.ǩand- mi.zad/</td>
</tr>
</table>

<table>
<tr><td colspan="2" align="center">**Simple Future**
مستقبل (آینده ساده)</td></tr>
<tr>
<td align="center">(ما) لبخند خواهیم زد
/(mă) lab.ǩand- ǩă.him- zad/</td>
<td align="center">(من) لبخند خواهم زد
/(man) lab.ǩand- ǩă.ham- zad/</td>
</tr>
<tr>
<td align="center">(شما) لبخند خواهید زد
/(šo.mă) lab.ǩand- ǩă.hid- zad/</td>
<td align="center">(تو) لبخند خواهی زد
/(to) lab.ǩand- ǩă.hi- zad/</td>
</tr>
<tr>
<td align="center">(آنها) لبخند خواهند زد
/(ăn.hă) lab.ǩand- ǩă.hand- zad/</td>
<td align="center">(او/آن) لبخند خواهد زد
/(u/ ăn) lab.ǩand- ǩă.had- zad/</td>
</tr>
</table>

<table>
<tr><td colspan="2" align="center">**Command**
امر</td></tr>
<tr>
<td align="center">لبخند بزنید!
/lab.ǩand- be.za.nid/</td>
<td align="center">لبخند بزن!
/lab.ǩand- be.zan/</td>
</tr>
</table>

to stand

ایستادَن

/is.tă.dan/

Plural	Singular
Simple Present مضارع اخباری(حال ساده)	
(ما) می ایستیم /(mă) mi.is.tim/	(من) می ایستم /(man) mi.is.tam/
(شما) می ایستید /(šo.mă) mi.is.tid/	(تو) می ایستی /(to) mi.is.ti/
(آنها) می ایستند /(ăn.hă) mi.is.tand/	(او/آن) می ایستد /(u/ ăn) mi.is.tad/
Present Subjunctive مضارع التزامی	
(ما) بایستیم /(mă) be.is.tim/	(من) بایستم /(man) be.is.tam/
(شما) بایستید /(šo.mă) be.is.tid/	(تو) بایستی /(to) be.is.ti/
(آنها) بایستند /(ăn.hă) be.is.tand/	(او/آن) بایستد /(u/ ăn) be.is.tad/
Present Progressive مضارع مستمر(در جریان)	
(ما) داریم می ایستیم /(mă) dă.rim- mi.is.tim/	(من) دارم می ایستم /(man) dă.ram- mi.is.tam/
(شما) دارید می ایستید /(šo.mă) dă.rid- mi.is.tid/	(تو) داری می ایستی /(to) dă.ri- mi.is.ti/
(آنها) دارند می ایستند /(ăn.hă) dă.rand- mi.is.tand/	(او/آن) دارد می ایستد /(u/ ăn) dă.rad- mi.is.tad/

239

Simple Past
ماضی مطلق (گذشته ساده)

(ما) ایستادیم	(من) ایستادم
/(mǎ) is.tǎ.dim/	/(man) is.tǎ.dam/
(شما) ایستادید	(تو) ایستادی
/(šo.mǎ) is.tǎ.did/	/(to) is.tǎ.di/
(آنها) ایستادند	(او/آن) ایستاد
/(ǎn.hǎ) is.tǎ.dand/	/(u/ ǎn) is.tǎd/

Imperfect Indicative
ماضی استمراری

(ما) می ایستادیم	(من) می ایستادم
/(mǎ) mi.is.tǎ.dim/	/(man) mi.is.tǎ.dam/
(شما) می ایستادید	(تو) می ایستادی
/(šo.mǎ) mi.is.tǎ.did/	/(to) mi.is.tǎ.di/
(آنها) می ایستادند	(او/آن) می ایستاد
/(ǎn.hǎ) mi.is.tǎ.dand/	/(u/ ǎn) mi.is.tǎd/

Present Perfect
ماضی نقلی

(ما) ایستاده ایم	(من) ایستاده ام
/(mǎ) is.tǎ.de.im/	/(man) is.tǎ.de.am/
(شما) ایستاده اید	(تو) ایستاده ای
/(šo.mǎ) is.tǎ.de.id/	/(to) is.tǎ.de.i/
(آنها) ایستاده اند	(او/آن) ایستاده است
/(ǎn.hǎ) is.tǎ.de.and/	/(u/ ǎn) is.tǎ.de- ast/

Past Perfect
ماضی بعید

(ما) ایستاده بودیم	(من) ایستاده بودم
/(mǎ) is.tǎ.de- bu.dim/	/(man) is.tǎ.de- bu.dam/
(شما) ایستاده بودید	(تو) ایستاده بودی
/(šo.mǎ) is.tǎ.de- bu.did/	/(to) is.tǎ.de- bu.di/
(آنها) ایستاده بودند	(او/آن) ایستاده بود
/(ǎn.hǎ) is.tǎ.de- bu.dand/	/(u/ ǎn) is.tǎ.de- bud/

<table>
<tr><td colspan="2" align="center">

Past Subjunctive

ماضی التزامی
</td></tr>
<tr>
<td align="center">

(ما) ایستاده باشیم

/(mă) is.tă.de- bă.šim/
</td>
<td align="center">

(من) ایستاده باشم

/(man) is.tă.de- bă.šam/
</td>
</tr>
<tr>
<td align="center">

(شما) ایستاده باشید

/(šo.mă) is.tă.de- bă.šid/
</td>
<td align="center">

(تو) ایستاده باشی

/(to) is.tă.de- bă.ši/
</td>
</tr>
<tr>
<td align="center">

(آنها) ایستاده باشند

/(ăn.hă) is.tă.de- bă.šand/
</td>
<td align="center">

(او/آن) ایستاده باشد

/(u/ ăn) is.tă.de- bă.šad/
</td>
</tr>
</table>

<table>
<tr><td colspan="2" align="center">

Past Progressive

ماضی مستمر(در جریان)
</td></tr>
<tr>
<td align="center">

(ما) داشتیم می ایستادیم

/(mă) dăš.tim- mi.is.tă.dim/
</td>
<td align="center">

(من) داشتم می ایستادم

/(man) dăš.tam- mi.is.tă.dam/
</td>
</tr>
<tr>
<td align="center">

(شما) داشتید می ایستادید

/(šo.mă) dăš.tid- mi.is.tă.did/
</td>
<td align="center">

(تو) داشتی می ایستادی

/(to) dăš.ti- mi.is.tă.di/
</td>
</tr>
<tr>
<td align="center">

(آنها) داشتند می ایستادند

/(ăn.hă) dăš.tand- mi.is.tă.dand/
</td>
<td align="center">

(او/آن) داشت می ایستاد

/(u/ ăn) dăšt- mi.is.tăd/
</td>
</tr>
</table>

<table>
<tr><td colspan="2" align="center">

Simple Future

مستقبل (آینده ساده)
</td></tr>
<tr>
<td align="center">

(ما) خواهیم ایستاد

/(mă) ḱă.him- is.tăd/
</td>
<td align="center">

(من) خواهم ایستاد

/(man) ḱă.ham- is.tăd/
</td>
</tr>
<tr>
<td align="center">

(شما) خواهید ایستاد

/(šo.mă) ḱă.hid- is.tăd/
</td>
<td align="center">

(تو) خواهی ایستاد

/(to) ḱă.hi- is.tăd/
</td>
</tr>
<tr>
<td align="center">

(آنها) خواهند ایستاد

/(ăn.hă) ḱă.hand- is.tăd/
</td>
<td align="center">

(او/آن) خواهد ایستاد

/(u/ ăn) ḱă.had- is.tăd/
</td>
</tr>
</table>

<table>
<tr><td colspan="2" align="center">

Command

امر
</td></tr>
<tr>
<td align="center">

بایستید !

/be.is.tid/
</td>
<td align="center">

بایست !

/be.ist/
</td>
</tr>
</table>

241

to start

شُروع کَردَن

/šo.ruʿ- kar.dan/

Plural	Singular
Simple Present مضارع اخباری(حال ساده)	
(ما) شروع می کنیم /(mǎ) šo.ruʿ- mi.ko.nim/	(من) شروع می کنم /(man) šo.ruʿ- mi.ko.nam/
(شما) شروع می کنید /(šo.mǎ) šo.ruʿ- mi.ko.nid/	(تو) شروع می کنی /(to) šo.ruʿ- mi.ko.ni/
(آنها) شروع می کنند /(ǎn.hǎ) šo.ruʿ- mi.ko.nand/	(او/آن) شروع می کند /(u/ ǎn) šo.ruʿ- mi.ko.nad/
Present Subjunctive مضارع التزامی	
(ما) شروع بکنیم /(mǎ) šo.ruʿ- be.ko.nim/	(من) شروع بکنم /(man) šo.ruʿ- be.ko.nam/
(شما) شروع بکنید /(šo.mǎ) šo.ruʿ- be.ko.nid/	(تو) شروع بکنی /(to) šo.ruʿ- be.ko.ni/
(آنها) شروع بکنند /(ǎn.hǎ) šo.ruʿ- be.ko.nand/	(او/آن) شروع بکند /(u/ ǎn) šo.ruʿ- be.ko.nad/
Present Progressive مضارع مستمر(در جریان)	
(ما) داریم شروع می کنیم /(mǎ) dǎ.rim- šo.ruʿ- mi.ko.nim/	(من) دارم شروع می کنم /(man) dǎ.ram- šo.ruʿ- mi.ko.nam/
(شما) دارید شروع می کنید /(šo.mǎ) dǎ.rid- šo.ruʿ- mi.ko.nid/	(تو) داری شروع می کنی /(to) dǎ.ri- šo.ruʿ- mi.ko.ni/
(آنها) دارند شروع می کنند /(ǎn.hǎ) dǎ.rand- šo.ruʿ- mi.ko.nand/	(او/آن) دارد شروع می کند /(u/ ǎn) dǎ.rad- šo.ruʿ- mi.ko.nad/

Simple Past ماضی مطلق (گذشته ساده)	
(ما) شروع کردیم /(mǎ) šo.ruʿ- kar.dim/	(من) شروع کردم /(man) šo.ruʿ- kar.dam/
(شما) شروع کردید /(šo.mǎ) šo.ruʿ- kar.did/	(تو) شروع کردی /(to) šo.ruʿ- kar.di/
(آنها) شروع کردند /(ǎn.hǎ) šo.ruʿ- kar.dand/	(او/آن) شروع کرد /(u/ ǎn) šo.ruʿ- kard/

Imperfect Indicative ماضی استمراری	
(ما) شروع می کردیم /(mǎ) šo.ruʿ- mi.kar.dim/	(من) شروع می کردم /(man) šo.ruʿ- mi.kar.dam/
(شما) شروع می کردید /(šo.mǎ) šo.ruʿ- mi.kar.did/	(تو) شروع می کردی /(to) šo.ruʿ- mi.kar.di/
(آنها) شروع می کردند /(ǎn.hǎ) šo.ruʿ- mi.kar.dand/	(او/آن) شروع می کرد /(u/ ǎn) šo.ruʿ- mi.kard/

Present Perfect ماضی نقلی	
(ما) شروع کرده ایم /(mǎ) šo.ruʿ- kar.de.im/	(من) شروع کرده ام /(man) šo.ruʿ- kar.de.am/
(شما) شروع کرده اید /(šo.mǎ) šo.ruʿ- kar.de.id/	(تو) شروع کرده ای /(to) šo.ruʿ- kar.de.i/
(آنها) شروع کرده اند /(ǎn.hǎ) šo.ruʿ- kar.de.and/	(او/آن) شروع کرده است /(u/ ǎn) šo.ruʿ- kar.de- ast/

Past Perfect ماضی بعید	
(ما) شروع کرده بودیم /(mǎ) šo.ruʿ- kar.de- bu.dim/	(من) شروع کرده بودم /(man) šo.ruʿ- kar.de- bu.dam/
(شما) شروع کرده بودید /(šo.mǎ) šo.ruʿ- kar.de- bu.did/	(تو) شروع کرده بودی /(to) šo.ruʿ- kar.de- bu.di/
(آنها) شروع کرده بودند /(ǎn.hǎ) šo.ruʿ- kar.de- bu.dand/	(او/آن) شروع کرده بود /(u/ ǎn) šo.ruʿ- kar.de- bud/

Past Subjunctive	
ماضی التزامی	
(ما) شروع کرده باشیم	(من) شروع کرده باشم
/(mǎ) šo.ruʿ- kar.de- bǎ.šim/	/(man) šo.ruʿ- kar.de- bǎ.šam/
(شما) شروع کرده باشید	(تو) شروع کرده باشی
/(šo.mǎ) šo.ruʿ- kar.de- bǎ.šid/	/(to) šo.ruʿ- kar.de- bǎ.ši/
(آنها) شروع کرده باشند	(او/آن) شروع کرده باشد
/(ǎn.hǎ) šo.ruʿ- kar.de- bǎ.šand/	/(u/ ǎn) šo.ruʿ- kar.de- bǎ.šad/

Past Progressive	
ماضی مستمر(در جریان)	
(ما) داشتیم شروع می کردیم	(من) داشتم شروع می کردم
/(mǎ) dǎš.tim- šo.ruʿ- mi.kar.dim/	/(man) dǎš.tam- šo.ruʿ- mi.kar.dam/
(شما) داشتید شروع می کردید	(تو) داشتی شروع می کردی
/(šo.mǎ) dǎš.tid- šo.ruʿ- mi.kar.did/	/(to) dǎš.ti- šo.ruʿ- mi.kar.di/
(آنها) داشتند شروع می کردند	(او/آن) داشت شروع می کرد
/(ǎn.hǎ) dǎš.tand- šo.ruʿ- mi.kar.dand/	/(u/ ǎn) dǎšt- šo.ruʿ- mi.kard/

Simple Future	
مستقبل (آینده ساده)	
(ما) شروع خواهیم کرد	(من) شروع خواهم کرد
/(mǎ) šo.ruʿ- ǩǎ.him- kard/	/(man) šo.ruʿ- ǩǎ.ham- kard/
(شما) شروع خواهید کرد	(تو) شروع خواهی کرد
/(šo.mǎ) šo.ruʿ- ǩǎ.hid- kard/	/(to) šo.ruʿ- ǩǎ.hi- kard/
(آنها) شروع خواهند کرد	(او/آن) شروع خواهد کرد
/(ǎn.hǎ) šo.ruʿ- ǩǎ.hand- kard/	/(u/ ǎn) šo.ruʿ- ǩǎ.had- kard/

Command	
امر	
* شروع بکنید !	* شروع بکن !
/šo.ruʿ- be.ko.nid/	/šo.ruʿ- be.kon/

* also: شروع کن!   شروع کنید!

244

to stay

ماندَن

/măn.dan/

Plural	Singular
Simple Present مضارع اخباری(حال ساده)	
(ما) می مانیم /(mă) mi.mă.nim/	(من) می مانم /(man) mi.mă.nam/
(شما) می مانید /(šo.mă) mi.mă.nid/	(تو) می مانی /(to) mi.mă.ni/
(آنها) می مانند /(ăn.hă) mi.mă.nand/	(او/آن) می ماند /(u/ ăn) mi.mă.nad/
Present Subjunctive مضارع التزامی	
(ما) بمانیم /(mă) be.mă.nim/	(من) بمانم /(man) be.mă.nam/
(شما) بمانید /(šo.mă) be.mă.nid/	(تو) بمانی /(to) be.mă.ni/
(آنها) بمانند /(ăn.hă) be.mă.nand/	(او/آن) بماند /(u/ ăn) be.mă.nad/
Present Progressive مضارع مستمر(در جریان)	
(ما) داریم می مانیم /(mă) dă.rim- mi.mă.nim/	(من) دارم می مانم /(man) dă.ram- mi.mă.nam/
(شما) دارید می مانید /(šo.mă) dă.rid- mi.mă.nid/	(تو) داری می مانی /(to) dă.ri- mi.mă.ni/
(آنها) دارند می مانند /(ăn.hă) dă.rand- mi.mă.nand/	(او/آن) دارد می ماند /(u/ ăn) dă.rad- mi.mă.nad/

Simple Past
ماضی مطلق (گذشته ساده)

(ما) ماندیم	(من) ماندم
/(mǎ) mǎn.dim/	/(man) mǎn.dam/
(شما) ماندید	(تو) ماندی
/(šo.mǎ) mǎn.did/	/(to) mǎn.di/
(آنها) ماندند	(او/آن) ماند
/(ǎn.hǎ) mǎn.dand/	/(u/ ǎn) mǎnd/

Imperfect Indicative
ماضی استمراری

(ما) می ماندیم	(من) می ماندم
/(mǎ) mi.mǎn.dim/	/(man) mi.mǎn.dam/
(شما) می ماندید	(تو) می ماندی
/(šo.mǎ) mi.mǎn.did/	/(to) mi.mǎn.di/
(آنها) می ماندند	(او/آن) می ماند
/(ǎn.hǎ) mi.mǎn.dand/	/(u/ ǎn) mi.mǎnd/

Present Perfect
ماضی نقلی

(ما) ماند ه ایم	(من) مانده ام
/(mǎ) mǎn.de.im/	/(man) mǎn.de.am/
(شما) مانده اید	(تو) مانده ای
/(šo.mǎ) mǎn.de.id/	/(to) mǎn.de.i/
(آنها) مانده اند	(او/آن) مانده است
/(ǎn.hǎ) mǎn.de.and/	/(u/ ǎn) mǎn.de- ast/

Past Perfect
ماضی بعید

(ما) مانده بودیم	(من) مانده بودم
/(mǎ) mǎn.de- bu.dim/	/(man) mǎn.de- bu.dam/
(شما) مانده بودید	(تو) مانده بودی
/(šo.mǎ) mǎn.de- bu.did/	/(to) mǎn.de- bu.di/
(آنها) مانده بودند	(او/آن) مانده بود
/(ǎn.hǎ) mǎn.de- bu.dand/	/(u/ ǎn) mǎn.de- bud/

Past Subjunctive	
ماضی التزامی	
(ما) مانده باشیم	(من) ماند ه باشم
/(mă) măn.de- bă.šim/	/(man) măn.de- bă.šam/
(شما) مانده باشید	(تو) مانده باشی
/(šo.mă) măn.de- bă.šid/	/(to) măn.de- bă.ši/
(آنها) مانده باشند	(او/آن) مانده باشد
/(ăn.hă) măn.de- bă.šand/	/(u/ ăn) măn.dc- bă.šad/

Past Progressive	
ماضی مستمر(در جریان)	
(ما) داشتیم می ماندیم	(من) داشتم می ماندم
/(mă) dăš.tim- mi.măn.dim/	/(man) dăš.tam- mi.măn.dam/
(شما) داشتید می ماندید	(تو) داشتی می ماندی
/(šo.mă) dăš.tid- mi.măn.did/	/(to) dăš.ti- mi.măn.di/
(آنها) داشتند می ماندند	(او/آن) داشت می ماند
/(ăn.hă) dăš.tand- mi.măn.dand/	/(u/ ăn) dăšt- mi.mănd/

Simple Future	
مستقبل (آینده ساده)	
(ما) خواهیم ماند	(من) خواهم ماند
/(mă) kă.him- mănd/	/(man) kă.ham- mănd/
(شما) خواهید ماند	(تو) خواهی ماند
/(šo.mă) kă.hid- mănd/	/(to) kă.hi- mănd/
(آنها) خواهند ماند	(او/آن) خواهد ماند
/(ăn.hă) kă.hand- mănd/	/(u/ ăn) kă.had- mănd/

Command	
امر	
بمانید!	بمان!
/be.mă.nid/	/be.măn/

to talk

حَرف زَدَن

/harf- za.dan/

Plural	Singular
Simple Present مضارع اخباری(حال ساده)	
(ما) حرف می زنیم /(mǎ) harf- mi.za.nim/	(من) حرف می زنم /(man) harf- mi.za.nam/
(شما) حرف می زنید /(šo.mǎ) harf- mi.za.nid/	(تو) حرف می زنی /(to) harf- mi.za.ni/
(آنها) حرف می زنند /(ǎn.hǎ) harf- mi.za.nand/	(او/آن) حرف می زند /(u/ ǎn) harf- mi.za.nad/
Present Subjunctive مضارع التزامی	
(ما) حرف بزنیم /(mǎ) harf- be.za.nim/	(من) حرف بزنم /(man) harf- be.za.nam/
(شما) حرف بزنید /(šo.mǎ) harf- be.za.nid/	(تو) حرف بزنی /(to) harf- be.za.ni/
(آنها) حرف بزنند /(ǎn.hǎ) harf- be.za.nand/	(او/آن) حرف بزند /(u/ ǎn) harf- be.za.nad/
Present Progressive مضارع مستمر(در جریان)	
(ما) داریم حرف می زنیم /(mǎ) dǎ.rim- harf- mi.za.nim/	(من) دارم حرف می زنم /(man) dǎ.ram- harf- mi.za.nam/
(شما) دارید حرف می زنید /(šo.mǎ) dǎ.rid- harf- mi.za.nid/	(تو) داری حرف می زنی /(to) dǎ.ri- harf- mi.za.ni/
(آنها) دارند حرف می زنند /(ǎn.hǎ) dǎ.rand- harf- mi.za.nand/	(او/آن) دارد حرف می زند /(u/ ǎn) dǎ.rad- harf- mi.za.nad/

248

Simple Past	
ماضی مطلق (گذشته ساده)	
(ما) حرف زدیم	(من) حرف زدم
/(mǎ) harf- za.dim/	/(man) harf- za.dam/
(شما) حرف زدید	(تو) حرف زدی
/(šo.mǎ) harf- za.did/	/(to) harf- za.di/
(آنها) حرف زدند	(او/آن) حرف زد
/(ǎn.hǎ) harf- za.dand/	/(u/ ǎn) harf- zad/

Imperfect Indicative	
ماضی استمراری	
(ما) حرف می زدیم	(من) حرف می زدم
/(mǎ) harf- mi.za.dim/	/(man) harf- mi.za.dam/
(شما) حرف می زدید	(تو) حرف می زدی
/(šo.mǎ) harf- mi.za.did/	/(to) harf- mi.za.di/
(آنها) حرف می زدند	(او/آن) حرف می زد
/(ǎn.hǎ) harf- mi.za.dand/	/(u/ ǎn) harf- mi.zad/

Present Perfect	
ماضی نقلی	
(ما) حرف زده ایم	(من) حرف زده ام
/(mǎ) harf- za.de.im/	/(man) harf- za.de.am/
(شما) حرف زده اید	(تو) حرف زده ای
/(šo.mǎ) harf- za.de.id/	/(to) harf- za.de.i/
(آنها) حرف زده اند	(او/آن) حرف زده است
/(ǎn.hǎ) harf- za.de.and/	/(u/ ǎn) harf- za.de- ast/

Past Perfect	
ماضی بعید	
(ما) حرف زده بودیم	(من) حرف زده بودم
/(mǎ) harf- za.de- bu.dim/	/(man) harf- za.de- bu.dam/
(شما) حرف زده بودید	(تو) حرف زده بودی
/(šo.mǎ) harf- za.de- bu.did/	/(to) harf- za.de- bu.di/
(آنها) حرف زده بودند	(او/آن) حرف زده بود
/(ǎn.hǎ) harf- za.de- bu.dand/	/(u/ ǎn) harf- za.de- bud/

Past Subjunctive
ماضی التزامی

(ما) حرف زده باشیم	(من) حرف زده باشم
/(mă) harf- za.de- bă.šim/	/(man) harf- za.de- bă.šam/
(شما) حرف زده باشید	(تو) حرف زده باشی
/(šo.mă) harf- za.de- bă.šid/	/(to) harf- za.de- bă.ši/
(آنها) حرف زده باشند	(او/آن) حرف زده باشد
/(ăn.hă) harf- za.de- bă.šand/	/(u/ ăn) harf- za.de- bă.šad/

Past Progressive
ماضی مستمر(در جریان)

(ما) داشتیم حرف می زدیم	(من) داشتم حرف می زدم
/(mă) dăš.tim- harf- mi.za.dim/	/(man) dăš.tam- harf- mi.za.dam/
(شما) داشتید حرف می زدید	(تو) داشتی حرف می زدی
/(šo.mă) dăš.tid- harf- mi.za.did/	/(to) dăš.ti- harf- mi.za.di/
(آنها) داشتند حرف می زدند	(او/آن) داشت حرف می زد
/(ăn.hă) dăš.tand- harf- mi.za.dand/	/(u/ ăn) dăšt- harf- mi.zad/

Simple Future
مستقبل (آینده ساده)

(ما) حرف خواهیم زد	(من) حرف خواهم زد
/(mă) harf- ǩă.him- zad/	/(man) harf- ǩă.ham- zad/
(شما) حرف خواهید زد	(تو) حرف خواهی زد
/(šo.mă) harf- ǩă.hid- zad/	/(to) harf- ǩă.hi- zad/
(آنها) حرف خواهند زد	(او/آن) حرف خواهد زد
/(ăn.hă) harf- ǩă.hand- zad/	/(u/ ăn) harf- ǩă.had- zad/

Command
امر

حرف بزنید!	حرف بزن!
/harf- be.za.nid/	/harf- be.zan/

to teach

یاد دادَن

/yăd- dă.dan/

Plural	Singular
Simple Present <div dir="rtl">مضارع اخباری(حال ساده)</div>	
<div dir="rtl">(ما) یاد می دهیم</div> /(mă) yăd- mi.da.him/	<div dir="rtl">(من) یاد می دهم</div> /(man) yăd- mi.da.ham/
<div dir="rtl">(شما) یاد می دهید</div> /(šo.mă) yăd- mi.da.hid/	<div dir="rtl">(تو) یاد می دهی</div> /(to) yăd- mi.da.hi/
<div dir="rtl">(آنها) یاد می دهند</div> /(ăn.hă) yăd- mi.da.hand/	<div dir="rtl">(او/آن) یاد می دهد</div> /(u/ ăn) yăd- mi.da.had/
Present Subjunctive <div dir="rtl">مضارع التزامی</div>	
<div dir="rtl">(ما) یاد بدهیم</div> /(mă) yăd- be.da.him/	<div dir="rtl">(من) یاد بدهم</div> /(man) yăd- be.da.ham/
<div dir="rtl">(شما) یاد بدهید</div> /(šo.mă) yăd- be.da.hid/	<div dir="rtl">(تو) یاد بدهی</div> /(to) yăd- be.da.hi/
<div dir="rtl">(آنها) یاد بدهند</div> /(ăn.hă) yăd- be.da.hand/	<div dir="rtl">(او/آن) یاد بدهد</div> /(u/ ăn) yăd- be.da.had/
Present Progressive <div dir="rtl">مضارع مستمر(در جریان)</div>	
<div dir="rtl">(ما) داریم یاد می دهیم</div> /(mă) dă.rim- yăd- mi.da.him/	<div dir="rtl">(من) دارم یاد می دهم</div> /(man) dă.ram- yăd- mi.da.ham/
<div dir="rtl">(شما) دارید یاد می دهید</div> /(šo.mă) dă.rid- yăd- mi.da.hid/	<div dir="rtl">(تو) داری یاد می دهی</div> /(to) dă.ri- yăd- mi.da.hi/
<div dir="rtl">(آنها) دارند یاد می دهند</div> /(ăn.hă) dă.rand- yăd- mi.da.hand/	<div dir="rtl">(او/آن) دارد یاد می دهد</div> /(u/ ăn) dă.rad- yăd- mi.da.had/

<table>
<tr><td colspan="2" align="center">**Simple Past**
ماضی مطلق (گذشته ساده)</td></tr>
<tr>
<td align="center">(ما) یاد دادیم
/(mǎ) yǎd- dǎ.dim/</td>
<td align="center">(من) یاد دادم
/(man) yǎd- dǎ.dam/</td>
</tr>
<tr>
<td align="center">(شما) یاد دادید
/(šo.mǎ) yǎd- dǎ.did/</td>
<td align="center">(تو) یاد دادی
/(to) yǎd- dǎ.di/</td>
</tr>
<tr>
<td align="center">(آنها) یاد دادند
/(ǎn.hǎ) yǎd- dǎ.dand/</td>
<td align="center">(او/آن) یاد داد
/(u/ ǎn) yǎd- dǎd/</td>
</tr>
</table>

<table>
<tr><td colspan="2" align="center">**Imperfect Indicative**
ماضی استمراری</td></tr>
<tr>
<td align="center">(ما) یاد می دادیم
/(mǎ) yǎd- mi.dǎ.dim/</td>
<td align="center">(من) یاد می دادم
/(man) yǎd- mi.dǎ.dam/</td>
</tr>
<tr>
<td align="center">(شما) یاد می دادید
/(šo.mǎ) yǎd- mi.dǎ.did/</td>
<td align="center">(تو) یاد می دادی
/(to) yǎd- mi.dǎ.di/</td>
</tr>
<tr>
<td align="center">(آنها) یاد می دادند
/(ǎn.hǎ) yǎd- mi.dǎ.dand/</td>
<td align="center">(او/آن) یاد می داد
/(u/ ǎn) yǎd- mi.dǎd/</td>
</tr>
</table>

<table>
<tr><td colspan="2" align="center">**Present Perfect**
ماضی نقلی</td></tr>
<tr>
<td align="center">(ما) یاد داده ایم
/(mǎ) yǎd- dǎ.de.im/</td>
<td align="center">(من) یاد داده ام
/(man) yǎd- dǎ.de.am/</td>
</tr>
<tr>
<td align="center">(شما) یاد داده اید
/(šo.mǎ) yǎd- dǎ.de.id/</td>
<td align="center">(تو) یاد داده ای
/(to) yǎd- dǎ.de.i/</td>
</tr>
<tr>
<td align="center">(آنها) یاد داده اند
/(ǎn.hǎ) yǎd- dǎ.de.and/</td>
<td align="center">(او/آن) یاد داده است
/(u/ ǎn) yǎd- dǎ.de- ast/</td>
</tr>
</table>

<table>
<tr><td colspan="2" align="center">**Past Perfect**
ماضی بعید</td></tr>
<tr>
<td align="center">(ما) یاد داده بودیم
/(mǎ) yǎd- dǎ.de- bu.dim/</td>
<td align="center">(من) یاد داده بودم
/(man) yǎd- dǎ.de- bu.dam/</td>
</tr>
<tr>
<td align="center">(شما) یاد داده بودید
/(šo.mǎ) yǎd- dǎ.de- bu.did/</td>
<td align="center">(تو) یاد داده بودی
/(to) yǎd- dǎ.de- bu.di/</td>
</tr>
<tr>
<td align="center">(آنها) یاد داده بودند
/(ǎn.hǎ) yǎd- dǎ.de- bu.dand/</td>
<td align="center">(او/آن) یاد داده بود
/(u/ ǎn) yǎd- dǎ.de- bud/</td>
</tr>
</table>

Past Subjunctive
ماضی التزامی

(ما) یاد داده باشیم	(من) یاد داده باشم
/(mă) yăd- dă.de- bă.šim/	/(man) yăd- dă.de- bă.šam/
(شما) یاد داده باشید	(تو) یاد داده باشی
/(šo.mă) yăd- dă.de- bă.šid/	/(to) yăd- dă.de- bă.ši/
(آنها) یاد داده باشند	(او/آن) یاد داده باشد
/(ăn.hă) yăd- dă.de- bă.šand/	/(u/ ăn) yăd- dă.de- bă.šad/

Past Progressive
ماضی مستمر(در جریان)

(ما) داشتیم یاد می دادیم	(من) داشتم یاد می دادم
/(mă) dăš.tim- yăd- mi.dă.dim/	/(man) dăš.tam- yăd- mi.dă.dam/
(شما) داشتید یاد می دادید	(تو) داشتی یاد می دادی
/(šo.mă) dăš.tid- yăd- mi.dă.did/	/(to) dăš.ti- yăd- mi.dă.di/
(آنها) داشتند یاد می دادند	(او/آن) داشت یاد می داد
/(ăn.hă) dăš.tand- yăd- mi.dă.dand/	/(u/ ăn) dăšt- yăd- mi.dăd/

Simple Future
مستقبل (آینده ساده)

(ما) یاد خواهیم داد	(من) یاد خواهم داد
/(mă) yăd- ǩă.him- dăd/	/(man) yăd- ǩă.ham- dăd/
(شما) یاد خواهید داد	(تو) یاد خواهی داد
/(šo.mă) yăd- ǩă.hid- dăd/	/(to) yăd- ǩă.hi- dăd/
(آنها) یاد خواهند داد	(او/آن) یاد خواهد داد
/(ăn.hă) yăd- ǩă.hand- dăd/	/(u/ ăn) yăd- ǩă.had- dăd/

Command
امر

یاد بدهید!	یاد بده !
/yăd- be.da.hid/	/yăd- be.de/

to thank

تَشَکُّر کَردَن

/ta.šak.kor- kar.dan/

Plural	Singular
Simple Present	
مضارع اخباری(حال ساده)	
(ما) تشکّر می کنیم	(من) تشکّر می کنم
/(mǎ) ta.šak.kor- mi.ko.nim/	/(man) ta.šak.kor- mi.ko.nam/
(شما) تشکّر می کنید	(تو) تشکّر می کنی
/(šo.mǎ) ta.šak.kor- mi.ko.nid/	/(to) ta.šak.kor- mi.ko.ni/
(آنها) تشکّر می کنند	(او/آن) تشکّر می کند
/(ǎn.hǎ) ta.šak.kor- mi.ko.nand/	/(u/ ǎn) ta.šak.kor- mi.ko.nad/
Present Subjunctive	
مضارع التزامی	
(ما) تشکّر بکنیم	(من) تشکّر بکنم
/(mǎ) ta.šak.kor- be.ko.nim/	/(man) ta.šak.kor- be.ko.nam/
(شما) تشکّر بکنید	(تو) تشکّر بکنی
/(šo.mǎ) ta.šak.kor- be.ko.nid/	/(to) ta.šak.kor- be.ko.ni/
(آنها) تشکّر بکنند	(او/آن) تشکّر بکند
/(ǎn.hǎ) ta.šak.kor- be.ko.nand/	/(u/ ǎn) ta.šak.kor- be.ko.nad/
Present Progressive	
مضارع مستمر(در جریان)	
(ما) داریم تشکّر می کنیم	(من) دارم تشکّر می کنم
/(mǎ) dǎ.rim- ta.šak.kor- mi.ko.nim/	/(man) dǎ.ram- ta.šak.kor- mi.ko.nam/
(شما) دارید تشکّر می کنید	(تو) داری تشکّر می کنی
/(šo.mǎ) dǎ.rid- ta.šak.kor- mi.ko.nid/	/(to) dǎ.ri- ta.šak.kor- mi.ko.ni/
(آنها) دارند تشکّر می کنند	(او/آن) دارد تشکّر می کند
/(ǎn.hǎ) dǎ.rand- ta.šak.kor- mi.ko.nand/	/(u/ ǎn) dǎ.rad- ta.šak.kor- mi.ko.nad/

Simple Past	
ماضی مطلق (گذشته ساده)	
(ما) تشکّر کردیم	(من) تشکّر کردم
/(mă) ta.šak.kor- kar.dim/	/(man) ta.šak.kor- kar.dam/
(شما) تشکّر کردید	(تو) تشکّر کردی
/(šo.mă) ta.šak.kor- kar.did/	/(to) ta.šak.kor- kar.di/
(آنها) تشکّر کردند	(او/آن) تشکّر کرد
/(ăn.hă) ta.šak.kor- kar.dand/	/(u/ ăn) ta.šak.kor- kard/

Imperfect Indicative	
ماضی استمراری	
(ما) تشکّر می کردیم	(من) تشکّر می کردم
/(mă) ta.šak.kor- mi.kar.dim/	/(man) ta.šak.kor- mi.kar.dam/
(شما) تشکّر می کردید	(تو) تشکّر می کردی
/(šo.mă) ta.šak.kor- mi.kar.did/	/(to) ta.šak.kor- mi.kar.di/
(آنها) تشکّر می کردند	(او/آن) تشکّر می کرد
/(ăn.hă) ta.šak.kor- mi.kar.dand/	/(u/ ăn) ta.šak.kor- mi.kard/

Present Perfect	
ماضی نقلی	
(ما) تشکّر کرده ایم	(من) تشکّر کرده ام
/(mă) ta.šak.kor- kar.de.im/	/(man) ta.šak.kor- kar.de.am/
(شما) تشکّر کرده اید	(تو) تشکّر کرده ای
/(šo.mă) ta.šak.kor- kar.de.id/	/(to) ta.šak.kor- kar.de.i/
(آنها) تشکّر کرده اند	(او/آن) تشکّر کرده است
/(ăn.hă) ta.šak.kor- kar.de.and/	/(u/ ăn) ta.šak.kor- kar.de- ast/

Past Perfect	
ماضی بعید	
(ما) تشکّر کرده بودیم	(من) تشکّر کرده بودم
/(mă) ta.šak.kor- kar.de- bu.dim/	/(man) ta.šak.kor- kar.de- bu.dam/
(شما) تشکّر کرده بودید	(تو) تشکّر کرده بودی
/(šo.mă) ta.šak.kor- kar.de- bu.did/	/(to) ta.šak.kor- kar.de- bu.di/
(آنها) تشکّر کرده بودند	(او/آن) تشکّر کرده بود
/(ăn.hă) ta.šak.kor- kar.de- bu.dand/	/(u/ ăn) ta.šak.kor- kar.de- bud/

Past Subjunctive	
ماضی التزامی	
(ما) تشکّر کرده باشیم	(من) تشکّر کرده باشم
/(mă) ta.šak.kor- kar.de- bă.šim/	/(man) ta.šak.kor- kar.de- bă.šam/
(شما) تشکّر کرده باشید	(تو) تشکّر کرده باشی
/(šo.mă) ta.šak.kor- kar.de- bă.šid/	/(to) ta.šak.kor- kar.de- bă.ši/
(آنها) تشکّر کرده باشند	(او/آن) تشکّر کرده باشد
/(ăn.hă) ta.šak.kor- kar.de- bă.šand/	/(u/ ăn) ta.šak.kor- kar.de- bă.šad/

Past Progressive	
ماضی مستمر(در جریان)	
(ما) داشتیم تشکّر می کردیم	(من) داشتم تشکّر می کردم
/(mă) dăš.tim- ta.šak.kor- mi.kar.dim/	/(man) dăš.tam- ta.šak.kor- mi.kar.dam/
(شما) داشتید تشکّر می کردید	(تو) داشتی تشکّر می کردی
/(šo.mă) dăš.tid- ta.šak.kor- mi.kar.did/	/(to) dăš.ti- ta.šak.kor- mi.kar.di/
(آنها) داشتند تشکّر می کردند	(او/آن) داشت تشکّر می کرد
/(ăn.hă) dăš.tand- ta.šak.kor- mi.kar.dand/	/(u/ ăn) dăšt- ta.šak.kor- mi.kard/

Simple Future	
مستقبل (آینده ساده)	
(ما) تشکّر خواهیم کرد	(من) تشکّر خواهم کرد
/(mă) ta.šak.kor- kă.him- kard/	/(man) ta.šak.kor- kă.ham- kard/
(شما) تشکّر خواهید کرد	(تو) تشکّر خواهی کرد
/(šo.mă) ta.šak.kor- kă.hid- kard/	/(to) ta.šak.kor- kă.hi- kard/
(آنها) تشکّر خواهند کرد	(او/آن) تشکّر خواهد کرد
/(ăn.hă) ta.šak.kor- kă.hand- kard/	/(u/ ăn) ta.šak.kor- kă.had- kard/

Command	
امر	
* تشکّر بکنید!	* تشکّر بکن!
/ta.šak.kor- be.ko.nid/	/ta.šak.kor- be.kon/

* also: تشکّر کن!   تشکّر کنید!

to think

فِکر کَردَن

/fekr- kar.dan/

Plural	Singular
Simple Present	
مضارع اخباری(حال ساده)	
(ما) فکر می کنیم /(mǎ) fekr- mi.ko.nim/	(من) فکر می کنم /(man) fekr- mi.ko.nam/
(شما) فکر می کنید /(šo.mǎ) fekr- mi.ko.nid/	(تو) فکر می کنی /(to) fekr- mi.ko.ni/
(آنها) فکر می کنند /(ǎn.hǎ) fekr- mi.ko.nand/	(او/آن) فکر می کند /(u/ ǎn) fekr- mi.ko.nad/

Plural	Singular
Present Subjunctive	
مضارع التزامی	
(ما) فکر بکنیم /(mǎ) fekr- be.ko.nim/	(من) فکر بکنم /(man) fekr- be.ko.nam/
(شما) فکر بکنید /(šo.mǎ) fekr- be.ko.nid/	(تو) فکر بکنی /(to) fekr- be.ko.ni/
(آنها) فکر بکنند /(ǎn.hǎ) fekr- be.ko.nand/	(او/آن) فکر بکند /(u/ ǎn) fekr- be.ko.nad/

Plural	Singular
Present Progressive	
مضارع مستمر(در جریان)	
(ما) داریم فکر می کنیم /(mǎ) dǎ.rim- fekr- mi.ko.nim/	(من) دارم فکر می کنم /(man) dǎ.ram- fekr- mi.ko.nam/
(شما) دارید فکر می کنید /(šo.mǎ) dǎ.rid- fekr- mi.ko.nid/	(تو) داری فکر می کنی /(to) dǎ.ri- fekr- mi.ko.ni/
(آنها) دارند فکر می کنند /(ǎn.hǎ) dǎ.rand- fekr- mi.ko.nand/	(او/آن) دارد فکر می کند /(u/ ǎn) dǎ.rad- fekr- mi.ko.nad/

Simple Past
ماضی مطلق (گذشته ساده)

(ما) فکر کردیم	(من) فکر کردم
/(mǎ) fekr- kar.dim/	/(man) fekr- kar.dam/
(شما) فکر کردید	(تو) فکر کردی
/(šo.mǎ) fekr- kar.did/	/(to) fekr- kar.di/
(آنها) فکر کردند	(او/آن) فکر کرد
/(ǎn.hǎ) fekr- kar.dand/	/(u/ ǎn) fekr- kard/

Imperfect Indicative
ماضی استمراری

(ما) فکر می کردیم	(من) فکر می کردم
/(mǎ) fekr- mi.kar.dim/	/(man) fekr- mi.kar.dam/
(شما) فکر می کردید	(تو) فکر می کردی
/(šo.mǎ) fekr- mi.kar.did/	/(to) fekr- mi.kar.di/
(آنها) فکر می کردند	(او/آن) فکر می کرد
/(ǎn.hǎ) fekr- mi.kar.dand/	/(u/ ǎn) fekr- mi.kard/

Present Perfect
ماضی نقلی

(ما) فکر کرده ایم	(من) فکر کرده ام
/(mǎ) fekr- kar.de.im/	/(man) fekr- kar.de.am/
(شما) فکر کرده اید	(تو) فکر کرده ای
/(šo.mǎ) fekr- kar.de.id/	/(to) fekr- kar.de.i/
(آنها) فکر کرده اند	(او/آن) فکر کرده است
/(ǎn.hǎ) fekr- kar.de.and/	/(u/ ǎn) fekr- kar.de- ast/

Past Perfect
ماضی بعید

(ما) فکر کرده بودیم	(من) فکر کرده بودم
/(mǎ) fekr- kar.de- bu.dim/	/(man) fekr- kar.de- bu.dam/
(شما) فکر کرده بودید	(تو) فکر کرده بودی
/(šo.mǎ) fekr- kar.de- bu.did/	/(to) fekr- kar.de- bu.di/
(آنها) فکر کرده بودند	(او/آن) فکر کرده بود
/(ǎn.hǎ) fekr- kar.de- bu.dand/	/(u/ ǎn) fekr- kar.de- bud/

Past Subjunctive
ماضی التزامی

(ما) فکر کرده باشیم	(من) فکر کرده باشم
/(mǎ) fekr- kar.de- bǎ.šim/	/(man) fekr- kar.de- bǎ.šam/
(شما) فکر کرده باشید	(تو) فکر کرده باشی
/(šo.mǎ) fekr- kar.de- bǎ.šid/	/(to) fekr- kar.de- bǎ.ši/
(آنها) فکر کرده باشند	(او/آن) فکر کرده باشد
/(ǎn.hǎ) fekr- kar.de- bǎ.šand/	/(u/ ǎn) fekr- kar.de- bǎ.šad/

Past Progressive
ماضی مستمر(در جریان)

(ما) داشتیم فکر می کردیم	(من) داشتم فکر می کردم
/(mǎ) dǎš.tim- fekr- mi.kar.dim/	/(man) dǎš.tam- fekr- mi.kar.dam/
(شما) داشتید فکر می کردید	(تو) داشتی فکر می کردی
/(šo.mǎ) dǎš.tid- fekr- mi.kar.did/	/(to) dǎš.ti- fekr- mi.kar.di/
(آنها) داشتند فکر می کردند	(او/آن) داشت فکر می کرد
/(ǎn.hǎ) dǎš.tand- fekr- mi.kar.dand/	/(u/ ǎn) dǎšt- fekr- mi.kard/

Simple Future
مستقبل (آینده ساده)

(ما) فکر خواهیم کرد	(من) فکر خواهم کرد
/(mǎ) fekr- ǩǎ.him- kard/	/(man) fekr- ǩǎ.ham- kard/
(شما) فکر خواهید کرد	(تو) فکر خواهی کرد
/(šo.mǎ) fekr- ǩǎ.hid- kard/	/(to) fekr- ǩǎ.hi- kard/
(آنها) فکر خواهند کرد	(او/آن) فکر خواهد کرد
/(ǎn.hǎ) fekr- ǩǎ.hand- kard/	/(u/ ǎn) fekr- ǩǎ.had- kard/

Command
امر

* فکر بکنید !	* فکر بکن !
/fekr- be.ko.nid/	/fekr- be.kon/

* also: فکر کن!   فکر کنید!

259

to touch

لَمس کَردَن

/lams- kar.dan/

Plural	Singular
Simple Present مضارع اخباری(حال ساده)	
(ما) لمس می کنیم /(mǎ) lams- mi.ko.nim/	(من) لمس می کنم /(man) lams- mi.ko.nam/
(شما) لمس می کنید /(šo.mǎ) lams- mi.ko.nid/	(تو) لمس می کنی /(to) lams- mi.ko.ni/
(آنها) لمس می کنند /(ǎn.hǎ) lams- mi.ko.nand/	(او/آن) لمس می کند /(u/ ǎn) lams- mi.ko.nad/
Present Subjunctive مضارع التزامی	
(ما) لمس بکنیم /(mǎ) lams- be.ko.nim/	(من) لمس بکنم /(man) lams- be.ko.nam/
(شما) لمس بکنید /(šo.mǎ) lams- be.ko.nid/	(تو) لمس بکنی /(to) lams- be.ko.ni/
(آنها) لمس بکنند /(ǎn.hǎ) lams- be.ko.nand/	(او/آن) لمس بکند /(u/ ǎn) lams- be.ko.nad/
Present Progressive مضارع مستمر(در جریان)	
(ما) داریم لمس می کنیم /(mǎ) dǎ.rim- lams- mi.ko.nim/	(من) دارم لمس می کنم /(man) dǎ.ram- lams- mi.ko.nam/
(شما) دارید لمس می کنید /(šo.mǎ) dǎ.rid- lams- mi.ko.nid/	(تو) داری لمس می کنی /(to) dǎ.ri- lams- mi.ko.ni/
(آنها) دارند لمس می کنند /(ǎn.hǎ) dǎ.rand- lams- mi.ko.nand/	(او/آن) دارد لمس می کند /(u/ ǎn) dǎ.rad- lams- mi.ko.nad/

	Simple Past		
	ماضی مطلق (گذشته ساده)		
(ما) لمس کردیم	/(mǎ) lams- kar.dim/	(من) لمس کردم	/(man) lams- kar.dam/
(شما) لمس کردید	/(šo.mǎ) lams- kar.did/	(تو) لمس کردی	/(to) lams- kar.di/
(آنها) لمس کردند	/(ǎn.hǎ) lams- kar.dand/	(او/آن) لمس کرد	/(u/ ǎn) lams- kard/

	Imperfect Indicative		
	ماضی استمراری		
(ما) لمس می کردیم	/(mǎ) lams- mi.kar.dim/	(من) لمس می کردم	/(man) lams- mi.kar.dam/
(شما) لمس می کردید	/(šo.mǎ) lams- mi.kar.did/	(تو) لمس می کردی	/(to) lams- mi.kar.di/
(آنها) لمس می کردند	/(ǎn.hǎ) lams- mi.kar.dand/	(او/آن) لمس می کرد	/(u/ ǎn) lams- mi.kard/

	Present Perfect		
	ماضی نقلی		
(ما) لمس کرده ایم	/(mǎ) lams- kar.de.im/	(من) لمس کرده ام	/(man) lams- kar.de.am/
(شما) لمس کرده اید	/(šo.mǎ) lams- kar.de.id/	(تو) لمس کرده ای	/(to) lams- kar.de.i/
(آنها) لمس کرده اند	/(ǎn.hǎ) lams- kar.de.and/	(او/آن) لمس کرده است	/(u/ ǎn) lams- kar.de- ast/

	Past Perfect		
	ماضی بعید		
(ما) لمس کرده بودیم	/(mǎ) lams- kar.de- bu.dim/	(من) لمس کرده بودم	/(man) lams- kar.de- bu.dam/
(شما) لمس کرده بودید	/(šo.mǎ) lams- kar.de- bu.did/	(تو) لمس کرده بودی	/(to) lams- kar.de- bu.di/
(آنها) لمس کرده بودند	/(ǎn.hǎ) lams- kar.de- bu.dand/	(او/آن) لمس کرده بود	/(u/ ǎn) lams- kar.de- bud/

<table>
<tr><td colspan="2" align="center">**Past Subjunctive**
ماضی التزامی</td></tr>
<tr>
<td align="center">(ما) لمس کرده باشیم
/(mă) lams- kar.de- bă.šim/</td>
<td align="center">(من) لمس کرده باشم
/(man) lams- kar.de- bă.šam/</td>
</tr>
<tr>
<td align="center">(شما) لمس کرده باشید
/(šo.mă) lams- kar.de- bă.šid/</td>
<td align="center">(تو) لمس کرده باشی
/(to) lams- kar.de- bă.ši/</td>
</tr>
<tr>
<td align="center">(آنها) لمس کرده باشند
/(ăn.hă) lams- kar.de- bă.šand/</td>
<td align="center">(او/آن) لمس کرده باشد
/(u/ ăn) lams- kar.de- bă.šad/</td>
</tr>
</table>

<table>
<tr><td colspan="2" align="center">**Past Progressive**
ماضی مستمر(در جریان)</td></tr>
<tr>
<td align="center">(ما) داشتیم لمس می کردیم
/(mă) dăš.tim- lams- mi.kar.dim/</td>
<td align="center">(من) داشتم لمس می کردم
/(man) dăš.tam- lams- mi.kar.dam/</td>
</tr>
<tr>
<td align="center">(شما) داشتید لمس می کردید
/(šo.mă) dăš.tid- lams- mi.kar.did/</td>
<td align="center">(تو) داشتی لمس می کردی
/(to) dăš.ti- lams- mi.kar.di/</td>
</tr>
<tr>
<td align="center">(آنها) داشتند لمس می کردند
/(ăn.hă) dăš.tand- lams- mi.kar.dand/</td>
<td align="center">(او/آن) داشت لمس می کرد
/(u/ ăn) dăšt- lams- mi.kard/</td>
</tr>
</table>

<table>
<tr><td colspan="2" align="center">**Simple Future**
مستقبل (آینده ساده)</td></tr>
<tr>
<td align="center">(ما) لمس خواهیم کرد
/(mă) lams- ǩă.him- kard/</td>
<td align="center">(من) لمس خواهم کرد
/(man) lams- ǩă.ham- kard/</td>
</tr>
<tr>
<td align="center">(شما) لمس خواهید کرد
/(šo.mă) lams- ǩă.hid- kard/</td>
<td align="center">(تو) لمس خواهی کرد
/(to) lams- ǩă.hi- kard/</td>
</tr>
<tr>
<td align="center">(آنها) لمس خواهند کرد
/(ăn.hă) lams- ǩă.hand- kard/</td>
<td align="center">(او/آن) لمس خواهد کرد
/(u/ ăn) lams- ǩă.had- kard/</td>
</tr>
</table>

<table>
<tr><td colspan="2" align="center">**Command**
امر</td></tr>
<tr>
<td align="center">* لمس بکنید !
/lams- be.ko.nid/</td>
<td align="center">* لمس بکن !
/lams- be.kon/</td>
</tr>
</table>

* also: لمس کن!   لمس کنید!

to translate

تَرجُمه کَردَن

/tar.jo.me- kar.dan/

Plural	Singular
Simple Present مضارع اخباری(حال ساده)	
(ما) ترجمه می کنیم /(mǎ) tar.jo.me- mi.ko.nim/	(من) ترجمه می کنم /(man) tar.jo.me- mi.ko.nam/
(شما) ترجمه می کنید /(šo.mǎ) tar.jo.me- mi.ko.nid/	(تو) ترجمه می کنی /(to) tar.jo.me- mi.ko.ni/
(آنها) ترجمه می کنند /(ǎn.hǎ) tar.jo.me- mi.ko.nand/	(او/آن) ترجمه می کند /(u/ ǎn) tar.jo.me- mi.ko.nad/
Present Subjunctive مضارع التزامی	
(ما) ترجمه بکنیم /(mǎ) tar.jo.me- be.ko.nim/	(من) ترجمه بکنم /(man) tar.jo.me- be.ko.nam/
(شما) ترجمه بکنید /(šo.mǎ) tar.jo.me- be.ko.nid/	(تو) ترجمه بکنی /(to) tar.jo.me- be.ko.ni/
(آنها) ترجمه بکنند /(ǎn.hǎ) tar.jo.me- be.ko.nand/	(او/آن) ترجمه بکند /(u/ ǎn) tar.jo.me- be.ko.nad/
Present Progressive مضارع مستمر(در جریان)	
(ما) داریم ترجمه می کنیم /(mǎ) dǎ.rim- tar.jo.me- mi.ko.nim/	(من) دارم ترجمه می کنم /(man) dǎ.ram- tar.jo.me- mi.ko.nam/
(شما) دارید ترجمه می کنید /(šo.mǎ) dǎ.rid- tar.jo.me- mi.ko.nid/	(تو) داری ترجمه می کنی /(to) dǎ.ri- tar.jo.me- mi.ko.ni/
(آنها) دارند ترجمه می کنند /(ǎn.hǎ) dǎ.rand- tar.jo.me- mi.ko.nand/	(او/آن) دارد ترجمه می کند /(u/ ǎn) dǎ.rad- tar.jo.me- mi.ko.nad/

263

<table>
<tr><td colspan="2" align="center">**Simple Past**
ماضی مطلق (گذشته ساده)</td></tr>
<tr>
<td align="center">(ما) ترجمه کردیم
/(mǎ) tar.jo.me- kar.dim/</td>
<td align="center">(من) ترجمه کردم
/(man) tar.jo.me- kar.dam/</td>
</tr>
<tr>
<td align="center">(شما) ترجمه کردید
/(šo.mǎ) tar.jo.me- kar.did/</td>
<td align="center">(تو) ترجمه کردی
/(to) tar.jo.me- kar.di/</td>
</tr>
<tr>
<td align="center">(آنها) ترجمه کردند
/(ǎn.hǎ) tar.jo.me- kar.dand/</td>
<td align="center">(او/آن) ترجمه کرد
/(u/ ǎn) tar.jo.me- kard/</td>
</tr>
</table>

<table>
<tr><td colspan="2" align="center">**Imperfect Indicative**
ماضی استمراری</td></tr>
<tr>
<td align="center">(ما) ترجمه می کردیم
/(mǎ) tar.jo.me- mi.kar.dim/</td>
<td align="center">(من) ترجمه می کردم
/(man) tar.jo.me- mi.kar.dam/</td>
</tr>
<tr>
<td align="center">(شما) ترجمه می کردید
/(šo.mǎ) tar.jo.me- mi.kar.did/</td>
<td align="center">(تو) ترجمه می کردی
/(to) tar.jo.me- mi.kar.di/</td>
</tr>
<tr>
<td align="center">(آنها) ترجمه می کردند
/(ǎn.hǎ) tar.jo.me- mi.kar.dand/</td>
<td align="center">(او/آن) ترجمه می کرد
/(u/ ǎn) tar.jo.me- mi.kard/</td>
</tr>
</table>

<table>
<tr><td colspan="2" align="center">**Present Perfect**
ماضی نقلی</td></tr>
<tr>
<td align="center">(ما) ترجمه کرده ایم
/(mǎ) tar.jo.me- kar.de.im/</td>
<td align="center">(من) ترجمه کرده ام
/(man) tar.jo.me- kar.de.am/</td>
</tr>
<tr>
<td align="center">(شما) ترجمه کرده اید
/(šo.mǎ) tar.jo.me- kar.de.id/</td>
<td align="center">(تو) ترجمه کرده ای
/(to) tar.jo.me- kar.de.i/</td>
</tr>
<tr>
<td align="center">(آنها) ترجمه کرده اند
/(ǎn.hǎ) tar.jo.me- kar.de.and/</td>
<td align="center">(او/آن) ترجمه کرده است
/(u/ ǎn) tar.jo.me- kar.de- ast/</td>
</tr>
</table>

<table>
<tr><td colspan="2" align="center">**Past Perfect**
ماضی بعید</td></tr>
<tr>
<td align="center">(ما) ترجمه کرده بودیم
/(mǎ) tar.jo.me- kar.de- bu.dim/</td>
<td align="center">(من) ترجمه کرده بودم
/(man) tar.jo.me- kar.de- bu.dam/</td>
</tr>
<tr>
<td align="center">(شما) ترجمه کرده بودید
/(šo.mǎ) tar.jo.me- kar.de- bu.did/</td>
<td align="center">(تو) ترجمه کرده بودی
/(to) tar.jo.me- kar.de- bu.di/</td>
</tr>
<tr>
<td align="center">(آنها) ترجمه کرده بودند
/(ǎn.hǎ) tar.jo.me- kar.de- bu.dand/</td>
<td align="center">(او/آن) ترجمه کرده بود
/(u/ ǎn) tar.jo.me- kar.de- bud/</td>
</tr>
</table>

<table>
<tr><td colspan="2" align="center">**Past Subjunctive**
ماضی التزامی</td></tr>
<tr>
<td align="center">(ما) ترجمه کرده باشیم
/(mă) tar.jo.me- kar.de- bă.šim/</td>
<td align="center">(من) ترجمه کرده باشم
/(man) tar.jo.me- kar.de- bă.šam/</td>
</tr>
<tr>
<td align="center">(شما) ترجمه کرده باشید
/(šo.mă) tar.jo.me- kar.de- bă.šid/</td>
<td align="center">(تو) ترجمه کرده باشی
/(man) tar.jo.me- kar.de- bă.ši/</td>
</tr>
<tr>
<td align="center">(آنها) ترجمه کرده باشند
/(ăn.hă) tar.jo.me- kar.de- bă.šand/</td>
<td align="center">(او/ آن) ترجمه کرده باشد
/(u/ ăn) tar.jo.me- kar.de- bă.šad/</td>
</tr>
</table>

<table>
<tr><td colspan="2" align="center">**Past Progressive**
ماضی مستمر(در جریان)</td></tr>
<tr>
<td align="center">(ما) داشتیم ترجمه می کردیم
/(mă) dăš.tim- tar.jo.me- mi.kar.dim/</td>
<td align="center">(من) داشتم ترجمه می کردم
/(man) dăš.tam- tar.jo.me- mi.kar.dam/</td>
</tr>
<tr>
<td align="center">(شما) داشتید ترجمه می کردید
/(šo.mă) dăš.tid- tar.jo.me- mi.kar.did/</td>
<td align="center">(تو) داشتی ترجمه می کردی
/(to) dăš.ti- tar.jo.me- mi.kar.di/</td>
</tr>
<tr>
<td align="center">(آنها) داشتند ترجمه می کردند
/(ăn.hă) dăš.tand- tar.jo.me- mi.kar.dand/</td>
<td align="center">(او/آن) داشت ترجمه می کرد
/(u/ ăn) dăšt- tar.jo.me- mi.kard/</td>
</tr>
</table>

<table>
<tr><td colspan="2" align="center">**Simple Future**
مستقبل (آینده ساده)</td></tr>
<tr>
<td align="center">(ما) ترجمه خواهیم کرد
/(mă) tar.jo.me- ǩă.him- kard/</td>
<td align="center">(من) ترجمه خواهم کرد
/(man) tar.jo.me- ǩă.ham- kard/</td>
</tr>
<tr>
<td align="center">(شما) ترجمه خواهید کرد
/(šo.mă) tar.jo.me- ǩă.hid- kard/</td>
<td align="center">(تو) ترجمه خواهی کرد
/(to) tar.jo.me- ǩă.hi- kard/</td>
</tr>
<tr>
<td align="center">(آنها) ترجمه خواهندکرد
/(ăn.hă) tar.jo.me- ǩă.hand- kard/</td>
<td align="center">(او/ آن) ترجمه خواهد کرد
/(u/ ăn) tar.jo.me- ǩă.had- kard/</td>
</tr>
</table>

<table>
<tr><td colspan="2" align="center">**Command**
امر</td></tr>
<tr>
<td align="center">* ترجمه بکنید!
/tar.jo.me- be.ko.nid/</td>
<td align="center">* ترجمه بکن!
/tar.jo.me- be.kon/</td>
</tr>
</table>

* also: ترجمه کن!   ترجمه کنید!

to travel

سَفَر کَردَن

/sa.far- kar.dan/

Plural	Singular
Simple Present مضارع اخباری(حال ساده)	
(ما) سفر می کنیم /(mǎ) sa.far- mi.ko.nim/	(من) سفر می کنم /(man) sa.far- mi.ko.nam/
(شما) سفر می کنید /(šo.mǎ) sa.far- mi.ko.nid/	(تو) سفر می کنی /(to) sa.far- mi.ko.ni/
(آنها) سفر می کنند /(ǎn.hǎ) sa.far- mi.ko.nand/	(او/آن) سفر می کند /(u/ ǎn) sa.far- mi.ko.nad/
Present Subjunctive مضارع التزامی	
(ما) سفر بکنیم /(mǎ) sa.far- be.ko.nim/	(من) سفر بکنم /(man) sa.far- be.ko.nam/
(شما) سفر بکنید /(šo.mǎ) sa.far- be.ko.nid/	(تو) سفر بکنی /(to) sa.far- be.ko.ni/
(آنها) سفر بکنند /(ǎn.hǎ) sa.far- be.ko.nand/	(او/آن) سفر بکند /(u/ ǎn) sa.far- be.ko.nad/
Present Progressive مضارع مستمر(در جریان)	
(ما) داریم سفر می کنیم /(mǎ) dǎ.rim- sa.far- mi.ko.nim/	(من) دارم سفر می کنم /(man) dǎ.ram- sa.far- mi.ko.nam/
(شما) دارید سفر می کنید /(šo.mǎ) dǎ.rid- sa.far- mi.ko.nid/	(تو) داری سفر می کنی /(to) dǎ.ri- sa.far- mi.ko.ni/
(آنها) دارند سفر می کنند /(ǎn.hǎ) dǎ.rand- sa.far- mi.ko.nand/	(او/آن) دارد سفر می کند /(u/ ǎn) dǎ.rad- sa.far- mi.ko.nad/

266

<table>
<tr><td colspan="2" align="center">

Simple Past

ماضی مطلق (گذشته ساده)

</td></tr>
<tr>
<td align="center">

(ما) سفر کردیم

/(mă) sa.far- kar.dim/

</td>
<td align="center">

(من) سفر کردم

/(man) sa.far- kar.dam/

</td>
</tr>
<tr>
<td align="center">

(شما) سفر کردید

/(šo.mă) sa.far- kar.did/

</td>
<td align="center">

(تو) سفر کردی

/(to) sa.far- kar.di/

</td>
</tr>
<tr>
<td align="center">

(آنها) سفر کردند

/(ăn.hă) sa.far- kar.dand/

</td>
<td align="center">

(او/آن) سفر کرد

/(u/ ăn) sa.far- kard/

</td>
</tr>
</table>

<table>
<tr><td colspan="2" align="center">

Imperfect Indicative

ماضی استمراری

</td></tr>
<tr>
<td align="center">

(ما) سفر می کردیم

/(mă) sa.far- mi.kar.dim/

</td>
<td align="center">

(من) سفر می کردم

/(man) sa.far- mi.kar.dam/

</td>
</tr>
<tr>
<td align="center">

(شما) سفر می کردید

/(šo.mă) sa.far- mi.kar.did/

</td>
<td align="center">

(تو) سفر می کردی

/(to) sa.far- mi.kar.di/

</td>
</tr>
<tr>
<td align="center">

(آنها) سفر می کردند

/(ăn.hă) sa.far- mi.kar.dand/

</td>
<td align="center">

(او/آن) سفر می کرد

/(u/ ăn) sa.far- mi.kard/

</td>
</tr>
</table>

<table>
<tr><td colspan="2" align="center">

Present Perfect

ماضی نقلی

</td></tr>
<tr>
<td align="center">

(ما) سفر کرده ایم

/(mă) sa.far- kar.de.im/

</td>
<td align="center">

(من) سفر کرده ام

/(man) sa.far- kar.de.am/

</td>
</tr>
<tr>
<td align="center">

(شما) سفر کرده اید

/(šo.mă) sa.far- kar.de.id/

</td>
<td align="center">

(تو) سفر کرده ای

/(to) sa.far- kar.de.i/

</td>
</tr>
<tr>
<td align="center">

(آنها) سفر کرده اند

/(ăn.hă) sa.far- kar.de.and/

</td>
<td align="center">

(او/آن) سفر کرده است

/(u/ ăn) sa.far- kar.de- ast/

</td>
</tr>
</table>

<table>
<tr><td colspan="2" align="center">

Past Perfect

ماضی بعید

</td></tr>
<tr>
<td align="center">

(ما) سفر کرده بودیم

/(mă) sa.far- kar.de- bu.dim/

</td>
<td align="center">

(من) سفر کرده بودم

/(man) sa.far- kar.de- bu.dam/

</td>
</tr>
<tr>
<td align="center">

(شما) سفر کرده بودید

/(šo.mă) sa.far- kar.de- bu.did/

</td>
<td align="center">

(تو) سفر کرده بودی

/(to) sa.far- kar.de- bu.di/

</td>
</tr>
<tr>
<td align="center">

(آنها) سفر کرده بودند

/(ăn.hă) sa.far- kar.de- bu.dand/

</td>
<td align="center">

(او/آن) سفر کرده بود

/(u/ ăn) sa.far- kar.de- bud/

</td>
</tr>
</table>

<table>
<tr><td colspan="2" align="center">**Past Subjunctive**
ماضی التزامی</td></tr>
<tr><td align="center">(ما) سفر کرده باشیم
/(mǎ) sa.far- kar.de- bǎ.šim/</td><td align="center">(من) سفر کرده باشم
/(man) sa.far- kar.de- bǎ.šam/</td></tr>
<tr><td align="center">(شما) سفر کرده باشید
/(šo.mǎ) sa.far- kar.de- bǎ.šid/</td><td align="center">(تو) سفر کرده باشی
/(to) sa.far- kar.de- bǎ.ši/</td></tr>
<tr><td align="center">(آنها) سفر کرده باشند
/(ǎn.hǎ) sa.far- kar.de- bǎ.šand/</td><td align="center">(او/ آن) سفر کرده باشد
/(u/ ǎn) sa.far- kar.de- bǎ.šad/</td></tr>
</table>

<table>
<tr><td colspan="2" align="center">**Past Progressive**
ماضی مستمر(در جریان)</td></tr>
<tr><td align="center">(ما) داشتیم سفر می کردیم
/(mǎ) dǎš.tim- sa.far- mi.kar.dim/</td><td align="center">(من) داشتم سفر می کردم
/(man) dǎš.tam- sa.far- mi.kar.dam/</td></tr>
<tr><td align="center">(شما) داشتید سفر می کردید
/(šo.mǎ) dǎš.tid- sa.far- mi.kar.did/</td><td align="center">(تو) داشتی سفر می کردی
/(to) dǎš.ti- sa.far- mi.kar.di/</td></tr>
<tr><td align="center">(آنها) داشتند سفر می کردند
/(ǎn.hǎ) dǎš.tand- sa.far- mi.kar.dand/</td><td align="center">(او/ آن) داشت سفر می کرد
/(u/ ǎn) dǎšt- sa.far- mi.kard/</td></tr>
</table>

<table>
<tr><td colspan="2" align="center">**Simple Future**
مستقبل (آینده ساده)</td></tr>
<tr><td align="center">(ما) سفر خواهیم کرد
/(mǎ) sa.far- ǩǎ.him- kard/</td><td align="center">(من) سفر خواهم کرد
/(man) sa.far- ǩǎ.ham- kard/</td></tr>
<tr><td align="center">(شما) سفر خواهید کرد
/(šo.mǎ) sa.far- ǩǎ.hid- kard/</td><td align="center">(تو) سفر خواهی کرد
/(to) sa.far- ǩǎ.hi- kard/</td></tr>
<tr><td align="center">(آنها) سفر خواهند کرد
/(ǎn.hǎ) sa.far- ǩǎ.hand- kard/</td><td align="center">(او/ آن) سفر خواهد کرد
/(u/ ǎn) sa.far- ǩǎ.had- kard/</td></tr>
</table>

<table>
<tr><td colspan="2" align="center">**Command**
امر</td></tr>
<tr><td align="center">* سفر بکنید!
/sa.far- be.ko.nid/</td><td align="center">* سفر بکن!
/sa.far- be.kon/</td></tr>
</table>

* also: سفر کن!   سفر کنید!

to understand

فَهمیدَن

/fah.mi.dan/

Plural	*Singular*
Simple Present مضارع اخباری(حال ساده)	
(ما) می فهمیم /(mă) mi.fah.mim/	(من) می فهمم /(man) mi.fah.mam/
(شما) می فهمید /(šo.mă) mi.fah.mid/	(تو) می فهمی /(to) mi.fah.mi/
(آنها) می فهمند /(ăn.hă) mi.fah.mand/	(او/آن) می فهمد /(u/ ăn) mi.fah.mad/
Present Subjunctive مضارع التزامی	
(ما) بفهمیم /(mă) be.fah.mim/	(من) بفهمم /(man) be.fah.mam/
(شما) بفهمید /(šo.mă) be.fah.mid/	(تو) بفهمی /(to) be.fah.mi/
(آنها) بفهمند /(ăn.hă) be.fah.mand/	(او/آن) بفهمد /(u/ ăn) be.fah.mad/
Present Progressive مضارع مستمر(در جریان)	
(ما) داریم می فهمیم /(mă) dă.rim- mi.fah.mim/	(من) دارم می فهمم /(man) dă.ram- mi.fah.mam/
(شما) دارید می فهمید /(šo.mă) dă.rid- mi.fah.mid/	(تو) داری می فهمی /(to) dă.ri- mi.fah.mi/
(آنها) دارند می فهمند /(ăn.hă) dă.rand- mi.fah.mand/	(او/آن) دارد می فهمد /(u/ ăn) dă.rad- mi.fah.mad/

269

<table>
<tr><td colspan="2" align="center">**Simple Past**
ماضی مطلق (گذشته ساده)</td></tr>
<tr>
<td align="center">(ما) فهمیدیم
/(mǎ) fah.mi.dim/</td>
<td align="center">(من) فهمیدم
/(man) fah.mi.dam/</td>
</tr>
<tr>
<td align="center">(شما) فهمیدید
/(šo.mǎ) fah.mi.did/</td>
<td align="center">(تو) فهمیدی
/(to) fah.mi.di/</td>
</tr>
<tr>
<td align="center">(آنها) فهمیدند
/(ǎn.hǎ) fah.mi.dand/</td>
<td align="center">(او/آن) فهمید
/(u/ ǎn) fah.mid/</td>
</tr>
</table>

<table>
<tr><td colspan="2" align="center">**Imperfect Indicative**
ماضی استمراری</td></tr>
<tr>
<td align="center">(ما) می فهمیدیم
/(mǎ) mi.fah.mi.dim/</td>
<td align="center">(من) می فهمیدم
/(man) mi.fah.mi.dam/</td>
</tr>
<tr>
<td align="center">(شما) می فهمیدید
/(šo.mǎ) mi.fah.mi.did/</td>
<td align="center">(تو) می فهمیدی
/(to) mi.fah.mi.di/</td>
</tr>
<tr>
<td align="center">(آنها) می فهمیدند
/(ǎn.hǎ) mi.fah.mi.dand/</td>
<td align="center">(او/آن) می فهمید
/(u/ ǎn) mi.fah.mid/</td>
</tr>
</table>

<table>
<tr><td colspan="2" align="center">**Present Perfect**
ماضی نقلی</td></tr>
<tr>
<td align="center">(ما) فهمیده ایم
/(mǎ) fah.mi.de.im/</td>
<td align="center">(من) فهمیده ام
/(man) fah.mi.de.am/</td>
</tr>
<tr>
<td align="center">(شما) فهمیده اید
/(šo.mǎ) fah.mi.de.id/</td>
<td align="center">(تو) فهمیده ای
/(to) fah.mi.de.i/</td>
</tr>
<tr>
<td align="center">(آنها) فهمیده اند
/(ǎn.hǎ) fah.mi.de.and/</td>
<td align="center">(او/آن) فهمیده است
/(u/ ǎn) fah.mi.de- ast/</td>
</tr>
</table>

<table>
<tr><td colspan="2" align="center">**Past Perfect**
ماضی بعید</td></tr>
<tr>
<td align="center">(ما) فهمیده بودیم
/(mǎ) fah.mi.de- bu.dim/</td>
<td align="center">(من) فهمیده بودم
/(man) fah.mi.de- bu.dam/</td>
</tr>
<tr>
<td align="center">(شما) فهمیده بودید
/(šo.mǎ) fah.mi.de- bu.did/</td>
<td align="center">(تو) فهمیده بودی
/(to) fah.mi.de- bu.di/</td>
</tr>
<tr>
<td align="center">(آنها) فهمیده بودند
/(ǎn.hǎ) fah.mi.de- bu.dand/</td>
<td align="center">(او/آن) فهمیده بود
/(u/ ǎn) fah.mi.de- bud/</td>
</tr>
</table>

Past Subjunctive
ماضی التزامی

(ما) فهمیده باشیم	(من) فهمیده باشم
/(mă) fah.mi.de- bă.šim/	/(man) fah.mi.de- bă.šam/
(شما) فهمیده باشید	(تو) فهمیده باشی
/(šo.mă) fah.mi.de- bă.šid/	/(to) fah.mi.de- bă.ši/
(آنها) فهمیده باشند	(او/آن) فهمیده باشد
/(ăn.hă) fah.mi.de- bă.šand/	/(u/ ăn) fah.mi.de- bă.šad/

Past Progressive
ماضی مستمر(در جریان)

(ما) داشتیم می فهمیدیم	(من) داشتم می فهمیدم
/(mă) dăš.tim- mi.fah.mi.dim/	/(man) dăš.tam- mi.fah.mi.dam/
(شما) داشتید می فهمیدید	(تو) داشتی می فهمیدی
/(šo.mă) dăš.tid- mi.fah.mi.did/	/(to) dăš.ti- mi.fah.mi.di/
(آنها) داشتند می فهمیدند	(او/آن) داشت می فهمید
/(ăn.hă) dăš.tand- mi.fah.mi.dand/	/(u/ ăn) dăšt- mi.fah.mid/

Simple Future
مستقبل (آینده ساده)

(ما) خواهیم فهمید	(من) خواهم فهمید
/(mă) kă.him- fah.mid/	/(man) kă.ham- fah.mid/
(شما) خواهید فهمید	(تو) خواهی فهمید
/(šo.mă) kă.hid- fah.mid/	/(to) kă.hi- fah.mid/
(آنها) خواهند فهمید	(او/آن) خواهد فهمید
/(ăn.hă) kă.hand- fah.mid/	/(u/ ăn) kă.had- fah.mid/

Command
امر

بفهمید !	بفهم !
/be.fah.mid/	/be.fahm/

to use

اِستِفاده کَردَن

/es.te.fă.de- kar.dan/

Plural	Singular
Simple Present مضارع اخباری(حال ساده)	
(ما) استفاده می کنیم /(mă) es.te.fă.de- mi.ko.nim/	(من) استفاده می کنم /(man) es.te.fă.de- mi.ko.nam/
(شما) استفاده می کنید /(šo.mă) es.te.fă.de- mi.ko.nid/	(تو) استفاده می کنی /(to) es.te.fă.de- mi.ko.ni/
(آنها) استفاده می کنند /(ăn.hă) es.te.fă.de- mi.ko.nand/	(او/آن) استفاده می کند /(u/ ăn) es.te.fă.de- mi.ko.nad/
Present Subjunctive مضارع التزامی	
(ما) استفاده بکنیم /(mă) es.te.fă.de- be.ko.nim/	(من) استفاده بکنم /(man) es.te.fă.de- be.ko.nam/
(شما) استفاده بکنید /(šo.mă) es.te.fă.de- be.ko.nid/	(تو) استفاده بکنی /(to) es.te.fă.de- be.ko.ni/
(آنها) استفاده بکنند /(ăn.hă) es.te.fă.de- be.ko.nand/	(او/آن) استفاده بکند /(u/ ăn) es.te.fă.de- be.ko.nad/
Present Progressive مضارع مستمر(در جریان)	
(ما) داریم استفاده می کنیم /(mă) dă.rim- es.te.fă.de- mi.ko.nim/	(من) دارم استفاده می کنم /(man) dă.ram- es.te.fă.de- mi.ko.nam/
(شما) دارید استفاده می کنید /(šo.mă) dă.rid- es.te.fă.de- mi.ko.nid/	(تو) داری استفاده می کنی /(to) dă.ri- es.te.fă.de- mi.ko.ni/
(آنها) دارند استفاده می کنند /(ăn.hă) dă.rand- es.te.fă.de- mi.ko.nand/	(او/آن) دارد استفاده می کند /(u/ ăn) dă.rad- es.te.fă.de- mi.ko.nad/

Simple Past
ماضی مطلق (گذشته ساده)

(ما) استفاده کردیم	(من) استفاده کردم
/(mǎ) es.te.fǎ.de- kar.dim/	/(man) es.te.fǎ.de- kar.dam/
(شما) استفاده کردید	(تو) استفاده کردی
/(šo.mǎ) es.te.fǎ.de- kar.did/	/(to) es.te.fǎ.de- kar.di/
(آنها) استفاده کردند	(او/آن) استفاده کرد
/(ǎn.hǎ) es.te.fǎ.de- kar.dand/	/(u/ ǎn) es.te.fǎ.de- kard/

Imperfect Indicative
ماضی استمراری

(ما) استفاده می کردیم	(من) استفاده می کردم
/(mǎ) es.te.fǎ.de- mi.kar.dim/	/(man) es.te.fǎ.de- mi.kar.dam/
(شما) استفاده می کردید	(تو) استفاده می کردی
/(šo.mǎ) es.te.fǎ.de- mi.kar.did/	/(to) es.te.fǎ.de- mi.kar.di/
(آنها) استفاده می کردند	(او/آن) استفاده می کرد
/(ǎn.hǎ) es.te.fǎ.de- mi.kar.dand/	/(u/ ǎn) es.te.fǎ.de- mi.kard/

Present Perfect
ماضی نقلی

(ما) استفاده کرده ایم	(من) استفاده کرده ام
/(mǎ) es.te.fǎ.de- kar.de.im/	/(man) es.te.fǎ.de- kar.de.am/
(شما) استفاده کرده اید	(تو) استفاده کرده ای
/(šo.mǎ) es.te.fǎ.de- kar.de.id/	/(to) es.te.fǎ.de- kar.de.i/
(آنها) استفاده کرده اند	(او/آن) استفاده کرده است
/(ǎn.hǎ) es.te.fǎ.de- kar.de.and/	/(u/ ǎn) es.te.fǎ.de- kar.de- ast/

Past Perfect
ماضی بعید

(ما) استفاده کرده بودیم	(من) استفاده کرده بودم
/(mǎ) es.te.fǎ.de- kar.de- bu.dim/	/(man) es.te.fǎ.de- kar.de- bu.dam/
(شما) استفاده کرده بودید	(تو) استفاده کرده بودی
/(šo.mǎ) es.te.fǎ.de- kar.de- bu.did/	/(to) es.te.fǎ.de- kar.de- bu.di/
(آنها) استفاده کرده بودند	(او/آن) استفاده کرده بود
/(ǎn.hǎ) es.te.fǎ.de- kar.de- bu.dand/	/(u/ ǎn) es.te.fǎ.de- kar.de- bud/

<table>
<tr><td colspan="2" align="center">

Past Subjunctive

ماضی التزامی

</td></tr>
<tr>
<td align="center">

(ما) استفاده کرده باشیم

/(mǎ) es.te.fǎ.de- kar.de- bǎ.šim/

</td>
<td align="center">

(من) استفاده کرده باشم

/(man) es.te.fǎ.de- kar.de- bǎ.šam/

</td>
</tr>
<tr>
<td align="center">

(شما) استفاده کرده باشید

/(šo.mǎ) es.te.fǎ.de- kar.de- bǎ.šid/

</td>
<td align="center">

(تو) استفاده کرده باشی

/(to) es.te.fǎ.de- kar.de- bǎ.ši/

</td>
</tr>
<tr>
<td align="center">

(آنها) استفاده کرده باشند

/(ǎn.hǎ) es.te.fǎ.de- kar.de- bǎ.šand/

</td>
<td align="center">

(او/آن) استفاده کرده باشد

/(u/ ǎn) es.te.fǎ.de- kar.de- bǎ.šad/

</td>
</tr>
</table>

<table>
<tr><td colspan="2" align="center">

Past Progressive

ماضی مستمر(در جریان)

</td></tr>
<tr>
<td align="center">

(ما) داشتیم استفاده می کردیم

/(mǎ) dǎš.tim- es.te.fǎ.de- mi.kar.dim/

</td>
<td align="center">

(من) داشتم استفاده می کردم

/(man) dǎš.tam- es.te.fǎ.de- mi.kar.dam/

</td>
</tr>
<tr>
<td align="center">

(شما) داشتید استفاده می کردید

/(šo.mǎ) dǎš.tid- es.te.fǎ.de- mi.kar.did/

</td>
<td align="center">

(تو) داشتی استفاده می کردی

/(to) dǎš.ti- es.te.fǎ.de- mi.kar.di/

</td>
</tr>
<tr>
<td align="center">

(آنها) داشتند استفاده می کردند

/(ǎn.hǎ) dǎš.tand- es.te.fǎ.de- mi.kar.dand/

</td>
<td align="center">

(او/آن) داشت استفاده می کرد

/(u/ ǎn) dǎšt- es.te.fǎ.de- mi.kard/

</td>
</tr>
</table>

<table>
<tr><td colspan="2" align="center">

Simple Future

مستقبل (آینده ساده)

</td></tr>
<tr>
<td align="center">

(ما) استفاده خواهیم کرد

/(mǎ) es.te.fǎ.de- kǎ.him- kard/

</td>
<td align="center">

(من) استفاده خواهم کرد

/(man) es.te.fǎ.de- kǎ.ham- kard/

</td>
</tr>
<tr>
<td align="center">

(شما) استفاده خواهید کرد

/(šo.mǎ) es.te.fǎ.de- kǎ.hid- kard/

</td>
<td align="center">

(تو) استفاده خواهی کرد

/(to) es.te.fǎ.de- kǎ.hi- kard/

</td>
</tr>
<tr>
<td align="center">

(آنها) استفاده خواهند کرد

/(ǎn.hǎ) es.te.fǎ.de- kǎ.hand- kard/

</td>
<td align="center">

(او/آن) استفاده خواهد کرد

/(u/ ǎn) es.te.fǎ.de- kǎ.had- kard/

</td>
</tr>
</table>

<table>
<tr><td colspan="2" align="center">

Command

امر

</td></tr>
<tr>
<td align="center">

* استفاده بکنید!

/es.te.fǎ.de- be.ko.nid/

</td>
<td align="center">

* استفاده بکن!

/es.te.fǎ.de- be.kon/

</td>
</tr>
</table>

* also: استفاده کن!   استفاده کنید!

to wait

صَبر کَردَن

/sabr- kar.dan/

Plural	Singular
Simple Present	
مضارع اخباری(حال ساده)	
(ما) صبر می کنیم	(من) صبر می کنم
/(mă) sabr- mi.ko.nim/	/(man) sabr- mi.ko.nam/
(شما) صبر می کنید	(تو) صبر می کنی
/(šo.mă) sabr- mi.ko.nid/	/(to) sabr- mi.ko.ni/
(آنها) صبر می کنند	(او/آن) صبر می کند
/(ăn.hă) sabr- mi.ko.nand/	/(u/ ăn) sabr- mi.ko.nad/

Plural	Singular
Present Subjunctive	
مضارع التزامی	
(ما) صبر بکنیم	(من) صبر بکنم
/(mă) sabr- be.ko.nim/	/(man) sabr- be.ko.nam/
(شما) صبر بکنید	(تو) صبر بکنی
/(šo.mă) sabr- be.ko.nid/	/(to) sabr- be.ko.ni/
(آنها) صبر بکنند	(او/آن) صبر بکند
/(ăn.hă) sabr- be.ko.nand/	/(u/ ăn) sabr- be.ko.nad/

Plural	Singular
Present Progressive	
مضارع مستمر(در جریان)	
(ما) داریم صبر می کنیم	(من) دارم صبر می کنم
/(mă) dă.rim- sabr- mi.ko.nim/	/(man) dă.ram- sabr- mi.ko.nam/
(شما) دارید صبر می کنید	(تو) داری صبر می کنی
/(šo.mă) dă.rid- sabr- mi.ko.nid/	/(to) dă.ri- sabr- mi.ko.ni/
(آنها) دارند صبر می کنند	(او/آن) دارد صبر می کند
/(ăn.hă) dă.rand- sabr- mi.ko.nand/	/(u/ ăn) dă.rad- sabr- mi.ko.nad/

<table>
<tr><td colspan="2" align="center">**Simple Past**
ماضی مطلق (گذشته ساده)</td></tr>
<tr>
<td align="center">(ما) صبر کردیم
/(mǎ) sabr- kar.dim/</td>
<td align="center">(من) صبر کردم
/(man) sabr- kar.dam/</td>
</tr>
<tr>
<td align="center">(شما) صبر کردید
/(šo.mǎ) sabr- kar.did/</td>
<td align="center">(تو) صبر کردی
/(to) sabr- kar.di/</td>
</tr>
<tr>
<td align="center">(آنها) صبر کردند
/(ǎn.hǎ) sabr- kar.dand/</td>
<td align="center">(او/آن) صبر کرد
/(u/ ǎn) sabr- kard/</td>
</tr>
</table>

<table>
<tr><td colspan="2" align="center">**Imperfect Indicative**
ماضی استمراری</td></tr>
<tr>
<td align="center">(ما) صبر می کردیم
/(mǎ) sabr- mi.kar.dim/</td>
<td align="center">(من) صبر می کردم
/(man) sabr- mi. kar.dam/</td>
</tr>
<tr>
<td align="center">(شما) صبر می کردید
/(šo.mǎ) sabr- mi.kar.did/</td>
<td align="center">(تو) صبر می کردی
/(to) sabr- mi.kar.di/</td>
</tr>
<tr>
<td align="center">(آنها) صبر می کردند
/(ǎn.hǎ) sabr- mi.kar.dand/</td>
<td align="center">(او/آن) صبر می کرد
/(u/ ǎn) sabr- mi.kard/</td>
</tr>
</table>

<table>
<tr><td colspan="2" align="center">**Present Perfect**
ماضی نقلی</td></tr>
<tr>
<td align="center">(ما) صبر کرده ایم
/(mǎ) sabr- kar.de.im/</td>
<td align="center">(من) صبر کرده ام
/(man) sabr- kar.de.am/</td>
</tr>
<tr>
<td align="center">(شما) صبر کرده اید
/(šo.mǎ) sabr- kar.de.id/</td>
<td align="center">(تو) صبر کرده ای
/(to) sabr- kar.de.i/</td>
</tr>
<tr>
<td align="center">(آنها) صبر کرده اند
/(ǎn.hǎ) sabr- kar.de.and/</td>
<td align="center">(او/آن) صبر کرده است
/(u/ ǎn) sabr- kar.de- ast/</td>
</tr>
</table>

<table>
<tr><td colspan="2" align="center">**Past Perfect**
ماضی بعید</td></tr>
<tr>
<td align="center">(ما) صبر کرده بودیم
/(mǎ) sabr- kar.de- bu.dim/</td>
<td align="center">(من) صبر کرده بودم
/(man) sabr- kar.de- bu.dam/</td>
</tr>
<tr>
<td align="center">(شما) صبر کرده بودید
/(šo.mǎ) sabr- kar.de- bu.did/</td>
<td align="center">(تو) صبر کرده بودی
/(to) sabr- kar.de- bu.di/</td>
</tr>
<tr>
<td align="center">(آنها) صبر کرده بودند
/(ǎn.hǎ) sabr- kar.de- bu.dand/</td>
<td align="center">(او/آن) صبر کرده بود
/(u/ ǎn) sabr- kar.de- bud/</td>
</tr>
</table>

Past Subjunctive	
ماضی التزامی	
(ما) صبر کرده باشیم	(من) صبر کرده باشم
/(mă) sabr- kar.de- bă.šim/	/(man) sabr- kar.de- bă.šam/
(شما) صبر کرده باشید	(تو) صبر کرده باشی
/(šo.mă) sabr- kar.de- bă.šid/	/(to) sabr- kar.de- bă.ši/
(آنها) صبر کرده باشند	(او/آن) صبر کرده باشد
/(ăn.hă) sabr- kar.de- bă.šand/	/(u/ ăn) sabr- kar.de- bă.šad/

Past Progressive	
ماضی مستمر(در جریان)	
(ما) داشتیم صبر می کردیم	(من) داشتم صبر می کردم
/(mă) dăš.tim- sabr- mi.kar.dim/	/(man) dăš.tam- sabr- mi.kar.dam/
(شما) داشتید صبر می کردید	(تو) داشتی صبر می کردی
/(šo.mă) dăš.tid- sabr- mi.kar.did/	/(to) dăš.ti- sabr- mi.kar.di/
(آنها) داشتند صبر می کردند	(او/آن) داشت صبر می کرد
/(ăn.hă) dăš.tand- sabr- mi.kar.dand/	/(u/ ăn) dăšt- sabr- mi.kard/

Simple Future	
مستقبل (آینده ساده)	
(ما) صبر خواهیم کرد	(من) صبر خواهم کرد
/(mă) sabr- kă.him- kard/	/(man) sabr- kă.ham- kard/
(شما) صبر خواهید کرد	(تو) صبر خواهی کرد
/(šo.mă) sabr- kă.hid- kard/	/(to) sabr- kă.hi- kard/
(آنها) صبر خواهند کرد	(او /آن) صبر خواهد کرد
/(ăn.hă) sabr- kă.hand- kard/	/(u/ ăn) sabr- kă.had- kard/

Command	
امر	
* صبر بکنید!	* صبر بکن!
/sabr- be.ko.nid/	/sabr- be.kon/

* also: صبر کن!   صبر کنید!

277

to wake up

بیدار شُدَن

/bi.dăr- šo.dan/

Plural	Singular
Simple Present مضارع اخباری(حال ساده)	
(ما) بیدار می شویم /(mă) bi.dăr- mi.ša.vim/	(من) بیدار می شوم /(man) bi.dăr- mi.ša.vam/
(شما) بیدار می شوید /(šo.mă) bi.dăr- mi.ša.vid/	(تو) بیدار می شوی /(to) bi.dăr- mi.ša.vi/
(آنها) بیدار می شوند /(ăn.hă) bi.dăr- mi.ša.vand/	(او/آن) بیدار می شود /(u/ ăn) bi.dăr- mi.ša.vad/
Present Subjunctive مضارع التزامی	
(ما) بیدار بشویم /(mă) bi.dăr- be.ša.vim/	(من) بیدار بشوم /(man) bi.dăr- be.ša.vam/
(شما) بیدار بشوید /(šo.mă) bi.dăr- be.ša.vid/	(تو) بیدار بشوی /(to) bi.dăr- be.ša.vi/
(آنها) بیدار بشوند /(ăn.hă) bi.dăr- be.ša.vand/	(او/آن) بیدار بشود /(u/ ăn) bi.dăr- be.ša.vad/
Present Progressive مضارع مستمر(در جریان)	
(ما) داریم بیدار می شویم /(mă) dă.rim- bi.dăr- mi.ša.vim/	(من) دارم بیدار می شوم /(man) dă.ram- bi.dăr- mi.ša.vam/
(شما) دارید بیدار می شوید /(šo.mă) dă.rid- bi.dăr- mi.ša.vid/	(تو) داری بیدار می شوی /(to) dă.ri- bi.dăr- mi.ša.vi/
(آنها) دارند بیدار می شوند /(ăn.hă) dă.rand- bi.dăr- mi.ša.vand/	(او/آن) دارد بیدار می شود /(u/ ăn) dă.rad- bi.dăr- mi.ša.vad/

<table>
<tr><td colspan="2" align="center">**Simple Past**
ماضی مطلق (گذشته ساده)</td></tr>
<tr>
<td align="center">(ما) بیدار شدیم
/(mă) bi.dăr- šo.dim/</td>
<td align="center">(من) بیدار شدم
/(man) bi.dăr- šo.dam/</td>
</tr>
<tr>
<td align="center">(شما) بیدار شدید
/(šo.mă) bi.dăr- šo.did/</td>
<td align="center">(تو) بیدار شدی
/(to) bi.dăr- šo.di/</td>
</tr>
<tr>
<td align="center">(آنها) بیدار شدند
/(ăn.hă) bi.dăr- šo.dand/</td>
<td align="center">(او/آن) بیدار شد
/(u/ ăn) bi.dăr- šod/</td>
</tr>
</table>

<table>
<tr><td colspan="2" align="center">**Imperfect Indicative**
ماضی استمراری</td></tr>
<tr>
<td align="center">(ما) بیدار می شدیم
/(mă) bi.dăr- mi.šo.dim/</td>
<td align="center">(من) بیدار می شدم
/(man) bi.dăr- mi.šo.dam/</td>
</tr>
<tr>
<td align="center">(شما) بیدار می شدید
/(šo.mă) bi.dăr- mi.šo.did/</td>
<td align="center">(تو) بیدار می شدی
/(to) bi.dăr- mi.šo.di/</td>
</tr>
<tr>
<td align="center">(آنها) بیدار می شدند
/(ăn.hă) bi.dăr- mi.šo.dand/</td>
<td align="center">(او/آن) بیدار می شد
/(u/ ăn) bi.dăr- mi.šod/</td>
</tr>
</table>

<table>
<tr><td colspan="2" align="center">**Present Perfect**
ماضی نقلی</td></tr>
<tr>
<td align="center">(ما) بیدار شده ایم
/(mă) bi.dăr- šo.de.im/</td>
<td align="center">(من) بیدار شده ام
/(man) bi.dăr- šo.de.am/</td>
</tr>
<tr>
<td align="center">(شما) بیدار شده اید
/(šo.mă) bi.dăr- šo.de.id/</td>
<td align="center">(تو) بیدار شده ای
/(to) bi.dăr- šo.de.i/</td>
</tr>
<tr>
<td align="center">(آنها) بیدار شده اند
/(ăn.hă) bi.dăr- šo.de.and/</td>
<td align="center">(او/آن) بیدار شده است
/(u/ ăn) bi.dăr- šo.de- ast/</td>
</tr>
</table>

<table>
<tr><td colspan="2" align="center">**Past Perfect**
ماضی بعید</td></tr>
<tr>
<td align="center">(ما) بیدار شده بودیم
/(mă) bi.dăr- šo.de- bu.dim/</td>
<td align="center">(من) بیدار شده بودم
/(man) bi.dăr- šo.de- bu.dam/</td>
</tr>
<tr>
<td align="center">(شما) بیدار شده بودید
/(šo.mă) bi.dăr- šo.de- bu.did/</td>
<td align="center">(تو) بیدار شده بودی
/(to) bi.dăr- šo.de- bu.di/</td>
</tr>
<tr>
<td align="center">(آنها) بیدار شده بودند
/(ăn.hă) bi.dăr- šo.de- bu.dand/</td>
<td align="center">(او/آن) بیدار شده بود
/(u/ ăn) bi.dăr- šo.de- bud/</td>
</tr>
</table>

Past Subjunctive	
ماضی التزامی	
(ما) بیدار شده باشیم	(من) بیدار شده باشم
/(mǎ) bi.dǎr- šo.de- bǎ.šim/	/(man) bi.dǎr- šo.de- bǎ.šam/
(شما) بیدار شده باشید	(تو) بیدار شده باشی
/(šo.mǎ) bi.dǎr- šo.de- bǎ.šid/	/(to) bi.dǎr- šo.de- bǎ.ši/
(آنها) بیدار شده باشند	(او/ آن) بیدار شده باشد
/(ǎn.hǎ) bi.dǎr- šo.de- bǎ.šand/	/(u/ ǎn) bi.dǎr- šo.de- bǎ.šad/

Past Progressive	
ماضی مستمر(در جریان)	
(ما) داشتیم بیدار می شدیم	(من) داشتم بیدار می شدم
/(mǎ) dǎš.tim- bi.dǎr- mi.šo.dim/	/(man) dǎš.tam- bi.dǎr- mi.šo.dam/
(شما) داشتید بیدار می شدید	(تو) داشتی بیدار می شدی
/(šo.mǎ) dǎš.tid- bi.dǎr- mi.šo.did/	/(to) dǎš.ti- bi.dǎr- mi.šo.di/
(آنها) داشتند بیدار می شدند	(او/ آن) داشت بیدار می شد
/(ǎn.hǎ) dǎš.tand- bi.dǎr- mi.šo.dand/	/(u/ ǎn) dǎšt- bi.dǎr- mi.šod/

Simple Future	
مستقبل (آینده ساده)	
(ما) بیدار خواهیم شد	(من) بیدار خواهم شد
/(mǎ) bi.dǎr- ǩǎ.him- šod/	/(man) bi.dǎr- ǩǎ.ham- šod/
(شما) بیدار خواهید شد	(تو) بیدار خواهی شد
/(šo.mǎ) bi.dǎr- ǩǎ.hid- šod/	/(to) bi.dǎr- ǩǎ.hi- šod/
(آنها) بیدار خواهند شد	(او/ آن) بیدار خواهد شد
/(ǎn.hǎ) bi.dǎr- ǩǎ.hand- šod/	/(u/ ǎn) bi.dǎr- ǩǎ.had- šod/

Command	
امر	
* بیدار بشوید!	* بیدار بشو!
/bi.dǎr- be.ša.vid/	/bi.dǎr- be.šo/

*   also: بیدار شوید!   بیدار شو!

to walk

راه رَفتَن

/răh- raf.tan/

Plural	Singular
Simple Present <div dir="rtl">مضارع اخباری(حال ساده)</div>	
<div dir="rtl">(ما) راه می رویم</div> /(mă) răh- mi.ra.vim/	<div dir="rtl">(من) راه می روم</div> /(man) răh- mi.ra.vam/
<div dir="rtl">(شما) راه می روید</div> /(šo.mă) răh- mi.ra.vid/	<div dir="rtl">(تو) راه می روی</div> /(to) răh- mi.ra.vi/
<div dir="rtl">(آنها) راه می روند</div> /(ăn.hă) răh- mi.ra.vand/	<div dir="rtl">(او/آن) راه می رود</div> /(u/ ăn) răh- mi.ra.vad/

Plural	Singular
Present Subjunctive <div dir="rtl">مضارع التزامی</div>	
<div dir="rtl">(ما) راه برویم</div> /(mă) răh- be.ra.vim/	<div dir="rtl">(من) راه بروم</div> /(man) răh- be.ra.vam/
<div dir="rtl">(شما) راه بروید</div> /(šo.mă) răh- be.ra.vid/	<div dir="rtl">(تو) راه بروی</div> /(to) răh- be.ra.vi/
<div dir="rtl">(آنها) راه بروند</div> /(ăn.hă) răh- be.ra.vand/	<div dir="rtl">(او/آن) راه برود</div> /(u/ ăn) răh- be.ra.vad/

Plural	Singular
Present Progressive <div dir="rtl">مضارع مستمر(در جریان)</div>	
<div dir="rtl">(ما) داریم راه می رویم</div> /(mă) dă.rim- răh- mi.ra.vim/	<div dir="rtl">(من) دارم راه می روم</div> /(man) dă.ram- răh- mi.ra.vam/
<div dir="rtl">(شما) دارید راه می روید</div> /(šo.mă) dă.rid- răh- mi.ra.vid/	<div dir="rtl">(تو) داری راه می روی</div> /(to) dă.ri- răh- mi.ra.vi/
<div dir="rtl">(آنها) دارند راه می روند</div> /(ăn.hă) dă.rand- răh- mi.ra.vand/	<div dir="rtl">(او/آن) دارد راه می رود</div> /(u/ ăn) dă.rad- răh- mi.ra.vad/

281

Simple Past
ماضی مطلق (گذشته ساده)

(ما) راه رفتیم	(من) راه رفتم
/(mǎ) rǎh- raf.tim/	/(man) rǎh- raf.tam/
(شما) راه رفتید	(تو) راه رفتی
/(šo.mǎ) rǎh- raf.tid/	/(to) rǎh- raf.ti/
(آنها) راه رفتند	(او/ آن) راه رفت
/(ǎn.hǎ) rǎh- raf.tand/	/(u/ ǎn) rǎh- raft/

Imperfect Indicative
ماضی استمراری

(ما) راه می رفتیم	(من) راه می رفتم
/(mǎ) rǎh- mi.raf.tim/	/(man) rǎh- mi.raf.tam/
(شما) راه می رفتید	(تو) راه می رفتی
/(šo.mǎ) rǎh- mi.raf.tid/	/(to) rǎh- mi.raf.ti/
(آنها) راه می رفتند	(او/آن) راه می رفت
/(ǎn.hǎ) rǎh- mi.raf.tand/	/(u/ ǎn) rǎh- mi.raft/

Present Perfect
ماضی نقلی

(ما) راه رفته ایم	(من) راه رفته ام
/(mǎ) rǎh- raf.te.im/	/(man) rǎh- raf.te.am/
(شما) راه رفته اید	(تو) راه رفته ای
/(šo.mǎ) rǎh- raf.te.id/	/(to) rǎh- raf.te.i/
(آنها) راه رفته اند	(او/آن) راه رفته است
/(ǎn.hǎ) rǎh- raf.te.and/	/(u/ ǎn) rǎh- raf.te- ast/

Past Perfect
ماضی بعید

(ما) راه رفته بودیم	(من) راه رفته بودم
/(mǎ) rǎh- raf.te- bu.dim/	/(man) rǎh- raf.te- bu.dam/
(شما) راه رفته بودید	(تو) راه رفته بودی
/(šo.mǎ) rǎh- raf.te- bu.did/	/(to) rǎh- raf.te- bu.di/
(آنها) راه رفته بودند	(او/آن) راه رفته بود
/(ǎn.hǎ) rǎh- raf.te- bu.dand/	/(u/ ǎn) rǎh- raf.te- bud/

<table>
<tr><td colspan="2" align="center">**Past Subjunctive**
ماضی التزامی</td></tr>
<tr>
<td align="center">(ما) راه رفته باشیم
/(mă) răh- raf.te- bă.šim/</td>
<td align="center">(من) راه رفته باشم
/(man) răh- raf.te- bă.šam/</td>
</tr>
<tr>
<td align="center">(شما) راه رفته باشید
/(šo.mă) răh- raf.te- bă.šid/</td>
<td align="center">(تو) راه رفته باشی
/(to) răh- raf.te- bă.ši/</td>
</tr>
<tr>
<td align="center">(آنها) راه رفته باشند
/(ăn.hă) răh- raf.te- bă.šand/</td>
<td align="center">(او/آن) راه رفته باشد
/(u/ ăn) răh- raf.te- bă.šad/</td>
</tr>
</table>

<table>
<tr><td colspan="2" align="center">**Past Progressive**
ماضی مستمر(در جریان)</td></tr>
<tr>
<td align="center">(ما) داشتیم راه می رفتیم
/(mă) dăš.tim- răh- mi.raf.tim/</td>
<td align="center">(من) داشتم راه می رفتم
/(man) dăš.tam- răh- mi.raf.tam/</td>
</tr>
<tr>
<td align="center">(شما) داشتید راه می رفتید
/(šo.mă) dăš.tid- răh- mi.raf.tid/</td>
<td align="center">(تو) داشتی راه می رفتی
/(to) dăš.ti- răh- mi.raf.ti/</td>
</tr>
<tr>
<td align="center">(آنها) داشتند راه می رفتند
/(ăn.hă) dăš.tand- răh- mi.raf.tand/</td>
<td align="center">(او/آن) داشت راه می رفت
/(u/ ăn) dăšt- răh- mi.raft/</td>
</tr>
</table>

<table>
<tr><td colspan="2" align="center">**Simple Future**
مستقبل (آینده ساده)</td></tr>
<tr>
<td align="center">(ما) راه خواهیم رفت
/(mă) răh- ǩă.him- raft/</td>
<td align="center">(من) راه خواهم رفت
/(man) răh- ǩă.ham- raft/</td>
</tr>
<tr>
<td align="center">(شما) راه خواهید رفت
/(šo.mă) răh- ǩă.hid- raft/</td>
<td align="center">(تو) راه خواهی رفت
/(to) răh- ǩă.hi- raft/</td>
</tr>
<tr>
<td align="center">(آنها) راه خواهند رفت
/(ăn.hă) răh- ǩă.hand- raft/</td>
<td align="center">(او/آن) راه خواهد رفت
/(u/ ăn) răh- ǩă.had- raft/</td>
</tr>
</table>

<table>
<tr><td colspan="2" align="center">**Command**
امر</td></tr>
<tr>
<td align="center">راه بروید!
/răh- be.ra.vid/</td>
<td align="center">راه برو!
/răh- bo.ro/</td>
</tr>
</table>

to want

خواستَن

/k̆ǎs.tan/

Plural	Singular
Simple Present	
مضارع اخباری(حال ساده)	
(ما) می خواهیم	(من) می خواهم
/(mǎ) mi.k̆ǎ.him/	/(man) mi.k̆ǎ.ham/
(شما) می خواهید	(تو) می خواهی
/(šo.mǎ) mi.k̆ǎ.hid/	/(to) mi.k̆ǎ.hi/
(آنها) می خواهند	(او/آن) می خواهد
/(ǎn.hǎ) mi.k̆ǎ.hand/	/(u/ ǎn) mi.k̆ǎ.had/
Present Subjunctive	
مضارع التزامی	
(ما) بخواهیم	(من) بخواهم
/(mǎ) be.k̆ǎ.him/	/(man) be.k̆ǎ.ham/
(شما) بخواهید	(تو) بخواهی
/(šo.mǎ) be.k̆ǎ.hid/	/(to) be.k̆ǎ.hi/
(آنها) بخواهند	(او/آن) بخواهد
/(ǎn.hǎ) be.k̆ǎ.hand/	/(u/ ǎn) be.k̆ǎ.had/
Present Progressive	
مضارع مستمر(در جریان)	
(ما) داریم می خواهیم	(من) دارم می خواهم
/(mǎ) dǎ.rim- mi.k̆ǎ.him/	/(man) dǎ.ram- mi.k̆ǎ.ham/
(شما) دارید می خواهید	(تو) داری می خواهی
/(šo.mǎ) dǎ.rid- mi.k̆ǎ.hid/	/(to) dǎ.ri- mi.k̆ǎ.hi/
(آنها) دارند می خواهند	(او/آن) دارد می خواهد
/(ǎn.hǎ) dǎ.rand- mi.k̆ǎ.hand/	/(u/ ǎn) dǎ.rad- mi.k̆ǎ.had/

<table>
<tr><td colspan="2" align="center">**Simple Past**
ماضی مطلق (گذشته ساده)</td></tr>
<tr><td align="center">(ما) خواستیم
/(mă) kăs.tim/</td><td align="center">(من) خواستم
/(man) kăs.tam/</td></tr>
<tr><td align="center">(شما) خواستید
/(šo.mă) kăs.tid/</td><td align="center">(تو) خواستی
/(to) kăs.ti/</td></tr>
<tr><td align="center">(آنها) خواستند
/(ăn.hă) kăs.tand/</td><td align="center">(او/آن) خواست
/(u/ ăn) kăst/</td></tr>
</table>

<table>
<tr><td colspan="2" align="center">**Imperfect Indicative**
ماضی استمراری</td></tr>
<tr><td align="center">(ما) می خواستیم
/(mă) mi.kăs.tim/</td><td align="center">(من) می خواستم
/(man) mi.kăs.tam/</td></tr>
<tr><td align="center">(شما) می خواستید
/(šo.mă) mi.kăs.tid/</td><td align="center">(تو) می خواستی
/(to) mi.kăs.ti/</td></tr>
<tr><td align="center">(آنها) می خواستند
/(ăn.hă) mi.kăs.tand/</td><td align="center">(او/آن) می خواست
/(u/ ăn) mi.kăst/</td></tr>
</table>

<table>
<tr><td colspan="2" align="center">**Present Perfect**
ماضی نقلی</td></tr>
<tr><td align="center">(ما) خواسته ایم
/(mă) kăs.te.im/</td><td align="center">(من) خواسته ام
/(man) kăs.te.am/</td></tr>
<tr><td align="center">(شما) خواسته اید
/(šo.mă) kăs.te.id/</td><td align="center">(تو) خواسته ای
/(to) kăs.te.i/</td></tr>
<tr><td align="center">(آنها) خواسته اند
/(ăn.hă) kăs.te.and/</td><td align="center">(او/آن) خواسته است
/(u/ ăn) kăs.te- ast/</td></tr>
</table>

<table>
<tr><td colspan="2" align="center">**Past Perfect**
ماضی بعید</td></tr>
<tr><td align="center">(ما) خواسته بودیم
/(mă) kăs.te- bu.dim/</td><td align="center">(من) خواسته بودم
/(man) kăs.te- bu.dam/</td></tr>
<tr><td align="center">(شما) خواسته بودید
/(šo.mă) kăs.te- bu.did/</td><td align="center">(تو) خواسته بودی
/(to) kăs.te- bu.di/</td></tr>
<tr><td align="center">(آنها) خواسته بودند
/(ăn.hă) kăs.te- bu.dand/</td><td align="center">(او/آن) خواسته بود
/(u/ ăn) kăs.te- bud/</td></tr>
</table>

Past Subjunctive	
ماضی التزامی	
(ما) خواسته باشیم /(mǎ) ḱǎs.te- bǎ.šim/	(من) خواسته باشم /(man) ḱǎs.te- bǎ.šam/
(شما) خواسته باشید /(šo.mǎ) ḱǎs.te- bǎ.šid/	(تو) خواسته باشی /(to) ḱǎs.te- bǎ.ši/
(آنها) خواسته باشند /(ǎn.hǎ) ḱǎs.te- bǎ.šand/	(او/آن) خواسته باشد /(u/ ǎn) ḱǎs.te- bǎ.šad/

Past Progressive	
ماضی مستمر(در جریان)	
(ما) داشتیم می خواستیم /(mǎ) dǎš.tim- mi.ḱǎs.tim/	(من) داشتم می خواستم /(man) dǎš.tam- mi.ḱǎs.tam/
(شما) داشتید می خواستید /(šo.mǎ) dǎš.tid- mi.ḱǎs.tid/	(تو) داشتی می خواستی /(to) dǎš.ti- mi.ḱǎs.ti/
(آنها) داشتند می خواستند /(ǎn.hǎ) dǎš.tand- mi.ḱǎs.tand/	(او/آن) داشت می خواست /(u/ ǎn) dǎšt- mi.ḱǎst/

Simple Future	
مستقبل (آینده ساده)	
(ما) خواهیم خواست /(mǎ) ḱǎ.him- ḱǎst/	(من) خواهم خواست /(man) ḱǎ.ham- ḱǎst/
(شما) خواهید خواست /(šo.mǎ) ḱǎ.hid- ḱǎst/	(تو) خواهی خواست /(to) ḱǎ.hi- ḱǎst/
(آنها) خواهند خواست /(ǎn.hǎ) ḱǎ.hand- ḱǎst/	(او/آن) خواهد خواست /(u/ ǎn) ḱǎ.had- ḱǎst/

Command	
امر	
بخواهید! /be.ḱǎ.hid/	بخواه! /be.ḱǎh/

to wash

شُستَن

/šos.tan/

Plural	*Singular*
Simple Present مضارع اخباری(حال ساده)	
(ما) می شوییم /(mǎ) mi.šu.yim/	(من) می شویم /(man) mi.šu.yam/
(شما) می شویید /(šo.mǎ) mi.šu.yid/	(تو) می شویی /(to) mi.šu.yi/
(آنها) می شویند /(ǎn.hǎ) mi.šu.yand/	(او/آن) می شوید /(u/ ǎn) mi.šu.yad/
Present Subjunctive مضارع التزامی	
(ما) بشوییم /(mǎ) be.šu.yim/	(من) بشویم /(man) be.šu.yam/
(شما) بشویید /(šo.mǎ) be.šu.yid/	(تو) بشویی /(to) be.šu.yi/
(آنها) بشویند /(ǎn.hǎ) be.šu.yand/	(او/آن) بشوید /(u/ ǎn) be.šu.yad/
Present Progressive مضارع مستمر(در جریان)	
(ما) داریم می شوییم /(mǎ) dǎ.rim- mi.šu.yim/	(من) دارم می شویم /(man) dǎ.ram- mi.šu.yam/
(شما) دارید می شویید /(šo.mǎ) dǎ.rid- mi.šu.yid/	(تو) داری می شویی /(to) dǎ.ri- mi.šu.yi/
(آنها) دارند می شویند /(ǎn.hǎ) dǎ.rand- mi.šu.yand/	(او/آن) دارد می شوید /(u/ ǎn) dǎ.rad- mi.šu.yad/

Simple Past	
ماضی مطلق (گذشته ساده)	
(ما) شستیم	(من) شستم
/(mǎ) šos.tim/	/(man) šos.tam/
(شما) شستید	(تو) شستی
/(šo.mǎ) šos.tid/	/(to) šos.ti/
(آنها) شستند	(او/آن) شست
/(ǎn.hǎ) šos.tand/	/(u/ ǎn) šost/

Imperfect Indicative	
ماضی استمراری	
(ما) می شستیم	(من) می شستم
/(mǎ) mi.šos.tim/	/(man) mi.šos.tam/
(شما) می شستید	(تو) می شستی
/(šo.mǎ) mi.šos.tid/	/(to) mi.šos.ti/
(آنها) می شستند	(او/آن) می شست
/(ǎn.hǎ) mi.šos.tand/	/(u/ ǎn) mi.šost/

Present Perfect	
ماضی نقلی	
(ما) شسته ایم	(من) شسته ام
/(mǎ) šos.te.im/	/(man) šos.te.am/
(شما) شسته اید	(تو) شسته ای
/(šo.mǎ) šos.te.id/	/(to) šos.te.i/
(آنها) شسته اند	(او/آن) شسته است
/(ǎn.hǎ) šos.te.and/	/(u/ ǎn) šos.te- ast/

Past Perfect	
ماضی بعید	
(ما) شسته بودیم	(من) شسته بودم
/(mǎ) šos.te- bu.dim/	/(man) šos.te- bu.dam/
(شما) شسته بودید	(تو) شسته بودی
/(šo.mǎ) šos.te- bu.did/	/(to) šos.te- bu.di/
(آنها) شسته بودند	(او/آن) شسته بود
/(ǎn.hǎ) šos.te- bu.dand/	/(u/ ǎn) šos.te- bud/

<table>
<tr><td colspan="2" align="center">**Past Subjunctive**
ماضی التزامی</td></tr>
<tr>
<td align="center">(ما) شسته باشیم
/(mă) šos.te- bă.šim/</td>
<td align="center">(من) شسته باشم
/(man) šos.te- bă.šam/</td>
</tr>
<tr>
<td align="center">(شما) شسته باشید
/(šo.mă) šos.te- bă.šid/</td>
<td align="center">(تو) شسته باشی
/(to) šos.te- bă.ši/</td>
</tr>
<tr>
<td align="center">(آنها) شسته باشند
/(ăn.hă) šos.te- bă.šand/</td>
<td align="center">(او/آن) شسته باشد
/(u/ ăn) šos.te- bă.šad/</td>
</tr>
</table>

<table>
<tr><td colspan="2" align="center">**Past Progressive**
ماضی مستمر(در جریان)</td></tr>
<tr>
<td align="center">(ما) داشتیم می شستیم
/(mă) dăš.tim- mi.šos.tim/</td>
<td align="center">(من) داشتم می شستم
/(man) dăš.tam- mi.šos.tam/</td>
</tr>
<tr>
<td align="center">(شما) داشتید می شستید
/(šo.mă) dăš.tid- mi.šos.tid/</td>
<td align="center">(تو) داشتی می شستی
/(to) dăš.ti- mi.šos.ti/</td>
</tr>
<tr>
<td align="center">(آنها) داشتند می شستند
/(ăn.hă) dăš.tand- mi.šos.tand/</td>
<td align="center">(او/آن) داشت می شست
/(u/ ăn) dăšt- mi.šost/</td>
</tr>
</table>

<table>
<tr><td colspan="2" align="center">**Simple Future**
مستقبل (آینده ساده)</td></tr>
<tr>
<td align="center">(ما) خواهیم شست
/(mă) ḱă.him- šost/</td>
<td align="center">(من) خواهم شست
/(man) ḱă.ham- šost/</td>
</tr>
<tr>
<td align="center">(شما) خواهید شست
/(šo.mă) ḱă.hid- šost/</td>
<td align="center">(تو) خواهی شست
/(to) ḱă.hi- šost/</td>
</tr>
<tr>
<td align="center">(آنها) خواهند شست
/(ăn.hă) ḱă.hand- šost/</td>
<td align="center">(او/آن) خواهد شست
/(u/ ăn) ḱă.had- šost/</td>
</tr>
</table>

<table>
<tr><td colspan="2" align="center">**Command**
امر</td></tr>
<tr>
<td align="center">بشویید!
/be.šu.yid/</td>
<td align="center">بشوی!
/be.šuy/</td>
</tr>
</table>

to wear

پوشیدَن

/pu.ši.dan/

Plural	Singular
Simple Present	
مضارع اخباری(حال ساده)	
(ما) می پوشیم	(من) می پوشم
/(mǎ) mi.pu.šim/	/(man) mi.pu.šam/
(شما) می پوشید	(تو) می پوشی
/(šo.mǎ) mi.pu.šid/	/(to) mi.pu.ši/
(آنها) می پوشند	(او/آن) می پوشد
/(ǎn.hǎ) mi.pu.šand/	/(u/ ǎn) mi.pu.šad/

Plural	Singular
Present Subjunctive	
مضارع التزامی	
(ما) بپوشیم	(من) بپوشم
/(mǎ) be.pu.šim/	/(man) be.pu.šam/
(شما) بپوشید	(تو) بپوشی
/(šo.mǎ) be.pu.šid/	/(to) be.pu.ši/
(آنها) بپوشند	(او/آن) بپوشد
/(ǎn.hǎ) be.pu.šand/	/(u/ ǎn) be.pu.šad/

Plural	Singular
Present Progressive	
مضارع مستمر(در جریان)	
(ما) داریم می پوشیم	(من) دارم می پوشم
/(mǎ) dǎ.rim- mi.pu.šim/	/(man) dǎ.ram- mi.pu.šam/
(شما) دارید می پوشید	(تو) داری می پوشی
/(šo.mǎ) dǎ.rid- mi.pu.šid/	/(to) dǎ.ri- mi.pu.ši/
(آنها) دارند می پوشند	(او/آن) دارد می پوشد
/(ǎn.hǎ) dǎ.rand- mi.pu.šand/	/(u/ ǎn) dǎ.rad- mi.pu.šad/

Simple Past
ماضی مطلق (گذشته ساده)

(ما) پوشیدیم	(من) پوشیدم
/(mă) pu.ši.dim/	/(man) pu.ši.dam/
(شما) پوشیدید	(تو) پوشیدی
/(šo.mă) pu.ši.did/	/(to) pu.ši.di/
(آنها) پوشیدند	(او/آن) پوشید
/(ăn.hă) pu.ši.dand/	/(u/ ăn) pu.šid/

Imperfect Indicative
ماضی استمراری

(ما) می پوشیدیم	(من) می پوشیدم
/(mă) mi.pu.ši.dim/	/(man) mi.pu.ši.dam/
(شما) می پوشیدید	(تو) می پوشیدی
/(šo.mă) mi.pu.ši.did/	/(to) mi.pu.ši.di/
(آنها) می پوشیدند	(او/آن) می پوشید
/(ăn.hă) mi.pu.ši.dand/	/(u/ ăn) mi.pu.šid/

Present Perfect
ماضی نقلی

(ما) پوشیده ایم	(من) پوشیده ام
/(mă) pu.ši.de.im/	/(man) pu.ši.de.am/
(شما) پوشیده اید	(تو) پوشیده ای
/(šo.mă) pu.ši.de.id/	/(to) pu.ši.de.i/
(آنها) پوشیده اند	(او/آن) پوشیده است
/(ăn.hă) pu.ši.de.and/	/(u/ ăn) pu.ši.de- ast/

Past Perfect
ماضی بعید

(ما) پوشیده بودیم	(من) پوشیده بودم
/(mă) pu.ši.de- bu.dim/	/(man) pu.ši.de- bu.dam/
(شما) پوشیده بودید	(تو) پوشیده بودی
/(šo.mă) pu.ši.de- bu.did/	/(to) pu.ši.de- bu.di/
(آنها) پوشیده بودند	(او/آن) پوشیده بود
/(ăn.hă) pu.ši.de- bu.dand/	/(u/ ăn) pu.ši.de- bud/

<table>
<tr><td colspan="2" align="center">

Past Subjunctive

ماضی التزامی

</td></tr>
<tr>
<td align="center">

(ما) پوشیده باشیم

/(mǎ) pu.ši.de- bǎ.šim/

</td>
<td align="center">

(من) پوشیده باشم

/(man) pu.ši.de- bǎ.šam/

</td>
</tr>
<tr>
<td align="center">

(شما) پوشیده باشید

/(šo.mǎ) pu.ši.de- bǎ.šid/

</td>
<td align="center">

(تو) پوشیده باشی

/(to) pu.ši.de- bǎ.ši/

</td>
</tr>
<tr>
<td align="center">

(آنها) پوشیده باشند

/(ǎn.hǎ) pu.ši.de- bǎ.šand/

</td>
<td align="center">

(او/آن) پوشیده باشد

/(u/ ǎn) pu.ši.de- bǎ.šad/

</td>
</tr>
<tr><td colspan="2" align="center">

Past Progressive

ماضی مستمر(در جریان)

</td></tr>
<tr>
<td align="center">

(ما) داشتیم می پوشیدیم

/(mǎ) dǎš.tim- mi.pu.ši.dim/

</td>
<td align="center">

(من) داشتم می پوشیدم

/(man) dǎš.tam- mi.pu.ši.dam/

</td>
</tr>
<tr>
<td align="center">

(شما) داشتید می پوشیدید

/(šo.mǎ) dǎš.tid- mi.pu.ši.did/

</td>
<td align="center">

(تو) داشتی می پوشیدی

/(to) dǎš.ti- mi.pu.ši.di/

</td>
</tr>
<tr>
<td align="center">

(آنها) داشتند می پوشیدند

/(ǎn.hǎ) dǎš.tand- mi.pu.ši.dand/

</td>
<td align="center">

(او/آن) داشت می پوشید

/(u/ ǎn) dǎšt- mi.pu.šid/

</td>
</tr>
<tr><td colspan="2" align="center">

Simple Future

مستقبل (آینده ساده)

</td></tr>
<tr>
<td align="center">

(ما) خواهیم پوشید

/(mǎ) ǩǎ.him- pu.šid/

</td>
<td align="center">

(من) خواهم پوشید

/(man) ǩǎ.ham- pu.šid/

</td>
</tr>
<tr>
<td align="center">

(شما) خواهید پوشید

/(šo.mǎ) ǩǎ.hid- pu.šid/

</td>
<td align="center">

(تو) خواهی پوشید

/(to) ǩǎ.hi- pu.šid/

</td>
</tr>
<tr>
<td align="center">

(آنها) خواهند پوشید

/(ǎn.hǎ) ǩǎ.hand- pu.šid/

</td>
<td align="center">

(او/آن) خواهد پوشید

/(u/ ǎn) ǩǎ.had- pu.šid/

</td>
</tr>
<tr><td colspan="2" align="center">

Command

امر

</td></tr>
<tr>
<td align="center">

بپوشید!

/be.pu.šid/

</td>
<td align="center">

بپوش!

/be.puš/

</td>
</tr>
</table>

to win

بُردَن

/bor.dan/

Plural	*Singular*
Simple Present مضارع اخباری(حال ساده)	
(ما) می بریم /(mǎ) mi.ba.rim/	(من) می برم /(man) mi.ba.ram/
(شما) می برید /(šo.mǎ) mi.ba.rid/	(تو) می بری /(to) mi.ba.ri/
(آنها) می برند /(ǎn.hǎ) mi.ba.rand/	(او/آن) می برد /(u/ ǎn) mi.ba.rad/
Present Subjunctive مضارع التزامی	
(ما) ببریم /(mǎ) be.ba.rim/	(من) ببرم /(man) be.ba.ram/
(شما) ببرید /(šo.mǎ) be.ba.rid/	(تو) ببری /(to) be.ba.ri/
(آنها) ببرند /(ǎn.hǎ) be.ba.rand/	(او/آن) ببرد /(u/ ǎn) be.ba.rad/
Present Progressive مضارع مستمر(در جریان)	
(ما) داریم می بریم /(mǎ) dǎ.rim- mi.ba.rim/	(من) دارم می برم /(man) dǎ.ram- mi.ba.ram/
(شما) دارید می برید /(šo.mǎ) dǎ.rid- mi.ba.rid/	(تو) داری می بری /(to) dǎ.ri- mi.ba.ri/
(آنها) دارند می برند /(ǎn.hǎ) dǎ.rand- mi.ba.rand/	(او/آن) دارد می برد /(u/ ǎn) dǎ.rad- mi.ba.rad/

Simple Past
ماضی مطلق (گذشته ساده)

(ما) بردیم	(من) بردم
/(mǎ) bor.dim/	/(man) bor.dam/
(شما) بردید	(تو) بردی
/(šo.mǎ) bor.did/	/(to) bor.di/
(آنها) بردند	(او/آن) برد
/(ǎn.hǎ) bor.dand/	/(u/ ǎn) bord/

Imperfect Indicative
ماضی استمراری

(ما) می بردیم	(من) می بردم
/(mǎ) mi.bor.dim/	/(man) mi.bor.dam/
(شما) می بردید	(تو) می بردی
/(šo.mǎ) mi.bor.did/	/(to) mi.bor.di/
(آنها) می بردند	(او/آن) می برد
/(ǎn.hǎ) mi.bor.dand/	/(u/ ǎn) mi.bord/

Present Perfect
ماضی نقلی

(ما) برده ایم	(من) برده ام
/(mǎ) bor.de.im/	/(man) bor.de.am/
(شما) برده اید	(تو) برده ای
/(šo.mǎ) bor.de.id/	/(to) bor.de.i/
(آنها) برده اند	(او/آن) برده است
/(ǎn.hǎ) bor.de.and/	/(u/ ǎn) bor.de- ast/

Past Perfect
ماضی بعید

(ما) برده بودیم	(من) برده بودم
/(mǎ) bor.de- bu.dim/	/(man) bor.de- bu.dam/
(شما) برده بودید	(تو) برده بودی
/(šo.mǎ) bor.de- bu.did/	/(to) bor.de- bu.di/
(آنها) برده بودند	(او/آن) برده بود
/(ǎn.hǎ) bor.de- bu.dand/	/(u/ ǎn) bor.de- bud/

<table>
<tr><td colspan="2" align="center">Past Subjunctive
ماضی التزامی</td></tr>
<tr>
<td align="center">(ما) برده باشیم
/(mǎ) bor.de- bǎ.šim/</td>
<td align="center">(من) برده باشم
/(man) bor.de- bǎ.šam/</td>
</tr>
<tr>
<td align="center">(شما) برده باشید
/(šo.mǎ) bor.de- bǎ.šid/</td>
<td align="center">(تو) برده باشی
/(to) bor.de- bǎ.ši/</td>
</tr>
<tr>
<td align="center">(آنها) برده باشند
/(ǎn.hǎ) bor.de- bǎ.šand/</td>
<td align="center">(او/آن) برده باشد
/(u/ ǎn) bor.de- bǎ.šad/</td>
</tr>
</table>

<table>
<tr><td colspan="2" align="center">Past Progressive
ماضی مستمر(در جریان)</td></tr>
<tr>
<td align="center">(ما) داشتیم می بردیم
/(mǎ) dǎš.tim- mi.bor.dim/</td>
<td align="center">(من) داشتم می بردم
/(man) dǎš.tam- mi.bor.dam/</td>
</tr>
<tr>
<td align="center">(شما) داشتید می بردید
/(šo.mǎ) dǎš.tid- mi.bor.did/</td>
<td align="center">(تو) داشتی می بردی
/(to) dǎš.ti- mi.bor.di/</td>
</tr>
<tr>
<td align="center">(آنها) داشتند می بردند
/(ǎn.hǎ) dǎš.tand- mi.bor.dand/</td>
<td align="center">(او/آن) داشت می برد
/(u/ ǎn) dǎšt- mi.bord/</td>
</tr>
</table>

<table>
<tr><td colspan="2" align="center">Simple Future
مستقبل (آینده ساده)</td></tr>
<tr>
<td align="center">(ما) خواهیم برد
/(mǎ) kǎ.him- bord/</td>
<td align="center">(من) خواهم برد
/(man) kǎ.ham- bord/</td>
</tr>
<tr>
<td align="center">(شما) خواهید برد
/(šo.mǎ) kǎ.hid- bord/</td>
<td align="center">(تو) خواهی برد
/(to) kǎ.hi- bord/</td>
</tr>
<tr>
<td align="center">(آنها) خواهند برد
/(ǎn.hǎ) kǎ.hand- bord/</td>
<td align="center">(او/آن) خواهد برد
/(u/ ǎn) kǎ.had- bord/</td>
</tr>
</table>

<table>
<tr><td colspan="2" align="center">Command
امر</td></tr>
<tr>
<td align="center">ببرید!
/be.ba.rid/</td>
<td align="center">ببر!
/be.bar/</td>
</tr>
</table>

to work

کار کَردَن

/kǎr- kar.dan/

	Plural	*Singular*
Simple Present مضارع اخباری(حال ساده)		
(ما) کار می کنیم /(mǎ) kǎr- mi.ko.nim/		(من) کار می کنم /(man) kǎr- mi.ko.nam/
(شما) کار می کنید /(šo.mǎ) kǎr- mi.ko.nid/		(تو) کار می کنی /(to) kǎr- mi.ko.ni/
(آنها) کار می کنند /(ǎn.hǎ) kǎr- mi.ko.nand/		(او/آن) کار می کند /(u/ ǎn) kǎr- mi.ko.nad/
Present Subjunctive مضارع التزامی		
(ما) کار بکنیم /(mǎ) kǎr- be.ko.nim/		(من) کار بکنم /(man) kǎr- be.ko.nam/
(شما) کار بکنید /(šo.mǎ) kǎr- be.ko.nid/		(تو) کار بکنی /(to) kǎr- be.ko.ni/
(آنها) کار بکنند /(ǎn.hǎ) kǎr- be.ko.nand/		(او/آن) کار بکند /(u/ ǎn) kǎr- be.ko.nad/
Present Progressive مضارع مستمر(در جریان)		
(ما) داریم کار می کنیم /(mǎ) dǎ.rim- kǎr- mi.ko.nim/		(من) دارم کار می کنم /(man) dǎ.ram- kǎr- mi.ko.nam/
(شما) دارید کار می کنید /(šo.mǎ) dǎ.rid- kǎr- mi.ko.nid/		(تو) داری کار می کنی /(to) dǎ.ri- kǎr- mi.ko.ni/
(آنها) دارند کار می کنند /(ǎn.hǎ) dǎ.rand- kǎr- mi.ko.nand/		(او/آن) دارد کار می کند /(u/ ǎn) dǎ.rad- kǎr- mi.ko.nad/

<table>
<tr><td colspan="2" align="center">**Simple Past**
ماضی مطلق (گذشته ساده)</td></tr>
<tr><td align="center">(ما) کار کردیم
/(mǎ) kǎr- kar.dim/</td><td align="center">(من) کار کردم
/(man) kǎr- kar.dam/</td></tr>
<tr><td align="center">(شما) کار کردید
/(šo.mǎ) kǎr- kar.did/</td><td align="center">(تو) کار کردی
/(to) kǎr- kar.di/</td></tr>
<tr><td align="center">(آنها) کار کردند
/(ǎn.hǎ) kǎr- kar.dand/</td><td align="center">(او/آن) کار کرد
/(u/ ǎn) kǎr- kard/</td></tr>
</table>

<table>
<tr><td colspan="2" align="center">**Imperfect Indicative**
ماضی استمراری</td></tr>
<tr><td align="center">(ما) کار می کردیم
/(mǎ) kǎr- mi.kar.dim/</td><td align="center">(من) کار می کردم
/(man) kǎr- mi.kar.dam/</td></tr>
<tr><td align="center">(شما) کار می کردید
/(šo.mǎ) kǎr- mi.kar.did/</td><td align="center">(تو) کار می کردی
/(to) kǎr- mi.kar.di/</td></tr>
<tr><td align="center">(آنها) کار می کردند
/(ǎn.hǎ) kǎr- mi.kar.dand/</td><td align="center">(او/آن) کار می کرد
/(u/ ǎn) kǎr- mi.kard/</td></tr>
</table>

<table>
<tr><td colspan="2" align="center">**Present Perfect**
ماضی نقلی</td></tr>
<tr><td align="center">(ما) کار کرده ایم
/(mǎ) kǎr- kar.de.im/</td><td align="center">(من) کار کرده ام
/(man) kǎr- kar.de.am/</td></tr>
<tr><td align="center">(شما) کار کرده اید
/(šo.mǎ) kǎr- kar.de.id/</td><td align="center">(تو) کار کرده ای
/(to) kǎr- kar.de.i/</td></tr>
<tr><td align="center">(آنها) کار کرده اند
/(ǎn.hǎ) kǎr- kar.de.and/</td><td align="center">(او/آن) کار کرده است
/(u/ ǎn) kǎr- kar.de- ast/</td></tr>
</table>

<table>
<tr><td colspan="2" align="center">**Past Perfect**
ماضی بعید</td></tr>
<tr><td align="center">(ما) کار کرده بودیم
/(mǎ) kǎr- kar.de- bu.dim/</td><td align="center">(من) کار کرده بودم
/(man) kǎr- kar.de- bu.dam/</td></tr>
<tr><td align="center">(شما) کار کرده بودید
/(šo.mǎ) kǎr- kar.de- bu.did/</td><td align="center">(تو) کار کرده بودی
/(to) kǎr- kar.de- bu.di/</td></tr>
<tr><td align="center">(آنها) کار کرده بودند
/(ǎn.hǎ) kǎr- kar.de- bu.dand/</td><td align="center">(او/آن) کار کرده بود
/(u/ ǎn) kǎr- kar.de- bud/</td></tr>
</table>

Past Subjunctive	
ماضی التزامی	
(ما) کار کرده باشیم	(من) کار کرده باشم
/(mă) kăr- kar.de- bă.šim/	/(man) kăr- kar.de- bă.šam/
(شما) کار کرده باشید	(تو) کار کرده باشی
/(šo.mă) kăr- kar.de- bă.šid/	/(to) kăr- kar.de- bă.ši/
(آنها) کار کرده باشند	(او/آن) کار کرده باشد
/(ăn.hă) kăr- kar.de- bă.šand/	/(u/ ăn) kăr- kar.de- bă.šad/

Past Progressive	
ماضی مستمر(در جریان)	
(ما) داشتیم کار می کردیم	(من) داشتم کار می کردم
/(mă) dăš.tim- kăr- mi.kar.dim/	/(man) dăš.tam- kăr- mi.kar.dam/
(شما) داشتید کار می کردید	(تو) داشتی کار می کردی
/(šo.mă) dăš.tid- kăr- mi.kar.did/	/(to) dăš.ti- kăr- mi.kar.di/
(آنها) داشتند کار می کردند	(او/آن) داشت کار می کرد
/(ăn.hă) dăš.tand- kăr- mi.kar.dand/	/(u/ ăn) dăšt- kăr- mi.kard/

Simple Future	
مستقبل (آینده ساده)	
(ما) کار خواهیم کرد	(من) کار خواهم کرد
/(mă) kăr- kă.him- kard/	/(man) kăr- kă.ham- kard/
(شما) کار خواهید کرد	(تو) کار خواهی کرد
/(šo.mă) kăr- kă.hid- kard/	/(to) kăr- kă.hi- kard/
(آنها) کار خواهند کرد	(او/آن) کار خواهد کرد
/(ăn.hă) kăr- kă.hand- kard/	/(u/ ăn) kăr- kă.had- kard/

Command	
امر	
* کار بکنید!	* کار بکن!
/kăr- be.ko.nid/	/kăr- be.kon/

* also: کار کن!   کار کنید!

to write

نِوشتَن

/ne.veš.tan/

Plural	Singular
Simple Present مضارع اخباری(حال ساده)	
(ما) می نویسیم /(mǎ) mi.ne.vi.sim/	(من) می نویسم /(man) mi.ne.vi.sam/
(شما) می نویسید /(šo.mǎ) mi.ne.vi.sid/	(تو) می نویسی /(to) mi.ne.vi.si/
(آنها) می نویسند /(ǎn.hǎ) mi.ne.vi.sand/	(او/آن) می نویسد /(u/ ǎn) mi.ne.vi.sad/
Present Subjunctive مضارع التزامی	
(ما) بنویسیم /(mǎ) be.ne.vi.sim/	(من) بنویسم /(man) be.ne.vi.sam/
(شما) بنویسید /(šo.mǎ) be.ne.vi.sid/	(تو) بنویسی /(to) be.ne.vi.si/
(آنها) بنویسند /(ǎn.hǎ) be.ne.vi.sand/	(او/آن) بنویسد /(u/ ǎn) be.ne.vi.sad/
Present Progressive مضارع مستمر(در جریان)	
(ما) داریم می نویسیم /(mǎ) dǎ.rim- mi.ne.vi.sim/	(من) دارم می نویسم /(man) dǎ.ram- mi.ne.vi.sam/
(شما) دارید می نویسید /(šo.mǎ) dǎ.rid- mi.ne.vi.sid/	(تو) داری می نویسی /(to) dǎ.ri- mi.ne.vi.si/
(آنها) دارند می نویسند /(ǎn.hǎ) dǎ.rand- mi.ne.vi.sand/	(او/آن) دارد می نویسد /(u/ ǎn) dǎ.rad- mi.ne.vi.sad/

299

<table>
<tr><td colspan="2" align="center">**Simple Past**
ماضی مطلق (گذشته ساده)</td></tr>
<tr>
<td align="center">(ما) نوشتیم
/(mă) ne.veš.tim/</td>
<td align="center">(من) نوشتم
/(man) ne.veš.tam/</td>
</tr>
<tr>
<td align="center">(شما) نوشتید
/(šo.mă) ne.veš.tid/</td>
<td align="center">(تو) نوشتی
/(to) ne.veš.ti/</td>
</tr>
<tr>
<td align="center">(آنها) نوشتند
/(ăn.hă) ne.veš.tand/</td>
<td align="center">(او/آن) نوشت
/(u/ ăn) ne.vešt/</td>
</tr>
</table>

<table>
<tr><td colspan="2" align="center">**Imperfect Indicative**
ماضی استمراری</td></tr>
<tr>
<td align="center">(ما) می نوشتیم
/(mă) mi.ne.veš.tim/</td>
<td align="center">(من) می نوشتم
/(man) mi.ne.veš.tam/</td>
</tr>
<tr>
<td align="center">(شما) می نوشتید
/(šo.mă) mi.ne.veš.tid/</td>
<td align="center">(تو) می نوشتی
/(to) mi.ne.veš.ti/</td>
</tr>
<tr>
<td align="center">(آنها) می نوشتند
/(ăn.hă) mi.ne.veš.tand/</td>
<td align="center">(او/آن) می نوشت
/(u/ ăn) mi.ne.vešt/</td>
</tr>
</table>

<table>
<tr><td colspan="2" align="center">**Present Perfect**
ماضی نقلی</td></tr>
<tr>
<td align="center">(ما) نوشته ایم
/(mă) ne.veš.te.im/</td>
<td align="center">(من) نوشته ام
/(man) ne.veš.te.am/</td>
</tr>
<tr>
<td align="center">(شما) نوشته اید
/(šo.mă) ne.veš.te.id/</td>
<td align="center">(تو) نوشته ای
/(to) ne.veš.te.i/</td>
</tr>
<tr>
<td align="center">(آنها) نوشته اند
/(ăn.hă) ne.veš.te.and/</td>
<td align="center">(او/آن) نوشته است
/(u/ ăn) ne.veš.te- ast/</td>
</tr>
</table>

<table>
<tr><td colspan="2" align="center">**Past Perfect**
ماضی بعید</td></tr>
<tr>
<td align="center">(ما) نوشته بودیم
/(mă) ne.veš.te- bu.dim/</td>
<td align="center">(من) نوشته بودم
/(man) ne.veš.te- bu.dam/</td>
</tr>
<tr>
<td align="center">(شما) نوشته بودید
/(šo.mă) ne.veš.te- bu.did/</td>
<td align="center">(تو) نوشته بودی
/(to) ne.veš.te- bu.di/</td>
</tr>
<tr>
<td align="center">(آنها) نوشته بودند
/(ăn.hă) ne.veš.te- bu.dand/</td>
<td align="center">(او/آن) نوشته بود
/(u/ ăn) ne.veš.te- bud/</td>
</tr>
</table>

Past Subjunctive ماضی التزامی	
(ما) نوشته باشیم /(mă) ne.veš.te- bă.šim/	(من) نوشته باشم /(man) ne.veš.te- bă.šam/
(شما) نوشته باشید /(šo.mă) ne.veš.te- bă.šid/	(تو) نوشته باشی /(to) ne.veš.te- bă.ši/
(آنها) نوشته باشند /(ăn.hă) ne.veš.te- bă.šand/	(او/آن) نوشته باشد /(u/ ăn) ne.veš.te- bă.šad/

Past Progressive ماضی مستمر(در جریان)	
(ما) داشتیم می نوشتیم /(mă) dăš.tim- mi.ne.veš.tim/	(من) داشتم می نوشتم /(man) dăš.tam- mi.ne.veš.tam/
(شما) داشتید می نوشتید /(šo.mă) dăš.tid- mi.ne.veš.tid/	(تو) داشتی می نوشتی /(to) dăš.ti- mi.ne.veš.ti/
(آنها) داشتند می نوشتند /(ăn.hă) dăš.tand- mi.ne.veš.tand/	(او/آن) داشت می نوشت /(u/ ăn) dăšt- mi.ne.vešt/

Simple Future مستقبل (آینده ساده)	
(ما) خواهیم نوشت /(mă) kă.him- ne.vešt/	(من) خواهم نوشت /(man) kă.ham- ne.vešt/
(شما) خواهید نوشت /(šo.mă) kă.hid- ne.vešt/	(تو) خواهی نوشت /(to) kă.hi- ne.vešt/
(آنها) خواهند نوشت /(ăn.hă) kă.hand- ne.vešt/	(او/آن) خواهد نوشت /(u/ ăn) kă.had- ne.vešt/

Command امر	
بنویسید! /be.ne.vi.sid/	بنویس! /be.ne.vis/

Index of English – Persian Verbs

A

accept	قبول کردن
answer	جواب دادن
ask	پرسیدن

B

be	بودن
be able to	توانستن
become	شدن
break	شکستن
bring	آوردن
buy	خریدن

C

call	تلفن کردن
catch	گرفتن
change	عوض کردن
choose	انتخاب کردن
close	بستن
come	آمدن
continue	ادامه دادن
cook	پختن
cry	گریه کردن

D

dance	رقصیدن
decide	تصمیم گرفتن
decrease	کم کردن
deny	رد کردن
do	کردن
drink	نوشیدن
drive	رانندگی کردن

E

eat	خوردن
empty	خالی کردن
enter	وارد شدن
exit	خارج شدن
explain	توضیح دادن

F

feel	احساس کردن
fill	پر کردن
find	پیدا کردن
finish	تمام کردن
fly	پرواز کردن
forget	فراموش کردن

G

give	دادن
go	رفتن

H

happen	اتّفاق افتادن
have	داشتن
hear	شنیدن

I

increase	زیاد کردن
introduce	معرفی کردن
invite	دعوت کردن

K

kiss	بوسیدن
know	دانستن

L

laugh	خندیدن
learn	یاد گرفتن
listen	گوش دادن
live	زندگی کردن

lose	گم کردن
love	دوست داشتن

M

measure	اندازه گرفتن
meet	آشنا شدن

N

need	احتیاج داشتن

O

open	باز کردن

P

pick up	برداشتن
play	بازی کردن
practice	تمرین کردن
prepare	آماده کردن
put	گذاشتن

R

read	خواندن
remember	به یاد آوردن
repeat	تکرار کردن
return	برگشتن
run	دویدن

S

say	گفتن
say good bye	خداحافظی کردن
say hello	سلام کردن
scream	فریاد زدن
see	دیدن
sell	فروختن
send	فرستادن
show	نشان دادن
sing	آواز خواندن
sit	نشستن
sleep	خوابیدن
smell	بوییدن
smile	لبخند زدن
stand	ایستادن
start	شروع کردن
stay	ماندن

T

talk	حرف زدن
teach	یاد دادن
thank	تشکّر کردن
think	فکر کردن
touch	لمس کردن

translate	ترجمه کردن
travel	سفر کردن

U

understand	فهمیدن
use	استفاده کردن

W

wait	صبر کردن
wake up	بیدار شدن
walk	راه رفتن
want	خواستن
wash	شستن
wear	پوشیدن
win	بردن
work	کار کردن
write	نوشتن

Index of Persian – English Verbs

آ

meet	آشنا شدن
prepare	آماده کردن
come	آمدن
sing	آواز خواندن
bring	آوردن

ا

happen	اتّفاق افتادن
need	احتیاج داشتن
feel	احساس کردن
continue	ادامه دادن
use	استفاده کردن
choose	انتخاب کردن
measure	اندازه گرفتن
stand	ایستادن

ب

open	باز کردن
play	بازی کردن

pick up	برداشتن
win	بردن
return	برگشتن
close	بستن
be	بودن
kiss	بوسیدن
smell	بوییدن
remember	به یاد آوردن
wake up	بیدار شدن

پ

cook	پختن
ask	پرسیدن
fill	پر کردن
fly	پرواز کردن
wear	پوشیدن
find	پیدا کردن

ت

translate	ترجمه کردن
thank	تشکّر کردن

decide	تصمیم گرفتن
repeat	تکرار کردن
call	تلفن کردن
finish	تمام کردن
practice	تمرین کردن
be able to	توانستن
explain	توضیح دادن

ج

answer	جواب دادن

ح

talk	حرف زدن

خ

exit	خارج شدن
empty	خالی کردن
say good bye	خداحافظی کردن
buy	خریدن
laugh	خندیدن

sleep	خوابیدن
want	خواستن
read	خواندن
eat	خوردن

س

travel	سفر کردن
say hello	سلام کردن

understand	فهمیدن

ق

accept	قبول کردن

د

give	دادن
have	داشتن
know	دانستن
invite	دعوت کردن
love	دوست داشتن
run	دویدن
see	دیدن

ش

become	شدن
start	شروع کردن
wash	شستن
break	شکستن
hear	شنیدن

ک

work	کار کردن
do	کردن
decrease	کم کردن

گ

put	گذاشتن
catch	گرفتن
cry	گریه کردن
tell	گفتن
lose	گم کردن
listen	گوش دادن

ص

wait	صبر کردن

ر

drive	رانندگی کردن
walk	راه رفتن
deny	رد کردن
go	رفتن
dance	رقصیدن

ع

change	عوض کردن

ف

forget	فراموش کردن
send	فرستادن
sell	فروختن
scream	فریاد زدن
think	فکر کردن

ل

smile	لبخند زدن
touch	لمس کردن

ز

live	زندگی کردن
increase	زیاد کردن

م

stay	ماندن
introduce	معرفی کردن

ن

show	نشان دادن
sit	نشستن
write	نوشتن
drink	نوشیدن

و

enter	وارد شدن

ی

teach	یاد دادن
learn	یاد گرفتن

Made in the USA
Middletown, DE
13 August 2017